R00047 99261

Due Return

D0734387

Sir Harry Vane

(Courtesy of the National Portrait Gallery)

Sir Harry Vane
His Life and Times (1613-1662)

by J. H. Adamson
and H. F. Folland

Let us now praise famous men
Ecclesiasticus
Nothing extenuate, nor set down ought in malice
Othello

Gambit
INCORPORATED
Boston
1973

DH
407
V2
H65

First printing

Copyright © 1973 by J. H. Adamson and H. F. Folland
All rights reserved including the right to reproduce
this book or parts thereof in any form
Library of Congress Catalog Card Number: 72–94005
International Standard Book Number: 0–87645–064–8
Printed in the United States of America

For
Gerald,
Hugh and Alice,
Jane and Edward,
who understand the men of stricken conscience

Foreword

As we came to know young Sir Henry Vane and the Puritan revolutionaries, we were continually beset by paradox. Some of the ideas and attitudes which had aroused in them the strongest emotions men can feel now seemed merely curious. But perhaps more often we encountered incidents and themes that echoed our own times so irresistibly that we had the sense of living through them a second time. We have tried to capture this double view, the mingling of the strange and the familiar.

We have allowed ourselves one invention, the not unlikely idea that the devout Lady Vane found solace in reading from her books of prayer at critical moments in her life. Three of those prayers Lady Vane could not have known in the exact form we have used.

In the interest of narrative, we have selected and combined details from various sources, and when they contradicted each other, we have trusted our own judgment to choose between them or reconcile them. As in our previous book, *The Shepherd of the Ocean: Sir Walter Raleigh and His Times*, we decided not to encumber the text with footnotes. We believe that the general reader will welcome this omission; for scholars we list our sources in a bibliography at the end of the volume. Generally we have modernized spelling and punctuation, but otherwise we have tried to be faithful to the record, to let the speeches, letters, diaries, and other documents speak for themselves.

J. H. ADAMSON
H. F. FOLLAND

Salt Lake City, Utah
March 1, 1973

Acknowledgments

We have acknowledged sources and scholarly obligations in the bibliography, but some particular debts require more personal appreciation. The scholarly writings of Professor J. H. Hexter on Vane and the Independent party are most illuminating; and the recent biography of Vane by Miss Violet Rowe was an invaluable source for the middle period of Vane's life.

We are also indebted to the other previous biographers of Vane whose industry made our work easier and whose views helped us formulate our own.

Finally we wish to thank the British Museum and the Widener Library at Harvard University for generously allowing us access to their collections; we are especially grateful to the Marriott Library at the University of Utah and to its staff, whose constant and cheerful attention to our needs made the writing of the book possible.

Contents

Illustrations

Our joy is like a narrow raft
Afloat upon the hungry sea.
Hereon is but a little space,
And all men, eager for a place,
Do thrust each other in the sea.
And each man, eager for a place,
Doth thrust his brother in the sea.
And so our joy is wan with fears,
And so the sea is salt with tears.
Ah, well is thee, thou art asleep!

Our life is like a curious play
Where each man hideth from himself.
"Let us be open as the day,"
One mask doth to the other say,
When he would deeper hide himself—
"Let us be open as the day,"
That he may better hide himself.
And so the world goes round and round,
Until our life with rest is crowned.
Ah, well is thee, thou art asleep.

Anonymous

Sir Harry Vane

(Courtesy of the Victoria and Albert Museum)

A Baptism (1613)

On a May morning in 1613 a coach pulled by two fine grays drew up at the parish church of Debden in County Essex. From it a nurse alighted, holding a sleeping infant in her arms. Then came a young woman in her early twenties, aristocratic in her bearing, Frances Darcy, Lady Vane, who was bringing her first child to be baptized. With her was her husband, Sir Henry Vane, for whom his son would be named.

In gentler times this ceremony might have been performed at home, but the hostility of the Puritans towards the mother church had impelled the clergy to urge the sons and daughters of the establishment to participate in public ceremonies, to cherish and encourage liturgy and ritual. For different reasons this father and mother were both willing to have it so. For while the mother was devout, hers was a mild, traditional devotion with no yearning for private ecstasy and no expectation of earthly utopia. The gemlike prose of the Anglican Prayer Book and her own book of private prayers expressed her moods and satisfied her religious needs. Whenever she sorrowed or suffered or hoped, she turned to those books and found mirrored there the states of her own inner life. When the time of her delivery had drawn near, she had read a particular prayer with quiet comfort:

> O most gracious workman, let thy pitifulness amend the thing which our sinfulness hath marred, and either abate my pain, that I may not need of so great strength, tendance, and cunning, or else increase my strength, power, and courage, that I may be able to overcome all the pain of my travail.

Now the baby had made the perilous journey from her womb to her arms; ahead of it lay an even more perilous journey, and so, on that day, she would deliver it into the arms of the church, to be infused with the grace which flowed through the sacraments in order that it might resist the world, the flesh, and the devil.

The father too approved of the public ceremony, but for different reasons. He intended to seek and improve his fortunes at the Court of a monarch who had espoused the established church. James I had said, "No bishop, no King," and those who wished to serve him knew the implications of that now famous proverb. Sir Henry Vane had a face that took the eye, a bold face with high features, the nose too large, lips sensual and disdainful, an undisguised arrogance in the eyes—a face that was ugly yet striking. Most of all it was a worldly face, startling to encounter in a church, the kind of face the child was that day to be armed against. There was no hint of humility in it, of dependence on God's grace during this weary pilgrimage; it spoke rather of beef and brandy, both rare, and of hawks and horses. There were no deflected lights, no hidden passages that suggested a nature crossed by an anxious will or a hidden strain of idealism. It was the face of a man who knew instinctively, as hounds know about rabbits and foxes, that power and status and money were the three flowers of life, and that they blossomed from a single root of calculating self-interest.

Sir Henry Vane already had a good start in life for one who meant to leave behind him a name and some lands with walls and towers. Brasenose College, Oxford, had given him manners and an accent; Gray's Inn had taught him all the law he needed to know; and in 1611 he had been knighted by a Scottish monarch known for the largesse with which, for a fee, he distributed English honors. New knights, it was said, swarmed in every corner, and everyone knew that those honors were achieved through the payment of money to an impecunious Crown. Still, it was a knighthood.

And Sir Henry Vane had something more behind him than a bargain dubbing, something intangible but even more impressive than his material advantages, and that was an ancestry that went back beyond the Norman Conquest to the Welsh Howell ap Vane, and a coat of arms that reflected one of the greatest moments of English history. In 1356, when Edward the Black Prince had led his men-at-arms and archers across the channel against the city of

Poitiers, there was in the ranks a yeoman archer who was called, by some of his friends who did not always voice their consonants, Henery Fane.

The Black Prince, it was said, had only 2,000 men-at-arms and 4,000 archers. There were 1,500 more, so nondescript in status and function that they were simply called "other." The French king, John II, was in a somewhat better state. According to a French chronicler, in addition to abundant "others" he had 60,000 horse; but what really stirred the heart was that the king's four sons were in the field, along with twenty-six dukes and earls, and at least sixscore banners. Finally, there was the king himself, mounted on a white courser, ready upon almost any occasion to shout, "God and Saint Denis." He was a most happy king, concerned only that the English might deny him glory by running away, and so he quickly assembled his army, terrible with banners, and "hasted sore to find the Englishmen."

Oddly enough, it had not occurred to the Black Prince to run away. "In the name of God," said he, "let us now study how we shall fight with them at our advantage." And so he felled trees for artificial barriers and he pushed supply wagons into the vines, hedges, and bushes that already provided natural fortifications. Along these strong places, he deployed his strong men, the archers, carrying bows of yew and arrows fletched with the feathers of the gray goose. In theory archers should not shoot down blooded knights, as the Black Prince well knew, but he felt that the need to survive took precedence over the rules of honorable warfare.

Seeing the fatal disparity in numbers between the two hosts, the Cardinal of Perigord, a man of God who felt that not even Englishmen should be so summarily slaughtered, did his best to make peace; but honor had been invoked, the rallying cry of the English had been heard, and blood was up. The King of France and his four sons, after hearing Mass, ordained that all manner of men should set forth into the field, display each his banner, cry "God and Saint Denis," and sweep the English off the field.

And so the flower of French chivalry charged in waves against the strong places. As they approached the hedges, the English archers drove their arrows into the horses, "which drew back and flang and took on so fiercely" that many fell on their riders or lay dead or wounded on the field, obstructing other waves of charging horse from reaching the English lines. When the archers had done their deadly work, the men-at-arms, until now impatiently abiding the command, leapt onto their horses and the Black Prince gave the order, "Advance, banner, in the name of God and Saint George."

Until Saint George entered the field, King John had done marvels in arms. If one-fourth of the French host had done their devoir as well as he, the field would have gone to them, but he could not do everything. He finally fled, honorably overcome with weariness and wounds, pursued by Denis of Morbeke, a Frenchman who some years ago had escaped to England to avoid prosectuion for murder. In good French, he said to King John, "Sire, yield you."

To whom shall I yield me? Where is my cousin, the Prince of Wales?

Sire, he is not here, but yield you to me and I shall bring you to him.

Trusting a man who spoke such good French, the king took the gauntlet from his right hand and gave it to Sir Denis as a token of surrender. In the meantime the Black Prince had ended his cavalry charge and set his banner high as a rallying point, where he had caused a red pavilion to be erected and red wine to be brought. Just then a mob of weary men, both knights and commoners, appeared on the crest of a hill with the French king in their midst. At least ten knights and squires were claiming the honor of his capture, and the commoners, too, had set up an infernal clamor, shouting, pushing, rioting, English and Gascons fighting one another harder than they had ever fought the French, trying to win some honor in the eyes of the Black Prince. Seeing that the marshals could do nothing with this excited mob, the Black Prince raised his voice and "on pain of their heads" stilled the tumult. When the uproar had subsided, it was Henery Fane who came forward with the king's right gauntlet. He did not consider it necessary to explain that he had taken it not from the king but from Sir Denis of Morbeke; he simply knelt and in eloquent silence handed it to his prince who in turn caused him to rise, a moment later, as Sir Henry Vane.

The French felt that the fabric of the universe had been torn when the gauntlet of their king fell into the sweating palm of a mere archer, but the archer cared not a whit. He was later given a coat of arms with a dexter-gauntlet on it, the same coat of arms the bold-faced man at the church was now displaying on his carriage.

Later, another Vane had tried to be a throne-shaker. The grandfather of the present Sir Henry, the baby's great-grandfather, a Protestant gentleman and rebel of the sixteenth century, had been implicated in Wyatt's rebellion of protest against Mary's Spanish marriage, and if his youth had not pleaded louder than his treason, he would have lost his head. That Sir Henry Vane had not been content merely to serve his prince; God was his prince, he said, and at any peril God must be served first.

His grandson with the beef-and-brandy face had rejected such nebulous idealisms. He intended, if possible, to present another gauntlet to his liege. Before his son was born, he had bought a small office in the Court for 5,000 pounds sterling, and when he married, he persuaded his compliant wife to give him 3,000 pounds to buy still another office. These places of civil service paid almost no salary and their purchase price was an indirect donation to the monarch, but a wise servant always got his own back, and more—a good deal more. For performing the duties of his office he received gratuities from those whom his influence benefited. The more influence, ultimately, the greater wealth.

When his son was baptized, it was known that Sir Henry Vane would stand for Parliament the following year; it would, of course, be for some borough where the king's known wish would be adequate to have him elected. But what Sir Henry really wanted was a position near the person of young Charles. Princes of Wales and Sir Henry Vanes, he thought, were a fortunate combination.

In 1617 he would win that position, becoming cofferer to the prince's household; then the money paid for food, clothing, housing, servants' salaries, jewels, royal entertainment—all would pass through his hands and he would not undervalue his services.

But what of the new son? Would he seize a gauntlet for his liege or would God be his only prince? There were no portents that day. Of those who saw the baby at his baptism, half said that he looked like his mother while the others said he resembled his father. Time would prove both right, although later Vane's detractors would say that the young Sir Harry had merely become the old Sir Harry.

> This son is thine with heaven's good leave,
> His tongue all people shall deceive.

> Folk shall thee curse for thy night's work,
> When thou him got'st, nor Christian nor Turk.

But despite such libels, what young Vane would inherit of his father's expedience would be tempered by the mother's inward motions of the spirit. On this baptismal day, after he was cleansed from sin and dedicated to the service of God, he opened his eyes and cried.

A few days later, the grateful mother, accompanied by a nurse, went to her "churching." After the incense was lighted, the priest, dressed in white, approached her and intoned,

> Inasmuch as it hath pleased almighty God of his goodness to give you safe deliverance and hath preserved you in the great danger of childbirth, ye shall therefore give hearty thanks unto God and pray.

And then Frances Darcy Vane offered her prayers and praises.

2

The Wonderful Year (1625)

An *annus mirabilis* is not necessarily a good year; it is, rather, a year of wonders, a year to be marveled at as if it were perhaps prophetic of things to come. In such a year, 1625, James I died. He had never been popular; his table manners, his pedantry, his weakness for whiskey, his effeminacy, and his Scotch burr were all against him. His subjects had more or less got used to him, as men come to live easily with their afflictions. When he died, there was a great storm in the heavens—a portentous wonder—and in a flurry of elegiac verses poets revealed not so much their private grief as a decline in occasional poetry since the days of Elizabeth.

> Our day being gone, no night hung o'er our eyes,
> For at sun-setting did the sun arise.

For James was living still in his son Charles, and Sir Henry Vane had suddenly risen to be the servant of a king.

James had trusted the elder Vane, knowing that no inexplicable pang of conscience would interfere with the steady pursuit of a self-interest which would also be the interest of the sovereign. He had therefore increasingly used Vane for more important tasks than that of cofferer; he had trusted him with some personal matters and had sent him on some confidential embassages. Vane, it seems, had become an unofficial member of the diplomatic corps, and even when the king died he was preparing to go on a confidential mission to Charles' sister, the Queen of Bohemia.

All the servants of the former prince were now entitled to gratuities and pensions, and the elder Vane duly received his, some

2,500 pounds. There could be no more certain sign of Charles' favor to this man who had now served him for eight years than his taking immediate steps to reconcile Vane with the Duke of Buckingham, who despised him. Vane never lost the unhappy knack of making enemies of powerful men; Buckingham, Gustav Adolf, the Earl of Strafford, all disdained him as a time server. Buckingham had first come into prominence when his epicene beauty had caught the eye of James; he soon became a living proof of the adage that it is a disadvantage to be too handsome, and dangerous to cultivate charm to the neglect of more substantial traits. Even his rather ordinary intellectual gifts he carelessly dissipated in rash and impulsive judgments, which would some day make him England's most hated man.

A year or two earlier he had persuaded Charles to journey to Spain to sweep the Infanta off her feet in a wild, romantic courtship. There, Buckingham soon learned, religion and statecraft were considered more important than the delightful impulses of the heart which were reserved for lovers, poets, and ladies; the charade he directed soured into farce, and when the projected marriage was angrily called off, Buckingham convinced Charles that the royal honor of England had been slighted. Whereupon James had called a Parliament which was easily persuaded to declare yet another war on its old enemy, a war emotionally satisfying but financially difficult. But now James was dead, and the war, so lightly entered into, lay heavy on Charles and Buckingham.

With the Infanta no longer a possible bride, James had found a match for his son in France: Henrietta Maria, daughter of Henri IV and sister of Louis XIII. She was then only fifteen, with large eyes, larger teeth, and a minimal figure. To look at her, men said, was no violation of Lent. To offset her physical mediocrity, she had a remarkable vivacity, a quick mind, a keen sense of noblesse oblige, and a profound belief that God favored monarchy over all other forms of government. The English poets, under no obligation to make love to her themselves, found her handsome:

> The royal youth, pursuing the report
> Of beauty, found it in the Gallic court.

Charles was now a graceful and delicate man, thin from natural abstemiousness, and the slightness of his figure gracefully offset the shortness of his stature. He ate daintily, drank only a small glass of watered wine with his meals, and was restrained and fastidious with women; morally he was the kind of man Puritans might well admire, except for a certain lack of energy and zeal. The wife of a Presbyterian colonel wrote of him:

> King Charles was temperate, chaste, and serious; so that the fools and bawds, mimics and catamites of the former court grew out of fashion; and the nobility and courtiers, who did not quite abandon their debaucheries, had yet the reverence to the king as to retire into corners to practise them.

Most observers commented on two things about Charles. One was a quality they called aloofness or disdain; but those who came to know him better felt a warmth, a somewhat faintly expressed but unmistakably human warmth. From strangers and from what he called "overconfident men," from the alien in spirit, he had created a private recess where he kept part of himself hidden and secure. Away from the expediencies of kingship he maintained an inner chamber of the spirit, remote from any Presence Chamber, where he remained immaculate and serene.

The second thing universally acknowledged was the sorrow in the expression of his face, sometimes even in the posture of his body. When Sir John Suckling saw Peter Lely's portrait of Charles, he wrote,

> See! What an humble bravery doth shine,
> And grief triumphant breaking through each line.

It was perhaps this portrait that led Bernini to say that of all the faces he had ever seen this was the most expressive of sorrow. It may simply have been the sadness of a man born in a wrong time and into a role he would gladly have relinquished to those more solidly and grossly created to fill it, but it seemed to those who knew him a more universal and pervasive grief, for in theory at least, there was

> no place
> For private sorrow in a prince's face.

Later, when men looked back, it seemed as if Charles had possessed some prophetic knowledge of the ugliness and futility of the times in which he would have to live, and of the graceless role a thoughtful and sensitive man must sometimes play on the public stage.

Charles appeared above all to love order, even in matters superficial. He was incessantly fussy about the conduct of those who surrounded him. Not only did he require moral behavior, but he also worried about decorum: what forms of address should be used; who should attend him at meals; how close courtiers might properly approach the royal personages. He put his attendants through a dainty, Dresden china minuet that seemed both pathetic and irrelevant when gauged against the titanic energies that were bursting around his throne. One of his petty regulations forbade the wives of minor officials to attend at Court, but the king made an exception for Lady Vane, perhaps in deference to the wishes of the queen, who would have prized in her not merely the aristocratic bearing but also her deep love for the old religion which, as practiced by mannerly aristocrats, seemed so much akin to her even older one.

But there was nothing superficial about the love Charles felt for the order and the form which he perceived in art. He had better taste and more appreciation of fine paintings than any other monarch, English or European, and he sent his envoys all over Europe to buy the works of the best painters. Especially he loved the order expressed in the language and ritual of the Anglican church service, an order he could not find in evangelical worship. The two-hour vociferations from the Presbyterian pulpit enervated him; the furious apocalyptic prophecies of the enthusiasts seemed to him a kind of madness; they also wearied him, draining his small reserve of spiritual energy. And so he cherished the Anglican establishment where sacred story was annealed in glass, where the priest chanted the prayers and litanies of Cranmer, and intoned the words of the Bible known by his father's name. Robe, choir and organ, candles, processions; the bodily expressions of worship in kneeling, bowing, crossing; everything suffused with incense and dim religious light—all this seemed to him not pagan mummery nor popish idolatry as the Puritans were saying, but rather the beauty of holiness.

To be understood, this fragile man, whose essence is almost lost under analytic scrutiny, must be viewed in relation to his brother, Prince Henry, who, when he had died at eighteen, had been immortalized by Puritans and poets as the paradigm of what might have been, as the Star of the North whose premature setting was a timeless tragedy. He had been idolized from birth, for England, without a male heir for so long, had begun to prophesy some great future for this prince; in Scotland, wherever he appeared, the people "were daft for mirth"; English poets, good ones, had invoked Henry to usher in another golden age. In response to the image the poets projected of a perfect, all-round prince, Henry cultivated his innate strength and versatility; he became one of the finest horsemen in the realm, superb at jousting or any game that simulated war. Politically shrewd and ambitious, he even became adequately learned. Possibly because his father was so devoted to the established church, Henry favored the Puritan dissidents; unerringly he sensed where the single-minded energies of the nation lay, and he realized that, as a monarch born for Arthur's throne, he must cultivate them. There was, he knew, a Protestant crusade to be undertaken on the continent someday, and beyond Rome lived the pagan Turks.

> Kings must be dauntless; subjects will contemn
> Those who want hearts and wear a diadem.

The contrast with his delicate brother was almost cruel, and the boy Charles never questioned his inferiority to that paragon of dexterity. He was slow learning to walk and talk. He had a stammer which, as he grew older, he almost overcame, but under great stress there was always that moment of hesitation, the inward struggle with a touch of humiliation. His legs, weakened by some deficiency of diet, became permanently bowed, and the Court, still Elizabethan in feeling and therefore not delicate in its humor, tended to laugh at such a deformity. Young Henry jested that the oval legs mattered little; he would give his brother a bishop's robe to hide them under. Thus he expressed at once his slight contempt for both his brother and the unzealous church.

Driven into an inner recess, Charles developed in that chamber of the spirit not only a resistance to taunts and slights, but also a stubborn loyalty to his own beliefs: that men who painted pictures counted for more than men who led armies, and that it was not necessarily admirable to despise one's church or one's father, both of whom it seemed so natural to love.

And so Charles became a sad and gentle man as the conviction was borne in upon him that what he most loved had little to do with commerce or war or political intrigue or the frivolous bawdry of the Court—with all the crude outwardness of things which would never approximate the fragile order of his inner life or its delicate beauty.

Yet, after the sudden death of Henry, knowing that the burdens his vigorous brother had been so eager and competent to bear would one day be his, he cultivated what strength God had given him. This delicate and private man, never at ease with hearty aggressiveness, always gentle, courteous, and vulnerable, steeled himself to do what he had to do: sustain the dignity and power of the throne, cherish and protect the rights of his people, and protect from philistine enthusiasts the beautiful, orderly worship in God's church.

Now, in the year of wonder, he became king. The first problem he faced was lack of money. Although he could not really afford a costly funeral for his father, he believed that the monarchy needed the kind of symbolic support such a funeral could provide, and so the body of his father lay in state some six weeks while elaborate ceremonies could be prepared. A hearse was fashioned by Inigo Jones; over 9,000 suits of mourning were given out, and when the stately theatricals were finished, Charles was in debt some 50,000 pounds for them.

At the same time, old debtors were hopefully presenting their bills to the new king. Charles learned with dismay that the embalming of his mother back in 1619 had not yet been paid for, the most shocking of hundreds of neglected accounts. And soon there would be the expenses of his wedding festivities, and then of his coronation. Before Charles had been in office four months, the Lord Treasurer wrote, "There is neither money in the Exchequer left, nor means to maintain the ordinaries for this year to come, nor any more credit at all." On July 9, Thomas Locke said there had never been such a want of money, and by August 29 there was a mountain of unpaid bills and only 608 pounds in the Exchequer. In the midst of a prosperous society, the new king was ominously poor.

Then, unfortunately, Buckingham began to think again, this time about raising money; and there came into his mind a grandiose scheme to capture the Spanish Plate Fleet. England had tried many times to capture it, but neither Drake, Ralegh, nor Essex had succeeded. If only it could be taken now, ancient glories would revive and there would be plenty of money almost painlessly acquired.

Charles listened hopefully, but he could not wait until the Spanish ships came in; he simply had to have money now. So like any other desperately impecunious man, he thought of the pawnbrokers. Soon Sir Sackville Crow, a faithful servant but an inexperienced jewelry salesman, went to Amsterdam with two bags filled with Crown jewels and one bag of gold plate, under sanguine instructions to raise 300,000 pounds. Pawnbrokers being what they are, it would have been easier for him to take the Spanish fleet. After much delay and many offers and counteroffers, the pawnbrokers, unimpressed either with Buckingham's character or Charles' credit, offered to buy some of the jewels for 43,000 pounds. That sum and the rest of the gems were returned to England. The amount was just slightly more than Queen Henrietta Maria spent on new jewels during the first two years of her marriage.

Perhaps the most desperate need for money was to refurbish and rebuild the royal Navy, the condition of which was so bad that Dunkirkers and Barbary pirates added to the wonders of 1625 by harrying the English coasts and shipping lanes. Against the daring raiders in their swift, maneuverable ships the British navy seemed helpless. Of its twenty-seven seaworthy ships, over half had been built before James came to the throne, and eleven had sailed against the Spanish Armada. The few new ships were overdecorated and underdesigned, not so much fighters as monuments of Elizabethan grandeur. And so the sea-borne predators, especially the Barbary pirates who were mostly Moors with a sprinkling of European rogues, descended on the tired lion, seizing plunder and slaves. Sometimes their landing parties would capture a single man plowing in his field or two girls on their way to market; sometimes they carried away the greater part of a village to be sold as slaves or held for ransom. The British navy, with its long guns that would have been decisive if the pirates had waited for them to come within range, lumbered along too late. The pride of England was thus becoming an object of scorn and derision.

It is hard to imagine anything which could arouse greater emotion among Charles' subjects than the capture and sale of English men and women. It was said that white Christian women were being raped by dark-skinned Muslims; it was only slightly less traumatic to hear that Englishmen were being forced to serve as galley slaves and at times to row the ships that attacked their own country. The Crown was deluged with petitions from wives seeking their husbands' ransom, from parents seeking return of their children, and from mayors who petitioned on behalf of the captured citizens of their town. One such petition was on behalf of 2,000 captured mariners, another for sixty people kidnaped during a church service in Cornwall. Occasionally captives would escape or be ransomed and publish angry, livid accounts of their sufferings, accounts which aroused the indignation of the nation.

> . . . the scorching heat now penetrates their brains, their flesh is burned off their backs . . . who has not his head and face broken, all their bodies pearled with a bloody sweat. . . . They are beaten to put on their clothes and beaten to take them off, they are beaten to eat, drink, sleep and wash, and are beaten for doing any of these. . . . They curse the day of their nativities, and the parents that engendered them, and if it were to die to curse God himself (I speak it with awful timor); in their passions they renounce heaven, Saint Peter and all sanctity.

So one former galley slave wrote of the barbarous treatment of enslaved Englishmen.

Charles was sensitive not only about the sufferings of his subjects, but also about the humiliation of being harassed and intimidated by a fourth-rate power. In the first year of his reign he doubled the amount of money appropriated for the navy and continued to seek ways to find money for ships. But that was not enough at this critical moment. The scourge of the Barbary pirates was a disaster which Charles needed somehow to rise to meet. But in this as in other matters, he turned instead to advisers and subordinates who were too often cynical, incompetent, or corrupt.

Bad as it was, the visitation of the Barbary pirates was less terrifying than the epidemic of the plague which, in that wonderful year of 1625, raged as furiously as at any time in English history. It began as it always did: in April a few people who lived near the docks or in the crowded tenements died of a virulent fever. Seekers after final causes agreed that these deaths were caused by sinfulness:

the more generous said it was the sinfulness of all; the more rigid said it was the private sinfulness of the departed. And if the poor in their hovels were not really more sinful than the wealthy in their pleasant homes, then one could account for the selectivity of disease by exalting the divine will over the divine reason or mercy.

The deaths from the plague in the more pungent areas of the city almost doubled in the week of May 1. On that same day Charles was married by proxy to the Catholic princess Henrietta Maria and issued an order that "all manner of prosecution against . . . Roman Catholics . . . be stayed and forborne." Presbyterian pulpiteers, angered and afraid, pointed out that the plague had increased immediately after the proclamation.

By May 14, the fever had reached beyond the sinful poor and was afflicting the godly and affluent; those responsible for James' funeral which was held on that day wondered how many dead this resplendent celebration of death would cost.

By mid-June, Divine Providence seemed to have lost all sense of decorum, and, regardless of rank, several hundred a week were dying throughout London. Parliament was therefore adjourned to the city of Oxford. Just two days later in a house at Windsor, two of the king's servants died of the infection. Now even the royal person had been exposed and a thoroughly alarmed Presbyterian thought he knew why: "This taking part against our own religion is one of the chief causes of God's hand that now hangeth over us." The burning in the flesh was no more intense than the spiritual fear, and in the minds of militant Protestants, toleration of Catholics and the spread of the disease were linked.

With 500 dying every week, some steps had to be taken. London authorities therefore ordered the arrest and imprisonment of all Irishmen; the English felt safer with the Irish confined. Then, just in case that was not enough, the city fathers also ordered the sewage ditches to be scoured.

In July the fever was destroying the city and every Londoner was both vulnerable and suspect. The town of Bristol refused to allow citizens of London to come to the fair unless they had proof of their freedom from contamination, a document obtainable only from the Lord Mayor of London, in whose own household the sickness had broken out. Other towns near London shut their gates and the people withdrew into their houses.

When the fever had begun in London it aroused at first a feverish activity. The volunteer "searchers" carrying their white wands, along with the red cross and the bell, would inspect each house, and wherever they found a flushed and pustuled face, would post on the door the inscription, "Lord have mercy on us." Then they would set two soldiers to watch at the door of the dwelling of fire and wrath. These two soldiers were to watch by turns for forty days; then, if the fever had burned out, the house was purged by lime. But inside those doors the people were terrified, and in the sleepy hours of the watch they would sneak out through a window. Then the soldiers, usually only citizens working temporarily at a soldier's job, could either shoot or wink. If there were dead in the house, the death cart rumbled up late at night or early in the morning and picked up the vessels of wrath and dumped them into pits filled with lime which could not quite consume all that were shoveled in, nor quite obliterate the stench.

By the beginning of August this frantic activity had subsided and a great silence had descended upon London. The theaters and the inns were closed; the markets were shut down. If any business was transacted the person paying money dropped it into a tub of water from which it was taken out by the seller. No hands touched. The streets were empty and overgrown with grass. William Lilly, the astrologer, went all the way from Strand Bridge to Saint Antholine's Church and met only three people on the way. Now the searchers themselves had fled or were dying; there were not enough makeshift soldiers to guard the infected houses; the death carts were fewer each day as the dead became more numerous. Panic sat down outside the walls, and the Lord Mayor saw her: "If the City be straitened of victuals," he wrote the Privy Council, "it will not be in the power of the few magistrates that remain to restrain the violence that hunger may enforce." And by mid-August, when 5,000 names appeared each week on the plaguey bills, London had become a mortal prison. It was decreed that no boat might go from Kingston to London; if it did it could not return. Terrified citizens began to flock to the highways, but the surrounding towns and cities, having no desire to share London's death agony, required all travelers to present a ticket indicating from where they had come. If from London or any of its plague-infested suburbs, they were turned away and left to die in the highways or fields. "The citizens fled away as out of a house on fire," John Donne wrote,

> and stuffed their pockets with their best ware, and threw themselves into highways, and were not received so much as into barns, and perished so, some of them with more money about them than would have bought the village where they died.

In September, the death count was still 5,000 a week and London houses had become futile hiding places from that fire in the flesh. The schoolmasters, forbidden to open their schools, petitioned the government for relief, saying it was as painful to starve as to burn. And there were now many alarms at the activities of the Catholics: it was said that not content with bringing the plague, they were taking advantage of it to arm themselves and conspire to turn England over to Rome.

When the heart of the nation was pulsing feebly, the ruler should have made some gesture. That he could do nothing substantial everyone would acknowledge. What can a man do when the hand of God is upon him? But Charles might have walked among the sick; he might have uttered words that sounded hope while the church bells tolled of death. He might simply have said "courage" or "faith" or "I suffer with you." But the fastidious and delicate Charles, repelled by the ugliness and frightened at his helplessness, did only three conspicuous things. He gave 100 pounds to be distributed among the poor; he ordered a fast to be held each Wednesday; and he hid himself from the fever at Woodstock, sixty-five miles west of London. Before the gate where God's vicegerent dwelt, his servants erected a gibbet which warned that no one from that dying city might approach his king who now, at the height of the infection, dissolved the Parliament. Some said it didn't matter because only sickness and death were ruling the land anyway.

November at last brought cool weather and relief; in the first week less than 100 deaths were recorded, most of them among the "rabble." Then the burgesses, the merchants, the gentry, and the royal household began moving back into the city. Schoolmasters opened their schools and so, for some, terror was replaced by tedium. In the palace festivities were resumed. It was announced in December that the demoiselles of the Court would present a French pastoral in which the queen would be one of the actresses. When a strident, atrabilious Presbyterian learned of this, he was outraged, and fearful of God's further judgment. For William Prynne such play-acting was fit only for harlots. Moreover, Henrietta Maria, the daughter of a one-time Protestant who had turned Catholic because he thought Paris worth a Mass, had been educated by equivocating Jesuits; she was, Prynne thought, the spiritual daughter of Cardinal Richelieu. The idea of a book, a long, furious, unreadable, godly book, began to form in his mind.

There was little gaiety to decry among the citizens of London who had gone down into the pit. They had called out to their monarch and he had erected his gibbet; they had cried out to their God and he had withdrawn. In His silence their confidence had been shaken, and now, to absolve that hidden God, they needed to indict their fellow humans. As the macabre dance of Dreary Death had passed by and the great fear had lifted, men seemed more quarrelsome than ever. As Sir John Eliot said, "The danger of the time [the plague] was a great cause of dislike. . . . The dislike ushered in most of the questions that have been raised."

There were in that wonderful year other catastrophes; there were, for instance, preternaturally violent storms, unseasonable wetness in which farmers tried to make hay while standing up to their ankles in water. But compared to the overriding curse of the plague, these troubles seemed humanly manageable.

In politics, too, there was arising a serious and complex problem that would eventually involve both the Vanes—the problem of the Palatinate, one of the small German states of the Holy Roman Empire. The elector of this little state, Frederick V, was a Protestant who had married Elizabeth of England, Charles' sister. And Frederick, neither very bright nor very valiant, had over-reached himself. The neighboring Bohemia was ruled by Ferdinand, a prince of Spanish descent, whose intolerance toward Protestantism had so estranged his nobles that they had deposed him and offered the vacant kingship to Frederick. It was a perilous vacancy to step into, just when it was rumored that Ferdinand would soon be elected emperor. But Frederick, believing that his election to the Bohemian kingship was probably a direct expression of God's wishes, went to Prague and was crowned.

His reign lasted one disastrous year. An iconoclastic Calvinist, as intolerant in his own way as Ferdinand, he deeply offended his Lutheran subjects by tearing the great crucifix out of the royal chapel, by ripping the pictures of saints from the walls, and by offering for sale royal treasures of art which he regarded as idols. In November, 1620, the Count of Tilly, general of the armies of the Catholic League, captured Prague and sent Frederick into exile, to begin a life of wandering and begging for help in regaining rule of the Palatinate.

Frederick's loss of both Bohemia and the Palatinate aroused the strongest feeling in England. Today, the Puritan fear of Catholics seems paranoid, but that fear can be understood when one looks at the state of Protestantism on the continent. Everywhere it appeared about to go under. In France, Louis XIII was denying that liberty of worship which his father had granted Huguenots; Germany was being over-run by the armies of the Catholic League; England's allies were dispirited; the King of Denmark had been checked and the King of Sweden seemed indifferent to the fate of his coreligionists. The Low Countries, though willing, were unable to give any assistance. That was how it looked to an English member of Parliament who observed that the House of Austria had rich territories in India and Africa and was the master of Spain, Italy, and Germany. Protestants everywhere, he thought, were about to be swallowed up, leaving the sceptered isle to stand alone against the formidable power of Rome and her temporal princes. That is why most Englishmen found it so desperately necessary to recover the Palatinate. In that first "wonderful" year of his reign, it was the most serious international problem Charles faced.

From the beginning, the only real hope for that recovery lay with Gustav Adolf, the King of Sweden, a charismatic leader about whom legends and prophecies were already beginning to cluster, the Lion of the North who would overcome the Dragon and perhaps even the Imperial Eagle. He was also a military realist who made demands of men and money from the hard-pressed Charles which, however urgently they were needed, England simply could not supply. Christian of Denmark, on the other hand, a less effective but more sanguine monarch, asked Charles for only 6,000 men and subsistence money of 30,000 pounds per month. Charles duly promised it all, but was never able to send more than 4,000 men, most of whom were promptly slaughtered, and a total of 46,000 pounds subsistence. In 1626 Tilly defeated Christian who complained that, if the King of England had kept his word, he would not have gone under.

And so those in England and abroad who were trying to forge a *Corpus Evangelicorum,* an informal, international Protestant League, persisted in seeing England as the key to the plight of Protestantism on the continent. But the English monarch, perhaps because of his advisers, seemed to lack the desire or the power to recover the Palatinate or to defend the "pure" religion. At all events, he did nothing effective.

Of all the wonders of that first year of Charles' reign, not even the plague or the failure to recover the Palatinate had such deep-seated consequences as the failure of the new king to come to terms with his Parliament. Through the Parliament of 1625 and two successive ones, the hostility and estrangement would grow as Charles sought funds and Parliament, instead of granting them, sought new policies and new leadership.

It was desperate need for money that led Charles to call his first Parliament, for, as one of the members observed, "subtle inventions may pick the purse, but nothing can open it but the Parliament." There was no one to tell Charles what old Burghley had once told Elizabeth, that if she would first win their hearts, the Commons would give her their money.

His first Parliament began in mid-June of that year, and all its business and debates were held against the background of the tolling, mournful bells. Charles needed money not merely for small matters like the funeral, the marriage, the wardrobe, but also for the payments promised to Christian, for the even greater amounts needed to prepare a naval expedition against Spain, and for the ruinous debts he had inherited. He must have needed between seven and eight million pounds, but he dared not say so.

At the joint session which opened the Parliament the king spoke modestly and briefly. He was a young man, he said, and the attempt to recover the Palatinate, along with the war against Spain, would be his first concern. It would dishonor him and the Parliament if these actions were aborted; only Parliament could provide the means for their success. He then added that because he was "unfit for much speaking" (it was the stammer), he would let the Lord Keeper of the Seal say more.

That worthy indulged his taste for rhetoric, the principal point of which was that the Palatinate must be recovered. Sir Thomas Carew was then chosen Speaker and he made some propitious remarks. He remembered that, like Charles, good King Hezekiah was twenty-five years old when he began to reign, and he too showed zeal for God and religion. Sir Thomas was glad that His Majesty was safely back from Spain and was sure that with the sword Parliament would put into his hands, Charles would recover the Palatinate.

But after these pleasant formalities, the old issue which had disrupted previous Parliaments was raised: redress of grievance should precede the voting of supply, the members said, and grievances were plentiful. Old Sir Edward Coke thought the king's household was out of order, which might have reflected on Sir Henry Vane except that he had little control over the specified extravagances such as those for costly diet, apparel, and expensive new buildings. It was alleged that 140,000 pounds had recently been given for places and offices, and there were complaints about increased pensions for the Court. Never in Elizabeth's time had more than 18,000 pounds been given to pensioners, but now the sum was 120,000 and still growing.

These grievances, real and deeply felt as they were, might have been resolved if the religious issues had not been so urgent. Compared to those, all else seemed ancillary. The first thing that Parliament demanded was the enforcement of the laws against Jesuits, popish priests, et cetera. It was probably the et cetera that concealed the most difficult problem, for while it was always safe to attack the Jesuits, the king had recently remitted penalties against ordinary Catholic worshippers. And the whole controversy was inflamed by two recent books written by the king's chaplain, Richard Mountagu, who was popularly called an Arminian. That term, when precisely used, meant one who in some way modified the Calvinistic doctrine of predestination to make some room for free will and good deeds, a modification in the direction of humanism. But as the term was popularly used it implied a dangerous heretic, usually some cunning dissimulator who was really bent on bringing in popery.

When the Parliament of 1625 saw Mountagu's books they were shocked, for they felt that he had made an unjustifiable attack on

Puritanism, which he did indeed regard with aristocratic distaste. Puritans, he said, were "saint-seeming, Bible-bearing hypocrites," the kind of fanatics that had always plagued the church. But more offensive to the Puritans of Parliament than these somewhat light-hearted insults were his conciliatory statements about Rome, for although he found much to criticize in the Roman monolith, he was essentially an intellectual liberal who believed that Rome was also a spouse of Christ. These views allied him with William Laud, said to be his close friend and recently made confessor to the Duke of Buckingham, son of a "notorious Catholic."

There is something amusing in the amount of time spent by Charles' first Parliament on Mountagu's books; never has an author been so searchingly reviewed by a legislative body. But if one looks behind the attacks and defenses of these thoughtful, harmless treatises, it seems that the debate was serving as surrogate for a question of supreme importance: who should monitor and reform the church? The hierarchy itself in a convocation called by the king, or the elected representatives of the franchised voters?

After this first Parliament, even the issue of religion receded slightly before the virulence of the attacks directed at Buckingham, who became for Parliament "the cause of causes." For this, two reasons superseded all others, both involving military and naval disasters. The first was his attempt to take the Spanish fleet. Shortly after the first Parliament was dissolved, some old ships were patched up, some men with no heart for battle were impressed, and finally a fleet sailed off to Cadiz. Once there, all coordination and leadership broke down. When the English landed, they forgot to take food ashore. In the first Spanish village, the soldiers found wine and, pouring it into their empty stomachs, were soon ingloriously drunk, sprawled out in the fields and on the roads. Ship's fever attacked the crews, and despair grew along with disorganization. Finally the fleet limped home, a clownish, humiliating contrast to the expedition that had once gone to Cadiz under Ralegh and Essex.

The humiliation intensified Buckingham's desperation, which led to an impulsive expedition in 1627 to assist the Huguenots besieged by Richelieu at La Rochelle. Buckingham managed to land on a small island near the city, but thanks to his incompetence and his uncertain knowledge of tactics, he failed to take the island's fortress.

Finally he tried to re-embark without adequate cover for his troops, without even an adequate rearguard; and the French slaughtered the English like sheep. Some 6,884 English troops drew pay on the French island of Rhé; only 2,989 returned home, most of them to die from sickness brought on by malnutrition and exposure. In the fleet there were mutinies everywhere.

Both the Parliament and the people wished to call Buckingham to account. There was in England a legal fiction that the king could do no wrong; consequently his subjects could demand redress only from his ministers. Knowing this, the Tudor monarchs had sometimes sacrificed a loyal servant to the necessities of state. But Charles refused. With the admirable but inexpedient loyalty which he would later manifest towards Strafford and Laud, he said,

> I must let you know that I will not allow any of my servants to be questioned amongst you, much less such as are of eminent place and near unto me.

However personally admirable such loyalty may be, Clarendon was right that

> for supreme power to interpose and shelter an accused servant from answering is an obstruct of justice and almost automatically convicts without trial.

And Charles' subjects responded predictably. A commoner said that England's only remedy was to kill the duke, set Charles aside, and bring in the Queen of Bohemia, a lady to whom distance was lending enchantment. A son of Hugh Pyne said it would never be well with England until the duke's head fell from his shoulders. But one of the most alarming signs of unrest came from a highly placed young gentleman, son of the headmaster of St. Paul's school. This young man, Alexander Gill, Jr., had written some tavern doggerel about the duke:

> And now just God! I humbly pray
> That thou wilt take the slime away
> That keeps my Sovereign's eyes from viewing
> The things that will be our undoing.

Gill also crudely attacked the king himself for being led by the duke, and in his cups he had said, "We have a fine, wise King. He has wit enough to be a shopkeeper, to ask, what do you lack? and that is all!" And one day a libel was found posted at St. Paul's Cross: "The first thing God doth when he determineth to dethrone a king is to take away from him the hearts of his subjects."

But Buckingham's real significance lay deeper than the king's blind loyalties or his own failures. He was a representative of a system that was decadent and ripe for overthrow. He represented that swarm of noblemen, civil servants, and ambitious climbers who, like the elder Vane, held office by virtue of favor from the king or of cash payments for which they received the right to squeeze those whom they served. Enormous fortunes were being made in this fashion: Clarendon alleged that the Earl of Carlisle, noted for excesses in clothes and diet, had taken during his lifetime more than 400,000 pounds, a sum enormously greater than Charles could hope to coax from a Parliament. This swarm of parasites, of whom Buckingham was only the most egregious, represented a form of indirect taxation as they drained money from the productive segments of society. The Crown tolerated and even encouraged this abuse because the selling of offices provided necessary income which could not be raised through Parliament. And so the Court, it was said, was full of excess, idleness, and luxury, while the country was full of pride, mutiny, and discontent.

The "wonders" of Charles' first year were, to be sure, mostly disasters. And of all his troubles, only the plague ameliorated; everything else worsened. But there was one good sign. For those who still believed in the old portents, it came as most welcome news that a lioness in the Tower had whelped. Since the lioness was emblematic of the queen, this event might suggest that there would be an heir to the throne even though he would be, as some grumbled, half French.

Looking back on it all, an aristocratic observer wrote,

So many miraculous circumstances contributed to the King's ruin that men might well think that heaven and the earth and the stars designed it.

Worse days were ahead for the king, for the two Vanes, and for England, but as time simplified and heightened events in the minds of living men, more and more it seemed that all the troubles were rooted in that first wonderful year.

3

Diplomacy and Conscience (1631–1634)

The elder Vane served in all three of the troubled Parliaments during the first four years of Charles' reign. As befitted a man determined to rise to power through the influence of his prince, he pursued a cautious policy of adherence to the interests of the Crown. Neither then nor later was he a notable Parliamentarian. That title was being won by men like Sir John Eliot and Thomas Wentworth, who had demonstrated both eloquence and courage in their insistence that redress of grievance should precede supply. In 1628 Wentworth had been elevated to the peerage, and, since that time, some said he was leaning in a new political direction.

In addition to his work at Court and in the Parliament, Vane was busily pursuing the principal activity of the landed gentry: he was acquiring more land. In one of his rare autobiographical allusions, Vane, typically enough, talks of nothing but purchases of lands and buildings. For these he felt a solemn reverence, much as his son was coming to feel about God.

Of his newly purchased holdings, the most impressive was Raby Castle far to the north in the county of Durham, and not even Vane was so blind to history as not to know that he had purchased something more than real estate. Portions of that old pile went back to the Danish invasions; since then it had been the seat of the Nevilles who, in Elizabethan times, had rebelled and thereby forfeited their demesnes to the Crown.

> Seven hundred knights, retainers all
> Of Neville, at their master's call
> Had sat together in Raby's Hall.

Although in some disrepair, it was a noble castle, with moat and strong battlements that would support mounted culverin, with towered masonry and a strong inner keep. There were cavernous fireplaces which could roast an ox whole and a staircase down which a company of men could march without breaking rank.

Unquestionably Vane felt that this castle would provide a suitable title for him if he were raised to the peerage. Baron Raby had a fine sound in those crass ears, and one day he would fiercely resent the man who snatched the title from him.

When Vane purchased Raby, in true burgher fashion he complained to the king of the bad bargain he had made. It was, he said, "a mere hullock of stone" for which he had paid too much. On his first progress to Scotland, in 1633, King Charles stopped at Raby and, upon first seeing it, remarked in his mild way, "Sir Henry, this is more than a heap of stones."

Living in a time when primogeniture was unquestioned, Sir Henry took careful thought for the education of his eldest son upon whom that land and its keeping would devolve. He decided, therefore, to send young Henry to Westminster School in the shadow of the great Abbey, within hailing distance of the Houses of Parliament.

By any standards, Westminster was a fine school. Ben Jonson had been taught there by the great master William Camden, who had been succeeded, among others, by Lancelot Andrewes, a model of Anglican learning and gentleness. Now the master was Lambert Osbaldeston, conceded to be the best headmaster in England. One day more than eighty of his former pupils would hold the title of doctor and would reverence his name.

Osbaldeston inherited a strict school and had no intention of altering its nature. Under him it was said to be more disciplined than Eton, which was saying a good deal. At five in the morning, the monitor would cry *Surgite!* and the sleepy, grumbling boys would arise and kneel to say the collect for grace—in Latin, of course.

After the prayer a service followed, one much like that of the Prayer Book except that it was all in Latin. It included a General Confession, the Lord's Prayer, suffrages, a hymn, lessons from the Proverbs, a *Te Deum,* readings from the Sermon on the Mount, the Apostles' Creed, and again the Lord's Prayer. On Holy Days there would be other formal religious exercises, each appropriate to the occasion. At Westminster School the boys practiced formal worship regularly.

After breakfast the headmaster would set a proposition or passage in Latin to be translated by the fourth form, varied or contradicted by the fifth, and turned into verse by the sixth and seventh. This was the same exercise that Ben Jonson had found to be so useful for a poet, the same kind of exercise that Milton had performed a few years earlier at St. Paul's.

Each year in December, after the entire school had been examined by the Dean, the prebendaries, and the masters, the industrious boys were promoted. Those who made it to the upper forms were given a theme in Latin prose on Monday, in Latin verse on Tuesday, in Greek prose on Wednesday, and in Greek verse on Thursday; and, in the seventh and last form, the students were introduced to Hebrew. All the students worked eight hours each day and, for their intellectual and spiritual health, were beaten frequently, lustily, and piously. Anyone who graduated from Westminster, even if he never went on to university (as Ben Jonson did not), was thought to be a highly educated man.

Eighteen regular monitors and another special one were assigned to guard the boys against outward and inward impurities. Those who remember their own adolescence may smile or shudder at the task.

Of the many things that happened during the years young Vane spent at Westminster School, two are especially notable. The first was that the headmaster took such an extreme dislike to the Duke of Buckingham that to some he seemed also disrespectful of the king. It is not easy to know how his boys responded to this: in addition to Vane, two other famous republicans were to emerge from the school, Arthur Haselrig and Thomas Scot, whose lives would be intertwined with his. But such a small incidence of budding republicans is surely nothing remarkable.

Osbaldeston also took an extreme dislike to William Laud, particularly when, after Laud became Dean of Westminster Abbey, he opposed lectures and scriptural exercises, insisting instead on the ritualistic and liturgical observances of Anglicanism. Later Laud believed that Osbaldeston was referring to him in a letter which spoke of some unnamed person as

> Vermin, little urchin,
> Meddling hocus-pocus.

Although Osbaldeston denied that he meant Laud, he prudently fled to escape arrest. What evidence remains suggests that although most of the boys may have shared their headmaster's dislike of Laud, they also tended to side with the king, at least initially.

While young Vane was in the sixth and seventh forms, he was enduring acute emotional and religious struggles. Though all his life he was articulate in argument and exposition, he was inept at symbolic and lyrical expression, precisely what his crisis at Westminster called for. In describing this struggle, Vane's words are so conventional an expression of the basic Puritan experience that they could apply to the experiences of thousands of men of his time. But the experience seemed intensely his own and was the formative experience of his life: all that followed is understandable only in relation to it.

In his youthful days at Westminster, he tells us, he was inclined to the vanity of the world: he had the doubts and fears of adolescence, that first sense of the disparity between what the world seems and what it is, between childhood complacency and adolescent agony. There are always those little urgings of palate, stomach, or glands and the little betrayals associated with them which, at the age of fifteen or thereabouts, take on dark shadings of hidden mysteries. At that age boys discover why young Augustine desired stolen pears—not for themselves but because they symbolized the surrender to the first sin, the renewed assent to whatever is meant by Adam's fall. At that age, everything for a sensitive young boy may seem tainted with the scent and the sweat and the rub of "the fecund ditch."

While God might forgive man his lusts, many Puritans would not, and so Vane, when recounting this inner crisis, assures those whose good opinion he was still courting that he had never fallen into "lewdness," though he had fallen into profaneness, into life without God, into "a way of sin and death." He could not have failed to grasp the terrible irony in this; though monitors were paid to guard him against impurities, against outward impurity he never felt the need of their restraint, and against inward impurity they were useless. Besides, there were those required daily exercises, formal prayers and services designed to provide those small daily accessions of grace that to the serene seem stronger than the arrows of desire. But it was not that way with young Vane: formal religion could not penetrate his inner life deeply enough to allay the fear or assuage the guilt.

What happened to him then was all inward. At almost the same time, Oliver Cromwell, fourteen years older but still unknown, was experiencing the same thing: he too was a voyager of the inner life.

> O, I lived in and loved darkness and hated light;
> I was a chief, the chief of sinners. This is true:
> I hated godliness, yet God had mercy upon me.

In all his pain and self-loathing, not once did young Vane find either hope or relief from a written prayer, a liturgical gesture, or a ritualistic exercise. But inwardly, deeply hidden from eye or ear, owing nothing to sense, he dimly felt some "signal impressions." These were followed by "awakening dispensations" which came from no priest, no book, no institution. They were begotten in him by the will of an inscrutable God who had decreed that young Vane, in all his deformity, should be a vessel of mercy.

Later, in imagery borrowed from the Old Testament, he described what had happened in that fifteenth year: wells and springs had opened in the wilderness; the desert of his life knew rain and dew; there came to him a "rich and free grace"; and his bitter self-reproach ended in joy and the relief of a flood of tears. From this first experience he never turned back; but neither did he rest in it. Rather he continued to enjoy ecstasies, an almost daily drama of the inner life by which he would orient all that he was later to learn or to suffer.

The resolution of his personal crisis through the Puritan experience of grace decisively alienated him from Laudian Anglicanism, from the communal piety of his mother and the expedient churchliness of his father, from the community of all those whose worship was expressed through liturgical forms. For him, he now knew, formalism was death; only in spontaneity could the life of his spirit flower.

And so it was not surprising that when he went to Magdalen Hall, Oxford, as a gentleman commoner at the age of sixteen, he was repelled by its formalities. To matriculate, he was required to swear the oath of allegiance and supremacy; since he could not do it, he was never matriculated. He took off his scholar's gown and put on a layman's cloak, wandering around Oxford for a time, unfrocked, unsworn, and uninterested. He soon gave it all up.

A recent photograph of Raby Castle, County Durham, purchased by the elder Vane from the Crown and settled upon Henry, Jr., at the time of his marriage. (*Country Life*)

The Peter Lely portrait of young Vane. (Courtauld Institute of Art)

He never again endured formal education. It was said that like his brothers later on he studied at Leyden, which some thought a Puritan seminary, but no record of his affiliation with that or any other European university has been found. Apparently he spent a year traveling in France, Switzerland, and the Low Countries, acquiring some French, though not enough that as an Englishman he needed to be ashamed; undoubtedly he became acquainted with Puritan congregations on the continent. The pastor at Rotterdam was Hugh Peter, a stocky, red-faced, jovial minister of the Word, a man of inner voices and outer eccentricities who had been driven abroad, he said, by the formalisms of the Bishop of London. He was an improbable combination of traits, a kind of Celtic Puritan, full of laughter, pranks, and spiritual ecstasies. If, as seems likely, Vane met Peter and worshiped in his congregation, he would have known of Peter's fifteen articles to which his flock subscribed. Article two was directed against Laudian reform: "Cleave in heart to the true and pure worship of God, and oppose all ways of innovation and corruption."

When the young man returned home a year later, his father suggested in high places that his son might now do well in the diplomatic service. Because of young Vane's Puritan leanings, it was thought unwise to send him with his father to Gustav Adolf in Sweden; instead he was placed in the train of Ambassador Anstruther and sent to Vienna to the Court of the Catholic emperor, Ferdinand II. By contrast, John Suckling, a young cavalier and poet who might have been unduly influenced at that Imperial Court, was placed in the train of Ambassador Vane and sent to Gustav Adolf.

It was typical of Charles that he should have sent out these two embassies at the same time: he almost never decided on a single course of action. The Palatinate might be restored to his unattractive brother-in-law either by Gustav Adolf through force of arms or by Ambassador Anstruther through bargainings with the emperor. So the father went on one errand, the son on the other.

In 1631, the Thirty Years War was already thirteen years old and Gustav Adolf had been on the throne twenty years, a mature, forceful man who had been humanistically trained and who gave the impression of immense energy under firm restraint. He was a handsome, imposing figure, a man who always wished to be humble but invariably gave the impression of pride, a monarch who lent credibility to the theory of divine right. Gustav Adolf was unlikely as a Messiah only because his kingdom was so small, consisting of no more than 900,000 people living in a land where climate and soil were always difficult and sometimes cruel. Because this small kingdom did not offer enough men to fill out an army, Gustav Adolf depended on a mercenary force, but he developed procedures and attitudes which made it highly effective. The mercenaries who composed most of the continental armies of his opponents, Tilly and Wallenstein, had no strong sense of allegiance. They followed standards rather than causes and if the standard was captured, they were likely to desert. But Gustav Adolf discovered a strange and, to him, wonderful thing: there existed a people who were morally earnest about money. They called themselves Scots and, if regularly paid, they developed a strong sense of loyalty. Unlike the English they found the Swedish food rather good, although being used to a drink with real character, they could never forgive the Swedes for schnapps.

In return for money and sensible leadership, Gustav Adolf demanded that his troops maintain puritanical standards of conduct. They attended prayers twice a day, sermons once a week. No swearing was allowed, no blasphemy or sacrilege, and the soldiers were forbidden the consolations of the flesh. Perhaps these demands were not all strictly met, but enough of them were so that something unique emerged in the Protestant world: an army with both a brisk standard of military efficiency and a tradition of piety, a combination which would later be manifested in the armies of the Scots covenanters and in the New Model of Oliver Cromwell. With such an army, Gustav Adolf conceived that he might march on Vienna and do what Turk and Slav had failed to do for centuries: cross the Danube and storm the Burghof.

After the assassination in 1628 of Buckingham, who had met with a broad knife in a narrow passage, Sir Thomas Roe had been sent as ambassador to Stockholm. Roe, an old Elizabethan, was a man of unimpugned integrity, a merchant and a Protestant who was deeply disturbed by the Imperialist threat. *Divide et impera,* he wrote, had now become *divide et eradica.* Choosing him for ambassador indicated that in London there was hope of arriving at Protestant solidarity.

But after a year or so the English Court had come to regard Roe with suspicion. Henrietta Maria, Lord Treasurer Weston, and the group known as the Imperialist faction believed that Roe had become tainted with the cult of Gustav Adolf whom, according to Wallenstein, the German people awaited as the Jews await their Messiah. And so Roe was withdrawn and sent into virtual exile in his country house, to be replaced by Sir Henry Vane, who could be counted on to be completely loyal to Charles and never to be swayed by mere charismatic lure.

Meanwhile young Vane arrived in Vienna in April of 1631. A few weeks later Tilly and the Imperialists not only took Magdeburg but sacked the city and savagely slaughtered Protestants in their worst massacre since the day of St. Bartholomew in Paris half a century earlier. When Magdeburg fell, it seemed that the Eagle had been too strong for the Lion, and a great fear fell on the minds of all Protestants.

But after Magdeburg, with the deposed Frederick always at his side, Gustav Adolf and his army began a triumphal progress down Priest's Lane into South Germany, overcoming a long string of ecclesiastical territories as far south as Munich. In September, at the Battle of Breitenfeld, he demolished Tilly's army; had he pushed ahead, he might have taken Vienna.

The elder Vane caught up with the Swedish king in November and stayed with him in the triumphant journey through Mainz. But from the first Gustav Adolf treated him coldly. He knew well enough why Roe had been recalled and his resentment was manifest in his brusque treatment of Vane. Sir Henry's English, he said, sounded more and more like Spanish, and once in Munich, when Vane was haggling with him over some point of diplomacy, Gustav Adolf lost control of his monumental temper and turned on Sir Henry in anger. Later Vane would write,

It is usual with the King to repent himself when the blow is given; for he hath often told me . . . that he would give all he had to be master of his passions, but when he began to be moved, he hath something that rises in his brain, that makes him forget what he saith or doth; that this he finds in himself . . . but yet he cannot get it mastered though he hath often designed the same; and therefore he hopes God and all the world will forgive him.

As might be expected, negotiations between Vane and Gustav Adolf came to nothing.

In March of 1632, Sir Henry sent young John Suckling as his confidential messenger back to London where the quick-witted poet saw that the Spanish–Imperial faction was in control. In his dispatches to Vane, Suckling tells him that many in England think he has been sent to undo the work of Sir Thomas Roe. There is much murmuring; Vane is not popular. Some women of the Court take it ill that his son should be a statesman ahead of their own sons. Finally there are unpleasant rumors of corruption on the part of the clerks he left in charge of his duties as Comptroller of the Household.

One gathers from Suckling's dispatches that the elder Vane, certainly of the Spanish party when he left London, had become convinced that the best hope for restoration of the Palatinate was through the military victories of Gustav Adolf. The Prince of Orange certainly thought so; he had said to Sir Henry, "Whenever either the upper or lower Palatinate is restored by treaty, I will give His Majesty my head."

When Vane received his letters of recall in August of 1632, Gustav Adolf apparently hoped he would be replaced by a more suitable negotiator. But just four months later, before another embassy had been sent, the Lion King was killed in the Battle of Lutzen. Thus ended the father's mission, a failure in every sense. The war would drag on vainly for sixteen more years and Frederick would die in exile; his heir would finally regain only the lower Palatinate.

The son's mission, although not successful, was at least relatively serene. For him it was primarily an educational experience like the "grand tour" which was then considered the final phase of a good education. But Vienna, like Madrid or Warsaw, was about the furthest conceivable extension of a continental tour, which was normally limited to more accessible cities richer in cultural attractions.

Sir Robert Anstruther had apparently been dispatched to Vienna with the offer that England would induce the Dutch to negotiate their quarrel with Spain if Spain in turn would persuade Ferdinand to restore the Palatinate to Frederick. But the Spanish, knowing how much restoration of the Palatinate meant to England and to

Charles, asked a higher price: a declaration of war by the English on the Dutch. It was hopeless from the beginning.

What was young Vane like, then just eighteen years old? Despite his aversion to Oxford formalism he had adopted the new Oxford style of long hair, a fashion considered by many to be both abhorrent and ungodly. Originally Laud himself had tried to arrest this fad, prescribing in his precise way that an Oxford student's hair must not be so long as to hide the tips of his ears. At least one undergraduate, to the eternal disgust of his parents, had elected to leave Oxford rather than visit his barber. On this point, if on no other, Laud agreed with his old enemy William Prynne, who had written another graceless book entitled *Unloveliness of Love-Locks or a Gag for Long-haired Rattleheads.* But exhortations seldom change a style and now young Vane was wearing rich, brown, waving hair that had long since passed the tips of his ears and which came to rest in a graceful fall on his shoulders. Ultimately the Puritans themselves would succumb to this new style, even Cromwell and Ireton, but at the moment the more zealous among them were cropping their hair as a counterprotest. Ben Jonson's Zeal-of-the-Land Busy expressed the Puritan view: "long hair . . . is an ensign of pride, a banner, and the world is full of these banners."

Young Vane's oval face was gracefully framed by his long hair. The nose, like his father's, was too large, but it was straight and finely molded. The lips were full and the eyes, though too large for classic beauty, were luminous. The portrait of the son expresses an inwardness, a reserve, that is quite alien to the father. The Earl of Clarendon quite rightly called young Vane "unbeautiful," but he also acknowledged that there was something in his looks that made men think him extraordinary. It was a hidden power, an inner glow, that contrasted with and set off the bold features.

If Vane had been a more conventional and worldly young man, less defensively insulated against Roman Catholicism and Spanish Imperialism, both of which he saw there in their purest forms, Vienna might have marked some real turning point in his life, for it was a city of legend and history.

As long as anyone could remember, Vienna had been a formidable but not always impregnable bastion against alien conquest. Originally a group of Celts had supposedly founded a small settlement around a holy grove which they called Vindomina, the alleged last survivor of which, a dead trunk filled with iron nails (the *Stock im Eisen*), stood then as now a witness of remote pagan beginnings. And surely a young Englishman who had read and translated Latin for the first fifteen years of his life might have been expected to feel something familiar in this city's past, for the Romans, seeing immediately what a fine outpost it was, had eventually annexed it and, according to tradition, Marcus Aurelius had died there.

After the Romans, Attila, that personification of chaos and brutality, had occupied the city, followed by the Slavs and Avars, who in turn were expelled by Charlemagne. During the Crusades Vienna had been the center of traffic, always mediating between the energies and cultures of East and West. But what gave it exceptional significance to a traveler in 1631 is that just two years earlier it had withstood a siege by Suleiman the Magnificent who, arriving before the outer bastion, had said that he would surely dine in the Hofburg within three days. But he did not. So, in the phrases of the time, Christianity was saved and the West was preserved. Vienna's holy heritage lay dimly in the consciousness of middle Europeans, but it meant little on the Scandinavian frontier and less in England, especially to Puritans, and it was alien to Vane's mind and sympathies.

Vienna was perhaps too much of a bastion of Spanish Imperialism in those days, too much of a fortress, to be what travelers thought of as a great city, but the Viennese knew that the grace of Paris had been created on the battlements of Vienna. The city looked unimpressive to Italian and French visitors because there was no spectacular expression of the Renaissance; the city was still medieval. Dominating it was the Cathedral of St. Stephen with its catacombs, its tombs of the princes, its thirty-eight altars, its fine groined ceiling, and its high Gothic spire which is still the principal landmark and symbol of the city. The Hofburg was already a huge complex of buildings expressing various epochs and styles; the Rathaus was there, and the new baroque University Church, erected by the Jesuits, was completed in the year Vane arrived, although its rich frescoes and ornate interior were still to be added. Baroque was just beginning to reach Vienna.

The oldest building in the city was likely the small Church of St. Ruprecht, first built around 740 and already reconstructed many times when Vane saw it. And there was the famous University of Four Nations (Bohemia, Poland, Bavaria, and Saxony), modeled on the University of Paris. When Vane arrived it was already two hundred years old.

The outer city was stark, surrounded by strong high walls on which stood little watchtowers, but on the walls to the south and east there were massive bulwarks of bricks and earth designed to resist artillery or massed assault. The inner city, by contrast, was pleasant. Although it was crowded, there were some fair and spacious places, and one English traveler admired the new buildings even though he thought they were more for show than convenience.

The siege of 1629 had proved suburban living to be dangerous, but the city was so much too small for its population that infection became more fearsome than the Turks, and now suburbs were again thriving. On the "other side" of the Danube lived the Jews who traded in town by day, but were not allowed to sleep there at night. On "this side" of the Danube, there were pleasant gardens and fine new homes. To a Londoner it must have appeared exotic, cosmopolitan, and heterogeneous.

In 1631, Vienna still did not have the feel of a capital city, but during the religious turmoil Ferdinand II knew that it was the safest place for him, and lived there continuously. He was an interesting man, at once similar to his great rival, Gustav Adolf, and strikingly different. Although corpulent, he was abstemious; bread, not wine, was his problem. He was faithful to his empress who, as young Vane disapprovingly observed, was almost completely dominated by the priests. Ferdinand was like Charles and unlike Gustav Adolf in his punctilious observance of forms in both religious and Court life. Highly aware that he was styled "ever Augustus," he apparently felt that the Roman order for which he was responsible was best preserved by outward observances. And so, on some holy days, he would visit every church in the city. Even in ordinary times he loved the ceremonials, the processions, all the nuances of courtly and church etiquette; it was his answer to what he regarded as the anarchy of Lutheranism. He lacked the spontaneity, the self-assured vigor of Gustav Adolf, but he went even beyond Charles in his love and reverence for forms.

Ferdinand had slowly but forcefully removed Protestants from the university which, in 1623, he had given over entirely to the

Jesuits whom Vane feared and distrusted. Ferdinand's condition for restoring Frederick to the Palatinate had been that his heir should be sent to Vienna to be educated, that is to be molded, by the Society of Jesus. Measures against Protestants were increasingly strict until, in 1627, all evangelical worshipers were banished from Austria. Yong Vane, who would not take an oath or wear a gown, seems to have come to some disturbing conclusions about formalists; the forms they loved could be maintained only by some degree of force. Ferdinand, like Laud, seemed willing to employ whatever force was necessary, and Vane was coming to believe that forms and force were inescapably wedded.

This was the city, this the Court to which the boy, with his spiritual self-assurance and his worldly naïveté, was sent in April of 1631. His father had not yet left England; when he did he would first go to the Court of Christian of Denmark, then try to find the field headquarters of Gustav Adolf. Some seven months would elapse before the son would see his father. During the latter months, July through November, young Henry wrote his father a series of letters in his own hand. To the biographer these letters are both significant and frustrating for, as young Vane complains, he was furnished in Vienna with shoddy paper and thin ink, and with time the writing has faded almost into illegibility. Further, the letters are written in a combination of cipher and French. The cipher is no barrier, for someone has already decoded it on the manuscript itself, but the French offers more difficulty. Vane obviously wished to write in the language of continental diplomacy, but his French vocabulary was limited and his grasp of idiom weak. If it were not for *que* he would have been at a loss for connectives. It was the kind of boyish French which English fathers have been proud of for centuries. While there is no courtly affectation in the letters, there is at times a certain pomposity. Whether this merely reflects the style of diplomatic French or whether it also reflects the great pride a ' young man was taking in his new position is difficult to say.

Young Harry is immensely excited by his new role. He is a servant of kings and an emissary to kings, and Sir Robert Anstruther admits him to secret conferences, keeping him informed of all developments. He finds himself entrusted with secrets of state, with matters of war and peace. And from time to time one senses a slight surprise as Harry discovers for himself, at such a distance, the respect men have for his father and his father's influence.

From the first, young Harry expresses the realistic attitude of the English towards their mission. He tells his father of the pettifogging delays, the ministerial red tape to which the English embassy is subjected. From this he draws the obvious conclusion:

> . . . this manner of treating makes us see their desire to play with us and make us draw out the affair until they see in what fashion the affairs of Germany will go, which so far as one can tell will never be finished until one or the other of the religions is eradicated.

Divide et eradica; he was seeing for himself the truth of old Roe's maxim.

For at least three months young Vane continues sending letters into the void, not knowing whether his father is receiving them or not. As he continues to receive no reply, an anxiety of tone creeps into his letters: he is worried about his father's safety, and besides, as he keeps saying with increasing annoyance, he doesn't have enough money. (It is reassuring to know that some things in human relations never change.) Young Vane points out that he started from London with only 100 pounds, and he had paid half of that for the voyage; the other half was scarcely enough to provide him with linens, books, stockings, boots, slippers, and "a thousand other necessary things." Prices are shocking in Vienna, at least twice as high as in Paris. He trusts that his father will speedily send not only money but also directions as to how it should be spent, both of which his dutiful son will value highly. That was in September.

Shortly afterwards, he hears that he is to receive a thousand thalers, by no means a staggering sum, but when he next wrote, the money had still not arrived. He has now been in Vienna, he reminds his father, "three whole months," and had brought with him only a single suit of clothing. Winter is approaching and soon the entire Court, with all its punctilios and elegances, will return from the summer wars and vacations to winter in Vienna. Unless young Henry can visit a tailor his appearance will reflect sorely on the family honor. Everyone knows that he is the son of the ambassador to the King of Sweden.

Happily the thousand thalers arrived, and it apparently saw Harry through the initial formalities of the Imperial Court. Then, in November, he received instructions to journey to Nuremberg to meet his father. In a fluid military situation, this was a journey of no little danger. He wrote his father pointing out that it would have been safer if, as the ambassador suggested, he had first been sent to England with dispatches and thence to his father, but now it was too late for that. Very early in his life young Vane acquired a reputation for timidity—some called it cowardice—that followed him through his political career. That the imputation was not without foundation leads to the reflection that men show their courage in different ways. The time would come when many would feel that the younger Vane was capable of immense moral courage, although his physical courage always remained in doubt, and that doubt became one of his vulnerabilities.

In November young Harry proceeded to Nuremberg, perhaps because the English had concluded that further negotiations with Ferdinand were either futile or undesirable in view of the disastrous losses suffered by the Imperialists. On his way to Nuremberg, Vane's coach overturned in a stream. The important diplomatic papers, fortunately carried in another pouch, were safe, but the accident increased his need for money. He had bought a second suit with his thousand thalers and now it was ruined. Even his books and papers were "strangely affected" as his faltering French has it. He had left Vienna with only 350 thalers and the trip cost 220.

Upon reaching Nuremberg he was furnished with a much better grade of paper and ink with which he immediately fired off another letter to his father, who had not yet arrived. He is being overwhelmed, he says, with gifts and courtesies by citizens of a now Protestant province who know him to be the son of a member of the Privy Council. How should he repay these? Men of title expect him to entertain them; he has received honors and favors. Is he simply to ignore them? Young Vane seemed to be having a hard time understanding how a man as highly regarded as his father could be so obtuse about the financial needs of his son.

The letters also contain deeper strains than these, presages of the future. One of the most interesting is the letter in which he discusses his impressions of a Baron Rusdorf, a man with whom the elder Vane might one day have to deal. Harry first makes his customary extravagant apologies for presuming to instruct his father and then proceeds to analyze the man who, he says, has many fine qualities, so many that young Vane cannot help feeling friendship for him. But friendship aside, the same man has other qualities which are like a dead fly in a box of precious ointment; he is an expedient man, a man who accommodates himself to times and seasons, and, in diplomatic bargainings, he must be so regarded.

The eighteen-year-old boy has evidently been sitting in diplomatic bargaining sessions, saying nothing but watching the participants carefully, forming wiser than adolescent judgments, realistic judgments in which he carefully separates emotion and intellect. His precocious shrewdness is impressive.

The most significant of all the letters is one written on August 20, 1631, before he left Vienna; young Harry was still sending correspondence into limbo, but something had been profoundly troubling him. Apparently before he left England, his father had recommended some course of action to him, perhaps a suggestion that he should join the armies of Gustav Adolf. The father was likely thinking of the advantage any statesman holds who has seen military action, what it can mean in terms of reputation at home, or what a young man can learn of princes, states, and the forces that move them.

But young Vane was finding within himself a profound distaste for this proposed course of action: *"Je ne peus pas disposer mon naturel et affections à une affaire que vous semblez tant approver."* As first son, as beneficiary of all that primogeniture entails, quite apart from his natural affection for his father, he experiences some despair in trying to reconcile his inner feelings with his father's advice. In spite of torment and trouble of spirit, he simply cannot accede to his father's instructions in this one thing: war is abhorrent to him, this present holy war included.

Thus, so early in life, young Vane rejected his father's way of measuring benefits and outward advantage in favor of a course dictated by inner affections and motions. Characteristically it was feeling that turned him away, not reasoned assessment.

Although it cannot be demonstrated, it seems likely that young Vane did meet his father in Nuremberg or in some other Protestant city under the control of Gustav Adolf. It is even possible that he met the Lion of the North, but if so no record survives.

In February of 1632 young Vane left Rotterdam for England. The narrow pink he sailed on was battered by a storm; for three days and three nights there was no sight of land, but finally the storm subsided and young Harry took his dispatches to the king. Later he wrote,

> His Majesty was pleased to give me a generous and attentive audience . . . and told me that I had acquitted myself well.

Young Vane never spoke bitterly of Charles nor did he ever join with those who later demanded his life. According to a not improbable story, however, he did once incur Charles' wrath. In 1631 Charles had again propounded some new rules of Court etiquette. One of these forbade entrance into the presence or privy chambers to anyone wearing boots; another forbade the inner closet to any man under the degree of baron. According to the story, young Vane, on one occasion, was in a room to which his rank did not entitle him, and, on hearing the king approach, he hid behind an arras where the king discovered him and spoke to him severely.

But at about the time this was supposed to have happened, young Vane himself said only that Charles had shown him favor and promised to make him one of the Privy Chamber in ordinary, that is, a minor servant of the Court. What seems certain is that Harry returned to England deeply confirmed in his Puritan convictions but with greater poise and assurance. Within a month of his return, Sir Tobie Matthew, a professed Catholic, wrote to Vane, Sr., that he saw a "great improvement" in his son, that his French was good, his discourse discreet, his fashion comely and fair. These impressions were confirmed when Sir Francis Crane wrote to Sir Henry congratulating him on his son's hopeful prospects. His style and expression, he said, were quite remarkable for a young man. The final compliment came from the Countess of Westmoreland who, in writing to thank Vane for some favor shown her own son, said that in the "improvement" of young Vane she saw hopes for her own offspring. Harry appeared to be a young man with promise of a future at the Court.

But these people saw only the outer man; they had no access to his inner life where all was not going quite so smoothly. The Earl of Clarendon would later say,

After his return into England, he contracted a full prejudice and bitterness against the Church, both against the form and government and the liturgy which was generally in great respect. . . .

His bitterness became so intense, his unwillingness to conform so strong, that he was ready to sever his ties in England and, with other men of stricken conscience, set out for New England where, he believed, worship was free. It must have been distressing for a worldly and ambitious courtier like Sir Henry Vane to see his eldest son, after a precocious start in diplomacy that prepared him for advancement at Court, espousing the ideas and manners of the dissenting minority, and antagonizing the clerics who could assist his advancement. His immortal soul was doubtless his own affair, but why should he embarrass his family and jeopardize his career? Why should he wish to exile himself in a rough and barbarous land?

Sir Henry urged William Laud, famed for his skill in disputation and recently elevated to the Archbishopric of Canterbury, to give young Harry an interview in which he would try to persuade him out of his Puritan fancies and save him for the Anglican church. Although the Puritans were coming to associate Laud with Antichrist and the pope, his own position was the classical Anglican stance: the English church, though not the sole way to salvation, was of all churches the most admirable, providing a middle way between the clashing infallibilities of Geneva and Rome, between Calvinistic scripturalism and Roman *traditio*. A moderate enough position, it would seem; if anyone could reclaim young Harry, surely Laud could.

But no dissenter would approach Laud with open confidence. In the religious conflict between Puritan and Anglican, elder and bishop, Laud was a powerful polarizing figure; to many Puritans he stood for all they loathed in ritual, for all the repression that was driving them underground or across the waters to the Netherlands or New England. And his personality antagonized them as much as his policy. Some were becoming a bit frantic about him. Lady Eleanor Davies, a zealous but somewhat bewildered Puritan, by some ingenious arithmetical manipulation had found in the letters of Laud's name the number of the Beast, 666. She also predicted—in vain—his early demise. But some courtiers contemptuously regarded him not so much as an oppressor as a funny little man. And he did have his ridiculous aspects, especially because he took himself very seriously. Even King James had found him annoying because he could never leave even the smallest matter to work itself out, but must thrust himself into it. He was, as one writer described him, a little, low, bustling man, much too busy about everything.

Despite his apparently firm position, Laud was inwardly insecure. His father had been a man of low degree, and after Laud had worked his way up in the scholarly university world, his political greatness had been thrust upon him. He bore it painfully. Upon his elevation to the Archbishopric he wrote,

> I have had a heaviness hang upon me ever since I was nominated to this place, and I can give myself no account of it, unless it proceed from an apprehension that there is more expected from me than the craziness of these times will give me leave to do.

It is not surprising that in public he was self-assertive, speaking in a sharp, hasty manner.

When Laud became primate of the English church and guardian of its liturgy, his great love was not power but order. What he most liked, he said, was "little noise and great order"; in Puritan conventicles, however, he found little order and great noise. For Laud, the "great light of the Christian world" was Lancelot Andrewes, a humanistic Christian who placed primary emphasis on God's reason. On the other hand, his *bête noire* John Calvin stressed God's will as primary. Of all Calvin's teachings Laud most abhorred the doctrine of reprobation, according to which most of mankind had been arbitrarily damned before the creation of the world by an act of God's inscrutable will. Nor could he endure its corollary that Christ died only for the elect. The doctrine was so inflammatory that Laud tried to ban all public discussion of predestination, as he might once have forbidden schoolboys to produce lewd plays. But given the religious energies of the time, it would have been easier to forbid the discussion of sex; and of course, once banned, the subject became more desirable than the apples of the sun.

Because he so loved the divine reason, Laud asserted the corollary of its primacy: that public authority, the embodiment of many minds both living and dead, was more rational and beautiful than private judgment, which was limited in time, scope, and experience. This was no doubt admirable, but in his insecurity he pressed the view too far, trying to persuade himself that the other side had no merit at all. Devotion to private judgment and private experience, he said, placed private interest over the common good. He would not allow for the kind of personal religious experience that the young Vanes and Cromwells were undergoing.

University man that he was, Laud's intellectual preferences lay with Aristotle, who had said that virtuous conduct was linked to habit, to the steady performance of the desirable. Activity and movement must accompany intellect and will until virtue insensibly becomes natural, desirable in itself, and sweet to perform. That was the rationale for liturgical worship, for the repetition of known rituals. But there was something deeper. Universals or forms, said Aristotle, can exist only in things, are expressed through objects, are best known and understood in particulars. Thus the essence of a university, one might conclude, is best known through the daily conduct and intellectual activity of countless individuals. Similarly, the essence of a church might best be known through its ritual, its buildings, sacraments, devotions, prayers, and activities.

And so, Laud asked, what is the state of the church if we judge it by the particulars of conduct? The replies he heard both shocked and terrified him. He received reports of men who sat in church with their hats on and would not bow at the name of Jesus which, they said, was nothing but five letters of the alphabet. In some churches the communion table had been removed from the east end where the altar traditionally stood, and placed in the center of the church, where the Puritans wanted it. There, dogs pissed on the legs of the table, worshipers placed their coats and hats on it, and Puritan businessmen cleared a space on which to figure their interest, sometimes while the service was going on. Once a dog which had come to sniff seized the loaf from which the sacrament was to be made. With a great halloo, half the congregation joined in pursuit of the dog and repossessed the loaf, which was then consecrated and given to the communicants. One Puritan had eased both his bladder and his conscience by pissing in Canterbury Cathedral, thus paying his compliments to the pope. In Bedford, cock-fighting and betting were conducted every Shrove Tuesday. In Stratford-on-Avon, the minister allowed his poultry to roost and hogs to lodge in the chancel. In Cumberland, villagers could neither recognize nor say the Lord's Prayer. Sarah Peck, in her cups, mocked ceremony by christening a dog. William Reaner likened a minister's surplice to a whore's smock. Thomas Peckington actually killed two brothers for interfering with his falcon, and escaped punishment by pleading benefit of clergy.

The situation could be seen in microcosm in the Cathedral of Saint Paul where the vaults were being used to store ale, books, and tons of wood and coal. Whenever a nearby alehouse needed beer, the carts would go rumbling through the church basement. At the same time, the west end was full of people carrying on business, completely oblivious to the service, while lads courted maids and children played in the aisles. The clergy complained that the uproar was so great that neither prayers nor sermons could reach the congregation. Great noise and little order, indeed!

A more probing mind than Laud's might have asked why the commercial class was so indifferent to the values embodied in a cathedral, why the Lord Mayor of London insisted on wearing his sword during divine worship there, why no one seemed to feel the sanctity of a place hallowed by the worship of ages. If he had asked, he might have learned that this class, having somehow lost its taste for adoration, now wanted instruction. They loved sermons, and even at their own expense would hire "lecturers" to instruct them in the Word. The old service appealed to the old order out of which it had risen and which it both supported and comforted. But the new mercantile class was seeking a worship suited to its new modes of life and habits of thought. Calvinism and republicanism, it was said, were congenial, for Calvinism provided the kind of independence and individual self-discipline that were becoming more relevant than communal euphoria. In the old order the clergy was one of the three pillars of society, along with the king and his nobles; but in that pattern the rising commercial class, which included most of the productive forces of the nation, had no power or function in the church. They were therefore receptive to the modes of the Calvinistic system, in which the laity were as important as the clergy. These new improvised forms, untouched with the mellow-ness of age or the graciousness of art, were often raw and crude, but they worked, especially for men like young Vane to whom forms of worship did not matter if the spirit was present.

Just as Laud believed that outer forms could not be severed from the spiritual reality, so he believed that church and state were interdependent, the health of each depending on the other. That is why he would not compromise even in small things. When Puritans wished to restrict ales and wakes because drunkenness accompanied them, he might have made some conciliatory gesture; instead he infuriated the Puritans by insisting that the detested *Book of Sports* be read from the pulpit. When Goody Taylor refused to approach the communion table of Walden because it had been elevated, altarlike, to the top of two or three stairs, the archbishop insisted that she must. Thereupon some twenty-five mothers complained that Laud did not know what it was like to be pregnant. Here stood the table, they said, at the top of "lofty and bleak stairs" (one gets the feeling that it must be in the belfry); all child-bearing women would pray for the archbishop if he would relieve them of this climb. A different man would have laughed, shrugged, and admitted he was beaten, but the harassed Laud seemed to regard such humble requests as challenges to his authority, and remained obstinate.

The Earl of Clarendon, torn between pity, exasperation, and admiration, said that Laud's greatest lack was a true friend who could have reasoned honestly and kindly with him and pointed out his mistakes; those who had tried failed because they did not love him enough. And so this isolated man, donnish, unmarried, with no close friends, timid, insecure, and with a stern sense of duty, felt a profound loss as he helplessly watched the beauty of holiness succumb to the ugliness and anarchy created by the unrestrained individual will.

Gradually the struggle resolved itself into the superficial question of whether Laud could or could not compel worshipers to perform certain physical actions. Should men bow at the name of Jesus, and kneel towards the altar when entering the church? (Was the altar the throne of an invisible king or merely a piece of furniture?) Should the minister cross the infant during baptism? Should men remove their hats? In matters of this kind, Elizabeth had always compromised. Keep the communion table in the east end, she had said, except on communion day. Then move it to the center of the church if that is your custom. But Laud said that now it must always be in the east end, railed in, and elevated to the top of some stairs, and that men must approach bowing and receive the sacrament kneeling.

This was the man whom Sir Henry Vane engaged to induce his intense and rebellious son to bend to what he considered sweet reason and sound common sense. The archbishop invited young Henry to an interview, and so the two met face to face: Laud dressed in his customary bands and cap, now corpulent and red-faced, inclined to be a little sharp and impatient; Vane dressed in the fashion of the Court with his long flowing locks that Laud despised. Laud began by engaging in what a contemporary called "a good-natured remonstrance," but the interview soon became heated and descended into anger. The clash occurred over a matter of ritual: Henry refused to take communion if he could not take it standing; he would neither bow nor kneel. Laud insisted that he must. Henry might have defended his refusal by citing scriptures as other Puritans did, but his reasons lay deeper; as in his rejection of military life, he was compelled by an inner resistance. Laud could not comprehend what happens when the body is forced to perform acts which the soul despises. And so the boy was unable to make Laud understand why he could not kneel, that his resistance to the act came from the voice of the Spirit crying betrayal, warning him of defilement.

Laud may well have been thinking of a shocking case reported to him shortly before. Because they had received the communion kneeling, a Welshman had murdered his mother and brother. Though he had himself at one time practiced such idolatry, he had been informed by private inspiration that one should bow rather than kneel at the Lord's supper. He had therefore killed his mother and brother in order to save them. That was how far private inspiration might lead a man.

And so the old order and the new, Laud and the boy with the long hair, each desperately sincere, each speaking from a different context, could never understand each other. If Laud could have found an image for his God it would have been reason incarnate: logos, architect, builder, creator and sustainer of order and beauty, the source of tradition, the ultimate source of the ways and words of Anglicanism. To young Vane such a god was an idol. His deity was flame or bride, a dark fountain, a *mysterium tremendum* whose decrees inspired both love and fear, who arbitrarily sent or withheld his grace, and who ministered without mediation to the individual soul. To kneel at that communion table would be to deny the God that whispered to him.

The interview terminated abruptly. The busy and exasperated archbishop dismissed the young man with the luminous eyes, unconverted and knowing now that Laud was the great adversary. Laud could see no way to reach the boy; perhaps it would be best to let him go to New England after all, as he must have informed both the elder Vane and the king. Sometimes it enlightens young revolutionaries if they are allowed to go to the land of the revolution where, with the enchantment of distance stripped away, they may measure reality against revolutionary rhetoric. So the king granted young Vane's petition, and he was given permission to leave for three years.

A friend wrote to Sir Thomas Wentworth, a man whose life would soon be so fatally linked to that of young Vane:

> Sir Henry Vane also hath as good as lost his eldest son, who is gone into New England for conscience' sake; he likes not the discipline of the Church of England; none of our ministers would give him the sacrament standing; no persuasions of our bishops nor authority of his parents could prevail with him; let him go.

And young Vane, knowing that he stood to lose everything, miserable, unhappy, perhaps also a little elated at the adventure ahead of him, wrote his father on July 7, 1635. After some items of business, after asking for a pass from the king and his father's written assurance that he approved his going to America, he concluded:

> And, Sir, believe this from one that hath the honor to be your son (though as the case stands adjudged a most unworthy one), that howsomever you may be jealous of circumventions and plots that I entertain and practise, yet that I will never do anything (by God's good grace) which both with honor and a good conscience I may not justify or be content most willingly to suffer for. And were it not that I am very confident that as surely as there is truth in God so surely shall my innocency and integrity be cleared to you before you die, I protest to you ingenuously that the jealousy you have of me would break my heart. But as I submit all other things to the disposal of my good God, so do I my honesty among

the rest; and though I must confess I am compassed about with many infirmities, and am but too great a blemish to the religion I do profess, yet the bent and intention of my heart I am sure is sincere, and from hence flows the sweet peace I enjoy with my God amidst the many and heavy trials which now fall upon me and attend me: this is my only support in my losses of all other things: and this I doubt not of but that I have an all-sufficient God able to protect me, and who in due time will do it, and that in the eyes of all my friends.

Your most truly humble and obedient son,

H. Vane

When he came to look back on the events that preceded the revolution and should have alerted men that it was coming, the Earl of Clarendon remembered the "unnatural antipathy" that arose in those times between parents and children; there had been nothing like it, he said, since the world began. He cited the Vanes as his prime example: a Privy Councilor had to send his son to the world's wilderness just because he would not kneel for the sacrament.

No record remains of how Lady Vane thought or felt; she must have suffered, as mothers always do, when husband and eldest son clash and separate. But in the Prayer Book was a prayer of comfort for those who had a loved one departing on a long sea voyage.

O Eternal God who alone spreadest out the heavens and rulest the raging of the sea; we commend to thy Almighty protection thy servant, for whose preservation on the great deep our prayers are desired. Guard him, we beseech thee, from the dangers of the sea, from sickness, from the violence of enemies, and from every evil to which he may be exposed.

And young Harry passed in safety from the old world to the new.

4

New England (1635–1636)

Among Puritans there had grown up a mystique of New England which had touched Vane in London. Even the soberest Puritans had felt it, among them John Winthrop, founder of the Massachusetts Bay Colony, a man trained in the law and not given to effusions. In England Winthrop had felt depressed and even a little unclean, for men there, he said, were being treated like cattle rather than like persons, and no one could engage in trade without becoming corrupt because money took precedence over morals. And as he viewed the sad condition of the Protestant churches on the continent as well as in England, true religion seemed about to perish everywhere; the only hope lay in the West where, Winthrop thought, men might raise a bulwark against Roman Imperialism "which the Jesuits labor to rear in all parts of the world." The saintly John Cotton believed that New England was the fulfillment of the Biblical prophecy: "Moreover I will appoint a place for my people." Boston was God's answer to Vienna.

It would be difficult to imagine two more different cities than the one where Vane had served as apprentice diplomat and the one where he was preparing to seek his fortunes. Vienna was all fortification and fortress; Boston was a harbor, arms open to the sea—it would never know a wall, never suffer siege. Within its walls, Vienna preserved artifacts of many vanished civilizations, whereas in Boston, where not even Indians had established a permanent settlement, men were starting afresh. Vienna was empire and the honor and glory of the past, whereas Boston was all future, a history waiting to be written.

The Puritan belief in New England as a providential refuge was strengthened by the fact that before Winthrop arrived to establish his colony, deadly plagues had decimated the natives. Indian villages were deserted and untilled; wandering through these habitations of desolation, the colonists became accustomed to seeing scattered skulls and corpses and sometimes wigwams filled with dead bodies. Later some thought that the Indians were descendants of Noah's accursed son Ham, and that was why those great plagues had occurred. As Cotton Mather said, "The woods were almost cleared of these pernicious creatures to make room for a better growth."

And to the oppressed dissenters New England appeared a land of incredible abundance. In a time of high prices and scarcity of food they heard that in New England milk was a penny a quart; blueberries, currants, raspberries, strawberries, and plums were free; Indian corn "grew like a wonder." Especially marvelous was the harvest of the sea: cod, sturgeon, eels, crabs, mussels, oysters, and lobsters—some weighing twenty-five pounds, "so great and fat and luscious" that the colonists were cloyed with eating them. But best of all, for Englishmen, New England was an unbelievably healthful place. The weak and sickly became strong in the new world where the air, it was said, was better than old England's ale. The disadvantages of the new world, though conscientiously recounted, seemed trivial in comparison to the abundance of fowl and deer on endless parks of free land where a servant could have a larger estate than a nobleman in England. Freedom and opportunity were alike unbounded.

A remarkable group of Puritans had, for various reasons, been drawn towards the new world where they held patents both in the Connecticut River Valley and in the West Indies. They had formed a corporation known as Saybrook, a combination of the names of Lords Say and Brook. Also in the group were John Pym, who was already friendly with young Vane, Nathaniel Rich, John Hampden, Arthur Haselrig and others. Most of these patentees, at one time or another, talked of emigrating to America, and John Pym especially had announced it as his intention. But they were also men of estates and affairs and the time never quite seemed propitious. In the meantime settlers were slowly filtering into the Connecticut Valley where they were now jeopardizing the rights and future profits of Saybrook. That group therefore issued commissions to Henry Vane,

John Winthrop, Jr., and Hugh Peter to proceed to Connecticut, negotiate with the settlers there, and act as Saybrook's agents in New England. Thus at a very early age, young Vane was drawn into a circle of friendship with England's leading Puritans.

As the mystique of the new world drew men, they felt that the journey to it was a rite of passage. The elder Winthrop may have been the first to give this feeling voice. As soon as his company stepped on the ships, everyone felt something quite wonderful: children as well as adults were cheered and felt a surge of trust in the Lord of Hosts. And beneath his account of the arrival of his ship, Biblical echoes are audible: from the shore was wafted an odor like the smell of a garden, and then, wondrously, a wild pigeon flew onto the ship, an auspicious omen.

During the voyage the emigrants delighted in beholding the works of the Lord in the deep waters: sometimes the sea, with terrible countenance, would form itself into high hills and deep valleys; when, at other times, it resembled a plain or meadow, the fishes would sport, the grampuses would leap, and the whales would go by in companies "puffing up water streams." Occasionally a beautiful and terrifying iceberg would sail silently past. Every morning and evening there were worship services with community singing and praying, and at night the watches were set with a psalm and "a prayer that was not read out of a book." After such an exercise, how could they help sleeping soundly, free as they now were? These first voyages were true rites of passage.

For young Henry Vane the westward voyage was both a spiritual liberation and an escape from a cul-de-sac, for despite his religious mysticism, Vane was an ambitious young man who wanted at once to better the world and to get ahead in it. In old England, the exorbitant price of advancement had been violation of his spiritual integrity, but in the New Jerusalem where godliness was a recommendation to status and power, all doors would be open to him. Remembering his promise to his father that he would demonstrate his sincerity and purity of motive, he embarked with confidence and hope.

The *Abigail* set sail from Plymouth in September of 1635 with 220 persons aboard. The greatest hazard of the voyage was an infection of smallpox, which in the confined and crowded conditions of the ship might have been disastrous. But no one died; it was, said

Governor Winthrop, when he heard about it, "a special goodness of the Lord." The infection left Vane untouched, but he did suffer from the unkind suspicions of some fellow passengers who took very seriously the Puritan sumptuary customs, soon to be transformed into laws in New England: one should show no silk, no linen, no gold or silver thread, no vain embroidery. Even greater was the antipathy to long hair. Though Vane thought and felt like a Puritan, he was dressed like an aristocrat, and many of the passengers thought he must be an Anglican spy come to destroy their liberties. Young Winthrop and Peter, themselves attired in the severe Puritan fashion, were able to allay the hostility that Vane had aroused, but young Vane was left puzzled that people who were fleeing the formalism of outward religion should be so concerned with his outward appearance.

On October 6, 1635, the little vessel threaded its way among the islands and promontories of Massachusetts Bay, now beginning to display the red and gold of maple and sumac, until it stood at anchor off the town dock of Boston, at the base of the triad of hills that were the spine of Shawmut Peninsula. Because of alarms and threats of invasion from England, on the highest of those hills, some 200 feet above sea level, a warning beacon sixty-five feet high had been erected; the hill was now being called Beacon Hill.

Originally the settlement had been called Trimountain, but the name was changed in 1630 in order, it was said, to encourage the renowned John Cotton to emigrate. Cotton was pastor of St. Botolph's Church in Boston, Lincolnshire, and was so famous for sanctity that an innkeeper at Derby once had to ask him to leave because, he said, he was unable to swear while "that man was under his roof," and this interfered with his duties.

As the colonists looked out from the harbor they saw the brush-covered slopes, the scattered boulders and rocks beyond them, and, near the site of the present State Street, a church of rough-hewn logs and a thatched sloping roof with no spire. From this undeclared and unofficial center of the town, rude frame houses, occasionally varied by "mansions" with Elizabethan timberings and overhanging gables, straggled along cow paths, without symmetry or design.

The peninsula that united Boston to the mainland was so narrow and low that, at spring tide, the sea dashed over it.

The rocky nook, with hilltops three,
Looked eastward from the farms,
And twice each day the flowing sea
Took Boston in its arms.

Out in the open bay, sprinkled with islands, was occasionally seen an Indian canoe, but almost never a sail.

The social life of Boston consisted of Sabbath services, church meetings and Thursday lectures. There were no newspapers, dances, concerts, theatres, libraries. It was a grim and dreary place, the sort of place in which utopian dreams abound, the only kind of place where they can long survive. Young Vane had chosen his city wisely.

Just about five years earlier, the elder John Winthrop's party, as its charter authorized, had taken possession of the land from three miles south of the Charles River to three miles north of the Merrimac, and from the Atlantic Coast to the Pacific, the latter being the only known western landmark. This same charter gave the colonists the power to transfer the government of the Company from England to New England and there to make new laws consistent with the laws of England and the will of the king. The implied independence from the mother country and the Anglican church contained in this charter was guarded most zealously by the colonists, for they intended to establish a Holy Community, that most potent of all Puritan myths. On the voyage over, Winthrop had described to his fellow passengers his vision of "a city upon a hill," where Christian justice could shape a community through the love of God and godly love of one's fellow men. In the center there was to be the meeting house, the home of religion and justice; about it would cluster residences beautified with gardens and trees; farms, the basis of a stable community, would extend out into the surrounding open country. Civil power and the church, two embodiments of the same divine idea, independent but working in unison, would shape the spiritual and temporal lives of men into a paradigm of the Holy City. This vision was in harmony with young Vane's desire, already defining itself, to bring the divine order into reality by creating a body politic shaped by, and illustrative of, the spirit of godliness. The Holy Community was to be based on Winthrop's right principles; and if the basic principles were right, how could the structure raised upon them be anything but harmonious?

Now, five years after Winthrop's small band had arrived, there were probably 5,000 English settlers from Cape Ann to Cape Cod settled in some twenty townships, but their order and unity had been disturbed by the facts of geography as well as those of human nature. Along the intricate contours of Massachusetts Bay, several tracts of land had invited settlement, and even in 1630 members of the colony had dispersed into several areas. Soon Governor Winthrop and Deputy Governor Thomas Dudley were at odds over whether Shawmut Peninsula (Boston) or Newtown (Cambridge) should be the capital of the commonwealth. Dudley, sternly rigid and opinionated, held out for Newtown, where, coincidentally, he had built his own house, but Winthrop settled the question in 1632 by taking up the foundations of the house he had begun to build in Newtown and transporting them to Boston; there he erected his home near the principal spring, between the hills and the docks. Dudley concluded that Winthrop was taking too much authority upon himself and a permanent disagreement began its long course.

After the dispersal of the settlers, the chances of drawing them into a unified community had passed. The flow of immigration from England, at the flood when Vane arrived, assured the rapid growth and thus the individual identity of all the settlements around the harbor. Boston had an area of only two-and-a-half square miles, most of which was not arable, and so the residents had to acquire farms elsewhere. Newtown, meanwhile, was established as an independent town, and each of the settlements organized its own church and selected its own preacher. Winthrop was helpless against the forces of colonization. Besides, the character of Boston was being geographically determined: it was a natural seaport, soon to be dominated by traders, merchants, sailors, dock hands, and brokers— a miscellaneous, independent, and not always pious lot.

The disadvantages of New England were also beginning to assert themselves. Worst was the winter cold when all suffered and many died. Then, when the steamy heat of summer descended on the coast, mosquitoes came in innumerable humming swarms; the rattlesnakes and cottonmouths proliferated. Wolves raided the small flocks and herds while Indian swine trampled down the corn.

Housing was always inadequate; newcomers often lived in wigwams made of wattles clayed over and covered with bark. Later they might build peak-roofed houses of timber with clapboard surfaces, but frequently the green timber warped out of shape; at best these wooden houses, their chimneys made of twigs daubed with clay, were dangerously inflammable and many burned. By the time Vane landed in 1635, all supplies were in heavy demand—wood, ironware, clothing, fabrics, housewares, and labor, especially skilled labor—and the magistrates had set bitterly resented ceilings on prices and wages.

As the settlers pushed inland, they encountered the hostility of the land from which, some grumbled, only stones would grow. They also encountered the hostility of Indian tribes unwilling to be pushed aside. Despite the efforts of the colonists to win friendship through fair dealing, many of the Indians were already embittered by white traders who, having no permanent interest in the colony, were free to swagger, cheat, and then leave. These traders had made the Indians even more dangerous by giving them whiskey, firearms, and ammunition in exchange for furs. So far only sporadic clashes had taken place between the Indians and the colonists, but omens were bad. The French threatened the security of the colony from the north, and the Dutch from the south. Both were eager to expand and to dispute the English right to hold New England.

Worst of all was the anxiety about whether or not the colonial charter would remain valid. The problem here was that Sir Ferdinando Gorges held an earlier patent that included some of the land of the Massachusetts Bay Colony; he was now seeking royal permission and military power to enforce his claims. The appointment of Laud as one of the Lords Commissioners of Plantations lent strength to the claim of Gorges, who was both Royalist and Anglican, especially now when Laud and the king were becoming alarmed at rumors of separation in the New England church and of civil independency in the Massachusetts Bay government. The magistrates, in turn, were alarmed at rumors that the charter was to be revoked and a governor general sent over to rule in the king's name. The rumors took on substance when, in 1634, Laud temporarily restrained shiploads of Puritan emigrants from leaving harbor and in June the Massachusetts General Court received an order from the council to send the patent back to England. It was one of the most critical and terrifying moments in the early history of the colonies. The magistrates wisely temporized, saying that nothing could be done until the next General Court in September. Soon Charles would have too many troubles in Scotland to worry about New England. But now, with this threat hanging over them, the magistrates were alarmed at any incident which might darken their case if it were reported unsympathetically in England, and were ready to engage the good will of any new arrival like Vane who might exert favorable influence at Court.

One such incident concerned the king's banner. Just a year earlier the belligerent John Endicott of Salem, the same who in 1628 had hacked down Thomas Morton's maypole at Merry Mount and dispersed his drunken orgiasts, excised the red cross from the royal banner of England. It was not proper, he said, for a reformed people to display this banner which had been given to England by the pope as an emblem of victory and was therefore "a superstitious thing, and a relic of antichrist." The assembly of ministers debated his action, for while it was safe to oppose popery, it might not be altogether safe to deface the king's colors. After postponing decision from meeting to meeting, they advised that all royal ensigns be laid aside for the time being and that the cross be left out of the regimental colors. So the matter was left, and when Vane arrived, the royal colors were nowhere being displayed in the colony, and as yet no royalist had taken offense.

Meanwhile, many unanticipated problems were beginning to take shape in the continually improvised and often ambiguous government, for the civil and religious structures of the new colony were being formed not by systematic application of theory, but by a series of specific actions and decisions from which general policies emerged. Not until 1640 would there be a written code of laws and penalties to define the rights of freemen and the limits of magisterial authority; each criminal or civil case was judged on its own merit in the light of the law of God as revealed in the Bible, particularly in the Old Testament. Accordingly, as the magistrates of the Massachusetts Bay Company also functioned freely as officers of a civil commonwealth, precedents for legal jurisdictions and proceedings gradually shaped the characteristic New England state and town governments. Freemen annually elected a governor, a deputy governor, and eighteen assistants soon to be called magistrates, who met at regular intervals in a General Court which combined administrative, legislative, and judicial functions. As the court functioned, certain tendencies became perceptible: impartial fairness, even generosity in civil and financial matters, especially between gentlemen, and a corresponding severity, even cruelty, in punishing moral and criminal offenses, especially among servants. One of the earliest courts summoned Thomas Morton from Merry Mount, put him in the bilboes, confiscated all his property, and held him close prisoner until he could be forced, on his way to exile in England, to watch the burning of his house in the presence of the Indians he had abused. Even more barbarous was the punishment of Philip Ratcliff, a servant convicted of "most foul, scandalous invectives against our churches and government," the kind of thing Puritans were being convicted of in England. He was whipped, had his ears lopped off, and was banished. Both of these judgments excited much outrage in England; Laud especially was angered at the mutilation of Ratcliff although he had helped to pass a similar judgment and execution on a Scotch Puritan named Alexander Leighton which, predictably, had been badly received in New England.

Although by Biblical authority the death penalty was assigned for adultery, Winthrop's court was hesitant to inflict this sentence even though, as his *Journal* indicates, there was some occasion for it. Even in the rigorous life of the new world, flesh stubbornly asserted itself, causing great perturbation when carnal sins were discovered among the elect. Captain Underhill, a useful but uncontrollable military roisterer, was accused of adultery after he had spent some afternoons, behind locked doors, in the house of a genial neighbor woman. The court was unable to disprove Underhill's assertion that he was conducting private prayers with her; he soberly acknowledged that locking the door was injudicious and might indeed give rise to evil rumor. The elders were unhappy but could do nothing more than rebuke and admonish.

There were darker sins, too. When at Pascataquack two men committed sodomy, "and that on the Lord's day, in time of public exercise," the local governor tried to induce the Massachusetts court to bring them to trial, but the court did not think fit to do so. And as for a wicked fellow who was "so given up to that abomination" of bestiality that he "never saw any beast go before him but he lusted after it," he was disposed of by his own conscience and God's Providence: he fled to Long Island and was drowned there. God's Providence took care of many offenders who escaped man's punishment, especially Sabbath breakers or defiers of authority; they were quite likely to fall through the ice or be burned in their houses or attacked by Indians or wolves. Archibald Tomson, for example, was "carrying dung to his ground in a canoe upon the Lord's day, in fair weather and still water" when his canoe "sank under him in the harbor near the shore and he was never seen after."

Any reading of the records of the Massachusetts General Court will destroy most of the stereotypes of the Puritan and his commonwealth. The frailer vessels in Massachusetts assaulted one another, fornicated, enticed Indian maidens, sold firearms and whiskey to the Indians, cursed the magistrates, shot one another's dogs and goats, profaned, blasphemed, and in general carried on remarkably like men in England or elsewhere. But they did not bow at the name of Jesus and they did not kneel for communion. Some things they would not do.

The authorities tried very hard to maintain order and enforce moral conformity, until it seemed that a man's whole life was regulated by either the civil government or the church. In theory the state was separated from the church, for it was agreed that the state had no jurisdiction over man's conscience or his relation to his God. But immoral actions could be prosecuted in the civil courts as matters of social concern. And the church had strong general influence over the civil powers if only because church membership was a prerequisite to voting. In theory everyone was to attend church on Sundays; in practice this was impossible, for the meeting houses could not hold half the population. Besides, the churches became steadily more selective in their membership, so that there were increasingly large numbers of colonists who were either indifferent to religion or excluded because they held heretical opinions or were troublemakers or otherwise undesirable. As a result, as the churches increased in power they became less inclusive of the whole people and came to constitute, in fact, although not in name or theory, a state church which was loudly antipapal, quietly anti-Anglican, and stubbornly Independent. No wonder Laud was disturbed.

The question of toleration arose almost at once, and the only workable answer was that, in this precarious infancy of the colony, in the face of threats from three major nations and from the Indians, opinions which were divisive and might lead to disruption would be silenced. Captain Edward Johnson spoke for the majority when he said that Massachusetts was "no place of licentious liberty." We have, he continued, given up everything to come to a wilderness and we will use whatever means the Word of God allows to maintain our commonwealth. Mr. Dudley's stern thoughts on this subject caused him to break into song.

> Let men of God in court and churches watch
> O'er such as do a toleration hatch.

With no archbishop to determine what was acceptable for all congregations, there came a kind of competition in exclusiveness. There was no conscious intention of limiting opinion, but opinions result in actions and if these in turn threaten political (or moral) stability, the danger has to be stopped at its source. Thus the exigencies and ironies of their situation led the colonists into a conformity quite as "thorough" as that of Laud; and one rueful, disillusioned colonist said as he departed, "Lord bishops and lord brethren."

The issue of toleration appeared most dramatically in the career of Roger Williams who was exiled from Massachusetts not long after Vane arrived. Williams, a minister who had himself suffered persecution for his beliefs before emigrating, was a gentle, loving, kindly, stubborn, and difficult man, to whom repression and cruelty were repellent; in most things it was natural for him to be tolerant. After Massachusetts evicted him, he established in Rhode Island a haven for those nonconformists who could not be endured elsewhere.

But on one issue he was strangely intolerant. He believed that all people who had ever been in communication with the Church of England should publicly repent. Until they did so, he considered them no true Christians and their assemblies no true churches. But the Massachusetts colonists had generally tried to maintain at least a fiction of nonseparatism. Consequently Williams denounced them all and finally would not even say a blessing at table in the presence of his wife because she continued to attend public worship. Thus Williams, who by nature would draw all men together in love, himself became a disruptive force. The tendency to make the church exclusive destroyed its strength as the unifier of the plantations; it had begun by offering the hand of fellowship to all but the hopelessly vicious and unregenerate, and ended by thrusting out all but the certainly elect, dividing man from man. Williams' refusal to admit that the civil powers could punish the breach of the Sabbath day or any of the first four commandments might have been accommodated, and his insistence that the settlers could not have clear right to their lands without compounding financially with the Indians was both defensible and right. But the corollary that King Charles had no right to issue the patent which was the very foundation of the colony could not be admitted, and when, in 1633, he accused the king of having told a "solemn public lie," and applied to him some passages in the Book of Revelation about the beast and Antichrist, even while the revocation of the charter was being urged in England, the magistrates had to call him to account. Like the question of the red cross in the banner, the question of what to do about Williams was still unsettled at Vane's arrival, but young Henry soon felt a kinship and a strong bond of sympathy with many of Williams' views. Williams responded warmly and there began in New England what would prove to be Vane's longest and most constant friendship.

These problems of the relations of church and state, of conscience and civil affairs, were intensified by strong religious feeling during the five years since the inception of the colony. In the earliest days, while men were held together in the fight against the stubborn land, recurrent epidemics of smallpox, hostile neighbors, and threats from the homeland, a kind of religious revival strengthened them in their struggles. But it also stirred many to profoundly religious experiences which were manifested in a diversity of private beliefs arising from sincere consciences but socially divisive; minor heresies swarmed, and eccentric sectaries proliferated. As Winthrop put it, "Satan bestirred himself to hinder the progress of the gospel" by arousing a spirit of jealousy and dissension in the churches. Toleration of such divisions was at the same time made more difficult when in mid-decade a wave of religious anxiety swept the community. It was all very well for the regenerate to hold together and exclude everyone else, but what of those earnest souls who longed for the light but feared that they would be cast out into darkness? Cases were reported of persons whose profound anxiety drove them over the edge of insanity to such desperate actions as suicide, or child murder by a mother who, unable to endure her uncertainty, drowned her infant in order to save it from misery and to give herself the assurance at least of damnation.

Among such people and in such an atmosphere of insecurity and crisis, Vane disembarked. While the elder Winthrop by now had come to some reluctant realization of the abyss between conception and flawed reality, Vane the much younger idealist, still hopeful of a clean correspondence between plan and execution, was about to learn that even in the politically blank slate of a new world, right principles and pure intentions were terrifyingly inadequate. The "city upon a hill," the model of godly unity in which Vane expected to find a secure place, was already dangerously splintered and insecure.

The absence of the king's banner was still unnoticed, and though the charter had not been returned to the king, no further demand for it had been received. But tension was still unrelieved, and the ministers had voted that if a royal governor should be imposed on New England, they would resist him by force. Vane's arrival at a time like this seemed a clear dispensation of Providence. Young Harry, it was believed, might make the difference between restraint and intervention by the Crown. Obviously they expected far too much from him, but at the time it seemed that God had sent him to the colonies in their moment of peril. What persuasions were then used with Vane we do not know, but when John Winthrop, Jr., proceeded to Connecticut, both Vane and Peter surprisingly stayed in Massachusetts. How much Vane was offered remains in doubt, but he must have been promised some position of influence in the colony if he would stay there.

Vane's reception in Boston was generally adulatory. Even the usually restrained Winthrop was elated.

Here came also one Mr. Henry Vane, son and heir to Sir Henry Vane, comptroller of the King's house, who, being a young gentleman of excellent parts, had been employed by his father (when he was ambassador) in foreign affairs; yet being called to the obedience of the Gospel, forsook the honors and preferments of the court, to enjoy the ordinances of Christ in their purity here.

His father, being very averse to this way (as no way savoring the power of religion) would hardly have consented to his coming hither but that, acquainting the king with his son's disposition and desire, he commanded him to send him hither and gave him license for three years' stay here.

While Vane was indeed courted for his father's influence, at the same time everyone commented on his grave demeanor, his sober carriage. True, his clothing was too elegant and there was always the matter of his hair. John Endicott, busy in all matters, had formed a society against long hair and young Vane was badgered until he visited the barber. While some thought his hair still too long, the majority consented to admit him to the church of Boston on November 1. This means that he must have given a fervent and convincing recital of his conversion for that was the primary criterion for membership. Neither then nor later was the slightest doubt ever raised in Boston about the reality or profundity of Vane's religious experience. They believed what he said about his wrestlings with God.

Vane quickly struck up a friendship with the subtle-minded and gentle-hearted teacher of the Boston church, John Cotton, who invited him to lodge in his house across town from the dock on the lower slopes of Trimountain. Sometimes called Cotton's Hill and sometimes Pemberton's Hill, this land was situated near the present Tremont Street and Pemberton Square. Surrounded by a large garden, Cotton's house was an old-fashioned mansion with small diamond-shaped glass panes. After a time Vane built a small house of his own adjacent to or perhaps even adjoined to Cotton's house. Later, when he left New England, he gave that house to Seaborn Cotton, the minister's son, born during the passage to the new world.

Before Vane had been in the colony two months, an order was passed that anyone who wished to sue another person at law should first submit his case for arbitration to Mr. Vane and two of the elders. Though this rapid elevation for a boy of twenty-three may have increased too much his confidence in his own wisdom and political acumen, it did not blind him to the signs of trouble in the colony. A clashing opposition had developed almost from the start between the elder Winthrop and Thomas Dudley, reaching a climax in the election of 1634 when Dudley had replaced Winthrop as governor. In 1635 Winthrop had failed even to be elected deputy governor. Though still enjoying high prestige and exerting great influence, he had lost power to the more rigid and dogmatic factions. As a result, it was increasingly dangerous for anyone to question the judgment or the power of the magistrates.

Already Vane was feeling what he would later formally assert, that harmony was the soul of political society, that it was the harmony of the people that mattered and not the form of government, however theoretically desirable. Therefore the present friction was painful to him and he decided to do something about it. Being rather naïve about the nature of political man, he thought that a face-to-face meeting would enable the disputants to see and follow right reason. Enlisting Hugh Peter's aid, he called a meeting at Boston of Governor Haynes, Deputy Governor Bellingham, and the ministers most concerned—John Wilson and John Cotton of Boston, and Thomas Hooker of Newtown. Winthrop and Dudley, the chief antagonists, though not then in office, were also present, as they would have to be if the roots of the problem were to be exposed. Vane opened the meeting with prayer and then made a speech explaining that the meeting was called to accomplish the friendly uniting of the minds of Mr. Dudley and Mr. Winthrop, men of great consequence on whom the principal weight of affairs in the colony rested. Having spoken this flattering truth, he went on to urge all present to speak their minds freely and openly, leaving nothing unspoken in their breasts which might cause any "jar or difference" thereafter. But not all were inclined to play this game of truth. Winthrop stood up and blandly said that he knew of no breach between his brother Dudley and himself; whatever differences there had been were long since reconciled, and he was unconscious of any "alienation of affection" from him in Dudley or anyone else, except for some newcomers who in choosing to live in Newtown rather than Boston were perhaps avoiding him. And he desired all the company to speak freely if anyone had seen anything to criticize in his government or any of his activities; he hoped they would deal "freely and faithfully" with him, and he would take it in good part, "and would endeavor, by God's grace, to amend it." No one could say fairer than that. Next Dudley contributed to the love feast, saying that he had come as a mere observer, with no intent to charge his brother Winthrop with anything; to be sure, there had been breaches between them in the past, but these were all healed and he had no wish to reopen them. If there were any complaints to be made, let someone else make them. Then Governor Haynes had his say. He and Winthrop had always been on good terms, and the last thing he wanted was to give him any offense, but since the purpose of the meeting was to tell truth, he would speak freely and hope Mr. Winthrop would take it in good part as he had promised. He did recall one or two minor matters of justice in which it seemed to him that Mr. Winthrop had erred on the side of lenience. Winthrop replied gently that although he was sure that what he had said and done in those cases was somewhat misunderstood, he would go so far as to say that in his opinion justice ought to be administered with more lenity in the infancy of a plantation than after it had reached a settled state, for after all, people were more apt to transgress in uneasy times, partly because they did not yet know and understand the new laws and orders, and partly because of difficulties of new business and other pressures. But if he could be shown that this policy was in error, he would undertake to follow a stricter course. The question was turned over to the ministers who, after pondering overnight, delivered their ruling in the morning. Each one then offered different reasons, but they all added up to the same conclusion: strict discipline, both in criminal and military affairs, was more needful in plantations than in settled states, "as tending to the honor and safety of the gospel." What they did not say, but must have had in their minds, was that stricter religious discipline was also needed for the survival of the plantation. In the face of this unanimous judgment, Winthrop acknowledged himself convinced, and promised to endeavor (by God's assistance) to take a more strict course hereafter.

Whether or not this issue is the one that Vane intended to bring out, no one can know. What is certain is that his attempt to give moral guidance to his elders left some residual resentment. And God was indeed to assist Winthrop henceforth to achieve a rigor of repression that was dissonant with his essential nature, and Vane's friends and Vane himself were to suffer from it.

Vane, however, suffered no loss of popularity by the meeting. Rather, he endeared himself by his religious earnestness and his willingness to act on his convictions; among both religious enthusiasts and political opponents of Winthrop, he was so highly regarded that they continued to press him into responsible positions. On March 3, 1636, the General Court made him a freeman of the colony and appointed him a member of the commission for military affairs, empowered to supervise the training and supply of the militia and to conduct any necessary war, offensive or defensive. Then at the annual election, on May 25, as Vane was entering his twenty-fourth year, he was elected governor with John Winthrop, Sr., as deputy governor, thus combining all factions into a single administration. It seems a likely mark of Winthrop's distaste for this situation that he does not mention the election in his *Journal*, but swallowing his pride, he undertook to support the new governor in the interests of communal harmony. Vane's disastrous term began auspiciously.

Whatever young Vane thought about forms in religion, he had learned in London and especially in Vienna that they play a significant role in political life. He therefore instigated a certain pomp and ceremony unprecedented in Puritan Massachusetts. Wherever he went officially, he was attended by four uniformed sergeants with halberds, stiffly military in their bearing and colorful in appearance. On the day of his election all of the fifteen great ships then in Boston Harbor honored the son of the Privy Councilor of England with a "volley of great shot." Vane at once made use of this tribute as a means to settle some vexing questions about the relation of the colony to the ships using its harbor. There had been much dispute about fair prices, and the usual wildness of sailors ashore who, after a long and confining voyage, had disturbed the peace of the city. Acknowledging the good will of the fifteen masters, Vane responded by inviting them all to dinner, and after they had been generously entertained, he offered three propositions for their consideration. First, all ships should come to anchor before passing the fort that guarded the entrance to the harbor unless they had sent ahead a boat to "satisfy the commander that they were friends." Second, before any trading started, they should send an invoice of their goods to the governor and give him twenty-four hours to grant or refuse permission to sell. And finally, the crewmen should not stay ashore after sunset except for urgent reasons. These were all sensible recommendations, and in the amicable atmosphere that Vane had created, the masters accepted them.

But soon afterwards Governor Vane was faced by an unexpected crisis. He might have been forewarned that the absence of the king's colors would cause trouble if he had recognized the implications of an embarrassing incident involving a ship belonging to Sir Thomas Wentworth, now Deputy of Ireland. On May 15, the lieutenant commanding Castle Island, the fort at the entrance of the harbor, had demanded that the *St. Patrick* strike its colors before passing the fort; the master resented being ordered to strike his colors to a fort which flew no royal colors, and he complained to the magistrates. Realizing the danger of insulting Wentworth and of failing to display any emblem of loyalty to the king, the court ordered the lieutenant to board the *St. Patrick* and make public apology before the entire crew. But the next incident was not so easily settled. Shortly after he became governor, Vane heard that the master's mate on the *Hector*, observing that the king's colors were not flying at the fort, had concluded that the colonists were all traitors and rebels and loudly said as much to the crew. Vane promptly sent for Mr. Ferne, the master, who agreed to turn over the mate for arrest. But when a marshal and four sergeants went to the ship to get him, the crew refused to deliver him up except to the master himself. So the master brought him to court, which committed him on the testimony of two witnesses. But the crew raised such a tumult that the master obtained permission to return the mate to the ship, and bring him back to court the next day for trial. There he publicly admitted his offense, signed a submission, and was discharged. The case of one loudmouth was settled, but Vane realized that the underlying problem remained: how much would reports of this incident intensify the Crown's hostility against the colony, and hasten the revocation of the charter and appointment of a governor general? He called the masters to meet with him and Winthrop, and asked them to speak candidly—did they take offense, as the crewmen had done? They admitted that if they were interrogated on their return to England, they would like to be able to report that they saw the king's colors spread at the fort. Told that the government did not possess the king's colors, two of the masters offered to supply a banner. Still the magistrates hesitated; they were convinced that they should not set the idolatrous emblem of the cross in their ensign. However, a distinction might be drawn: since the fort was maintained not in the Company's name but the king's, it might be proper to show the royal colors there. Accordingly Vane accepted a banner from Captain Palmer and promised to fly it at Castle Island. The masters were satisfied, but among the colonists there was still doubt. Some, including Winthrop, could not be persuaded that it was lawful to display the cross even at the king's fortress; others simply couldn't decide what was right. But all agreed not to interfere if Vane and Dudley exercised their power as councilors to fly the flag on their own responsibility. They did so and in retrospect their decision seems both courageous and wise. Vane liked the cross no better than Winthrop, but he also knew what the banner of St. George meant to England, and he had no wish to arouse all that latent emotion.

A more agreeable event occurred when the General Court, under Vane, decided to give 400 pounds towards the erection of a public school at Newtown. In August of 1636 Governor Vane gave ten pounds towards the establishment of this same school. In 1638, after Vane was back in England, John Harvard, a minister of Charlestown, left some 800 pounds to the same use, and the school, by order of the court, was given his name.

Twice Vane had succeeded in settling delicate problems, but he had yet to meet his real tests as governor: the colony was being threatened from within by religious schism and from without by the Indians. The colonists had dealt fairly with the Indians and had maintained amicable relations with the neighboring tribes, especially the Narragansetts. But the Pequots—an Algonquian word for "destroyer"—were hostile. These aggressive and warlike Indians had forced their way down from the north some years before to take possession of lands on the Connecticut River, and they had driven clear to the coast, thrusting aside the local tribes who feared them as much as the white newcomers did. In the spring of 1634 they had committed an act of open hostility against the settlers. A Captain Stone, like many of the independent fur traders plying the coast an intemperate and disorderly man, was sailing from Boston to Virginia; he anchored in the mouth of the Connecticut River while three of his seven men went ashore to kill fowl. A band of Pequots boarded his ship, killed him, set the powder afire, and after killing the three hunters returned to the ship and slaughtered the rest of the crew. These ominous murders called for retaliation, but since Stone was a Virginian, Governor Winthrop passed the responsibility for punishing them to the governor of Virginia.

A year later, being at war with both the Narragansetts and the Dutch, the Pequots requested a treaty with Massachusetts. The court told their emissaries that friendship was possible only if they delivered up the men who had murdered Stone and if they paid for the destroyed pinnace. The Indians replied that, except for two, the guilty men were all dead and that if it were proved that these two deserved death, they would deliver them. They also countered with a story of Stone's trickery and aggression which, if true, extenuated the guilt of the Pequots. They further agreed to surrender to English settlers the Pequot rights to some land in Connecticut and to give much wampum and many skins in return for trade with the English.

The Narragansetts, meanwhile, attempted to assassinate the Pequot ambassadors, but the English made peace between the two tribes who then went home with faces saved while the English, holding a written agreement signed by Pequot emissaries, were temporarily relieved of a nagging danger. But though the English neither hastened to settle in Connecticut nor sent a ship to trade, and though the Pequots delivered no murderers, the matter nevertheless rested for nearly two years.

In the meantime, Vane's duties in Massachusetts entirely precluded his giving any attention to Saybrook affairs. Therefore, on July 1, 1636, he wrote to young John Winthrop, now governor of Connecticut, dissociating himself from the affairs of that province except for those which affected all the English in New England. One of these was that uneasy truce with the Pequots, although Connecticut, being in Pequot territory, was more urgently concerned than Boston or even Plymouth. Vane therefore commissioned young Winthrop to call a solemn conference with the head sachem of the Pequots in order to cement the treaty and forestall future conflict. But Vane knew also that since the signing of the treaty the Pequots had participated in killing some Englishmen on Long Island and had tried to seize a Plymouth ship that had entered their harbor to trade. So the instructions to Winthrop covered the possibility that the Pequots would refuse to come to a meeting; in that event he was to give back the "present" of wampum and skins, and inform them that the English held themselves free from any league with a people guilty of shedding English blood. If they did come to the conference, they should be charged with breaking the treaty of peace in that they had neither turned over the two murderers of Captain Stone nor delivered the additional "presents" they had promised. They should also be charged with other depredations and the killing of the men on Long Island. They must be allowed to defend themselves, however, and made to understand that the English did not take vengeance on those who had not been given a full opportunity to answer for themselves. Finally, if the Pequots cleared themselves of the charges, they should be told that the English were ready to confirm the peace; if not, relations would be severed and the English would avenge the blood of their countrymen.

Vane thus hoped to bring about either a firm peace or an open war, and to unite the settlements against their common enemy. But nothing came of his statesmanlike attempts at negotiation for in mid-July another incident occurred too outrageous to be overlooked: John Oldham, a planter of Watertown who had been out trading with two English boys and two Narragansetts, was brutally murdered in his ship by some Indians from Block Island. That the victim, like Captain Stone, was a loose wheeling rascal who had for years made trouble was beside the point; he was an Englishman and, if his death went unpunished, the Indians might draw some dangerous and uncomfortable conclusions. One John Gallop was out on the waters near Block Island with a man and two boys when he saw Oldham's pinnace drifting, its deck swarming with Indians, and a canoe full of Indians and goods making for the shore. When he hailed the ship, there was no reply; rather, the Indians made sail. Gallop's party, their firearms loaded only with duck shot, maneuvered to get ahead of the pinnace and collided with it so hard as almost to overset it. Six of the Indians leaped overboard. Gallop discharged his shot at the others, got his boat loose and stood off; four or five more Indians then jumped into the sea. Now, with only four Indians left aboard, Gallop boarded the pinnace. Immediately two of the Indians surrendered and were bound; two others hid below decks as Gallop proceeded to search the ship and found Oldham "under an old seine," his body still warm, his hands and legs partially hacked off, his head cleft open to the brain.

The news reached Boston when the two Indians who had accompanied Oldham came as emissaries from the chief sachem of the Narragansetts, Canonicus. They bore a letter from Roger Williams which certified what had happened and assured the governor that Canonicus was grieved and that he had dispatched another sachem, Miantonomo, with a party to punish the Block Islanders, who were subject to the Narragansetts. But it soon came out that all the Narragansett sachems, except these two, had a share in instigating the killing of Oldham because he had broken an agreement with them by making his own peace and trading with the Pequots. Finally it was learned that even the two emissaries were accomplices, but since they were also official ambassadors, the court did not imprison them; protocol was being maintained as if the Indians were a European nation. As war threatened, Williams was authorized to act as ambassador to the Narragansetts. Vane instructed him to tell them that they must send back the two boys captured on Oldham's ship, and must punish the Indians of Block Island who were guilty of the raid. As a result of these negotiations the boys were returned along with Oldham's goods, and the guilty Indians, most of whom had been drowned, were accounted for. Vane then cleared Canonicus and Miantonomo of guilt, but demanded that any guilty sachem still living should be sent to Boston for trial.

Whether or not the temperate negotiation of Vane and Williams could have averted the Pequot war is uncertain. Williams desperately hoped it would, uttering "daily cries" to God "for a merciful issue. . . ." The pacifistic and cautious Vane was equally eager for peace and so, for a month, emissaries went back and forth. But soon "God stirred up the hearts" of Vane and the magistrates and the ministers. Assembled in council, under stress of emotion, they decided that immediate retaliation was necessary to prevent more murderous raids. Their hysterical intensity is understandable, for the Indians, striking from ambush, mutilated and murdered men, women, and children indiscriminately, customarily killing them in exquisite torments not as a matter of judicial procedure—which the English could have understood—but for sheer and savage pleasure. The council therefore sent out a body of ninety men under four leaders, headed by that self-righteous, hot-headed bungler, John Endicott. Their commission was to sail to Block Island and avenge the death of Oldham; they were to spare the lives of women and children, but kill all the men and take possession of the Island. Then they were to sail to Pequot country and demand the murderers of Captain Stone and other English, confiscate the wampum the Pequots had promised as damages, and carry off some children as hostages. They were to use force only if the Indians would not comply with their demands. The temper of the expedition is sufficiently indicated by the fact that the company was composed entirely of volunteers. Meanwhile, William was still trying to persuade Miantonomo to deliver Oldham's two complicit Indians and cut off relations with the guilty Block Islanders.

On August 1, 1636, Endicott's party reached Block Island in four ships and tried to land in a hard wind and a heavy surf. They were welcomed by a barrage of arrows from about forty Indians. By the time a few of them got ashore the Indians had disappeared. On this little island—ten miles by four—barren of timber and covered only by thick scrub oak, they searched unsuccessfully for two days without finding the warriors. They contented themselves with destroying the plantations, burning the wigwams, mats and corn, staving in the canoes, and killing a few dogs. They believed they had wounded a few warriors but if so their fellows had carried them away.

Having punished the Block Islanders, the grim Endicott, reinforced by twenty men from the Saybrook plantation, turned to make ultimate demands against the Pequots. After four windbound days, the party sailed into the Pequot harbor where an Indian paddled out in a canoe to ask what they wanted. General Endicott announced that he came from the governor of Massachusetts to speak with their head sachem. On being told that Sassacus had gone to Long Island and the English must not land, he ordered the Indian emissary to go and bring other sachems. Meanwhile the English did land, with difficulty, on the high rocky shore. While the messenger was going back and forth bearing commands and returning with excuses, a menacing crowd of 300 Indians gathered around the hill on which the English forces stood. After four hours of delay, Endicott loudly stated the English demands and announced that unless the sachems would meet him and accede to those demands, he would fight. The messenger responded that if the English would lay down their arms, the Indians would also drop their bows and then the sachems would come. At this dallying and playing for time, Endicott's limited patience gave way. The Indians, he shouted, had dared the English to come and fight with them and now the English were here to fight. He ordered his men to stand steady until the enemy had withdrawn and then, expecting that they would retreat into a defense formation and stand their ground, he led his men in a charge. But the Indians failed to follow the tactics Endicott had devised for them: they dispersed and hid in ambushes, shooting their arrows from rocks and thickets and then disappearing. Because they wore armor, the Englishmen were uninjured by the feeble flights of arrows, while they, on the other hand, killed two Indians and wounded some others. Finding no opposing army to attack, they did their valiant best, marching upon a Pequot town where they burned the mats and wigwams; the corn being still green and tasseled, they could not burn that. When night fell they returned to their vessels and the next morning landed on the other side of the river where they burned all the wigwams and destroyed all the canoes they could find. Then they set out for home. The men of Saybrook, however, could not resist the temptation of the undefended corn; they had stowed a load of the ripe ears in their boats and returned to gather more when the Indians showered them with arrows. But the high trajectory made them easy to dodge and the soldiers fired back, probably killing a few Pequots. Then they dumped the corn from their sacks and ran to the safety of their boats.

Meanwhile, having carried out few of their instructions, Endicott's avengers returned in triumph to Boston, alive and unharmed, "a marvelous providence of God." In one thing, however, Endicott had succeeded: he had aroused the fury of the Pequots against all Englishmen, and now the dwellers in Connecticut would have to suffer for it. Besides, the foray had shaken the confidence of the relatively friendly Narragansetts, who were now apparently listening with some interest to a Pequot proposal for a league to exterminate the English before the English exterminated them. Roger Williams faithfully reported this rapprochement and, at Vane's request, set out alone, risking his life in a night voyage in a canoe through high winds and heavy waters to persuade the Narragansett sachem not to join the Pequots. For three nights, he says, he remained there, in nightly fear of the Pequot ambassadors, until Miantonomo finally decided to hold off the Pequots until he could confer with the English at Boston. There a treaty was agreed upon on October 22, 1636, and written out; Vane gave Roger Williams a copy so that he could interpret and explain the terms by which the Narragansetts and their posterity were pledged to maintain peace with Massachusetts and its confederates: neither party was to make peace with the Pequots nor to harbor any of them; the Indians were to put to death or deliver over any murderers and to return fugitive servants; the English were to give notice before attacking the Pequots, and the Narragansetts were to furnish them with guides; trade was to be free between them. After the treaty had been settled, the Indian ambassadors were ceremoniously dined, convoyed out of town by musketeers, and dismissed with the honor of a volley of shot. Vane now had one firm alliance.

But Endicott's abortive foray had aroused the Pequots to mounting reprisals against the fort at Saybrook. When five men went out to fetch hay in a meadow, the Pequots attacking from the high grass captured "a godly young man called Butterfield" and wounded some of the others. And two weeks later a hundred of them attacked from ambush three young men who, contrary to orders, had gone fowling. The young men were made captives, the nearest house and haystack were burned, and arrows were driven into the grazing cows. Thus began a long campaign of harassment—burning, capturing, and killing—that finally drove the Connecticut settlers into open war.

Endicott's heroics had also raised the ire of Governor Bradford of Plymouth who rebuked Massachusetts for stirring up a war by provoking the Pequots and then withdrawing without finishing anything. It was certainly a disastrously blundering action, hastily conceived and ineptly carried out; the elder Winthrop's irritated and ineffectual reply on behalf of Massachusetts shows his defensive embarrassment as he tried to justify the failure. Endicott's men, he said, did as much as could be expected with an enemy that always ran away; it was not possible to pursue in heavy armor. The English had prepared for a fight, not a footrace; besides, they had no guides to strange territory. They had not set out to make a war anyway, only to do justice, and they had managed to kill twice as many men as they were avenging. Anyhow, even if the English had killed all except a hundred Pequot warriors, that hundred could now do as much harm as the surviving tribe. Finally the Pequots would have realized the English advantage over them and made peace "if God had not deprived them of common reason." Uneasily Winthrop put the stamp of the Almighty on the outcome and let the matter rest.

But could Vane so let it rest? A mere boy, he must have been overwhelmed by the general sentiment of the deputies and the court. But still, as governor, he had issued the order which had set forces in motion that now neither he nor Williams nor anyone else could control. Vane's struggle with the Pequots raises the question of what a young man should do who has decided that war is wrong. Can a man in authority permit his countrymen to be slaughtered because his conscience will not sanction the use of force? In a crisis can he afford the luxury of neutrality if, at the same time, he seeks political position and power? Or are withdrawal and asceticism the only courses which can avert the ironies of corruption? It is a dilemma Vane would face almost until the day he died.

As far as Massachusetts was concerned, the matter did rest for several months, but the dwellers at the mouth of the Connecticut River had to endure the ever more bloody and atrocious reprisals of the Pequots. All in all it was turning out to be a bad year and even a more experienced and disillusioned politician than Vane might have been disheartened. Back in July he had written a revealing, despondent letter to his father about the state of the colony and, inadvertently, about the state of his own mind.

> The present face of things here is very tumultuous. The French continually encroach, and by vending of pieces and powder strengthen the natives for civil wars, and gain all the trade. The natives themselves are very treacherous, cruel, and cunning and let slip no advantages of killing and pilfering, if they may do it and not be discovered. The common report is also that the patent is damned, in which regard much unsettlement is like to grow amongst ourselves and great discouragement to the whole plantation. For those that are truly sincere, and are come out to advance the kingdom of the Lord Jesus must either suffer in the Cause or else labor for such retreat as God shall direct them to. In either of which cases I do not doubt but within two years this plantation, which is now flourishing, would become desolate, and either possessed again with Indians or emptied by pestilence. For it is not trade that God will set up in these parts, but the profession of His truth; and therefore if God's ends be not followed, men's ends will never be blessed nor attained.

Despite Vane's fear, the godly were never driven to a new asylum and while God may have been opposed to trade, he did not check its growth. It might have occurred to young Vane that the inner light does not always illuminate man's way in the temporal world, but apparently it did not, either now or later. But the antinomian promptings of his own inner light were soon to tear the colony almost in two.

5

Mistress Anne (1635–1637)

> Whate'er men speak by this new light,
> Still are they sure to be I' th' right.
> 'Tis a dark lantern of the Spirit,
> Which none see by but those that bear it.

Before Vane came to New England something had happened in his inner life that would forever separate him not only from Anglicans but also from "orthodox" Puritans. The latter had presumably undergone the same transforming experience that he had known at Westminster School, but with that one accession of grace, their inner spiritual lives apparently ended. It seemed to Vane that such men, after the first birth of the spirit, lived in the past, always harking back to that one experience and depending for current spiritual sustenance on "outward dispensations," that is, signs, visible manifestations of a Divine Providence whose least whisper they magnified into a cannon's roar. But Vane had undergone a second birth of the spirit; Christ, he would later say, had been born in him a first and then a second time, and it was this second coming of Christ in a man's soul that mattered most, even more than his incarnation in Jerusalem or his second coming in millennial glory—these were only outward dispensations, manifestations of the inner mystery.

Nor did Vane's spiritual life end with that second coming of Christ in his soul; as he was continually given grace, he experienced recurring inner motions and ecstasies, and for him these were all-sufficient. To these his intellect must bow; around these tenuous ascetic delights he organized the patterns of his life. His trust in these inner motions was reinforced by the observations he had made first in London and then in Vienna, where set forms had choked out the spontaneity of the spirit, and where the unregulated inner life of individuals was looked upon with suspicion and official disapproval. Thus, although Vane had said nothing openly, he had already espoused a mode of religious thinking and feeling known as antinomianism, the root of which term was *nomos,* the Greek word for law. And it was an antinomian spirit that was now disturbing the Bay Colony.

It was easy to see why antinomianism was feared, for it is the denial of the validity of law in the life of the spirit: it implies a distrust of all forms or rites of worship and stated rules of morality. The divine spirit which flows freely into the soul of a true believer is his only reliable guide, and true sanctity is an inner state, not a mode of conduct. What distressed the orthodox was not only the abrogation of all moral law, but the antinomian belief that the Holy Spirit dwelt *personally* within the elect, for that implied that by becoming one with God in a personal way, man had also made himself equal to God.

In long perspective, it seems that the antinomians, mostly unschooled and unconcerned with logical or theological distinctions, were trying to set forth the core of all mystical faiths: as the Hindus put it, *Atman* (God immanent in man) and Brahman (God transcendent) are the same; or, as the Transcendentalists of New England would later say, soul and Oversoul are one, which means that the inmost soul of man is one with God.

Harmless enough, one would think; but such views, especially when held by illiterate people, may become socially dangerous, for if a man in whom the Holy Spirit dwells is above the demands of the law and freed from social imperatives, it follows that whatever he does is sanctified, and the moral laws by which people manage to live together are irrelevant. And some enthusiasts did interpret this heady freedom as privilege to do whatever impulse suggested. An early Gnostic named Marcus had proclaimed that some divine spirit dwelt personally within him and that he had discovered a pleasant way to transmit it to women receptive to holiness. Some Christian females all too eagerly volunteered, and scandal still echoed through the corridors of centuries.

The most fearful example of the dire social consequences of

jettisoning the rules of morality was the notorious community of John of Leyden, with its holy promiscuity and sanctified murders. Martin Luther, although he nailed the moral law to the Cross with the rest of the Old Testament, still believed it was a useful guide by which Christians should examine their lives, and those who rejected it wholly, like John of Leyden, he called antinomians. So the term came to mean believers who thought that the Holy Ghost, personally dwelling within them, sanctioned personal immoralities. When antinomianism began to be felt in New England, the more sober colonists remembered John, and they knew that in England there had been outrages like that of the antinomian who had persuaded a young woman that all ceremonies, including marriage, were late inventions of the pope. By the time this foolish virgin had puzzled her way through his persuasive rhetoric, she found herself both pregnant and deserted. So in the minds of both Archbishop Laud and the graver Puritans, antinomianism meant libertinism.

In New England, as elsewhere, most antinomians were sober and even ascetic, but to men like the elder Winthrop, concerned with social peace and stability in the precariously balanced colony of Massachusetts, the antinomian doctrines were frightening because a social consequence of throwing over all rules and laws is likely to be anarchy, strife, and chaos. After all, Winthrop's commonwealth was to be a realization of the models of the scriptures which, to the orthodox, were the foundations of faith. As a Presbyterian tag put it, *bonus textuarius est bonus theologicus*: a good text man is a good divine. And not long after, the Westminister Confession would hold that the scriptures contained the whole gospel; nothing was to be added either by new revelations of the spirit or by the traditions of man. So the antinomians, every man of whom felt entitled to supplement or reinterpret the gospel by his own inner promptings, seemed as dangerous as the Catholics with their rites and traditions.

Some antinomians went so far as to maintain that the scripture was not even the real word of God; it was only the dead letter of it, containing merely the "Covenant of Works"; the living scripture was the voice within, the revelation of the indwelling spirit. Even the historical passages of the Bible were merely allegories to be interpreted by the indwelling Holy Ghost. And historical events themselves were of no greater consequence. That business in Jerusalem some 1,600 years ago, an antinomian reportedly said, was a small matter. What really counted was that Christ should continually reunite himself with man—that God should be made flesh not in history but in the present by manifesting himself in men's souls—as he had in the soul of Henry Vane.

These sanctified persons held themselves apart from other Christians in what was sometimes a spiritual arrogance. They were not as other men, they said, and hence the antinomians became a socially divisive and polarizing group, unlike the Hindus or Transcendentalists who, as universalists, maintained that the immanence and transcendence of God was true for all mankind, not merely for themselves.

In this new, struggling establishment, real differences in thought and feeling were beginning to alienate the antinomians from the orthodox Puritans, but the differences were difficult to define and the attempts to clarify them generated even greater differences. From the darkling struggle to define positions in the theological jargon of the times, some commonly understood terms emerged: for instance, the term designating holiness of conduct, "sanctification," as apart from the condition of the indwelling Holy Ghost, "justification." But even there lay conflict, for how could one tell a man who seemed sanctified because he followed the rules—mere hypocrisy—from those whose sanctified conduct flowed naturally and intuitively from grace of spirit? The orthodox, fearful of antinomian excesses, generally held that sanctification preceded justification—that is, a man must live a holy life before the Holy Ghost would enter his soul—a proposition the antinomians would by no means allow.

Their self-righteous exclusiveness, coupled with their assertion of the elect individual's right to oppose his own judgment to both church and state, made the antinomians dangerous enough; but they also entertained some minor tenets that were loathsome to the majority. One was mortalism, the doctrine that the soul died with the body. God would then resurrect together the soul and body of those whom he chose. The rest were utterly dead. Those who believed they would not be punished in hell but simply obliterated after death were irresponsibly free to sin deliciously, so the orthodox charged.

Some of the customs of the antinomians were exasperating too. Since they rejected ritual, they were much given to talk and discussion and encouraged unofficial weekday services in which laymen gathered to recount the previous Sunday's sermon and comment upon it. Laud himself might have warned the New Englanders that members of a small ecstatic sect, denied pulpits, would find some way to propagate their doctrines and advance their persons, and that those Thursday exercises could be seedbeds of dissension. He might have pointed out, too, that women were particularly given to antinomianism, perhaps because they are more emotional than men and tend to be more easily exalted or depressed. But there were more practical reasons: women were denied training for the ministry, and indeed had no assigned roles at all in the religious life of the churches. Only in the antinomian movements was there a way for a woman of strong religious sensibility to let the tongue speak something of what the heart felt. And in New England Mrs. Anne Hutchinson was one of those who felt strongly and spoke well.

She had come to Boston in the autumn of 1634 with her husband and children in order to be near her beloved teacher and guide, the Reverend John Cotton. She was evidently a woman of keen mind and strong character, with a husband who, as Winthrop observed, was a man of very mild temper and "weak parts." In fact, roles were reversed in the Hutchinson home, the husband being ruled by the wife. This seemed to both Hugh Peter and John Winthrop an inversion of the natural order, and many noted that like the unnatural rivalries of father and son, this emergence of woman from her traditional role into unnatural prominence might be a symptom, or even a cause, of the increasing upheavals in the state.

Mistress Anne quickly made herself loved and needed among the women of the colony by her medical and nursing skill, by the affectionate care she lavished on the sick and especially on women in childbirth. Finding the women she worked among generally illiterate and trapped in a life of uninspiring drudgery, Anne began to hold meetings for them on weekday afternoons in which she would recapitulate the sermons of Mr. Cotton, who was temporarily the occupant of the Boston pulpit, the Reverend Mr. Wilson having gone to England for a visit. Gradually she began to state her own feelings, adding her own exegesis and interpreting the teachings according to her own inner light; undoubtedly she distorted

Cotton's intricate theology into a more simplistic, less balanced, and more potentially explosive doctrine.

Cotton, a subtle theologian, had built his thought on the doctrine of free grace, but like other responsible evangelical theologians, he was also responsive to the claims of ethical and moral behavior. He consequently sought ways to relate and balance the two contrary pulls of grace and works. Once man was "justified" by God's grace, said Cotton, his actions, all being performed under the direction of the Holy Ghost, would inevitably be good. Thus he seemed to be upholding the antinomian position that justification preceded sanctification. Cotton also said that after justification the Holy Ghost became one with man; but, troubled by antinomian excesses, he drew a very fine distinction: if we infer from this that the Holy Ghost communicates some "personal propriety" of its own, we have then fallen into "vile Montanism." It is doubtful if anyone in New England fully understood this distinction, but all sensed his intent: he was trying to avoid the ultimate blasphemy. But such a distinction neither Mistress Anne nor Henry Vane would ever acknowledge. They joined in asserting that the truly justified believer was in some sense himself the Holy Ghost.

Anne's tendency to simplify the doctrine of grace without being aware of its social implications was a natural result of the intensity of her inner conviction, for she was by nature a mystic and enthusiast who had suffered through a series of religious crises that culminated in a kind of personal revelation. She was a martyr in search of an executioner.

She came quite naturally by her stubborn independence and her intense concern for religion, for her father had been denied a pulpit, had even been imprisoned for a time because he had attacked the bishops for ordaining unlearned men as priests. He was basically a reformer of Anglicanism, however, rather than a Separatist, and so when James purged the Puritan preachers in 1605, he was called to a church in London where he served for six years before he died in 1611, leaving his daughter troubled and adrift. A year later she married William Hutchinson, a kind man, loving father, and uxorious husband. Weak parts or not, he gave her fifteen children, only one of whom died in infancy.

Anne became so troubled at the formalism of the Anglican church that she considered separating, but before doing so, she set aside a day for humiliation and prayer in which to seek direction from God. In her distress God spoke to her, telling her that the Anglican churches were indeed unfaithful, that none of the ministers could "preach the Lord Jesus aright." He directed her mind to a passage in John's second epistle: "Every spirit that confesseth not that Jesus Christ is come in the flesh is the spirit of Antichrist." The Lord then directed her to a second passage: "He that denies the Testament, denies the Testator." From this she concluded that anyone who did not preach the new covenant of grace denied the death of the Testator; it followed, then, that it was the ministers of the Church of England who were these Antichrists. In this wholly unhistorical approach to the scriptures, in which each passage was judged solely by the light of the spirit, Anne was already demonstrating her antinomian tendencies.

But this terrifying perception left her shaken with a sense of her own atheism which haunted her through a long, tormented year. At last God granted her a clarifying revelation, leading her to understand that her own atheism lay in her reliance upon a covenant of works whereby she opposed Jesus Christ. So now she knew where Antichrist was to be discerned—he was in all those who preached or lived a covenant of works; and she could now distinguish, by the seal of the spirit, the very inflections of the different teachers, whether they spoke in the voice of John the Baptist, or Christ, or Antichrist. And of all the preachers the only ones who aroused within her an elevation of spirit, an ecstasy like the kiss of the Spouse, were Mr. John Cotton of Boston, Lincolnshire, and her distant relative, John Wheelwright.

But soon Wheelwright was silenced, and a year later, in 1633, Cotton fled Laud's threatened arrest and was secretly conveyed aboard the *Griffin* in which he escaped to the new world. Again bereft of the refreshings of the spirit, Anne turned to God who did not fail her. He "revealed himself" to her in Isaiah 30:20: "Though the Lord give thee adversity . . . yet thine eyes shall see thy teachers," at the same time revealing that she would be persecuted and suffer much trouble. She took this to mean that she should follow Cotton to Boston, Massachusetts.

During her first year in Massachusetts, with Wilson gone, Anne listened again to her beloved Mr. Cotton, the old quiet ecstasy returning each time he spoke; then she paraphrased and interpreted his words to the devoted women who came to her meetings. So many wished to come that she began holding two meetings a week, and then some of the men asked if they too might listen. Vane joined her following soon after he arrived, attracted by her eloquence, the intensity of her conviction, and his pleasure at finding her views reinforcing his own.

But there was more: in Mistress Anne he sensed an inner world that was intensely alive and free of all formalism. Here was no tedious recital of some past event, but a continual outpouring of spiritual force, unregulated, not really conscious of itself, and therefore unpredictable and exciting. Soon Anne was also drawn to young Vane. He was, after all, a man of rank soon to become governor of the colony; he was potentially her benefactor and protector. As she lectured she was particularly aware of the sensitive face, the brooding eyes, those soft hands that would never grip a musket or a sword or a dagger, hands made only for the pen and the book. And even more she was aware of his attentive empathy, the nuances and shifts of mood that matched her own. Vane was the young Seeker, drawn to a woman who was mother and sister and in some remote and subtle way lover, with whom he could share distant mutual ecstasies.

But the same ship which brought Vane to Massachusetts and to Anne Hutchinson also brought back the Reverend John Wilson to his parish. He was a tall thin man with a bony face, a harsh grating voice, and a dogmatic mind that easily drew distinctions of right and wrong, who assiduously preached the moral life, and was touchy about the prestige of his person and the sacredness of his function. He was an epitome of the Puritan preachers who had developed certain formalistic manners: they spoke with a nasal twang, wore their hair absurdly short, and appeared always in plain dress and with a severe countenance; the irreverent said they appeared to have been weaned on a pickle.

On Wilson's return, Cotton was relegated to his former position as teacher, a mere assistant; and Mistress Anne now had to listen to John Wilson each Sabbath. As he dwelt interminably on the holy wars of Israel, the caprices of Jehovah and his unfailing vengeance, she began receiving urgent signals from the Holy Spirit within: this man, so harsh and incisive in manner, so sternly moralistic, was not sanctified, he was merely sanctimonious; and his sanctimony was accepted by the people of Boston as evidence of his rebirth. So sanctimoniousness evidences justification! It was ridiculous. She came to realize that Wilson taught a doctrine of works, lived a covenant of works, and was himself unregenerate and without the seal of the spirit. Soon, in her meetings, she was invidiously comparing the two ministers in the light of her own revelations. Then, as she traveled about the colony to hear the other preachers, the Spirit bore witness that they too preached a covenant of works, were themselves obscurantistic legalists who had never known the flame or the kiss or the ecstasy or the seal. Thus they were the voice of Antichrist, ironically no different from the Anglican churches which they had fled.

Soon she was actively proselytizing in neighboring churches, spreading discontent, turning the people against their own ministers. The ugly suspicion of hypocrisy, of outer mannerism without inward correspondence, soon spread, and now the flocks were looking at their ministers with a critical eye; especially they were asking themselves if they felt anything, if there was any seal of the spirit, and the answer for many was no. Soon two parties began to shape up, the orthodox and the "opinionists," who tried to attract the new immigrants into their coterie.

When Edward Johnson landed in Boston he was buttonholed by a "little, nimble-tongued woman" who warned him against the "company of legal professors" whose preachings centered on the "Law which Christ hath abolished," and offered to lead him to a "woman that preaches better Gospel than any of your black-coats that have been at the Ninnyversity, a woman of another kind of spirit, who hath many revelations of things to come . . . [and] speaks from mere motion of the spirit, without any study at all."

It was impossible that men like Wilson and Winthrop could be unaware that such antiestablishment ideas were circulating among the women and even infecting some of the men, nor could they fail to be alarmed about the possible effects of them on the anxious commonwealth. But it was not until the Reverend John Wheelwright came to join the faction and stand as spokesman for them that the issues assumed clear definition. In May of 1636, soon after Vane had been elected governor, Wheelwright spoke as a private brother at the Boston meeting house and articulated the doctrines on which the conflict balanced. Strengthened by the presence of this eloquent and persuasive preacher and by having one of their influential disciples in the governor's seat, the opinionists increased in number and in boldness, but it was not until October that Deputy Governor Winthrop, who rightly saw Anne Hutchinson as the instigator and dominant force of the movement, set down his misgivings in his journal: dissent in the church, he wrote, must lead to dissension in civil government and a young colony surrounded by dangers could not afford to be divided against itself. Yet, having once fled persecution for conscience' sake, he was reluctant now to resort to it; he hoped he could bring the factions into harmony before heresy grew into sedition.

His first step was to hold a conference of the disagreeing parties along with other ministers of the Bay area. Mr. Cotton, with his usual kindly skill at bringing differences into accommodation, got all to agree that sanctification might "help to evidence justification," but neither Cotton nor many others, though they agreed about the indwelling of the Holy Ghost in a justified person, could agree with Mrs. Hutchinson's and Governor Vane's view that this was a personal union which implied a measure of godhood in the creature.

On October 30, the opinionists made a polarizing move: they proposed that Wheelwright be called as teacher in the Boston church. Winthrop, sensing this as an attack on Wilson as well as a move to gain power in the Boston church, refused consent on the grounds that inasmuch as the church was already furnished with able ministers whose spirit and quality were known, it would be unfit to add a man whose spirit was yet untested, and who held dissident views on two important points: Wheelwright believed that "a believer was more than a creature," and that the "person of the Holy Ghost and a believer were united." Henry Vane responded impulsively to Winthrop's attack; he marveled that the deputy could speak thus against Mr. Wheelwright whose doctrine had lately been approved by Mr. Cotton himself. And poor Cotton, beginning to find that the reconciler must also be the buffer, hedged. He could only say lamely that if it were fully thrashed out, he thought he and Wheelwright "might likely agree," and that he had the greatest respect for his godliness and abilities. Yet, since he was "apt to raise doubtful disputation," he could not endorse him as teacher in Boston. As a compromise it was agreed that Wheelwright might be called to the new church in Braintree.

But Winthrop's uncompromising speech had so offended Vane and other Hutchinsonians that they rebuked him sharply for bringing charges against a brother for utterances long past, and for doing it in a tone of bitterness and in public. Winthrop defended himself at length but tried to conciliate by arguing that the disagreement was not so much substantial as semantic, centering upon the terms "person of the Holy Ghost," and "real" union, neither of which is scriptural; if their use could be foreborne, the peace of the church might be maintained. His placatory speech was received in silence.

As the dispute continued and spread, Winthrop came more and more to feel that Vane, with whom he necessarily worked closely, was a principal antagonist. Though with typical generosity he acknowledged him as a "wise and godly gentleman," he and others entered into written controversy with Vane "for the peace sake of the church." Both sides agreed that the Holy Ghost dwells in believers, but they could not agree on precisely how, for Vane continued to insist on personal union. He finally conceded, however, that all should avoid the word "person" as of human invention and "tending to doubtful disputation."

But on points of doctrine Vane gave no ground, nor did he cease to support Mrs. Hutchinson. God had revealed himself to them both in an inward pillar of fire and both had drawn the same conclusions. They did not avow that they had a personal union with God because of scriptural or intellectual reasons; they avowed it because it had happened. It had not happened to the orthodox elders, and how could Vane and Mistress Anne match private experience against united disapproval and the weight of scriptural interpretations?

So young Governor Vane, for whom social harmony was the unfailing sign of political health, was caught between the claims of personal convictions and public responsibilities. Rationally he knew that what had started as a difference of opinion had grown out of all proportion, that he had become the leader of a divisive faction, that he was universally blamed for the division that was paralyzing the colony. While thus torn apart by anxiety, he received letters from England which spoke of difficulties in his personal estate; it is a measure of his desperation that he decided to seize on this excuse to resign his office and escape. Then he would not have to force the moment to its crisis. On December 7 he showed the letters to Winthrop and others on the council; as glad to be rid of him as he was eager to go, they gravely testified at the meeting of the court which Vane called that although his reasons were too private to be divulged, they were indeed urgent enough to justify his release from office.

But it was not to be carried so blandly. One of the assistants felt an inner motion to arise and speak "some pathetical passages" of lament that they would lose such a governor in times of great danger from Indians and French. Up to this point Vane had resisted hostility very well, but he was not prepared for words of sympathy which, like Aaron's rod, touched his emotions and released a flood of tears and confession. He would, he said, gladly risk the utter ruin of his estate rather than desert his people at such a time were it not that he feared the danger of God's judgments coming upon them for their differences and dissensions. Considering the "scandalous imputations brought upon himself, as if he should be the cause of all," he thought he should remove himself for a time. If he was really the disturber, he believed, his absence would help to heal the rift; if not, he would be exonerated.

And so the boy with his deeply wounded pride poured out justification and apology, interrupted by sobs, while the composed elders listened with stony faces. And that day young Vane learned a bitter thing: a man who strips himself emotionally naked in the presence of his enemies has delivered himself into their hands. That day the court gave him no flattering assurances, only the cold conclusion that it was not fitting to approve his departure on those grounds. Regaining control of himself, Vane apologized for speaking improperly from passion rather than from judgment, and since he was satisfied that the troubles with his estate were sufficient grounds, he still requested to be relieved. Most of the members of the court would be happy to have him gone on any terms, so they signified consent by cool silence and, moving at once to the question of his replacement, decided to call a general court of elections the following week.

But the Hutchinsonians were unwilling to surrender their champion for any reason. They sent a deputation to inform the court that the church membership did not approve of the governor's departure. Moved by this demonstration of approval and aware of the pain and problems his return to England would create, Vane decided to stay and fight; as an "obedient child of the church," he said, even with the permission of the court, he "durst not go away." The election was accordingly deferred until the normal time, the following May of 1637, and the court declared a recess of several days.

Before the court reconvened, the orthodox party summoned the ministers from the outlying towns to Boston where they held a preliminary meeting with John Cotton, taxing him with responsibility for the inflammatory opinions of his female disciple and suggesting she should be dealt with by the magistrates. Cotton countered by suggesting they first send for Anne and ask her to explain just how Cotton's doctrine differed from that of the other ministers. She responded to the summons and came to Cotton's house for her first confrontation with the opponents who would ultimately cast her out, a lone woman surrounded by powerful and suspicious men whose power she was challenging.

Hugh Peter led off by bluntly charging that Mrs. Hutchinson had made it common talk that the assembled ministers were different from true ministers of the gospel. She was hesitant and evasive. Peter assured her that this was a private communion of minds, not punitive but a quest for information only. "I pray," said he, "answer the question directly as fully and as plainly as you desire we should tell you our minds."

And then she cried out as passionately and unguardedly as Vane had done: "The fear of man is a snare; why should I be afraid?" Then rushed out all the words that would be used against her in the court. Mr. Cotton, she said, preached a covenant of grace but the rest a covenant of works; they were not "able ministers of the new testament"; they did not have "the seal of the spirit." Taken aback by this frank admission, they departed, admonishing Mr. Cotton to speak with her further.

When the court reconvened on Tuesday afternoon December 13, the magistrates first addressed themselves to such essential business as reorganizing the army into three regiments, with Governor Vane acting as chief general for the time being. But Vane's feelings were still precariously near the surface, and when the meeting of the ministers was spoken of he "took great offence" because it had been held without his knowledge. The next day the ministers attended their appointed meeting with the court, and Governor Vane, presiding, announced that their purpose was to try to settle the differences of opinion among the churches. Mr. Dudley urged everyone to speak out freely and openly. Vane pettishly interrupted to say that he would be only too glad to do so were it not that the ministers had already undertaken the matter. In the face of this second outburst, Hugh Peter, no longer able to hold his peace, told Vane plainly, though "with all due reverence," that the ministers were much saddened that he should be jealous of their meetings or seem to wish to restrain their liberty. Vane recognized his blunder (he had given the other side occasion to use the talismanic word "liberty"), and tried to excuse his ill-natured speech which, he said, was sudden and on a mistake. But refusing to be placated, Peter continued the attack: before the governor came, less than two years ago, the churches were at peace. Vane, angry and confused, countered with some approximations of scripture: "The light of the gospel brings a sword," and "the children of the bondwoman would persecute those of the freewoman." Peter refused the gambit and instead of countering with scripture, lectured him condescendingly, begging him, humbly, to consider how young he was, how inexperienced in the things of God, and he admonished him to beware of jumping to "peremptory conclusions, which he perceived him to be very apt unto." Vane made no reply and Peter went on to moralize about the principal causes of the dispute: pride, idleness, and ignorance. Seizing the advantage that Peter had gained, Pastor Wilson launched into a "very sad speech" about the perilous condition of the churches and how they might break into separatist sects if the alienation was not remedied. Finally, Wilson made an explicit charge: the cause of all the trouble was the new opinions that had arisen, and at that moment the magistrates shouted their approval, all except Vane, two deputies, and Cotton and Wheel-wright.

Those who had demurred took Wilson's speech very ill and went to his house to admonish him. He refused to give ground; he had been within his legal rights for he had been called to the court and, like the rest, had been invited to speak freely and faithfully. He denied, however, that he had pointed at the members of the Boston church more than at anyone else.

Dissatisfied with this explanation, Vane publicly called Wilson to account on December 31, indicting him in violent language which was echoed by many of the congregation, who reproached their pastor bitterly. Even the mild Mr. Cotton, with "much wisdom and moderation," joined in too, but he persuaded the congregation not to vote a formal censure. He did, however, subject Wilson to a grave exhortation. Wilson, shaken at finding himself so nearly rejected by his own church, "with the Lord's assistance" spoke the next day in his sermon with such temperance and gentleness that the congregation was satisfied and Vane himself expressed approval. Hoping to effect the reconciliation that now seemed possible, Winthrop wrote to Cotton to remind him of his own failing and to defend Wilson, who had indeed been roughly used. Cotton's answer was "very loving and gentle," but he still maintained his own good intentions and enlarged his arguments against Wilson. "In like loving manner," Winthrop wrote back, but spared Cotton his further arguments, which he showed instead to Wilson and the two ruling elders. The leaders were all suitably loving but their differences lay beneath, stubbornly unresolved.

Meanwhile the controversy was raging like a brush fire. Wild attacks on the Covenant of Works were being made, including a condemnation of all ten commandments; in a heated moment it was said that a person might be damned even though his conduct was fully sanctified and he remained in spiritual communion with Jesus Christ. People who formerly had been assured of their salvation now began to experience exquisite doubts: a Weymouth man leaped out of bed one night crying, "Art thou come, Lord Jesus?" He jumped from a window, and ran seven miles in the freezing cold, desperately stopping every now and then to kneel in the snow and pray, until he froze to death.

The ministers, too, were deeply troubled, for the opinionists, especially the women, were badgering them and openly contradicting their teachings in meeting. Mrs. Hutchinson and her followers more than once stood up and stalked out while Mr. Wilson was exhorting; and after sermons, when questions were in order, the women, enjoying their new freedom, asked edged questions that were really speeches or insults, aimed to discredit the speaker. As Thomas Weld bitterly wrote later:

> Now the faithful ministers of Christ must have dung cast on their faces, and be no better than legal preachers, *Baals'* priest, Popish factors, scribes, Pharisees, and opposers of Christ himself. . . . Now, after our sermons were ended at our public lectures, you might have seen half a dozen pistols discharged at the face of the preacher (I mean) so many objections . . . against our doctrine delivered; . . . yea, they would come when they heard a minister was upon such a point as was like to strike their opinions, with a purpose to oppose him to his face.

Nothing, it seemed, could assuage the bitterness and recriminations that were souring life in God's commonwealth. On January 8, 1637, in desperation the Boston church closed its rolls, and no new members would be admitted for nearly two years. Now there was nothing left to do but turn to God. The people placed their hopes in the general fast day that Vane and the court had set, a day of self-examination, prayer, and humiliation, a day to remember the miserable condition of the Protestant churches in Europe; the persecution of the faithful and the advance of papistry in England; the famine and plague and the depredations of the Pequots in Connecticut; but the most urgent of all was the "dissensions in our churches."

Cotton opened the fast day service on January 19, 1637, with a discourse on fasting which by-passed the bogs of controversy, after which John Wheelwright was invited to speak as a lay brother. Wheelwright had apparently received peremptory signals from the Holy Ghost, and so with the heedless and bungling sincerity of a certified fanatic, he contemptuously thrust aside the idea that a fast should be called for any reason other than the overriding fact that Christ was absent from his people in New England. He exhorted his listeners to seize the word of the Lord and kill the enemies of truth, to break them in pieces as with a rod of iron. As for these "wondrous holy people" who live under a covenant of works, they were enemies to Christ. Such talk, he acknowledged, might cause a combustion; so let it be. Christ came to send fire and the wicked must be burnt by it. Warming to his theme of fire he shouted that "the whore must be burnt" and Antichrist consumed.

Vane and the opinionists may have been gratified at these inspired rantings, but Wilson, Winthrop, and the orthodox were outraged, tight-lipped and deeply resolved. After the Wheelwright speech the disputes became so acrimonious that some feared if Laud were to hear how unity and discipline were being shredded, he might find excuse to reach across the sea. As Winthrop observed, every occasion increased contention, and men began distinguishing those under a covenant of grace from those under a covenant of works as in Europe they distinguished between Protestants and papists.

The orthodox party opened fire in the General Court session that began on March 9, with Vane in the chair. First they questioned the propriety of the attack on Wilson for his "sad speech" in the last court and voted to approve his good and timely advice. Then they indirectly rebuked Vane by voting that without the consent of the court no member should be publicly called to question about any utterance made during a session. Then they cleared a way to move against Wheelwright by voting that when any heresy endangered the state, the court had a right to act against it without waiting for the church to move. A majority of Boston church members presented a petition on behalf of Wheelwright, which Vane strongly supported. But the court rejected it, and rebuked the petitioners for their "presumptuous act."

Then Wheelwright was summoned and presented with the text of his sermon. He refused to evade the question; yes, this was what he had said, and would still say. The ministers who were called to testify all agreed that they preached the doctrine which he called a Covenant of Works. It followed, then, that he had called them antichristian. The court, after bitter debate, adjudged him guilty of sedition and contempt for defying the intention of the fast which was to reconcile differences. Governor Vane protested vehemently and, with the support of the small minority of the court that shared his views, not only justified Wheelwright but strongly condemned the proceedings of the court. When his protest was rejected, he and Cotton roused the Boston church to submit a second petition in defense of Wheelwright. The majority in the court reacted by moving to silence Wheelwright and to deny him his pulpit. But then they began to have second thoughts: this was reminiscent of the tyranny they had fled. Some of them had been denied pulpits in England by Laud, and many had been denied the right to worship as they wished, and so they decied to leave spiritual discipline to the authority of the Boston church.

The opinionist party, though now a small minority in the court, was intransigent. Wheelwright was to be sentenced on the civil charge of sedition at the next meeting of the court, and it appeared that a hot and vicious fight was shaping up. The majority therefore moved that the next court, at which the annual election would also take place, be moved from Boston to Cambridge where opinionists were less numerous, where the atmosphere was cooler, and where it would be easier for the conservative freemen of the outlying towns to come. Seeing the drift of the motion, Governor Vane, although it was his obligation to put the question to a vote, refused to do so. Then the impetuous John Endicott seized the chair and put the question. The motion was passed.

Thus Vane and his party were defeated all along the line, but he continued to keep himself unsullied from any contact with the covenant of works. He, Cotton, and Wheelwright refused to attend a meeting of the Concord church to ordain some ministers who had preached in England under the regime of the bishops. They considered these "legal preachers," they said, and would not lend their approval to the ceremonies by attending. At the same time they were preparing a new document, *Petition and Remonstrance*, in which they vindicated Wheelwright's sincerity as a healer of strife: his doctrine could not be seditious for his words had been "the very expressions of the Holy Ghost himself." They admonished the court to consider that Satan, the ancient enemy of free grace, was still attacking the prophets of God by his old methods, and concluded by saying that even if they were repulsed by the magistrates they knew they would find grace with the Lord. And so the strife seemed endless.

And always accompanying the internal strife, like an antiphonal theme, was the outer strife against the Pequots who were continuing to harass the settlers in the Connecticut Valley. Their attempt to make the Narragansetts their allies had failed, and, worse for them, a group of Pequots under the leadership of Uncas, calling themselves Mohegans, had seceded and were now hostile to their former brothers. Despite these difficulties, the Pequots raided with increasing frequency and ruthlessness, and soon accounts began filtering into Boston about the torture of captives. The most appalling case was that of John Tilley and a comrade who had landed to go fowling within a few miles of the fort at Saybrook. The Indians attacked them from ambush and, after killing his comrade, took Tilley captive and cut off his hands. He lived afterwards for three days during which they cut off his feet too. It was reported that they also tied him to a stake, peeled off strips of his skin, and put hot coals between skin and flesh. The Pequots looked on with pleasure and admiration that were increased by Tilley's courage; he was a stout man, they confessed, and "cried not at his torture."

The Pequot militancy had been intensified by Endicott's raid of the previous summer, and now they seemed to be pressing for a showdown with the English. Among Vane's last acts as governor was an alliance of Massachusetts Bay Colony with Connecticut and Plymouth and the Narragansett Indians to make war on the Pequots. All the New England colonies had been building fortifications, organizing their armies, and establishing regular watches; the Massachusetts court required all freemen to carry muskets or other arms whenever they attended public gatherings. On April 18, 1637, Vane called a special session of the court to make preparation for war. It was agreed that the war, being "undertaken upon just ground," should be prosecuted fully.

And thus irony was heaped upon irony. Vane had opposed formalisms in Vienna and London only to find them flourishing, under different forms, in Boston. And refusing to take up arms himself, he was forced by circumstances to set in motion the forces that would soon culminate in America's first national crime against conscience. It was a pacifist in principle who gave the orders that would result in the obliteration of the Pequot nation.

And so Governor Vane ordered 160 men to be assembled from various towns, organized, armed, and trained, ready to be sent to Connecticut to reinforce the twenty Massachusetts men already there under Captain Underhill, that man of private prayers. The council was also empowered to treat with Plymouth and Connecticut for aid. The governor of Plymouth, still annoyed about having had no voice in planning Endicott's campaign, finally agreed to send some men, but they arrived when the battles were over. On April 23, two hundred Pequots attacked a group of colonists working in a field, killing nine persons including a woman and a child; they also slaughtered cattle and carried off two young women who, they believed, could teach them to make gunpowder. The Connecticut court, thoroughly alarmed, decided to counter immediately and vigorously; they could not even wait for the Massachusetts contingent under Israel Stoughton which was then being mustered.

So Captain John Mason immediately set sail for Saybrook with ninety men while his Indian allies, sixty braves under the command of Uncas, marched there to meet them. When Mason and his men arrived, they were reassured to learn that Uncas had already destroyed a party of Pequots except for one captive who contemptuously laughed and "braved the English as though they durst not kill a Pequot." But the English, remembering the recent massacre and the torture of John Tilley, found a savage streak within themselves. They tied one of the captive's legs to a post, roped the other, and twenty of them seized the rope and began to pull the Indian apart. But Captain Underhill, too professional a soldier to enjoy civilian rages, pulled out his pistol and decently killed his enemy.

With the fierce support of the Mohegans and the timorous support of the Narragansetts, Mason then moved to his major objective—the Pequot fort and village on the Mystic River. Disobeying the instructions of the court to attack from the sea, but with the approval of God, certified by the chaplain after a night of prayer, Mason took a long way by land and came up to the fort undetected just when 150 Pequot braves had arrived from their other fort to join in the attack on the English. During that night Mason and his men could hear the Indians revelling, "singing and dancing and blessing their God for that the English were gone away." At dawn, Mason and his men burst in at the two opposite gates of the circular fortifications, achieving complete tactical surprise. They fired into the wigwams and as the Indians resisted with bow and arrow, set fire to the wigwams. Out of their burning homes the Indians ran in blind terror to find that the English soldiers had completely ringed their village. Inside this ring, the Indians milled in panic, wholly vulnerable to the controlled fire of the soldiers. A few warriors, with the final bravery of desperation, burst through the English encirclement only to find a second ring of enemies, the Mohegans and Narragansetts. Many of the Pequots were burned; most of the others were shot. It was an overwhelming and completely ruthless victory, the result, the colonists were certain, of God's providence. It effectively ended the Pequot nation.

Sassacus, a chief, and a few demoralized remnants of the Pequots took refuge in the forests, unable to harass Mason as he marched his army, some of them wounded, through Pequot country to the harbor whence they sailed back to Saybrook for the victory celebration. Israel Stoughton's Massachusetts men arrived too late for the slaughter but were given the responsibility of hunting Sassacus and pursuing the fugitives. It was in July that his men trapped most of them in a swamp and killed or captured them. Now there were Indian slaves to be distributed and Hugh Peter was quick to see an opportunity for lawful gain. He would like, he wrote, "a young woman or a girl and a boy" if that were possible. Too pure to sit in a church where a popish candle burned, he did not recoil from acquiring slaves.

The colony of Massachusetts immediately called for a day of thanksgiving, not forgetting while the festive spirit was upon them that their contribution to the war entitled them to some of the Pequot lands, for which they sent an embassy to negotiate. Vane was left to reflect on the primal curse that attended political affairs—that actions set in motion for the best of reasons and by the most idealistic men always went further than was intended or could have been foreseen. Actions, it seemed, developed lines of force quite independently of the wishes of those who initiated them. The Pequots were fierce, cunning human predators who had to be controlled; but if given some abstract choice, would anyone in New England have wished to see the entire tribe destroyed? John Endicott, perhaps, but not the Winthrops or the Cottons, not Roger Williams or Hugh Peter, not Anne Hutchinson and certainly not Henry Vane. And yet he had issued the orders and would have to live with the consequences. The Pequots were quiet enough now and the only trouble they would ever cause again would be in the consciences of later Americans who would regard the Pequot war as a symbolic paradigm of a universal cannibalism with man as the ultimate predator.

Vane had barely set the last phase of the Pequot war in motion when he lost his governorship; the massacre at Mystic came eight days after his own defeat at the polls. Even then the Massachusetts war effort was being hampered by the antinomian controversy. John Wilson had been chosen chaplain for Stoughton's army and the

Boston quota was filled with great difficulty, even during the anti-Pequot hysteria, because none of the opinionists would accompany the "legalist" pastor to the war. The Boston church sent only a few men whom they did not mind being rid of temporarily or permanently, men "of the most refuse sort." Not even the victory at Mystic could end the war at home.

May 17, 1637, the day of the fateful General Court election, dawned fair; all morning the freemen from the outlying towns were gathering in the meadow that is now Cambridge Common. The interval since the last court had done nothing to reconcile or relax the internal hostilities, and excitement grew as the magistrates, deputies, ministers, and freemen thronged the Common. Vane, realizing that this large turnout was inimical to the Boston faction, tried to delay the election, vaguely hoping for some unforeseen turn of fortune. Flanked by the four halberdiers who had made his comings and goings ceremonious, at about one o'clock in the afternoon he took his position at the base of a large oak tree on the north side of the Common. No sooner had he formally opened the meeting than a member of the Boston church presented a petition on behalf of John Wheelwright. This was a shrewd move, for the petition was in effect an appeal from the magistrates who had condemned Wheelwright to the judgment of the full and open court. Vane accepted the petition and was about to read it when Winthrop loudly objected: the motion was out of order, for this was a meeting held according to the charter specifically for election, and that must be the first order of business. He was supported by many other voices objecting to the setting of a bad precedent. But the Bostonians shouted their insistence and Vane announced that no further business would be transacted until the petition had been heard. As the argument became louder and more biting, words gave way to fists and it appeared that the meeting might break up in a riot. Then a most unexpected thing happened. The sedate, precise, and formal John Wilson, as though the antinomian Holy Ghost had unexpectedly seized him, climbed up on a limb of an oak tree and, shouting mightily over the tumult, exhorted his fellows to look to the charter, next to the word "liberty," the most potent word in all of Massachusetts. The suggestion that the Boston petition might threaten the charter was an inspired one. In that critical moment, Wilson was outdoing the Hutchinsonians. Cries of "election,

LIBRARY
EISENHOWER COLLEGE

election" rose from the crowd and Winthrop took hold of the situation by appealing to the majority to settle the point of order. He called for a division, and the greater number gathered in the group that favored proceeding to election. Vane still refused until Winthrop threatened to go ahead without him. Seeing that he had no option, Vane sullenly left his group of followers, resumed the chair, and conducted the elections. As he feared, his party was completely defeated. Winthrop was chosen governor and Dudley his deputy. The three office holders who belonged to the antinomian faction, Vane, Coddington, and Dummer, were eliminated.

But Boston had decided not to select its deputies until after the general election and, the next morning, they returned Vane, Coddington, and Hoffe to the General Court. On a technicality the court refused to seat them, so they went back to Boston and called a full meeting which voted again for the same three men. Not finding any grounds on which to reject them, the court now admitted them. For Vane, although it was a considerable comedown it was better than nothing. But for Wheelwright, Anne Hutchinson, and their party, it was the turning point towards disaster.

When Wheelwright made his appearance before the court he was unyielding about the charges of sedition and contempt; if he had committed sedition, he said, he ought to be put to death, and if they meant to proceed thus against him, he would "appeal to the king's court, for he could retract nothing." The court denied the legal possibility of appealing beyond its jurisdiction, but deferred his sentence so that he might have an opportunity to think over and retract his errors.

Then, under Winthrop's lead, the court passed an order which disturbed Vane profoundly. This order was in fact an act of exclusion, providing that no new person could be admitted to the colony without the permission of the magistrates, and it imposed a penalty upon any persons who should extend hospitality to unapproved newcomers for more than three weeks. While the expressed intent of the act was to exclude persons potentially dangerous to the commonwealth, a sensible enough thing, it took no great percipience to see who would in fact be excluded. Winthrop explained the anger of Vane and his party by saying that "they expected many of their opinion to come out of England." Ultimately this act passed.

Winthrop's election as governor, although it returned his party to power in the court, left him isolated in Boston where Vane and his friends did not accept defeat gracefully. As soon as Winthrop was chosen, the four sergeants who had attended Vane laid down their halberds and refused further attendance, saying they had attended Vane voluntarily and out of respect for his person. But if Boston would not honor Winthrop, the outsiders would: the neighboring towns offered to send men to carry the halberds. Then Boston made a belated offer to send two men, though not of the rank of sergeant. Choosing not to accept this slight, Winthrop appointed two of his own servants to act as guard of honor. And when he returned to Boston, he passed through the town to his own house in silence, attended only by his servants, and was welcomed by none. But Winthrop bore these petty insults as magnanimously as he had conducted himself a year ago when young Vane had defeated him. It was Vane who did not know what became a defeated man; like a wounded adolescent, he set an emotional tone for his followers, who stared coldly at Winthrop, or pointedly ignored him. The next Sunday at the meeting house, Vane pettishly refused to sit with Winthrop in the magistrates' seat where he had sat since his arrival, even before he was elected governor. He and his friend Coddington conspicuously seated themselves among the deacons and refused to move when the governor sent an attendant to invite them to join him. But the discourtesy of the Boston opinionists was offset by the honor paid Winthrop when he journeyed to Saugus, Salem, and Ipswich, where the townsmen crowded to meet him and escorted him triumphantly from town to town.

At about this time, Lord Ley, a nineteen-year-old aristocrat, son and heir to the Duke of Marlborough, landed in Boston on a visit to the new land. Governor Winthrop invited Vane and Lord Ley to a dinner but Vane refused, explaining that his "conscience withheld him." Not content with that, he boorishly stole the guest of honor and took him over to Noddle Island to dine with Mr. Samuel Maverick instead. Winthrop calmly recorded this insult merely as an instance of how wide the religious divisions had become.

The bitterness now centered around the Act of Exclusion. It flared to new intensity when the act was actually enforced against a shipload of new arrivals, among whom were relatives of Anne Hutchinson. Now the colonists felt on their own pulses how bitter a thing it was to turn away dear friends who had fled the Laudian persecution as they had done. Resentment of the act grew so strong that Winthrop felt compelled to justify it. He published a "Defense of the Order of the Court . . ." to which Vane published in reply, "A Brief Answer to a Certain Declaration." This, Vane's first published work, contains a tentative formulation of his ideas about the relation of liberty of conscience to the governance of a Christian commonwealth.

Nineteenth-century liberal admirers of Vane, who idealized him as a premature prophet of civil liberty and religious toleration, saw this as a first brave manifesto in the fight against tyranny; and there are indications that Vane had begun to learn that a dissident group that wishes to be tolerated must think about extending toleration to others, a necessary first step to the doctrine that toleration of dissent is itself good. It also displays certain basic qualities of Vane's mind. He demonstrates a gift for abstract thought which, throughout his life, enabled him to discern general principles in the chaos of debate, to argue from them, and sometimes to act upon them. It is this side of his thinking that has appealed to moderns, for some of the principles he enunciated and defended were generally accepted only in later centuries. But if in this way at times he offered a statesmanlike breadth and impartiality of thought, at other times he argued as a partisan exploiting fine principles for the immediate advantage of his party. The principle he here defends, attractive to later times, is that a state should not have the power to exclude or eject persons because their opinions differ from those of the majority. But one is a little dismayed to see that the grounds of this generous proposition are theological rather than political, that Vane's real reason for defending the dissenters is not that dissent is valuable, but that these particular dissenters are right: they have the Truth.

In this written exchange, Vane appears as a subtle theorist who still believes that "true principles" are directly workable in practical politics. Of course, one must remember his youth. Winthrop, on the other hand, thinks pragmatically, and behind his arguments lie not general principles but the compelling need to prevent the new commonwealth from destroying itself. Vane stands on principles; Winthrop, aware of principles, stands for actions that will ensure the security and growth of the colony. Vane argues as a thinker whose ideas are based on the absolute of an overwhelming religious experience; Winthrop argues as a doer who, whatever he may profess, is very much at home in a covenant of works. For theological differences do work out into different modes of political action. The stubborn man of principle is willing to countenance violence for Christ's sake, to let the gospel bring a sword, for that is what the scripture says it will do. Winthrop, the practical man, though he will pay respect to scripture, will always seek compromise; in extremity he will stretch a principle and interpret the gospel in a way which sanctions peace. Vane seems ready to sacrifice the whole civil structure in order to witness for the "true" Christ that was born in his soul. The crux of the disagreement is an old dilemma: if heretical opinion threatens the stability of the government, it is not a matter of conscience, but of sedition; so spoke William Laud and Ferdinand of Vienna; so had spoken Elizabeth of England. On the other hand, God's truth must not be excluded from the commonwealth by human judgment even if that truth tears the state apart. Winthrop's ultimate appeal is to political reality, Vane's to something that happened in his soul. Later, England would fight a civil war over these same issues, the relation of religion to politics, of conscience to the magistrate, and church to state.

Vane opposes Winthrop's definition of a commonwealth as a merely social contract: "a certain company of people consenting to cohabit together under one government, for their mutual safety and welfare." Vane's first objection to this, an objection he will maintain all his life, is that it defines a purely secular commonwealth, whereas nothing should be justified in a commonwealth except by the word of God and the sanction of the spirit of Christ. His second objection, one he would later qualify, is that the commonwealth derives its charter from the king and is therefore subject to the king's will. On these two propositions he bases most of his case, exploring some of their implications in depth and with much subtlety. For instance, he argues that though the commonwealth may decide who may or may not join, it may not exclude His Majesty's subjects without royal sanction, nor may magistrates exclude even dangerous persons for religious reasons without more than secular authority. Even churches have no right to receive or reject at their own discretions, but only "at the discretion of Christ."

Perhaps the most modern touch in this section is the imaginative sympathy he shows when he observes that by Winthrop's definition the societies of the Indians too are commonwealths, whose citizens may believe that "cohabitation of the English with them tends to their utter ruin," yet Vane doubts that Winthrop will say that they may lawfully keep the colonists out on that ground.

Winthrop had said it was worse to admit a man and then cast him out than simply to deny admittance in the first place. Vane seized on this, saying that it implied that the colony intended to eject the opinionists—"which if it must be, the Lord's will be done." Although young Henry would not be there to see it, it would be done before very long.

Winthrop, replying to common objections that under the new act some "profane persons" were received while other religious persons were rejected, had said in his practical way that this was justifiable because some profane persons were less dangerous than religious ones who were confirmed in erroneous opinions. Vane objects: this act gives magistrates liberty to refuse not only religious people but even those who are "truly and particularly religious"; besides, even those who walk in error should be reformed and pitied rather than simply excluded. As for Winthrop's contention that no good Christians have actually been refused, Vane flatly contradicts it: "divers Christians have been already rejected," and in such instances, Christ himself is rejected.

Winthrop would not admit that the law was directed particularly against those who held Wheelwright's ideas, but he maintained that even if it had been, there would be no evil in it, for those ideas caused strife and made people look upon their magistrates, ministers, and brethren as enemies to Christ, "more dangerous than the opinion of Mr. Williams." Vane replied that Jesus came not to send peace but a sword, and whoever preached the true gospel would "cause divisions by accident. . . . If he be blamed for this, Christ cannot be excused." If the ministers admit that what Wheelwright describes as a "way of works" is their way, then of course they are antichristian ministers. And if Wheelwright's opinions are more dangerous than those of Roger Williams it is because the true gospel is more dangerous than the gospel according to Williams.

Vane concludes with three reasons for thinking the law of exclusion wicked and sinful: it rejects men according to the judgment of other men, whereas the judgment should be God's; it gives magistrates liberty to reject eminent Christian persons, so that

Christ himself might be turned away from New England. Finally, the law contradicts the injunctions of Christ to render unto Caesar that which is Caesar's (in this case King Charles) and to do good to all, but "especially to them of the household of faith."

Vane's first writing is clearly organized, cogently argued, and responsive to the issues of the immediate controversy; it also looks beyond it. That almost all the supporting evidence is quotation from scripture merely places it in its time. But it was Winthrop who had the last word in print as the court did in fact. Roused by the force of Vane's attack, he countered in "A Reply to An Answer to a Declaration . . . "; if he deals here more sharply than his own disposition would lead him, he says, "the blame must fall upon him" who forced him into reluctant reply.

The merits of the dispute are difficult to assess. The law was harsh. It imposed humiliation and distress upon decent emigrants in search of a haven; it levied excessive fines on friends or relatives who wished to harbor them; it was arbitrary, discriminatory, applied a doctrine of prior restraint, and smacked of bigotry. On the other hand, the stiff-necked dogmatism and self-righteous intransigency of the Hutchinsonians did set brother against brother and did imperil the commonwealth so seriously that its guardians were forced to take some action. The fact that the religious grounds of controversy seem to us trivial and the theological distinctions too fine even to be understood, let alone fought over, has nothing to do with the case. Our indifference to theological trivia may render us insensitive to the feelings that ran so strong, although our own irrational and driving passions about minute distinctions of political ideology should help us understand the emotions and actions of these troubled men.

As the stifling summer wore on, the long anxiety about being overrun by Indians was put to rest by news of the final obliteration of the Pequot tribe; the scalp of the defeated sachem, Sassacus, was received in Boston, and disconsolate captives, mostly women and children, were again common sights on the streets.

On August 1, 1637, when the General Court reconvened after the adjournment of May 17, a replacement was selected for young Harry Vane as deputy from Boston. For Vane, believing that his career in Massachusetts was at a dead end, had arranged to sail for England with Lord Ley. On August 3, while the court was still sitting, Vane and Ley boarded the boat in Boston Harbor that was to carry them to their ship riding at anchor. Vane's party turned out in force to escort him to the boat; some of them crowded in to accompany him to the ship. As the boat left the dock, his friends, who had come armed, "gave him divers volleys of shot," and as the ship passed Castle Island, five pieces of ordnance were fired. However relieved he may have been to see the last of Vane, Winthrop did not take leave of his duties in court to see him off.

As Vane sailed out into the Atlantic, returning home with a full year of his royal leave still to run, he must have realized that his career in the new world was an abortive failure. Did he also realize that in a moment of greatest need he was abandoning his friends and supporters who had trusted his leadership? For his own good he got out of New England just in time. As one of the protagonists of the antinomian drama, he was stepping out of his role in the fourth act, just before the catastrophe into which he certainly would have been drawn. The events that took place after his departure were no longer his story, but they were in part the story of the effects of his presence and actions; he had helped to arouse the forces which now would crush the opinionists.

After Vane left there was one more attempt to bring the warring parties together. On August 30 began the synod, at which all the teaching elders of the country assembled to discuss eighty erroneous opinions and a number of "unwholesome expressions" and abuses of passages of scripture. And discuss they did, with such "jealousies, heats, and paroxysms of spirit" that it was necessary to threaten the police power of the magistrates to quiet them, and many of the Bostonians walked out and boycotted the synod. Finally the points of dispute were reduced to five, on which Cotton and Wheelwright opposed all the rest. Then Cotton, after long wooing by the conservatives and a dawning realization of how drastically the Hutchinsonians had warped his doctrines and how disruptively they had used them and him, worked over these five points until they were so expressed that the ministers could agree. Wheelwright was thus left isolated. Henceforth Cotton, with grief and misgivings, was obliged by mind and conscience to side with Wilson against Wheelwright and even Anne Hutchinson.

Once the points of doctrine were settled, the synod resolved that regular meetings of women in which one woman held forth in a "prophetical way" were "disorderly and without rule." And tendentious questioning which was not intended to seek information about the sermon but rather to contradict and reproach the elders was "utterly condemned."

Hopes that this synod would pacify the dissension were short-lived, for Wheelwright kept preaching the same doctrines and Mrs. Hutchinson's contentious tongue refused to rest. By the next meeting of the General Court on November 2, the elders were ready to stop temporizing and take action. Convinced that two parties so bitterly opposed could no longer be contained in the same body, they decided to banish some of the principal agitators. Two deputies were first called to account: William Aspinwall (who later became a Fifth Monarchy Man in England) had signed the Wheelwright petition, and John Coggeshall, although he had not signed it, had approved it and publicly maintained that Wheelwright was being persecuted for the truth. Both men were dismissed from office. Then John Wheelwright, who had been convicted several months ago, was called in and given one more chance to acknowledge his errors. But since he still maintained that he "had delivered nothing but the truth of Christ," Winthrop wearily argued the case once more, though he insisted that the court had condemned Wheelwright not for his doctrine but for sedition. Then the court pronounced the long-delayed sentence: he was disfranchised and banished, and given fourteen days to settle his affairs and leave the colony. Meanwhile, Coggeshall and Aspinwall had talked so angrily and loudly that they were now called in again. Coggeshall was disfranchised and enjoined to keep the peace on pain of banishment; Aspinwall talked back so defiantly that he was not only disfranchised but peremptorily banished.

The court then turned towards the source from which all dissension had flowed—Anne Hutchinson. She had long been known for her generosity to the sick, her comfort to the disheartened, but also for her neurotic self-assertion and obsessive preaching, her outgoing warmth and her self-centered pride. She was a remarkable, even brilliant woman who had been given almost all gifts except the humble one of rest. Now, as she faced the hostile court alone and almost unfriended, she was all dignity and icy self-control; in extremity she showed herself what Winthrop said she was, "a woman of ready wit and bold spirit." If she was frightened, she betrayed no sign of it. She listened to Winthrop's opening statement: she had been summoned to answer charges that she had spread opinions that were the cause of all these troubles, she had cast reproach upon the ministers and had continued her meetings even after they were prohibited. She must either acknowledge and reform these and other offenses or the court would take steps to assure that she should trouble no further.

About this time Mistress Anne, who was pregnant and who, according to usage, was required to stand before the court, began to show signs of pain in her sensitive face. The elders, until this moment unaware of her pregnancy, immediately ordered a chair to be brought. But the incident gave her a little moral edge which she was not unwilling to use.

Anne demanded that the elders specify the charges, and as they did so, trying to provoke her into unconsidered and incriminatory speeches, she calmly refused to be drawn, but parried their thrusts and matched scripture against scripture until it looked as if she might be superior in debate to the whole formidable power drawn up against her. Women are forbidden to teach, said the elders. A passage from Titus was her defense: "The aged women . . . may teach the young women to be sober, to love their husbands," and so on. One after another the aroused elders tried to trap her, but she could be neither silenced nor corrected. Again and again she put her interrogators on the defensive by saying, "Prove that. Prove that I said that." This examination was not going to be easy.

The court called as witnesses the ministers who had long ago interrogated her at Cotton's house, and invited her to speak to them in confidence. She indignantly objected that it is not the same thing to speak before a magistracy as "in a way of friendship privately." Soon she had the ministers uneasily evading the implication that they were betraying confidence. Their memories were not only at variance with hers but also with each other's, and it was with some difficulty that they reached a consensus that however she had phrased it, she had said that the ministers "preached a covenant of works and were not able ministers of the new testament."

"Prove that I said it," she replied.

"Did you say so?" asked the governor.

"No sir, it is your conclusion from what I said," she responded. Here were six ministers who agreed on the import of her speech and she still denied it; since they could not agree on her phrasing, they could not quite pin her down. Had she merely said that some preached the covenant of grace more fully than others? But it was getting late, so the court adjourned, the elders adjuring her to use the interim to think over the error of her ways.

The next morning, after the governor had summarized what the ministers had said, she tried a new tactic. The ministers, she said, were not impartial witnesses but had come in their own cause, nor were they speaking under oath. "Now the Lord hath said that an oath is the end of all controversy," so let them be put under oath that they may be believed. That did start them buzzing: was the word of men of God to be impugned? Some were reluctant to swear because anyone who disbelieved their assertions would hardly be convinced by their oaths; Hugh Peter said they were ready to swear if they could "see a way of God in it"; some could see no need of an oath when so many agreed at least on the import of her speeches. Behind their reluctance lurked a conscientious dread of swearing to words about which their memories were not wholly clear. They knew what she had been driving at and still smarted from it, but to swear to her very words? They haggled and niggled and split half-hairs while Mistress Anne sat poised and assured.

And then suddenly and surprisingly Anne lost control. After the ministers had argued long and tediously about who remembered what, the governor again tried to summarize: she *did* say "that they were not able ministers of the new testament," and Cotton honestly responded, "I do not remember it." Touched by the affectionate concern her old teacher was still showing for her, Mistress Anne lost that impersonal poise and poured out the whole story of her conversion and her revelations from God while the elders listened, their masked faces hiding their inner elation. The passionate flood reached a climax in a threatening jeremiad. The Lord had revealed to her that she would suffer affliction in the new world, but he had also said, "I am the same God that delivered Daniel out of the lion's den. I will also deliver thee. . . ." Then Anne faced the elders, her eyes animated, her voice tense:

> Therefore I desire you to look to it, for you see this scripture fulfilled this day and therefore I desire you that as you tender the Lord and the church and the commonwealth to consider and look

what you do. You have power over my body but the Lord Jesus
hath power over my body and my soul and assure yourselves thus
much, you do as much as in you lies to put the Lord Jesus from
you, and if you go in this course you begin, you will bring a curse
upon you and your posterity, and the mouth of the Lord hath
spoken it.

There was a moment of incredulous, stunned silence, then bedlam.
Emboldened by her disclosures the ministers were now loudly
recalling other frightful things she had said in the past such as that
"she had never had any great thing done about her but it was
revealed to her beforehand."

"I say the same thing still," she cried.

Did she really expect to be delivered by a miracle now? she was
asked.

"I do speak it before the Court," she replied.

Poor Cotton was called upon to say what he thought of these
miracles she claimed, and, even in all this hubbub, he tried to be
loyal, drawing a distinction which would save her: if she meant
Divine Providence he could not deny her words; if she meant a
suspension of the law of nature he would suspect them. He was then
asked about her revelations. Still refusing to condemn, he drew
another of his distinctions, this time between direct revelations of
the spirit and revelations through the ministry of the word, but all
had heard her: she spoke of immediate revelation, and had often
spoken so. Now many voices were heard: she is deluded by the
devil; she is the ground of all our disturbances. Certainly, in a
moment of passion or impulse, on signal from the inner voice, Anne
had condemned herself out of her own mouth and the court was
now free to banish her. Still, the magistrates were strangely
reluctant to do so; there was further argument, many voicing their
scruples about the legality of the ministers' testimony. Finally, late
in the evening, Deputy-Governor Dudley growled, "We shall all be
sick with fasting." And almost at once they found their way: if the
ministers would testify under oath, all scruples would be gone.
There was then "a great whispering among the ministers," and
Winthrop impatiently called upon two of Anne's most unrelenting
enemies, Thomas Weld and Hugh Peter. They swore the oath and
repeated their testimonies, and the governor called for a vote that

she should be "banished out of our liberties and imprisoned till she be sent away." All but three raised their hands and the governor pronounced the sentence. Anne was cast down, but not silenced. "I desire to know wherefore I am banished," she demanded.

Winthrop, who had been censured for his judicial lenience two years before, must have suffered torment of mind now; at any rate, the court did not send Anne away into the freezing winter that had already set in hard, but remanded her to the custody of Roxbury until spring. Even so, her supporters were enraged, and they were not a negligible group. They included a majority of the prosperous merchants and landholders, and several officials and military leaders. Had not some of her most active proponents been men of substance, the orthodox party would probably have disposed of her earlier. The wave of indignation and protest among these people so alarmed the court that they moved against the whole sect. First they disfranchised and removed from office all who commanded military units and then disarmed all those who had signed or approved the Wheelwright petitions. Fifty-nine Boston men and a scattering from adjacent towns were ordered to turn in all their weapons and ammunition, and forbidden to buy or borrow any guns until they acknowledged their sins and renounced the *Petition*. Anyone who defamed any court or any sentence of the court was to be fined, imprisoned, or banished. And the agents of the court went from house to house to serve the order on each petitioner and assign time and place for him to deliver up his arms.

Thus the power of the Hutchinsonians was broken. Some few bowed to the court and admitted their error; most grimly surrendered their weapons but not their opinions. A few of the most influential of them, led by William Coddington, who had held out against the verdict, could see nothing ahead but more contention and governmental suppression. They decided, therefore, to seek a better life outside the colony. By spring, a group of nineteen organized into a "body politic" and emigrated south to Rhode Island where Roger Williams offered a perpetual refuge. Meanwhile, Mistress Anne, under house arrest in Roxbury, could neither repress her exegetical impulses nor keep her mouth shut, and her studies in the prophetic books hatched out more erratic and disturbing propositions which drew many ministers to reason with her in her lodging. As "opinions" began swarming again, Cotton became fully convinced that irresponsible heretics had in truth made him a "stalking horse" for their wild notions by maintaining that what they believed was only what he taught. It was almost in self-defense that he joined the elders of the Boston church to proceed against Anne Hutchinson in a church trial, for though the secular court had punished her seditious harassment of the leaders, her unorthodox doctrines, so attractive and unsettling to emotional minds, now must be put to rest once and for all.

When Anne was summoned in March of 1638 to face trial by the congregation of her church, she was frightened and troubled, anxious to make her peace with her teacher. She was now willing to listen and be occasionally convinced; when her errors were explained to her, she frequently admitted that she had been mistaken or misunderstood. But still unsatisfied on many points, the church was preparing to subject her to admonition, the second most serious discipline it could impose. But the congregation was not unanimous —her son and son-in-law held out. However, the elders found a way to achieve unanimity: they would admonish her sons along with her. Mr. Cotton would deliver the admonition.

Mr. Cotton adjured the young men to realize that in defending their mother they were like serpents in her bowels, keeping her from the repentance that the brethren sought to induce in her. He admonished the sisters of the congregation to accept what was good in Mrs. Hutchinson's teachings but to reject what was unsound and dangerous. Finally, he admonished Mistress Anne to ponder the dishonor she had brought upon Christ and His ministers; he said how frequently he had feared for her arrogant spirit, her tendency to be "puffed up with her own parts." Now she must understand how her ideas, like a gangrene or leprosy, had infected near and far. But Cotton's most biting words came when he addressed himself to her heresy of mortalism, that the soul dies with the body. Through all the disturbances he had been sweet and gentle, slow to condemn, slow to judge, but now it seemed that mortalism gave him the opening to vent his own long-controlled emotions and perhaps to still some ugly rumors.

Mortalism, said Cotton, was a vile doctrine used by the Familists and other libertines to justify the common use of women. He was convinced that Anne had been faithful to her husband, but that did not alter the fact that her heresy opened the door to wickedness, abomination, and lust. It must have stung Anne harder than anything else that was said or done to her.

When she next faced the congregation and the elders, she again made an effort, against her nature, to accept correction and rebuke meekly; she read a written recantation of some errors and admitted that she had sometimes spoken rashly. But soon, under concerted baitings, she returned to her dangerous defenses: she had fallen into error only through the distress of her imprisonment, though she would admit that she had sometimes failed to state her thoughts accurately: "I confess that my expressions [sic] was that way, but it was never my judgment." Anne knew that she had not lied; if only she could make them understand. She continually tried to tell them of a revelation which came without words, an inner noetic assurance which, whenever it descended to words, always falsified the experience. Her words might be wrong but the ineffable experience she was trying to express by them was true. But as she tried to refine and rephrase, to make word and revelation agree, the impassioned elders could only hear hysteria and falsehood.

Even Mr. Cotton was at last decisive: they no longer needed to vex themselves about her gossamer webs of heresy, for now it was a matter of fact or practice, "as the making and holding of a lie." In silence the congregation assented to her excommunication and Brother Wilson formally cast her out. In the name of Christ, he delivered her up to Satan to be accounted a heathen and a publican; he commanded her to withdraw herself from the congregation as a leper, and have no more part in the holy ordinance of God.

Now, firmly committed to her martyrdom, Anne "gloried in her suffering," saying that "it was the greatest happiness, next to Christ, that ever befell her." And as she walked proudly out of the door of the meeting house, accompanied only by her loyal friend Mary Dyer, an attractive woman given to revelations of her own, Anne's last words were, "Better to be cast out of the Church than to deny Christ."

Anne and her family first sought security and welcome in Rhode Island, but trouble followed her. Word got about that when Anne had assisted Mary Dyer at her lying-in about a month before her trial, she had concealed the fact that the stillborn child was a "monster," more like a grotesque devil than a human creature. This charge raised a cloud of superstitious folklore about witchcraft, for it was familiarly believed that since Satan was incapable of creating life and had no sperm of his own, he stole the cold semen of dead men and with this impregnated the women who followed him. From such an impregnation only a monster could be born. In the spring of 1634 a "huge pack" of witches had been discovered in Lancashire, at least one of whom confessed that a "black man, Manelion," had frequently had the use of her body. For this she was condemned to death. Winthrop himself was very earnest about all this; he seemed almost as interested in all the sordid and sensational details of alleged witchcraft as King James had once been. He therefore ordered the monster exhumed and examined. Though "much corrupted," the horns and claws and the holes in its back were still clearly visible. The midwife, who had been alone with Anne and Mary when the foetus was aborted, had previously been suspected of witchcraft, including the selling of magic potions, and now she had left the colony, but she was recalled and interrogated. The elders, so ready to condemn Anne for lying, blandly lied to the midwife, telling her that Mrs. Hutchinson had already confessed everything and she therefore might as well tell the truth.

The same elders asked Roger Williams to find out why Anne, now in refuge in Rhode Island, had conspired to hide this manifestation of Divine Providence. She had done it, of course, to spare her friend from the kind of ugly sensationalism she was now being subjected to, and she had done it with Mr. Cotton's consent.

But the last cruel stroke fell when Anne herself, in August, 1638, aborted a strange mass of intertwined globular lumps (recently diagnosed as a hydatiform mole such as sometimes results from menopausal pregnancy). Now she too had borne a monster and there were those willing, even happy, to believe that she had been tupped by some devil. Others, less superstitious, saw providential correspondence between the monstrous ideas of the two women and their physical offspring. Then when God caused an earthquake in Rhode Island it was said that he was shaking the very ground under Anne Hutchinson.

There was a subtler irony, too, in all this, cruelty piled on cruelty. Back in England it had long been known that witches loved to attend sick and dying persons, hoping to snatch their souls in those last crucial and agonized moments. So, while in normal circumstances attending the sick was a Christian charity, once a woman was accused of witchcraft, such attendance became highly suspicious. And so even Mistress Anne's natural kindness and compassion were turned against her by the priesthood. She was like another Joan before the bishops; what the charge of heresy did not accomplish the charge of witchcraft did.

Groping for help in her desolation, her mind turned to her lost friend and counselor, Henry Vane, and she impulsively said things that could be misinterpreted. Roger Williams reported to John Winthrop of the exiled opinionists:

> I find their longings great after Mr. Vane, although they think he cannot return this year: the eyes of some are so earnestly fixed upon him that Mrs. Hutchinson professeth if he come not to New England she must to old England. . . .

Just so she had followed Mr. Cotton to Massachusetts earlier, always looking for a man who understood, who had some inward correspondence with her, whose presence strengthened her assurance of the seal of the spirit.

Nor was she alone in remembering Vane with idealizing trust. Many other colonists, Williams said, were hoping that if the king did impose an appointed governor-general on the colony, it might be Henry Vane, a hope that Williams tried to discourage, for he knew that even if Vane were to accept the office for life, it would not work out well.

Even in tolerant Rhode Island, Anne's obsessive mystical inventiveness and compulsive preaching at length stirred conflict, and she moved once again, this time to the borders of the Dutch settlements on Long Island. There she crowned her martyrdom with an irrelevant, violent death: she and five of her children were massacred by a band of marauding Indians who probably thought they were slaughtering their Dutch enemies. Only one of her daughters escaped to tell the story which was considered the final vindication of the Boston elders.

Anne Hutchinson and Henry Vane were an unlikely pair, and yet for a short time they shared mystical experiences and doctrines, and together resisted a government's attempt to suppress their divisive teachings. And their names continued to be associated in strange ways: a few years after Vane had lost his head on the scaffold, a secretary to a noble lord jotted on a document relating to America a note that shows how persistent unsavory gossip can be.

> Sir H. Vane in 1637 went over governor to New England with two women, Mrs. Dyer and Mrs. Hutchinson . . . where he debauched both, and both were delivered of monsters.

This is not much stranger than the portraits of sentimental biographers, who still later canonized these two as saints in the cause of freedom of religion, democratic government, and civil rights. The crown cannot really be made to fit Mistress Anne, for though she was a gifted, sincere, and courageous woman, standing almost alone against the elders and magistrates, she did not seem to believe in toleration except for her own beliefs; to what she knew was error she could give no quarter. Toleration, one feels, requires a sense of humor, and an ability to mistrust oneself, neither of which Mistress Anne—or Henry Vane—possessed.

For Vane a somewhat better case can be made, even though very little of it can be made on his record in Massachusetts. He did eventually work out and defend a theory of toleration that might include even Catholics—the acid test for a Puritan—and a theory of government which, while asserting God as the ultimate fountain of all power, placed immediate secular power in the people. But Vane's theories often clashed painfully with his actions, for again and again the exigencies of political life drove him into strangely intolerant positions.

Although Vane's major work was done in England, it is America that has apotheosized him. Wendell Phillips called him "the noblest human being who ever walked the streets of yonder city." And although apparently no statue has been erected to him in England, in the entryway of the Boston Public Library there stands an idealized bronze figure of a graceful, elegantly clothed, handsome young man, with long hair flowing from beneath a Cavalier hat; under the statue is a pedestal bearing the inscription, "An ardent defender of civil liberty and advocate of free thought in religion, he maintained that God, Law, and Parliament are superior to the King. This statue was placed here at the request of James Freeman Clarke, D. D., an honored citizen of Boston, who nobly labored for the abolition of slavery in America."

But the adulation came after Vane was safely dead and the Age of Godliness had been superseded by the Age of Enlightenment. Those who wrote of him in his own time tended to be uncharitable. A letter from New England said that young Vane's disgrace had made a deep impression, and partly from that and partly from his awareness of his own rashness he had gone back to England. After he arrived there Lord Saye and Sele wrote to Cotton saying that he had tried to show young Vane the error of his ways but the noble lord no longer had much converse with the Vane family. Most of the brothers were in Holland, he said, and the rest would likely go there soon. Another letter from England, this time to Winthrop, said that young Vane's ill behavior in New England had lost him all reputation. The talk was that he would soon leave England and go to Germany to live.

An unnamed New Englander judged him very harshly:

Truly by his aspect you would judge him a good man. Yet I am persuaded he has kindled those sparks among us, which many ages will not be able to extinguish. . . . All men are not fit for government, and none so dangerous as one that makes his affection his rule.

Later, Cotton Mather thought that "Mr. Vane's election will remain a blemish to their judgment who did elect him while New England remains a nation."

Yet Vane retained his interest in New England. On January 8, 1638, he was allotted by the General Court 200 acres of ground at Running Marsh, now Revere, and Winthrop, at the same time, was given 150 acres bordering that. As time and distance softened anger, Vane would prove a staunch and continuous champion of the colony, even though, as Winthrop acknowledged, "he might have taken occasion against us for some dishonor which he apprehended to have been unjustly put upon him here, yet . . . he showed himself a true friend to New England, and a man of noble and generous mind."

Vane came to the assistance of the Bostonians when they were in financial and legal difficulties in England. He gave lodgings and aid to Roger Williams, and that Rhode Island became a secure and chartered colony was partly due to Vane's intercessions as a member

of the Council for Plantations. As Williams would one day testify in
a letter:

> It was not price and money that could have purchased Rhode
> Island, but it was obtained by love—that love and favor which
> that honored gentleman, Sir H. Vane, and myself had with the
> great Sachem Miantonomo. . . . This I mention as the truly
> noble Sir H. Vane had been so good an instrument in the hands of
> God for procuring this island from the barbarians, as also for
> procuring and confirming the charter that it may be recorded
> with all thankfulness.

In 1653, when Cromwell's dictatorship had forced Vane into
personal retirement, many of the principal personages of Rhode
Island wrote him a letter, thanking him for his interest in their
internal problems, hoping "that when we are gone and rotten, our
posterity and children after us shall read in our town records, your
pious and favorable letters, and loving kindness to us."

Vane also exercised an influence on behalf of toleration in the
colony after he left. Years later, he could not altogether deny
charges by Presbyterians in the Westminster Assembly that
toleration had broken down in New England: give the Independents
power, the taunt went, and they will use it exactly as other men do.
Vane thereupon wrote Winthrop that he hoped the congregational
way in New England, backed with power, would not through its
own practice teach its oppugners in England to extirpate it there.

Vane left New England not only with the profit of some bitter
lessons learned in humiliation and defeat, but also with some
understanding of the kind of political activity—cautious, shrewd,
unemotional negotiation—that would make him a decisive force in
the far greater turbulence of England's civil and religious upheavals.
In the meantime the colonies needed Vane too much to humiliate
him further, and he was too magnanimous to insist on feeling
humiliated.

6

Young Harry and Black Tom
(1638–1641)

Vane returned to England to face many unanswered questions and not a little jubilation from those who were happy to see the young revolutionary defeated and disenchanted with his utopian adventure. It was not an easy time for him, and he may well have considered going to Germany and allying himself with the continental Protestants. Whatever his thoughts, he wisely said nothing and for a year and a half he disappeared from public view. His anxious father was casting about for suitable employment for him, but for the moment he was acceptable neither to the Crown nor to those English Puritans who looked towards New England.

During that year and a half he began developing ideas that later events would confirm and strengthen. He could still see, with Sir Thomas Roe, that English and continental Protestantism were engaged in a crucial struggle against a Catholicism allied with enormous secular power. And he believed still that the Separatist struggle in England against an established church that used its power to enforce doctrine and worship and to control conscience was part of that greater struggle. But his thoughts now went much further. The struggle was indeed global and final, he believed, a kind of spiritual Armageddon, and it was even now being carried on in America, the supposed bastion of the faithful. It was a far more complex struggle than any of the Puritan apologists had hitherto realized; no longer could Vane conceive of it in denominational terms. Within every denomination he perceived a calcified orthodoxy that strove to suppress those who lived spontaneously by the light of the spirit. He could see now that the conflicts within

Protestantism were more perilous and crucial than the traditional struggle against Catholicism or Anglicanism, and he was dimly aware that his own war would be increasingly waged against that formalism which the New England elders so efficiently represented. There was a terrible danger for Vane in this view of the world he was forming, for it allied him with a precariously small and tenuously defined minority. But it was also an inspiriting view for it made him the champion of Christ's elect whose consciences must be liberated from the oppressive power of secular magistrates and made free to receive their only master. He could not possibly have yet revealed these views to anyone, even privately. To suggest that papistry was not the ultimate enemy would have been enough to keep him out of public life in a time when the antipapal hostility burned as feverishly as any plague; to suggest that orthodox Protestants were the real antagonists of the Holy Spirit might very well have resulted in his imprisonment. Yet after that bitter experience in New England he was thinking such deadly, silent thoughts.

These ideas were still inchoate, only beginning to ripen into settled conviction. For the present, as long as Laud was Primate of England, the first imperative was to unseat the established state church with its extensive secular power. Once it was overthrown, he could give his full energies to the developing internecine conflict within Protestantism itself.

When he arrived home in the autumn of 1637, conditions in both church and state were worse than when he had left. No Parliament had been called, and therefore the royal prerogative was being stretched to dispense justice, to administer the affairs of the realm, and even, illegally many thought, to raise revenue. Three manifestations of the royal prerogative were especially disturbing to most Puritans: the Court of High Commission, the Court of Star Chamber (both prerogative courts), and the tax known as ship money. And Archbishop Laud was, or seemed to be, the prime mover in the first two.

The Court of High Commission, an ecclesiastical court, had been active in Elizabeth's time but until recently had receded quietly into the background. Now, under the encouragement of Laud, it was attaining an awesome prominence. Because it was an ecclesiastical body, the Commission answered neither to Parliament nor the

Common Law, but only to God or his representative on earth, King
Charles, in whose voice could frequently be detected the anxious
and angry tones of Archbiship Laud. This court was empowered to
inquire into and punish infractions of the canon law, libels against
the king, heretical opinions, profane speeches, fanatical pamphlets or
books, whether Puritan or popish, and schismatical behavior.
Though this jurisdiction seems rather wide, it comprised only the
religious function of the court, which also enjoyed a broad moral authority to look into incest, adultery, gambling, cruelty to wives,
drunkenness, and the entire array of depressing or amusing human
frailties.

When the court assembled it encouraged and even solicited
information against members of a parish or county. From this
information, secretly submitted, written accusations were drawn up.
The person informed against was then summoned to appear before
the commissioners and if necessary was "attached and brought into
custody." He was told neither the specific nature of the accusations
leveled against him, nor the identity of his accusers. Before learning
of the charges, he was required to take a solemn oath before the
court that he would make "full, true, and perfect answers" to all
questions. If he refused to take this oath, he was fined for contempt
of court. If he took it, he was examined and released under bond. If
the answers of the defendant were unsatisfactory, he was called to a
hearing which proceeded whether he was present or not; from its
sentence the only appeal was a direct petition to the king. It has
been said that those whom the court proceeded against could either
submit or be ruined, and often even submission was of no avail. It is
ironic that in fact, if not in theory, the ex-officio proceedings of this
court, inquisition under oath with judges as prosecutors, were
precisely the methods by which those fanatical anti-Laudians, the
General Court of Massachusetts, had proceeded against Anne
Hutchinson. Men apparently find it easier to discover injustice in
political forms when they are victims than when they themselves
wield the power.

The Court of High Commission was not entirely wrongheaded.
It frequently punished the cruelty of husbands to wives, while
insisting that they support separated spouses and dependent children. One can scarcely demur at their sentencing the Vicar of
Bristock, who locked his church door in the dead of winter and kept

his entire congregation inside the freezing church to hear a sermon on hell fire in which he asserted that God had created the greatest part of mankind for the express pleasure of damning them. Similarly one understands why they took away a license to preach from Mr. Peartree of St. Edmundsbury who customarily preached with "stentorian vociferations" and whose learning did not extend even to a knowledge of what *ecclesia* signified.

They quite rightly objected to Dr. Denison, clerk and curate of St. Katherine's, London, when he reviled his parishioners, comparing them among other things to "frogs, dogs, and devils; knaves, villains, rascals, queans, she-devils, pillory whores." Six married women came forward and testified that only with Christian fervor, augmented by blows and screams, could they repulse the muscular attentions of this doctor when he had attempted their chastity.

But for every legitimate case there seemed to be many doubtful ones, attempts to coerce conscience or enforce minor conformities. Parson Edward Williams was accused of engaging in "a high kind of terrification" when he preached against the *Book of Sports*. Other ministers were accused of not bowing, not kneeling, not using the sign of the cross, or not putting the communion table in the right place. James Nalton confessed that once in a baptism, instead of saying according to the Prayer Book, "I sign thee with the sign of the cross," he had said, "I sign thee with the seal of the covenant." The Vicar of Ware could not bring himself to say in the marriage ceremony, "With my body I thee worship"; such requirements, he said on one occasion, were driving people away to New England.

To many it seemed that this court existed primarily to harass Puritans. To a confirmed champion of the free conscience like young Vane it must have been the worst of abominations. The alien congregations in London such as the Walloons or Huguenots were ordered to send their children to parish church instead of to their own traditional congregations; the alien Protestants themselves had to conform to the Prayer Book in their services. A vigilant censorship was exerted by the court against books, pamphlets, even almanacs, and when the saintly Anglican George Herbert wrote,

> Religion stands on tip-toe in our land,
> Ready to pass to the American strand,

an Anglican censor at first refused permission to publish his book.

While ecclesiastical harassment was bad enough, inquiries into moral offenses were at once more ludicrous and more dangerous. Gentlemen seldom care to hazard much in the cause of the long sermon, the fanatical prophecy, or the hat either on or off the head. They have, however, their own set of peccadilloes which include gambling, guzzling, falconry, and fornication, which, as men of power and wealth, owners of land and Parliamentary seats, they do not care to have looked at too closely. The Court of High Commission proceeded against them with the same moral fervor that had marked its attacks on liturgical deviations. An informer told the court, for example, that a married woman other than his wife lodged in Sir John Astley's chamber. Sir John was summoned, but there appeared instead an outraged Lady Astley who said that because her husband was over seventy and afflicted with gout, Mrs. Bridges slept in his bedroom not as paramour but as custodian of the bedpan. Nevertheless Sir John was judicially admonished by the Archbishop of Canterbury himself to eschew all appearance of evil.

Augustine Moreland, a gentleman of Kent, was accused of excessive drinking and swearing. George Curtis, gentleman, was charged with adultery committed some eighteen years before, but since the court limited itself to charges not older than ten years, it regretfully released him with no worse punishment than embarrassment. In this and many other cases involving sexual offenses, the court was often puzzled that though both participated in the same event, the women should have so much clearer memories of it than the men, who seemed only too often to feel,

> That thing for which we woo
> Is not worth so much ado,

an attitude the clerics thought frivolous and the women maddening.

Offensive as its procedures were to lawyers and its liturgical rigidity to Puritans, its prurient prying into private morality most of all brought this court into contempt. The Earl of Clarendon said later that "persons of honor and great quality, of court and country," were every day cited into this ill-conceived tribunal; and Thomas Hobbes, no friend of revolution, would one day affirm that the Court of High Commission was among the offenses that cost Charles his life.

But even worse, as far as coercion of conscience was concerned, was the Court of Star Chamber, a court which suffers under a modern stereotyped disapproval which it does not wholly deserve. This court, named from the stars painted on the roof of the chamber in which it met, was the secular arm of the Privy Council. Generally composed of two chief justices and the entire Privy Council and never, in Elizabeth's time, including more than one bishop, it brought the highest legal authority and political power to bear on titled offenders too powerful to be reached by an ordinary jury or lesser judges. In nonpolitical matters it had generally been considered a good tribunal, but now it was thought to devote itself too much to political affairs. Also, more than one bishop frequently sat in the court, and in the public mind these churchmen seemed unduly influential. This court also proceeded by inquisition under oath; the defendant was not previously informed of charges, was allowed no counsel, and had no appeal from decisions.

Always much resented, this court aroused loathing and even terror when in 1630 it judged Alexander Leighton, a Scotch Presbyterian who had written a book, the main thesis of which was that all the evil that had occurred in England for over 1,000 years was directly attributable to the bishops. He also said that God had suffered the king to marry with the daughter of Heth, an insult to the daughter of Henri IV, and he urged cryptically that Hazael be smitten in the fifth rib, which might mean almost anything, including the assassination of Charles. His most revolutionary proposal, however, was that Parliament should resist dissolution and constitute itself a permanent body.

Though Laud did not vote on the condemnation of Leighton, he did speak before the court for two hours, and his notes were later published and bought up in large quantities. Later Leighton maintained that of all the judges in Star Chamber, the bishops were harshest to him. His punishment, designed "to show His Majesty's mercy and goodness," was to pay 10,000 pounds, to be set in pillory at Westminster and whipped, then to have one of his ears cut off, one of his nostrils slit, and his face branded with a branding iron forged for the occasion, bearing the letters SS for "sower of sedition." And unless the king "enlarged" him, Leighton was to be taken from prison at some future time to have the other ear cropped, the other nostril slit. It was reported, whether libelously or not, that when sentence was pronounced, Laud, peculiarly insensitive to this outrageous mutilation, took off his cap, raised his hands, and thanked God for this victory. At about the same time—to Laud's great indignation—Philip Ratcliffe was being similarly mutilated by the Massachusetts General Court.

Sir Henry Vane the elder did not participate in the deliberations against Leighton, for he was not made a member of the Privy Council until 1631, but thereafter when he was in England he acted as judge in the Star Chamber. While his son was fighting for toleration of antinomians in New England, he was joining in the persecution of dissenters in England.

The most famous Star Chamber case in which both Laud and the elder Vane participated was that of William Prynne, a Presbyterian lawyer who believed that he had been called into the world to seek out sin and to write books against it. From the standpoint of sheer production, he was triumphantly successful in this calling. As Anthony Wood said, "I verily believe, that if rightly computed, he wrote a sheet for every day of his life."

Each day Prynne addressed himself to the numerous and alarming problems of the world. He found little anywhere that could be called neutral or indifferent; follies and fashion were sinful and wicked. He condemned effeminate mixed dancing, dicing, stage plays, lascivious pictures, face painting, lewd clothing, health drinking, long hair, love locks, periwigs, women's curling, powdering, and cutting of their hair. He was opposed on moral grounds to bonfires, New Year's gifts, May games, amorous pastorals (such as the queen had appeared in), lascivious effeminate music, excessive laughter, luxurious disorderly keeping of Christmas, all of which were to God's dishonor. Plays were one of the principal recreations of the Court, but he condemned them and all who delighted in them.

> What else are the residue of our assiduous play-haunters, but adulterers, adulteresses, whoremasters, whores, bawds, panders, ruffians, roarers, drunkards, prodigals, cheaters, idle, infamous, base, profane and godless persons, who hate all grace, all goodness, and make a mock of piety.

Not only had the queen appeared in a pastoral, but about the time Prynne's book was published, she and her ladies performed in *Shepherd's Paradise*, a play by Walter Montagu; naturally it was believed that Prynne was glancing at her. At the same time passages referring vaguely to Nero and other historical tyrants were thought to be glancing at King Charles.

For this and other authorial offenses the Star Chamber sentenced Prynne to pay a 5,000 pound fine, to be expelled from Lincoln's Inn, to be deprived of his Oxford degree, to be imprisoned for life, and to have his ears cropped at the pillory. His book was a bad one, all could agree, but hardly that bad. The mutilation was duly carried out.

About this time Laud was reported to have said that Star Chamber had become his pulpit. After the Leighton sentence, he had received from one of the Temples an anonymous threat against his life, but that was nothing compared to the outcry aroused by the Prynne case. For even in prison Prynne, a true fanatic, continued to produce tracts and books which finally brought him again to the Star Chamber, where he was sentenced to have his cropped ears removed entirely, to pay another fine, to serve another term of life imprisonment, and to be branded SL (seditious libeler) on both cheeks. Again he went to the pillory, this time along with two other dissenters, Henry Burton and John Bastwick, who were also to be mutilated. A huge crowd assembled to see this crowning of the martyrs, and although a few callous men laughed, others wept; and whenever an ear came off or a puff of pungent smoke arose from the branding iron, the people roared as if they were themselves being hurt. The commoners strewed flowers before these mutilated martyrs, and with great veneration they collected and saved the bloody sponges and cloths discarded by the hangman.

With amazing stamina and courage, Prynne composed a Latin epigram on his return from the pillory; SL, he said, meant not seditious libeler but the scars of Laud, which he bore proudly. His epigram was translated and circulated widely:

> Triumphant I return. My face descries Laud's scorching scars—
> God's grateful sacrifice. S.L. *Stigmata Laudis*.

These cuttings and brandings, assented to, some said even provoked by, the bishops of the church, engendered disgust and loathing even among those who did not love Puritans. What were men of God doing so hideously disfiguring the image of God? The pillory, it seems, was becoming Prynne's pulpit.

William Prynne, a lawyer of rigid and limited views, achieved a certain heroic stature by fearlessly advocating his principles and suffering terribly for them. He was an intransigent Presbyterian in both religion and politics. (Radio Times Hulton Picture Library)

Hugh Peter, man of God and of the world, was both Puritan madcap and revolutionary fanatic. He served for a time as chaplain in Cromwell's New Model Army and was executed after the Restoration. (Courtauld Institute of Art)

A fastidious man of exquisite taste, Charles I was saddened and repelled by the role history had given him to play. He lacked the energy and foresight to resist the forces that assailed his throne. Portrait by Van Dyck. (Radio Times Hulton Picture Library)

Soon the elder Vane would be caught up in the trial of John Lilburne, who refused to take the ex-officio oath before the Chamber. Apparently somewhat self-taught in the law, Lilburne said no one had a right to make a man incriminate himself. He was found guilty, whipped from the Fleet to the Palace Yard, then placed in the pillory and finally put in prison, where he might have starved except for the affection and sympathy of the common people. Soon Lilburne would be the leader of the Levellers, those early champions of a modified democracy who wished to extend the franchise and give more power to the commoners. He would remember bitterly "that guilty old traitor, Sir Henry Vane," who had urged the bloody sentence against him in Star Chamber, and he would remember too, unfairly, that "crafty Machiavel," his son, who, Lilburne said, secretly supported the father in his injustices.

But young Vane would surely have been repelled by this and by another cruel sentencing in which his father concurred. His old headmaster, Lambert Osbaldeston, was sentenced by Star Chamber to have an ear cut off and nailed to the door of his school. But having no desire to emulate William Prynne or to trade his flesh for schoolboy acclaim, he fled with both ears intact.

In addition to the Court of High Commission and Star Chamber there was one other grievance impelling England towards rebellion—the imposition of ship money. When Charles came to the throne the navy had been in desperate condition; now, since the king was steadily improving it, the navy was a cause of much expense, and with no Parliamentary grants, money was exceedingly elusive. The attorney general at that time was William Noy, of whose name someone had made an anagram: *I moil in law.* While moiling, it occurred to him that in time of national emergency the king had an established right to require each maritime county to equip a ship and present it to the fleet. Counties that had no ship-building facilities could discharge their obligation by paying money. Noy therefore recommended that the king should issue writs of ship money to coastal counties, and in 1634 he did so. This action posed a number of problems: first of all, since the required ships were too large to be built anywhere except in royal shipyards, the counties had no real alternative to taxing their citizens. Further, everyone wondered just what the national emergency was. Had Charles truthfully been able to point to some danger from Spain he would have aroused much patriotism, but at the moment his principal enemy was Holland, a Protestant nation traditionally friendly to England. But the overriding issue was simply that one more way had been found to get money without Parliamentary consent, and that way seemed illegal taxation.

In 1635, the king decided to extend the tax of ship money to the inland counties, sensibly arguing that a threat against the whole nation should not fall solely on maritime counties. Everyone in these days of federalism would agree with that position; many then did not, and the Puritans used this issue to challenge the government. In 1637, just as young Vane was returning from Massachusetts, the legality of ship money was formally challenged by Lord Saye and Sele and by John Hampden. Possibly because Hampden was a commoner and because his case was a simpler one, the government decided to proceed against him. Ultimately seven of twelve judges found against Hampden and for the king, but his was a Pyrrhic victory, for it turned Hampden into a national hero, a symbol of justified resistance to tyranny. From a practical point of view, other consequences were worse. Although men had grumbled about the first writs, they usually paid them. But after Hampden's challenge a new temper was discernible in the nation: more people not only resented but resisted paying, and there were huge arrears for 1637 and even larger ones in 1638. In the Hampden trial, Charles lost more in the hearts of his subjects than he gained in the courts—and without filling the treasury.

As usual the elder Vane was unimpressed by the ethics of the case or its potential historical importance. He knew that the Treasurer of the Navy, Sir William Russell, was entitled to a commission of threepence in each pound on all the money collected and disbursed for the navy. The writs of ship money, Sir Henry perceived, would make the post of naval treasurer a most valuable position with an income too great for the deservings of even a good man like Russell. So in January of 1639 he obtained for his eldest son a joint treasurership just at the time when ship money was being used to equip the fleet for action in the unpopular Scottish war.

Thus while Hampden was publicly placing principle above property or life, young Vane was forced to do something that his inner spirit detested: he was collecting the despised ship money to support what he regarded as an arbitrary tyranny. Every week he would submit to the king and Privy Council the amount of ship money collected and the amount in arrears. He carried out his duties efficiently, quietly, and without protest. Edward Hyde, later Earl of Clarendon, thought him much reformed, a man well satisfied and composed to the government. But what a disparity there was between what he wished to do—what that inner voice required of him—and what his duties forced upon him; between the promptings of his heart and the requirements of his expedient father. It is not too much to suppose that he felt unclean, in need of purgation, of demonstrating publicly where his true allegiance lay. He would soon have occasion to.

The prerogative courts and ship money were not minor irritations; they were national offenses. And yet in retrospect they seem small when compared to the ongoing struggle with Scotland that was leading inevitably towards war. Again it was Laud, backed now by Thomas Wentworth, who urged the king along a fatal course. In the first three Parliaments of Charles, Wentworth had been a strong Parliamentary leader. A gaunt man with muscular limbs and dignified bearing, his thick dark hair and sallow complexion had earned him the name of Black Tom. Black, it was said, suited him. Yet he was an intelligent man whose principal characteristic was a driving energy, an incandescent inner flame that was frequently intensified by pain. He suffered chronically from gout and other ailments, and while pain debilitates some men, he was one of those whom it enkindles.

In his first Parliaments he had led the opposition in demanding reform before granting subsidies. "Unless we be secured in our liberties," he had said, "we cannot give." But then he had been elevated to the peerage, and in December of 1628 he had been made President of the Council of the North. There was no immediate change in his bearing or opinions; indeed, Sir Francis Nethersole wrote about that time to the Queen of Bohemia that "Thomas Wentworth has the greatest sway in Parliament."

But he had never been quite enough of a Parliament man to suit John Eliot and some others. Intensely interested in domestic reform, he cared little for continental politics and religious wars. He was in a sense medieval in his political thought, for he was willing to assert and uphold each sphere of power but not willing to alter those spheres. As dissent in Parliament grew and mingled with Puritan religiosity, he sensed an intent to transfer power from king to Parliament. He disliked that trend for two reasons: he simply did not trust the wisdom and restraint of the revolutionaries, and he came to feel that in the long term, order was more important to the state than change. As he put it,

> The authority of a king is the keystone which closeth up the arch of order and government, which contains each part in due relation to the whole, and which once shaken, infirmed, all the frame falls together into a confused heap of foundation and battlement.

Wentworth spoke strongly in Star Chamber against all the noncomformists. When the men he had helped to condemn were pilloried and cut, Wentworth called them trash and said that, if left unpunished, they would do irreparable harm to sovereignty. This attitude, though it caused the people to despise him, won him the friendship of Laud and the confidence of Charles. The delicate king, so hesitant in speech and action, seemed always to be seeking for a strong man who could make his hard decisions for him. He had leaned on the attractive but incompetent Buckingham with disastrous results; no one could accuse Wentworth of beauty or charm, but neither could anyone accuse him of incompetence.

So in January, 1632, Wentworth was appointed Lord Deputy of Ireland. He intended his government there to be "thorough," that is, efficient, loyal, and free of corruption. In all of the English government, it was Laud who most understood and sympathized with this goal, and both he and Wentworth consistently worked for it, each in his sphere. But soon the admirable word was turned by Puritan sarcasm into a byword of contempt, and to his enemies "thorough" meant only "tyrannous."

Ireland had traditionally been the testing ground of English patience and character, and few administrators had survived the test; it was a graveyard of promising careers. Wentworth ruled there by and through a Parliament. He brought about order, raised and trained an army which was eyed with some fear from England, and he brought economic prosperity; but he did all this with harshness and arrogance, with too much awareness of his own abilities, and he alienated most of the powerful interests there. He aroused admiration and fear in Ireland, but never affection. He could see in ancient

Irish civilization nothing of value, and in his impatience he seemed to have anticipated the sentiment of Milton's Samson, that weakness is wickedness. And weakness he could not tolerate in himself, in his king, or in Ireland. Of his administration there, Sir Thomas Roe wrote to the Queen of Bohemia that he was doing "great wonders" and governing like a king. He was "severe abroad and in business but sweet in private conversation; retired in his friendships but very firm; a terrible judge; a strong enemy; a servant violently zealous of his master's ends and not negligent of his own." He was, Sir Thomas concluded, a man never born for the middle region of fortune; he would either be the greatest man in England or he would fall. In 1637, Wentworth was admitted to the informal position of the king's chief counselor, and he was still rising.

Laud and Charles had first visited Scotland in 1633 and observed the practices and policies of the church there. They were offended by what they saw. The outside of the Scottish churches, Laud said, looked like pigeon houses and the inside like theatres. The Articles of Perth required communicants to kneel when taking communion, and the enforcement of this requirement, which had sent young Vane to New England, often drove entire congregations out of the church. The red-faced, extemporaneous prayers, the strenuous sweating sermons, repelled both Laud and Charles, and so they determined to provide the Scottish church with a Book of Common Prayer, a uniform service, and with bishops instead of elders. Over several years Laud caused to be prepared both canons and a Prayer Book, neither of which was ever submitted to an ecclesiastical body, even in England; and no one who helped produce them had any feeling for the temper of the Scots religion. Yet these new works were intended to supersede John Knox's Book of Common Order.

In the spring of 1637, this long-dreaded Prayer Book reached Scotland without being discussed either in an Assembly of the Scottish church or a Scottish Parliament. When the Dean of St. Giles tried to read the first service from the new Prayer Book, his voice was lost in the wails and outcries of the women. "The Mass is amongst us," one of them cried. "Baal is in the Church," shrieked another. But such biblicized outcries were drowned out by saltier native imprecations. And when the Bishop of Edinburgh arose and tried to still the tumult, a stool was thrown at his head. After that the service was abandoned. When the service was read again that afternoon, no women were allowed in the building.

In all this disturbance, the violence of the women puzzled, amused, or shocked observers. Sir Francis Botwright wrote that the women were swearing they would "beat out the bishops' brains with stones." Armies of women, he said, surrounded the soldiers in Edinburgh, and for their own safety the soldiers had to be removed. As the disturbances led towards armed conflict, the Countess of Westmoreland wrote to Secretary Windebank that the women of Scotland were the chief stirrers of the war; and when in June, 1639, the armies were in the field, the Marchioness of Hamilton, an "old lady" as she was called, led her own troops into the field, daggers hanging from her girdle. She carried with her a silver bullet and said that if her son, the Duke of Hamilton, landed his English troops, she would personally shoot him with it.

Another correspondent wrote home that in Scotland a new "housewifery" was being practiced by ladies and gentlewomen: they were taking up arms instead of brooms. Most shocking of all was the language these women used. Everywhere they were cursing, saying they wished the flesh of their husbands and children to be converted into dogs and their souls damned if they ever consented again to admit the bishops.

All this failed to impress Laud, possibly because he had never been married. The bishops, he hoped, would not be downcast because a few milkmaids had scolded them. But Traquair advised him that the new Prayer Book would require an army of 40,000 men.

The agitation in Scotland finally resulted in the renewal of the covenant which had been entered into first in 1581 to resist Spanish and papal pressures. Now, in 1638, the Scots pledged again before God, angels, and the world that they would constantly adhere to and defend the "true religion"; that they would renounce and resist all errors, corruptions, and innovations with whatever force was required. They confidently expected God's blessings on their avowals and believed that their proceedings were an honor to the king.

Through these difficulties the elder Vane manifested his usual caution. He supported the peace party and counseled negotiations, but the king turned away towards Wentworth and Ireland. Could the army which the Lord Deputy had so brilliantly trained there be used to reduce Scotland? Wentworth, with his fierce loyalty, with his pain and his passion, insisted that if the insolence of the Scots were not punished there would be no end of evil consequences.

The alarmed Scots now began to arm themselves, choosing for a commander Alexander Leslie, a tough little campaigner who had been personally knighted by Gustav Adolf. He, in turn, persuaded many professional soldiers at home and in Germany to take the covenant, and from Germany he received some first-rate military supplies.

Against the Scots force, modeled on the methods and tactics of Gustav Adolf, disciplined, tough, morally earnest, the English raised a badly equipped army with no campaign experience and no real desire to fight a bishops' war. Some of the romanticists of the Court wrongly believed that the king's presence in the field would make up for logistic failures, but this king, alas, had little military presence. When the two forces were assembled, Wentworth could see the inevitable outcome, and advised Charles not to join battle that year. Dismayed and shaken, Charles had no choice but to sign the humiliating Treaty of Berwick.

On January 12, 1640, the king elevated Wentworth to the Earldom of Strafford. At this crucial moment in his life, high in the king's favor and unofficial ruler of England, he did something strange—and, as it proved, deadly. Reminding the king that Lord Cleveland's heir also carried the title of Lord Wentworth, the Earl of Strafford persuaded his monarch to create a new barony which he might pass on to his son. Wentworth asked for, and received, the vacant Barony of Raby. The elder Vane, owner of Raby Castle, of course desperately hoped that some day he too might be elevated to the peerage and that the title would become his along with the castle.

Many believed that Wentworth had acted from pure arrogance because he despised Vane. Not only had they disagreed about war and peace, but the queen, who had taken a violent dislike to the strong and able Strafford, had taken a corresponding fancy to Vane, in whom she perceived a rather ordinary mind and a pliant will. Later Clarendon would say that this pettish act of revenge cost Strafford his head, and at the time the Court was divided into two factions over it. But the wiser men, it was said, wondered why the new earl "should so palpably affront Sir Henry Vane," as to cause a "fiery feud" between them.

The feud was intensified when Sir John Coke was relieved of his secretaryship. For this office, Strafford supported the Earl of Leicester, a nobleman who was Protestant without being Puritan, who, like Strafford, was disposed to support the king without being an arbitrary asserter of the prerogative. The queen, on the other hand, supported Vane and she had her way: on February 3, 1640, he was appointed secretary.

A month later Strafford crossed to Ireland, assembled the Parliament, and asked on the king's behalf for four subsidies (180,000 pounds) which were granted without a single negative voice. Charles was impressed, for he intended to punish the Scots, and he needed support of a kind that only his Parliament could grant. He had no recourse but to call one.

Young Vane stood for election to this, the Short Parliament, from the city of Hull. In March of 1640 the former mayor of that city wrote to the elder Vane explaining that he had received a letter from the Lord Admiral requiring them to accept young Vane for the ensuing Parliament. The Lord Admiral had haughtily asserted that it was his right to select a member from Hull, and the city was disposed to resist that claim. But when the seconding letter came from Secretary Vane, the City Council understood the situation better. The mayor reminded them that the king had recently discharged suits in the Exchequer against the city. All were sensible of "deep engagements," and so young Vane had been unanimously chosen to represent Hull as a burgess. Having reassured the anxious father, the former mayor concluded piously, "The Lord Almighty give his blessing."

The Short Parliament began on April 13, 1640, and within three or four days petitions of grievances were coming in from all over the country. John Pym voiced these grievances in a two-hour speech in which he attacked impositions of duty without Parliamentary consent; compositions for knighthood; monopolies; ship money; enlargement of forests; new customs; impressment of men against their will. He singled out, one by one, every device, every administrative shift by which Charles and his counselors had tried to evade Parliamentary approval for raising money. But his most impassioned attacks were reserved for the clergy, particularly those royal ministers who preached the divine right of kings.

The ministers in the meantime, assembled in convocation, voted the king six subsidies from the clergy, but on April 23, the House of Commons said that until "the liberties of the House and kingdom were cleared, they knew not whether they had anything to give or no." The distraught Charles now summoned his council. Strafford, just back from Ireland, urged that the king address himself to the peers and plead for the ancient royal right of subsidies first and then redress on the pledge of the royal word. He did so and the loyal peers voted overwhelmingly to support the king's plea, but the House of Commons, irritated at this violation of its ancient privilege to vote the money supply, denounced the other house. While this animosity was stirring, Strafford in the Lords and the elder Vane in Commons began to drop hints of dissolution. The queen was now completely won over by Strafford's loyalty and his fierce defense of royal prerogative; she averred that Strafford was the most faithful servant her husband had and the most capable.

The king, listening to the tenor of the debate in Commons, understood well enough that ship money was currently the prime grievance. He therefore determined to use it as a bargaining counter, and sent the elder Vane to Commons on May 4, to offer to surrender any claim to future levies of ship money in exchange for twelve subsidies. It was a daring offer but extremely costly, and in the ensuing debate men began feeling for a compromise. The elder Vane then arose and said that there was no point in further debate for the king would not accept less than twelve subsidies which, according to general calculation, would come to some 840,000 pounds. Strafford himself, and later Clarendon, blamed the breakdown of negotiations on Vane's unauthorized rigidity. But all this is hard to accept. Everything we know of the elder Vane tells us that he was a politic tool; it is hardly thinkable that he would have done anything so bold and outrageous as this on his own initiative. He might, however, have given sounder advice to his monarch. If he had possessed more intelligence, more insight, more courage, he might have urged conciliation on Charles, but he was the queen's man. She was not about to truckle to the Commons, and Vane was the last man in England to advise the king to set aside her wishes. And so, one day later, the Privy Council voted to dissolve this Short Parliament which had sat for some three weeks and accomplished nothing.

Shortly after the dissolution of the Short Parliament, Lady Vane wrote in her gentle, pious way to her husband, "I know your business is great; God bless you in all your proceedings that you may be an instrument of good for this kingdom, which I fear was never in greater want of faithful hearts than at this time." Did she suspect, one wonders, that her eldest son bore no loyal heart? If she did, she said nothing but contented herself with the Prayer Book.

> O almighty and everlasting God, which dost govern all things in heaven and earth: mercifully hear the supplications of thy people and grant us thy peace all the days of our life.

With Parliament dissolved, the Privy Council was faced with the urgent question of how to deal with Scotland. The elder Vane advocated a defense of the English borders, but Strafford counseled a quick, sharp blow; an invasion of Scotland, he thought, would bring that recalcitrant nation down in a matter of months. While all this discussion was going on, as secretary of the council, Vane was trying as best he could to copy down the sense of each speaker. When the queen had so vigorously advocated him for the secretaryship, he had confessed that his ear and hand were really not quick enough for taking complete notes. Now he struggled, and while his enemy, the new Baron of Raby talked, Vane wrote:

> Go on vigorously or let them alone. No defensive war; loss of honor and reputation. The quiet of England will hold out long. You will languish as betwixt Saul and David. Go on with a vigorous war as you first designed, loose and absolved from all rules of government; being reduced to extreme necessity, everything is to be done, that power might admit, and that you are to do. They refusing, you are acquitted towards God and man. You have an army in Ireland you may employ here to reduce this kingdom. Confident as anything under heaven, Scotland shall not hold out five months. One summer well employed will do it. Venture all I had, I would carry it or lose it. . . .

Then Laud spoke, echoing the impetuous and strong-willed Strafford.

Tried all ways and refused all ways. By the law of God and man you should have subsistence, and ought to have it, and lawful to take it.

When the meeting was over, Vane put these highly sensitive jottings safely away in a red velvet cabinet which he locked inside the strong room of his London house.

Somehow the suggestion got abroad that the government was considering bringing over an Irish army. In May the French agent wrote that "the King of England thinks of making use of 10,000 Irishmen as well to bring to terms his English subjects as for the Scottish war." There was always in the English mind a certain fear of the Catholic Irish, irrational but strong, and now Black Tom was being called Black Tom Tyrant, and he and Laud were considered the twin pillars of arbitrary and despotic government. His enemies observed, not without admiration, that Black Tom would not "suffer a guard to attend him, knowing he hath terror enough in his bended brows to amaze the prentices."

Matters were no better in Scotland. On July 23 the Scots army was said to be contemplating the seizure of Newcastle. In desperation the king sent the elder Vane and Cottington in to London to promise not to debase the coinage—a device contemplated for raising money—if the city would lend him 200,000 pounds. But the burgesses refused. At the same time Strafford was negotiating with the Spanish for a loan and the queen had written to the pope, foolishly believing that he would give financial as well as moral support. All these efforts came to nothing, and on August 29, after a small skirmish at Newburn, the English abandoned Newcastle to the Scots. Later, political libels would say that the younger Vane had shown himself a coward in that skirmish by running away, but it is not possible that the joint Treasurer of the Navy would have been sent to command a company in the Scots war. It is true that his brother William was in command of such a troop, and inasmuch as all English troops at Newburn retreated, William undoubtedly did also. Later he carried himself bravely in many engagements. But a legend of young Vane's physical cowardice was growing. In a lampoon written much later in the mock-heroic manner of *Don Quixote*, the high priest asks Sir Vane, Knight of the Most Mysterious Allegories, "whether he could fight or no? To which Sir Vane reply'd, that he never could nor never would fight."

After the defeat at Newburn, the elder Vane wrote to Secretary
Windebank from Raby Castle, "It is strange to see how Leslie steals
the hearts of the people in these northern parts. You shall do well to
think of timely remedies to be applied, lest the disease grows
incurable." But the disease still spread. On September 4, the Scots
occupied Durham and forced the counties of Northumberland and
Durham to support the invading army. Strafford remained confident
that English patriotism would be aroused by this invasion, for like
Charles he still trusted in the old mystique of kingship. Charles
personally reviewed his troops at York, and as the elder Vane wrote,
"Braver bodies of men and better clad have I not seen anywhere, for
the foot. For the horse, they are such as no man that sees them, by
their outward appearance, but will judge them able to stand and
encounter with any whatsoever." But this brave army was now
costing Charles 40,000 pounds a month that he did not have.

Through all these troubles, young Vane had continued to
perform his duties with quiet efficiency and things went well for
him. On June 23, 1640, he had been knighted, perhaps a tribute to
his inconspicuousness in the Short Parliament and to his father's
influence at Court. His knighthood was a precursor of his marriage
on July 1 to Frances, daughter of Sir Christopher Wray. The
Wrays of Glentworth were a wealthy and distinguished family.
Frances's grandfather had been the Chief Justice of the Queen's
Bench, known for his severity in cases that threatened the royal
prerogative; he also held seven manors in addition to the Hall of
Glentworth. Her father, a man of Puritan leanings, had resisted
payment of ship money in 1636 and would become a member of the
Long Parliament. Subdued now and too cautious to defy the
conservative religious feeling of the two families, young Vane
allowed himself to be married in an Anglican chapel. His father
responded handsomely, settling on him large properties including
Raby Castle in Lincolnshire and the elegant Fairlawn in Kent. From
his father's point of view, the marriage thus began auspiciously. The
elder Vane perhaps did not realize that this daughter-in-law tacitly
shared his son's dangerous religious views; she too was to be known
as a Seeker who, like her husband, distrusted organized churches and
listened to an inner voice. For young Vane this marriage would turn
out to be a relationship of close spiritual intimacy and affectionate
understanding, a spiritual anchorage, the happiest and most enduring

relationship of his stormy life, though it must have been distressing at times to the conservative Vanes and Wrays. But it was young Harry's great good fortune to marry a woman who was well-born, well-to-do, with the sensitivity of an Anne Hutchinson but without Anne's hungry and aggressive ego.

Because Vane was in the north at the time of his son's wedding and certain details of the marriage settlement had not been legally concluded, he sent word to his steward in the London house that his oldest son should be admitted to the treasure room to search for the necessary papers. Young Henry was given the key, and as he was looking for the papers, he noted a little cabinet covered with red velvet. Suddenly he was overwhelmed by a powerful urge to open it and see what it contained.

The details of what happened and of Vane's inner motives are not entirely clear, for the story was told somewhat differently by Parliamentary diarists who, seeing the hand of God in what Vane did, wished to justify him, and by the Royalists who wrote in anger, more concerned to demonstrate young Vane's seamy character than to discover God's ways. Later, the Earl of Clarendon wrote an account of young Vane's own testimony before the Commons, testimony which brings us as near to the truth as we are likely to come.

Young Harry did not explain why he felt impelled to look into that red cabinet, but he must have suspected that it contained secret papers concerning his father's role as secretary to the king and the Privy Council. And he knew, of course, that members of the Privy Council were sworn to secrecy about what was said and done in meetings, that these papers were, by authority of the king, privileged communications, that they were, as we would say, "Top Secret." And it was axiomatic that men spoke guardedly when they knew that their utterances would be published; only in the assured confidence of privacy could counselors, speaking in utter candor, give intimate, deeply felt, and disinterested advice. The values of state secrecy were evident, and the concept of the "public's right to know" did not yet exist. Equally strong against his snooping was the claim of family loyalty: he owed a duty to his father, whose consent to pry into matters of state he did not have and surely could not obtain.

On the other hand, the promptings of the inner voice might be urging him to some service in God's cause. Times were dangerous, and he had doubtless heard those disturbing rumors that Strafford had promised an Irish army; perhaps as Treasurer of the Navy which would transport such an army he had heard something even more substantial.

Besides, according to the strongly antinomian doctrine that he enunciated later, a truly justified believer who had received the second birth of Christ in his soul became the "Lamb's wife," higher even than the angels; his association with Christ was so intimate, his union with the Holy Ghost so personal, that he mysteriously participated in the godhead. The final, the most sacred, and the most difficult task of a Lamb's wife was to surrender to the divine will the "reasonable powers" and the personal will, even as Abraham offered up Isaac. Having accepted this ultimate sacrifice, God would transform such a man from an unreliable human, capable of erring as Adam had been before the fall, into an "absolute and unchangeable harmony with His will." Then the inner impulse would be the manifestation of God's voice and mere human reason would be irrelevant. So young Henry put aside the temptation of doubt, the dictates of reason, and the claims of family loyalty, and ceasing to argue with himself, he surrendered to impulse. He would spend a good part of his life attempting to justify this surrender.

He again sought out the steward and blandly lied that to complete his business he would need to borrow the keys once more, and the steward trustingly handed them over. Vane returned to the treasure room, opened the red cabinet, and took from it the secret papers, written in his father's hand and in his disjointed style of note-taking. He glanced at many sheets, but stopped with a constriction of the heart when he saw the notes of Strafford's advice in that conference held the day after the dissolution of the Short Parliament. He read the words again and again: "You have an army with which you may reduce this kingdom." Now he saw that his dissimulation and violation of trust were justified, that the very life of the nation had rested on his decision to obey the voice of the Holy Spirit.

Had he not surrendered his reasonable powers, certain reservations might have suggested themselves: Could it be self interest, at least in part, that was speaking to him now? Strafford was the ally of Laud, the enemy of the saints; Strafford had taken a title that belonged to him. Could this impulse, that coincided so closely with his antagonisms and his family's advantage, be wholly disinterested? And there might have been an even deeper level of questioning. He had failed in New England, and his inner integrity had been compromised when he agreed to collect the despised ship money. Could he now be seeking some way of publicly redeeming his diminished image of himself? How does any listener to inner voices distinguish the voice of God from his own desperate cries? Young Henry Vane, who needed so very much to believe in himself and the validity of inner promptings, could hardly permit such questions to rise into the realm of conscious inquiry. He had effected a personal union with the Holy Spirit; of that at least he was certain.

But he at once realized that if this discovery were to save the nation, it must be made public, and public disclosure would be an immensely greater betrayal of his father's trust, might even ruin the elder Vane's reputation and destroy his public usefulness along with the reputations of those corrupt ministers whose warlike advice was a peril to the life and liberty of citizens and soldiers alike. His filial betrayal would be absolute, yet the voice of God required it.

He hesitated for a time, baffled and confused, but soon he knew that he must follow that inner voice even through dissimulations and betrayal. However wrongly he came by that information he now possessed it and needed to act on it.

At just this time young Vane fell into an ague, into a burning, shaking fever which may well have been psychosomatic, induced by the terrible struggle within him between exultation and guilt. When he was recovering, John Pym, as leader of Parliament, called on the young member to comfort him in his illness. It was Pym's persuasion, many believed, that had finally sent Vane off to the new world, and unlike some of the Puritan leaders, he had not turned away from him after his homecoming; rather, he had become his guide and sponsor in Parliament. Now the two of them fell into a talk about "the sad condition of the kingdom," and though young Vane was bursting to tell what he knew, he could not yet bring himself to do it. It is a measure of the restraint that he had acquired that he postponed the disclosure. He asked Pym to call again tomorrow, when he would show him something that might indicate the imminent ruin of the kingdom.

The precise John Pym was punctual the next day, and there, in his father's house, the feverish young Vane showed Pym the notes.

Pym, seeing that the matter was "of counsel so prodigious," asked that a copy be made for himself. Vane at first refused, remembering that disclosure could bring his father under the greatest prejudice, but he was no match for the older, wholly committed Pym, who said that this discovery was God's way of preserving church and state. A flood of gratification poured through the mind of Harry, for he was hearing what he desperately needed to believe—that his urge to open the box had proceeded not from simple curiosity or even mortal prescience, but from concordance with the divine will. Now he had no choice; he allowed Pym to make a copy which both men carefully collated with the original. Pym then left, knowing that he had with him a document that might, at the proper time, expose the mind of Black Tom Tyrant and subject him to an aroused national conscience. And without Strafford, Charles somehow did not seem very frightening. Perhaps Pym hoped that he would not have to make the document public, for he would be glad to spare his young protegé embarrassment, and anyhow the mere knowledge of what the document contained constituted an enormous advantage. But in such a high matter, if he had to disclose it he would do so, and young Vane might then make what peace he could with his father and the world. Pym had no real doubt that, if necessary, the young idealist would think it right to sacrifice himself for the greater good.

Meanwhile, the English army in the north, realizing the increasing futility of its position, sought a treaty, and on October 21, 1640, the Scots agreed to a cessation of hostilities pending further negotiations, provided they were given 25,000 pounds a month for support of their army. Charles agreed to these terms primarily to gain both time and persuasive reasons to seek Parliamentary support once more. He therefore called for a new Parliament to meet on November 3, 1640, a Parliament to which both of the Vanes were returned. This was the Long Parliament, and it met under the shadow of fear and suspicion of Strafford, the "dark-browed apostate," who was the focus of obsessive hatred. The City remembered how he had tried to debase the coinage; Puritans had long since realized that he was more deadly, more powerful, and more to be feared than Laud; the whole nation blamed him for the terror of Star Chamber, the threat of the Irish army, and that immoral war with the Scots.

Strafford knew this, knew that his own safety could best be

preserved in Yorkshire at the head of the English army, but he nevertheless returned to London. Later his family would say that the elder Vane, preparing to shift his allegiance from Charles to Parliament, persuaded the king to send for him, but it is more likely that the delicate Charles simply needed the strength of Strafford to see him through the ordeal of facing Parliament. In any event, he asked his strongest man to return, promising that he "should not suffer in his person, honor, or fortune." Strafford knew that he was putting himself in jeopardy. He knew the malice and the fear of Parliament and the people, but he tested his heart and found it good. There was nothing cold there, he said, and so he came at his king's bidding.

Parliament opened amid all the old outcries against grievances and with all the appeals for redress, only now it was Ireland and Strafford that were the emotional issues. Not yet ready to impeach Charles or require his abdication, the Parliament was eager to call to account Strafford, Laud, Hamilton, and the ship-money judges.

The king was uneasy, for he knew that an attack on his ministers was inevitable, and feeling that anything they had said under the pledge of secrecy should not be available to be used against them, he ordered the elder Vane to burn his notes of council meetings. The secretary emptied the red cabinet and burned everything, unaware that John Pym had a true copy of one paper which he had read and pondered until he knew every word in it, that Pym knew Strafford had advised the king that he was "absolved from all rules of government," and that an Irish army was available "to reduce this kingdom." Inasmuch as the council meeting had occurred after England's first defeat by the Scots, a generous interpretation of the notes would have suggested that "this kingdom" meant Scotland, but Pym thought, or affected to think, otherwise. Therefore one of his first major actions was to impeach Strafford, who was arrested in late November and committed to the Tower.

Secretary Windebank, with the king's connivance, fled to France fearing to be caught in the net cast for Strafford; many wondered why the other secretary, Sir Henry Vane, surely equally culpable and vulnerable, was spared. The new Parliament scarcely questioned his role, even though Lady Vane had attended the queen's Catholic chapel and was known to be a compliant woman, and Vane himself had openly consorted with Catholics and stood high in the queen's favor. The reason for his immunity, some thought, lay in the influence his son had lately acquired with John Pym.

There was a good deal of delay as articles of impeachment against Strafford were read and passed in the House, sent on to the Lords, and then as Strafford's reply was read. It was not until March 23, 1641, that Pym opened the case against Strafford in the House, putting the worst possible constructions on his actions and motives. The Irish army, Pym thought, was the crucial point in the case, so he put the elder Vane on the stand. At first Vane's memory was hazy, but in Pym's very pointed questions he began to recognize phrases that he himself had once written. Always shrewd where his own survival was concerned, he quickly assumed that some other member of the Privy Council had already passed on exact information to Pym. He thereupon began to equivocate and soon his memory became wondrously clear as he repeated, for the House, the sense of his notes as he remembered them. He felt no great sorrow at seeing the Baron of Raby in trouble, and every effort of Strafford's friends to get the elder Vane to say that "this kingdom" meant Scotland failed. Vane refused to construe the words, but gave the impression that he thought they probably meant England.

The accusation of treason had now been supported by one witness, and the lack of a second one was an embarrassment to Pym and his Puritan friends. They could not forget that some two decades earlier their hero Ralegh had eloquently pleaded reason, scripture, and law against his own conviction by the mouth of a single witness; the Bible, if nothing else, required that all truth be established in the mouths of two or three witnesses. But now they were not to be had. Of those present at that impassioned council meeting, Laud, suddenly a weak and pitiable old man, had been committed to the Tower; Windebank had fled; the other four Privy Councilors—Hamilton, Northumberland, Bishop Juxon, and Cottington—all affirmed that Strafford had not, to their remembrance, said or proposed anything of the kind alleged by Pym.

But this negative testimony was not altogether convincing. If the notes were so harmless, why had the king ordered them to be burned? And Vane's suddenly improved memory could be accounted for if he had read Strafford's words once more just before he burned them. Still, almost as eloquently as Ralegh and with equal tenacity, Strafford held that a single witness could not establish treason.

By April 10, Strafford had borne himself so well and the evidence of treason had proved so tenuous that the prosecuting lawyers, Glyn and Maynard, called on Pym to disclose the secret evidence which he said he possessed. Pym then arose in the House and explained how he had procured from young Vane the document which he read aloud, explaining as he went all ciphers and ambiguities. He concluded by saying that this paper had the force of a second witness. It is difficult to see why he thought so. The elder Vane's oral testimony was now supported by an uncertified, unofficial, and surreptitiously acquired document, and both written testimony and oral testimony were that of the same man who was an obviously biased witness and an avowed enemy to the accused.

When Pym finished, young Vane arose "in seeming disorder." Some believed that such a suave, purposive, emotionless man would have to feign confusion, but those who had known him five years earlier in New England would not have thought so. Young Harry told his story, concluding that

> he knew this discovery would prove little less than his ruin in the good opinion of his father; but having been provoked by tenderness of conscience towards his common parent, his country, to trespass against his natural father, he hoped he should find compassion from that house [of Commons] although he had little hope of pardon elsewhere.

Then he sat down, and his father, with great sternness replied that he knew now what he had already come to suspect, that the confidential meeting of the Privy Council had been betrayed. What hurt was that his own son had been the betrayer.

Clarendon, Laud, and other Royalists believed that the whole scene had been staged by John Pym in order to destroy Strafford, and that he had coached and rehearsed both Vanes in their parts. It was well acted, they said, with such passion and gestures that Parliament was deeply moved. Certainly speakers rose to their feet to commend young Vane, assuring him that he had done right in listening to conscience, and a motion was passed enjoining the father to be friends with the son.

The elder Vane did not demur, but reconciliation came hard to him after his public humiliation. Still, while listening to the speeches, his mind had been racing: Strafford was probably now as good as dead, and without Strafford, it was not difficult to see which of the two parties would be stronger. He was riding a narrow raft, and for his life and property's sake he would have to move to the other side. Gradually the breach between the Vanes was closed, but it was the son who stood firm politically and the older man who had to shift his ground. Both suffered loss of prestige with the king, and both were relieved of office. And for some time a great coldness was noted between father and son.

Striking hard on the heels of this new disclosure, Parliament dropped judicial procedure against Strafford and resorted to a Bill of Attainder. By this ancient and cruel device, unused for centuries, a man could be convicted of treason by a simple vote of Parliament, without concern for rules of evidence or any formal legal processes at all. And young Vane's disclosures had pretty well determined which way the aroused Parliament would now vote.

The moderates tried in vain to prevent this legal murder. Edward Hyde talked to the Earl of Essex who merely replied that "stone dead hath no fellow." And then came a petition signed by 20,000 Londoners demanding "justice" upon Strafford, and for the first time the phrase "the People" began to be heard everywhere. The law was for a moment in abeyance while the voice of the people was heard: Strafford was condemned to be beheaded as a traitor. But pressed by those tender of the law, Parliament passed a rider which affirmed that this Bill of Attainder should not be considered a precedent. After agonizing long between his vowed promise to Strafford and a ruthless political necessity, Charles set pen to the death warrant of his most faithful friend and wisest counselor. On Tower Hill, an enormous crowd which some estimated at 200,000 assembled in triumph to see their enemy die. He had learned not to put his trust in princes, Strafford had earlier said, but now he seemed to trust firmly in his God, and so he died bravely and with dignity.

Once Strafford was dead there was a wave of sympathy with his courage, a revulsion at the manner of his conviction, and a growing suspicion and even hatred of those responsible for his death. Strafford, some said, could not be legally convicted, but nevertheless an innocent man had suffered because young Harry Vane, with his hypocritical tender conscience and his readiness to invoke the inner spirit to justify his own desires, had betrayed his father, Strafford, and the king. After the Restoration, when the no-longer-young Vane would suffer from the long-delayed malice and rage of the Royalists, some would say that his own unjust conviction and execution owed much to the bitter remembrance of what he had done to Strafford.

The poets soon began to echo popular sentiments. John Cleveland wrote of the "glorious Strafford,"

> Here lies wise and valiant dust,
> Huddled up twixt Fit and Just.
>
> Here lies his blood; and let it lie
> Speechless still and never cry.

Incensed by the mob that had screamed for Strafford's head and would shout its way to new prominence under the Parliamentary reign, another poet wrote,

> There by the malice of the great and proud,
> And unjust clamors of the frantic crowd,
> The great, the learned Strafford met his Fate.
> O sacred Innocence! what can expiate
> For guiltless blood but blood?

Though the testimony of the Vanes had not been sufficient to convict Strafford legally, many believed they were morally guilty of his death because it was the notes of the council meeting that had convinced many members that Strafford had really intended treason. But even if he were guilty, his execution without due process was widely disturbing, as John Denham made plain:

> They after death their fears of him express,
> His innocence, and their own guilt confess.
> Their legislative frenzy they repent,
> Enacting it should make no precedent.

But was not Charles the real betrayer? He had promised Strafford his life on the honor of a king, and whatever the pressures, he was weak to bend under them. To the day of his death his conscience was tormented and he might well have prayed, as Thomas Stanley later imagined his doing:

> Thou whose mercies know no bound,
> Pardon my compliant sin.
> Death in me the guiltless found,
> Who his refuge should have been.

Royalists were dismayed and disheartened. A great man had died, they said, that birds of prey might live. But the Puritans were breathing easier. Thanks to young Harry Vane there was now a little more room on their narrow raft. And yet young Vane must have been sickened too. He was not a man of blood, he said, and to the end of his life he protested that there was no blood on his hands, a strange protestation from one whose orders had doomed the Pequot nation. It is true, however, that never once in all his life did he personally commit a violent act. Certainly he had not meant to kill Strafford, but Strafford was dead. Although he was certain, desperately certain, that he had acted from the promptings of the Holy Spirit, it had all gone further than he had foreseen or intended.

7

The Parliamentary Revolution (1640–1642)

The Long Parliament had begun on November 3, 1640, and continued in session until September 9, 1641, when a short recess was declared. At the end of that first session, one observer wrote that young Vane was a favorite everywhere, largely because of the blow he had given Strafford. As personal tragedy and high drama, the execution of the earl was the emotional climax of the period; yet in the months preceding and following his execution, many matters less sensational but more portentous were being discussed in Parliament with unanimity of feeling and sentiment that it would never know again.

There was a Scots army inside English borders which, since it could not be resisted, had to be bought off. Neither the tribute required to keep that army quiet nor the money to build a force to drive it home could be raised by any shifts of the royal prerogative. The king therefore urgently needed Parliament and could not afford to dismiss it. With a clearly observable shift of power from king to Commons, there spread a strong feeling of suppressed excitement and of rising hope which was felt even in New England, inciting a number of exiles there to return home. Among these were Hugh Peter and an obscure wine-cooper named Thomas Venner, whom Vane would some day know to his cost.

Looking back on the early days of this Parliament, Edward Hyde, who had become Lord Clarendon, said that there had been eight or nine who set the "designs," of whom Pym was chief; then there had been a number of "stout seconders" of whom young Vane was one. A few weeks after the Parliament opened, he had coolly and efficiently read a report on the navy in which, to the House's dismay, he said that 60,000 pounds was needed immediately if the fleet was to be made seaworthy. He also spoke in favor of impressing men for the navy, asserting that the quality and numbers of the seamen had deteriorated below the point of safety. At that time, Parliamentary fervor for the "liberties of the subject" over-rode his recommendation. Sooner or later, however, revolutionary fervor would have to measure the luxury of passion against the cold demands of necessity, and so, in May, 1641, just before Strafford's execution, an ordinance for naval impressment was passed. Never quite so concerned about the liberty of the outward man as about the inner liberty of private belief and individual experience, Vane would later favor the impressment of soldiers too.

In those euphoric days of the early Long Parliament, men naturally thought of redressing the cruel personal injustices inflicted by the Court of Star Chamber. John Pym therefore moved that William Prynne and Henry Burton be freed and returned to London. The elder Vane, obtuse and insensitive to what was happening around him, demurred. He had been a member of the court responsible for the mutilation of the two men, and it had been observed that ever since he became secretary, priests and Jesuits had been attracted to his house "as iron to loadstone." Yet after the death of Strafford he could hardly expect the king's party to trust him. Even so, he had no glimmer now of the dangerous edge on which he walked, and was wholly surprised at the savagery of the replies directed against him. Nor did he or other members of Commons yet know how strong the friendship between young Vane and Pym had grown since the transmission of the secret document. Later the elder Vane would recognize that friendship as his invisible shield, and even now his alert instinct for survival suggested that he should be silent for a time, while he observed a puzzling new world in the making.

Cromwell demanded the release of John Lilburne along with Prynne and Burton; others pleaded for John Bastwick and for Alexander Leighton who had now been in jail for eleven years and who had suffered terribly, stoically, but not silently in his imprisonment. To these and other prisoners the Parliament said "go forth," and to those in darkness they said "show yourselves," thus fulfilling the scriptures.

When Prynne and Burton arrived in London, they were greeted by a thousand horse, a hundred coaches, and "a world of foot," everyone carrying, for remembrance, rosemary branches whose gray-green leaves would soon come to symbolize the liberty of the people and the reign of King Jesus. Robert Baillie, one of the Scots commissioners who witnessed the homecoming, said he had never seen such affection showered on men. Soon all those who had once galled the bishops returned and lent their presence and their sense of undying grievance to the cry for a settlement of the church which would diminish or exclude the "prelatical parasites."

Parliament also moved to redress older, more general grievances. John Hampden, fitting enough, spoke against ship money with strong seconding speeches from Lord Falkland, the gentle courtier, and Edward Hyde, foremost of the constitutional lawyers. Sir Harbottle Grimston, knight of the shire from Essex, spoke against Star Chamber; others spoke against the Court of High Commission, against religious innovations, and the past dissolutions of Parliament. These speeches expressed the common feelings so fully that frequently there were no negative voices and therefore no debate.

Want of money, the most persistent enemy of any state, remained Parliament's principal problem. In his urgent desire to provide for the fleet, young Vane proposed Parliamentary subsidies, but though he was supported by his father and a few others, the Commons, prepared for minor expediencies, were not yet ready for major ironies. After they had just declared ship-money illegal, a tax on Englishmen for the support of the navy seemed too paradoxical. It was decided therefore that tonnage and poundage, a revenue derived from a tax on imported wine and other commodities, would be used for that purpose. Sir Symonds D'Ewes suggested that the navy's need for funds might be attributed in part to the negligence of Lord Russell, then ill at home with the gout; and he observed that Russell had acquired substantial wealth in his position, although he said nothing about young Vane's having done so. Concerned at these attacks, Lord Russell offered a personal loan to the navy of 6,000 pounds, while he and young Vane both pledged their personal credit for 20,000 more, to be repaid when revenues came in.

In January of 1641 Pym gave young Vane his first significant committee assignment on a committee charged with obtaining money for the army. In March, having been informed that the City entertained a good opinion of young Vane, the House sent him, along with some other members, to the City Council to obtain a loan for 100,000 pounds. It was granted, and this expedient temporarily saved Parliament from acceding to Pym's embarrassing proposal of a forced loan. They remembered that in 1626, after dissolving a recalcitrant Parliament, Charles had imposed such a loan, and a number of men had gone to the Tower for refusing to pay it. Sir Symonds D'Ewes spoke for the majority when he objected that a Parliamentary tyranny was as bad as a Royalist one. A voluntary loan guaranteed by Parliamentary subsidies obviated for a time another cruel, ironic necessity.

While Vane played a relatively minor role in these events, it was inevitable that he would soon work his way into the emotional center of the revolution. The attack on the bishops gave him his opening. About a month after the Long Parliament began, some 15,000 citizens of London had signed a petition which went beyond any notion of mere church reform: it embodied the revolutionary proposal that episcopacy should be abolished "with all its dependencies, roots and branches." It was accompanied to Westminster Hall by a noisy, enthusiastic mob of some 1,500 apprentices and citizens.

This petition caused perhaps the first significant rift in Parliamentary unanimity. Pym, Hampden, St. John, young Vane, and the other future leaders of the Parliamentary party wished to consider the petition. Among those who opposed it was the elder Vane, who found nothing more to say than that the petitioners were no better than Brownists, that is, proponents of separation from the English church. Of course they were separatists—that was the point of the petition. Vane's obtuse remark was received with annoyance and resentment.

The future leaders of the Royalist party, Hyde and Falkland, also opposed this proposal, although for other reasons. It offended Hyde's sense of the need for continuity and order; it was too abrupt, too final. Such sudden and violent change, he said, would commit the ship of state to uncharted waters. Falkland, though he supported reform measures and opposed Laud, preferred a compromise in which the power of the bishops should be curtailed, especially their power to prosecute, and their authority should be shared with ministers in the dioceses. And while he was willing to abolish some offensive ceremonies, he disliked and distrusted the Puritan manners. Himself the very model of a courtier, learned in books and language, admired for his "humanity, courtesy, and affability," loved for his benevolent and charitable nature, he saw in the new men something inimical to most of the things he loved. He agreed with Edmund Waller that both good poems and good lives needed form and style, and he found little of either in the noisy petitioners or in their intemperate petition. John Selden, an Erastian lawyer and probably the most brilliant mind in Parliament, also mistrusted extreme solutions. Such men as these formed a group in Commons, resembling a modern political party, which opposed another Parliamentary group on a matter of high principle.

Not long after the petition was submitted, Pym announced to the House that he believed there were sufficient grounds to indict Laud for treason, and when the indictment was sent up to the House of Lords in February, 1641, young Vane was one of the members designated to carry it, a certain sign of Vane's sympathies with the indictment and of Pym's favor and trust in him. At about the same time he was one of six new members added to the Grand Committee on Religion and one of the three known to favor the abolition of the bishops.

Now young Harry began to extend his friendships and his political influence. He allied himself with Oliver Cromwell, a little-known Huntingdon man, with Oliver St. John, who had been appointed solicitor-general by the king, and with Arthur Haselrig, whose extreme and "absurd views," as some called them, leaned toward republicanism.

Cromwell and St. John were related by marriage, but worlds apart in temperament and character. St. John was a skilled lawyer with an incisive mind, a man, it was said, "of dark and clouded countenance, very proud and conversing with very few, and those men of his own humor and inclination." Neither appalled by bishops nor pleased by Puritans, he thought that priest and preacher alike tended to be meddlesome nuisances and that the entire apparatus of religion should be subjected to state control.

Cromwell, on the other hand, was passionately religious, emotionally fervent, incapable of concealing an idea or a feeling. Sir Philip Warwick, a courtly young gentleman much inclined to judge by appearances, described his first view of Cromwell in 1640.

I came one morning into the house well clad, and perceived a gentleman speaking (whom I knew not) very ordinarily apparelled; for it was a plain cloth suit, which seemed to have been made by an ill country-tailor; his linen was plain and not very clean, and I remember a speck or two of blood upon his little band, which was not much larger than his collar; his hat was without a hat band: his stature was of a good size, his sword stuck close to his side, his countenance swollen and reddish, his voice sharp and untunable, and his eloquence full of fervor.

Warwick noted with some surprise that in spite of this unseemly appearance Cromwell was "much hearkened unto."

To Warwick's description, others have added details. Cromwell had a large nose and a wart under the left side of his lower lip. He cared less for books, some thought, than most other men. Richard Baxter noted with some uneasiness that Oliver when cold sober had the same "vivacity, hilarity and alacrity" that in any other man would have indicated he had drunk a cup too much.

These four men, young Vane, Haselrig, Cromwell, and St. John, collaborated on a bill which would destroy episcopacy "root and branch," abolishing bishops entirely. They timed its introduction to coincide with another and lesser attack. Some members of Commons thought that the bishops of England, who by virtue of their titles were members of the House of Lords, should be excluded from the upper House, at least during the discussion of church reform in which they had so powerful and settled an interest. All the bishops had taken the infamous "et cetera oath" propounded by the Convocation of Divines, which bound the clergy to support the institution of episcopacy as instituted with "Archbishops, Bishops, Deans, Archdeacons, et cetera." This oath finally alienated the thoughtful and devout Richard Baxter from the established church. "Oh cursed oath," Nehemiah Wallington had cried. Young Vane believed that having taken this oath, the bishops could not fairly discuss religious reform without the risk of perjuring themselves. Other members, more apprehensive about shattering historical precedents, had argued that there were no legal grounds for excluding the bishops. The final decision lay with the House of Lords itself.

On May 27, 1641, when the Commons learned that the Lords had resolved to retain the bishops, the four young Parliamentarians brought forth their Root and Branch Bill. A vigorous, angry, and partisan debate followed, after which, according to John Nalson, speeches in favor of episcopacy were suppressed, while those opposed were printed and disseminated. Falkland spoke against this bill which, he said, was so violent that it resembled a "total massacre" of men, women, and children, and Edward Hyde strongly objected even to the reading of the bill. But by 135 to 108 the Commons voted a first reading and then laid it aside.

Of the speeches disseminated and printed, Nalson believed the most significant one was by young Vane "who was now become not only the proselyte but the favorite of the faction." On June 11, he delivered his first major public address in England.

There is a good deal of expediency and political rhetoric in it; perhaps only one paragraph is fully characteristic of the man. When he confronts the crucial question of whether episcopacy should be abolished or merely amended and reformed, he resorts to an analogy between a man and an institution, the old, familiar comparison of the microcosm to the macrocosm. When a man is regenerated, Vane argued, he is not by degrees amended and reformed; rather, there is a wondrous moment when old things pass away and all becomes new. So it must be in the church; it is regeneration and not reformation that is needed.

Otherwise, the speech is structured on two main points: episcopacy has been found prejudicial both to religion and to the civil state. Taking up the religious issue first, Vane says that the root of episcopacy grows in "the Pope's Paradise." Any argument, therefore, which can be made for bishops can be adduced even more strongly in favor of the pope, for the two differ only in degree, not in kind. The hierarchical structure of episcopacy, he says, grew from a spirit of pride,

> first exalting itself above its fellow presbyters under the form of a bishop; then over its fellow bishops under the title of archbishops, and so still mounting over those of its own profession, till it come to be Pope, and then it sticks not to tread upon the necks of princes, kings, and emperors.

Episcopacy, Vane believes, was not established by Christ and must therefore represent the spirit of Antichrist. Through it, superstition and corruption in worship and doctrine have been introduced with the design of "hastening us back again to Rome."

Episcopacy was also a sower of civil strife, for the bishops taught the "lawfulness of arbitrary power." They also ignored the common law in their church courts and, worst of all, were responsible for the war between England and Scotland. In sum, they had tried to deprive Englishmen of their civil freedom, "desiring to make us grind in their mill, as the Phillistines did Sampson, and to put out both our eyes. O let us be avenged of these Phillistines for our two eyes."

As long as episcopacy exists, Vane warns, religion will be in danger; similarly while the bishops have votes in the House of Lords, they can obstruct "good and wholesome laws tending to salvation." Then he touched on a practical matter. The Scots army had demanded the abolition of episcopacy as one of its terms for withdrawal; Vane is therefore certain that there is little chance of "durable peace so long as the cause of the war yet continues."

He concludes with an emotional peroration. This Parliament, he says, "has been called, continued, preserved, and secured by the immediate finger of God, as it were, for this work." If episcopal government is not pulled down Divine Providence will be given a check.

Let us not then halt any longer between two opinions, but with one heart and resolution give glory to God in complying with his providence, and with the good safety and peace of this Church and State, which is by passing this bill we are now upon.

It is a politically powerful and effective speech. If judged against the pulpit fulminations of the time it is also restrained in tone, despite its inflammatory plea. But, judged against the best speeches on the same subject, it is neither magnanimous nor tolerant. There were countless devout Anglicans who, believing that grace flowed to them through the sacraments of the church, felt their consciences as severely violated by what Vane proposed as his had been by the elders of Massachusetts. Even Henry Burton, who had greater cause than Vane to despise episcopacy, proposed an established national church surrounded by voluntary ones, essentially the solution accepted during the Revolution of 1688 when after a civil war and 100,000 dead, common sense came for a time into fashion.

During the debate the question had arisen several times as to what form of church government should succeed that now established. On June 21, Vane proposed that a commission, consisting of an equal number of laity and clergy, be appointed in each diocese to manage religious affairs. But the Commons were so opposed to giving the clergy any voice at all that they rejected Vane's moderate proposal and voted to appoint nine lay commissioners to exercise all ecclesiastical jurisdiction in England. This proposal could only have distressed Vane, who believed that the state should not meddle in the religious life of man and who was still young enough to expect that a Parliament should recognize the evident rightness of his solution and vote for it.

To the dismay of Parliament, while the debate was still continuing on the church settlement, the king decided early in August to visit his subjects in Scotland and bring the charm and regality of his person to bear on settlement of what disputes remained. Since no one knew what this visit might lead to, it was thought best to postpone discussion of the divisive issue of episcopacy. Nevertheless in the debate on the Root and Branch Bill, Vane had come a long way toward achieving his first goal in the religious reform of the English nation. The bill and his supporting speech had met with some formidable opposition but less than anyone had expected. At the same time Parliament had displayed a strong opposition to Laudian Anglicanism. Now with Strafford attainted and Laud impeached, Vane, Cromwell, and others could afford to pause and see what might result from the actions they had initiated.

They did not have to wait long. On September 1 the House of Commons passed a resolution that communion tables should be moved from the east end of churches and chapels to the center, and that in the future no rails should surround the table. Further, crucifixes and "scandalous pictures" such as those of any member of the Holy Trinity and all images of the Virgin Mary should be taken away; at the same time, tapers, candlesticks, basins, and bowing at the name of Jesus were proscribed.

Now the Root and Branch mob—known to some as The People—taking the hint from this resolution and frustrated at the delay in passing Vane's bill, began to act. Entering churches, they broke altar rails, shattered stained-glass windows, and tore up any monuments to the dead that savored of such idolatry as inviting prayers for the departed. Clergymen in cloth or vestments were ridiculed and sometimes assaulted. Up in Nottingham, Lucy Hutchinson said that within two miles of her home was a church where Christ on the Cross, the Virgin, and St. John had been "fairly set up in a window" over the altar. Other "superstitious pictures" had hung upon the walls. The priest, tender of these sacred objects, gently removed the heads from the images and hid them in a closet, persuading the church officer that he had carried out the Parliamentary orders. But zealots complained to Colonel Hutchinson, who "persuaded" the parson to destroy all the images, to blot out all the superstitious paintings and to break the glass windows.

The new barbarism was everywhere. In London, according to a merchant named Nehemiah Wallington, an idol in the wall was cut down at Leonard's Eastcheap, superstitious pictures in the glass were broken in pieces, and the picture of the Virgin, mounted on candlesticks, was pulled down and ground beneath the heel of the righteous. "And some of those pieces of broken glass," Wallington continued, "I have to keep for a remembrance to show to the generations to come what God hath done for us, to give us such a reformation that our forefathers never saw the like: His name ever have the praise." And he proudly carried in his pocket the shattered glass fragments of what had once been a serene and compassionate face. At. St. Margaret's Church in new Fleet Street, the glass windows were broken to pieces, the pictures on the doors cut off, and some "idolatrous, superstitious brass" was hacked off the gravestones. And now, to the astonishment of literate people, ignorant ranting preachers began to proclaim that Latin was the language of the Beast.

Fortunately, some men and women were repelled by the stupidity of these excesses. The churchwarden at St. Giles Cripplegate said that all asses disliked rails, including those members of Parliament who had ordered them torn down. And Mr. Grant of Middlesex, who thought that pictures belonged in the chapel because they were layman's books, also said that an organ was better ten to one than singing of psalms, which he called "Hopkins his jigs." Sir Symonds D'Ewes, having heard that the churchwarden in Woolchurch, London, had not only obediently defaced all those mortuary statues which appeared in a praying posture but had torn up the brass inscriptions, told the House of Commons in shocked tones that antiquity was being destroyed. History has claims beyond the present, he said, and the tombs should be repaired.

Soon it was doubtful whether the greater tumults raged in favor of or in opposition to the House order. To oppose lordly, wealthy, and powerful bishops was one thing; to destroy the few objects of grace and beauty that illuminated the lives of ordinary people was another. Although some things were spared, there was one major disaster. The chief symbol in the city of London of Laud's attempt to restore episcopal grandeur was St. Paul's Cathedral, for which he had made "a noble portico"; now the carved work on it was broken down with axes and hammers. It took no more than a walk around London to see how the Root and Branch issue had polarized and divided both a Parliament and a nation. Thus some took notice that a strikingly new situation had arisen. In normal times the political life of a nation resembles a drugged and drowsy giant, slow to respond, insensitive to the need for change, accustomed to taunts and complaints. But when a revolutionary fervor burns in the people's hearts, everything becomes magnified: the minds of men become so excited and agitated that pin pricks feel like rapier thrusts; a pebble dropped into the aroused waters generates storms; the normal relationships between political cause and effect are suspended; predictability is lost. Action begets heightened reaction which in turn generates fiercer and more impulsive action. Events race from crisis to crisis to conflict. So it was in England now.

The forces the Parliamentary revolution had released continued to rage unchecked during the recess of Parliament from September 8 to October 20, 1641. The elder Vane had already accompanied the king to Scotland, visiting Raby Castle on the way. Young Vane was acting on a large committee appointed to carry on the duties of government while Parliament was adjourned and the king absent. He who had once governed a commonwealth in America had now become in England one of the rulers of a nominal monarchy.

During the Parliamentary recess, there came disturbing reports from Scotland where Charles was engaged in his characteristic double-dealing. He was probably not consciously dishonest, but he was weak and aggrieved. What therefore seemed to others dissimulation seemed to him only a justifiable policy. In Edinburgh he listened to everything and assented to much of what the Assembly and the Scotch Estates had to say. He attended the Presbyterian

Kirk, where he managed to convey an impression, if not of zeal, at least of interest and concern. While he had no money either to give or pledge, his lavishness with his large treasury of honors and titles gained him a national popularity which disturbed Pym and his party. But all the while Charles was courting the Scotch establishment, he was also engaged in intrigue with the Earl of Montrose, an ardent Royalist, perhaps the best military man in Scotland who, as a result of this intrigue, would some day shake Scotland to its roots.

When Charles had heard in Scotland of the Root and Branch debates and the iconoclastic tumults, he sent a message to Parliament that read like a manifesto:

> I hear it is reported that at my return I intend to alter the government of the Church of England, to bring it to that form as it is here. Therefore I command you to assure all my servants that I am constant to the discipline and doctrine of the Church of England established by Queen Elizabeth and my father, and that I resolve, by the grace of God, to die in the maintenance of it.

During the recess, the matter of the church settlement continued to seethe. In October, someone sent John Pym a "plague rag," a filthy cloth which had been seeped in the purulent flume of a pestilent corpse, with an accompanying note even uglier than the rag. And then, as the recess ended, there came news of what seemed the final and overwhelming disaster. The Irish, who had been outwardly quiet but inwardly burning from centuries of oppression, men whose memories of their long woe gave them no rest, men more recently repressed by the disciplined rule of Strafford, now took alarm at the anti-Catholic rhetoric and the legislative acts of the Long Parliament: they arose and began a wild, unsystematic, disorderly slaughter of the English. Soon incredible stories of mass slaughters began reaching English shores. Along with the terrifying news of the Protestant and English dead came stories of atrocities. Women had been stripped naked, it was said, raped, and then left to wander in the near-winter cold until they died; children had been clubbed and thrust through with the sword. Catholic mobs had in fact seized Protestant churches and desecrated them with a fury that could have taught the London iconoclasts something. Finally the Irish had published a resolution not too unlike the Scottish covenant, in which they resolved to defend "the public and free exercise of the true and Catholic Roman religion." This especially inflamed certain factions in the Parliament and angered the Scots.

For some reason, the king was slow to proclaim the Irish rebels and traitors; already refugees from Ireland were reporting that the Irish were saying they would come over and help the king against the Parliament. Charles fatuously announced, "I hope this ill news of Ireland may hinder some of those follies in England," and the Irish leaders now were displaying a commission purported to have been issued by the king at Edinburgh, a forgery, but rendered believable by Charles' statement. And still he had issued no proclamation against the Irish. To some of the Parliamentary leaders in England, it looked like a design on the grand scale: the Scots army had been withdrawn, and Charles had wooed Scotland while encouraging Ireland to rebel.

The women, who had been silent for a time, were aroused by the news from Ireland. Their leaders presented to Parliament a violent and hysterical petition attacking Laud and popery and lamenting that the "accursed and abominable idol of the mass" was permitted in England while "rapes are exercised on our sex in Ireland."

Are we to see our children dashed against stones, and mother's milk, mingled with infants' blood, running down the streets?

The petition acknowledges that "it may be thought strange, unbeseeming our sex" that women should thus engage in political strife, but religious equality is the basis for political equality: "Christ hath purchased us at as dear a rate as a man." Pym received the petition politely, thanked the women for it, and then counseled them to go home and pray for the men in Parliament who, with the aid of God, would set all right.

At the first news of the Irish rebellion, all other Parliamentary business was suspended, and the first action taken was to name a committee, of which young Vane was a member, to manage Irish affairs. At the same time the rebellion apparently crystallized in Pym's mind a project he had long been considering, a Grand Remonstrance accusing and denouncing Charles' government. This document took on massive proportions. Consisting of 204 items, it was, as Clarendon said, an account of every error, every misuse of royal power, every grievance that could be remembered or imagined since the year 1625: laxity in the treatment of Catholics, ecclesiastical innovations, haughty bishops, forced loans, ship money, Star Chamber, the Court of High Commission, monopolies, dissolutions of Parliament. Pym and those who helped him had good memories.

Toward the end, a section of the Grand Remonstrance deals with religion, a section written in a different style from the rest. Some modern historians have attributed it to Vane, but it is inconceivable that he could have either written it or agreed to it. Section 184 reads,

> And we do here declare that it is far from our purpose or desire to let loose the golden reins of discipline and government in the Church, to leave private persons or particular congregations to take up what form of Divine Service they please, for we hold it requisite that there should be throughout the whole realm a conformity to that order which the laws enjoin according to the Word of God.

John Pym could have assented completely to this proposition—it expressed exactly what he felt—and the Presbyterians too would have been gratified. But Seekers like Vane, in fact the entire Puritan left consisting of the Separatists, the Quakers, Anabaptists, Antinomians and all the sects or brethren of the inner light, would have been proscribed by it. Thus Vane's elation at his victory in the Root and Branch debate was tempered by this document which would have legalized in England the treatment accorded to Mistress Anne and himself in America. The enthusiasm with which Pym and his followers accepted this point of view again warned young Vane that the real struggle might not, after all, be with pope and bishop, but with the Protestant orthodox who always wished to throw nets of laws and rules over the human spirit. Vane took no part in the debate on the Grand Remonstrance. Whatever the spirit may have been whispering he repressed for the time being. He had learned in America that unseasonable expression was worse than silence, that an uncautious crusader might never arrive at the Holy City.

Meanwhile the bill for the exclusion of the bishops, which had passed the Commons almost unanimously, was again rejected by the Lords. Thereupon unprecedented crowds pressed to Westminster, among them the furious women. As the baiter of Puritans would later write,

The oyster women locked their fish up,
And trudged away to cry, "No Bishop."

The mobs heckled and harassed the bishops until in fear of their persons or their lives, many of them stayed away from Parliament. Any member known to favor the continued sitting of the bishops was also thréatened. On November 29, Sir John Strangways said that the privileges of Parliament, the issue which had precipitated the Parliamentary revolution, were "utterly broken if men might not come in safety to give their votes freely." Bulstrode Whitelocke agreed. The wild disorderliness among the great numbers of people gathered around Whitehall "was a dismal thing to all sober men" to see and hear, and especially to members of Parliament.

The incipient Royalists naturally cried out against these tumults, but John Pym replied, "God forbid that the House of Commons should proceed in any way to dishearten people to obtain their just desires in such a way." Even Sir Symonds D'Ewes, a conservative, did not wish "to discontent the citizens of London, our surest friends." As the massed people thundered in unison, "No bishops, No bishops," the chilling sound of the howling mob could be heard a mile away. D'Ewes consoled himself that perhaps the cry meant only no bishops sitting in the House of Lords. When it was pointed out to him that many of the mob wore swords, he suggested that possibly they did so because it was evening time. Sir Symonds was determined not to be disillusioned—not yet.

While the king was in Scotland, the execution of Strafford had been very much on his mind. Therefore when he returned to England in early December, 1641, one of his first acts was to dismiss the elder Vane from office; a day or so later, on December 10, he also relieved young Vane from his post as Treasurer of the Navy, allowing him one month in which to clear his accounts. Captain George Carteret wrote that Parliament was taking the recall of young Vane very badly for "he is much esteemed there," but that his father had lost the good opinion of both sides.

It was at this time that Philip Stapleton reported to Commons that a guard has been set around Parliament. The king, responding to appeals from the supporters of the bishops, had decided to stop intimidation by the people. The new guard was composed of 200 men armed with halberds, which "occasioned great fear and trouble in the House."

When news of the king's guard reached London, vast crowds surged once more towards Westminster. On December 23, the apprentices presented a Root and Branch petition containing 30,000 signatures. One day in late December, a mob broke into Westminster Hall, where the king's officers drew their swords and chased them out. The mobs continued to increase. On December 28 only two bishops took their seats in Lords, and some of the king's followers gathered troops of officers and soldiers of fortune who had come to London seeking employment in the Irish war, and pitted them against the people. Everywhere there were brawls, agitations, and tumults.

In Commons, however, other business than that of the bishops was going forward. It had previously been decided to supply the navy from tonnage and poundage and, while the exact nature of that tax was being debated, Mr. Yonge of Devonshire asked that a rider be appended to the tax bill requiring young Vane to be retained as Treasurer of the Navy. It is likely the first instance in English Parliamentary history in which a provision for an individual was proposed to be added to a revenue bill. The lawyers quickly defeated it.

Debates on the Grand Remonstrance also continued during December. Feeling inside Commons ran even higher than it had during the debate on the bishops, and it was expected that swords would be drawn before these debates finished. The Remonstrance finally passed by a vote of 159 to 148, Sir Symonds D'Ewes abstaining on the grounds that it lacked a precedent. After an even more bitter struggle the House voted 135–83 to print the document and send it throughout England. This decision showed that the Remonstrance was intended not so much for the king as for the people of England, to convince them that he had conspired against public liberties and had lost the right to select his own counselors or to control the militia. The printing of the Remonstrance was the ultimate humiliation for Charles, whose French queen was generous with reminders to him about how her father or her brother would have handled things.

The situation was now as tense as it could get without breaking. The mob and the guard faced each other at Westminster. Commons were divided from Lords, both houses from the king, and the Commons among themselves. Such a situation could not continue long; it only remained to see who would first lose nerve or who would impulsively make the irretrievable mistake.

Charles made it. As a counterthrust to the Remonstrance, some of his advisers proposed that he should impeach five members of Commons and one of Lords: Pym, Hampden, Holles, Strode, Haselrig, and Baron Montagu of Kimbolton, who would later become the Earl of Manchester. On January 3, 1642, the king's attorney appeared at the bar of the Lords and accused the impeached members of high treason because, it was alleged, having been in correspondence with the Scots while England was at war, they had traitorously invited and encouraged a foreign power to invade England. The Commons, who had not been too careful of legal forms themselves, now declared this demand illegal, but promised to take it into consideration. At the same time they requested a guard to protect them from the Cavalier bands. "I will reply tomorrow," said King Charles.

No man finds it easy to share a bed with a woman who impugns his manhood, and the king did not have a pleasant night. He heard once again how things would have been done in France, his wife saying, according to one account "that if he were King of England he would not suffer himself to be baffled about these persons." According to a more lively version, she said, "Go you coward and pull out these rogues by the ears, or never see my face any more."

Nor was Charles happy about the rumors he had heard that Commons intended to impeach his queen, and the possible danger to her made him somewhat desperate. Without consulting Hyde or his council, urged on by Digby and his furious queen, he set out for Westminster, joined along the way by some three or four hundred armed persons. Someone sent word to the Commons at about three of the clock in the afternoon that His Majesty was on his way with a company of armed men.

The House persuaded the five members to leave, and they slipped out into a boat waiting on the Thames. When the king and his party arrived at Westminster, his retainers filled the Hall but remained there; only the king passed through that door which no king had ever before passed uninvited.

"Mr. Speaker," said Charles to Lenthall, "I must for a time borrow your chair." Then he addressed the House in his restrained and delicate way, trying to bring all his poise and strength to a focus in this moment when it was so important that he should be a visible monarch.

Gentlemen, I am sorry for this occasion of coming unto you. Yesterday I sent a Sergeant-at-arms upon a very important occasion, to apprehend some that by my command were accused of high treason, whereunto I did expect obedience, and not a message.

Treason, he continued, had no privileges, and therefore he wished to know if the accused persons were present. Already his heart must have been cold with misgiving when he realized that they were gone, for he had not prepared for that contingency, and he did not quite know what to do.

"Is Mr. Pym here?" he asked; there was no reply from the House, only an ominous silence. Charles then turned to the Speaker and asked him if the five men were there. Lenthall, never a very forceful man, was granted a moment of grace that would establish his reputation forever. He knelt before the slight figure of his king, bowed his head courteously, and said gently, "I have neither eyes to see nor tongue to speak in this place, but as this House is pleased to direct me."

This dignified and wholly appropriate action contrasted strongly with Charles' nervous, hesitant manner, and he became petulant: "Well, well," he said, "tis no matter. I think my eyes are as good as another's. I see all the birds are flown. I do expect from you that you will send them to me as soon as they return hither."

He then bethought himself to say that he had never intended any force to the Parliament itself. He also perhaps remembered the queen who was awaiting a report, and left "in a more discontented and angry passion than he came in."

He left, too, with the cries of "privilege, privilege" ringing in his ears along with less restrained expressions. The next day there was a meeting of the City, attended by the Parliament men, in Guildhall. Although it was not a regular session of the House, business was transacted, and it was voted a breach of privileges of Parliament for anyone to arrest any of the five members. In all the confusion and anger and passion, young Vane was very cool. With an eye on the public record and on the future, he moved a short declaration that the Commons did not wish to protect any guilty man, but wished only to see the accused proceeded against in a legal way. It was precisely the right thing to say. Thereupon young Vane, Mr. Glyn, Sir Harbottle Grimston, Fiennes, and Stapleton were appointed a subcommittee to draw up a declaration which asserted that the five members could not be arrested without consent of the House.

The Lord Mayor, in this moment of extreme crisis, wisely refused to call out the Trained Bands. Nevertheless the city and suburbs were aroused. Over 40,000 men appeared armed with halberds, swords, and clubs. Some estimated the total number of the mob at 100,000 people. The cry of "arm, arm" was heard in every street. The Cavaliers who had affected to despise the contemptible mobs now hurriedly left the City; the guards around Parliament house quietly dispersed, leaving the king faced with a situation that perhaps not even Henrietta Maria's relatives could have handled—an armed and aroused city.

Then young Vane and the Lord Admiral, Earl of Warwick, a Puritan nobleman, went to work with all their energy to bring the navy into the affair on the Parliamentary side, and they were successful. Soon 200 barges appeared on the Thames, filled with armed sailors, some 2,000 of them ready to disembark and go into action on behalf of Parliament. There were no precedents by which anyone, let alone Charles, could decide what to do in such a situation, and so he took his queen and went to Hampton Court. He would never return to Whitehall again except as a prisoner.

No one knew what to expect now. Sir Symonds D'Ewes, a lawyer to the last, went home and made his will. Richard Bulstrode said that many of the king's friends resented the attempt on the five members because it rose from passion rather than reason. In a few days, he said, the king "had sunk from the height of all greatness." William Lilly, the astrologer, noted sadly that by that "unparalleled demand of his, he utterly lost himself and left scarce any possibility of reconcilement."

The most significant statement came from Lord Clarendon later.

> The truth is it cannot be expressed how great a change there appeared to be in the countenance and minds of all sorts of people, in town, and country, upon these late proceedings of the King. All that had been said before of plots and conspiracies against Parliament, once laughed at, was now believed."

Clarendon also believed that the key to Pym's policies in the days ahead was his remembrance of the attack on the five members and the inferences he drew from it.

Charles had two opposite policies, urged on by two sets of advisers: Hyde urged moderation and restraint; Henrietta Maria and some of the courtiers pressed the king to assert his royal power. The king might have followed either policy with some hope of success but that would have required the kind of firm decision he could not make. A little tired, more than a little uncertain, and painfully aware from the beginning of his reign that he might have been marked by destiny as the king who would lose it all, he had generally acted as others had directed him, which, as Richard Bulstrode said, "was, in a manner, reigning by courtesy." The bent of his temperament was to delay, to hope where hope was not justified, to deceive where necessary, and to vacillate. Still, there was something in that fragile poise, that sense of personal honor, which sometimes suggested that, given the right setting, this Dresden china figure might yet prove to be the manliest of men. That Vane, Cromwell, and the others could now change the nature of his government, even he would have conceded, but to destroy root and branch the church he loved might prove more difficult. If only Vane and the other revolutionaries had possessed some feeling for the "honorable stop," England might have been spared a long agony.

8

The Drift to War (1642)

After the king's attack on the five members, both sides waited for sentiment to crystallize and for the will of the country to assert itself. Charles sent his wife to the Low Countries with the Crown jewels, ostensibly for her safe-keeping but also to solicit support. She sailed on February 23, 1642; as the wind stood fair for the crossing and the *Lion*'s sails bellied, the king galloped along the cliffs, keeping the ship in sight until she had fallen below the steel-gray waves of winter.

There were still three major unreconciled differences between the king and Parliament: how the church should be settled, whether Parliament should have a voice in appointing the king's counselors, and who should control the militia and the strong places of the kingdom. On this last crucial question the Lords were more conciliatory than the Commons. When they sent down amendments which softened the proposals of the House, Vane proposed, in turn, that Commons should consent to these amendments provided that Lords also consented to whatever additions they might make. Sir Symonds D'Ewes opposed this startling suggestion as illegal. Commons had no right, he thought, to bind the upper House in this fashion. In his rather cavalier treatment of the peers, Vane was following the lead of Pym who had said,

The Commons will be glad to have your concurrence and help in saving the kingdom; but if they fail of it, it should not discourage them in doing their duty. And whether the kingdom be lost or saved, they shall be sorry that the story of this present Parliament should tell posterity that in so great a danger and extremity the House of Commons should be enforced to save the Kingdom alone.

As time went on, Vane's opposition to the House of Lords would intensify.

Frustrated by the attack on the five members, the rebellion in Ireland, and the expectation of papistical plots in England, on March 5 the Parliament issued its own Militia Ordinance according to which it would appoint Lords Lieutenants in every county, with power to assemble and arm the citizens. Sir Henry Vane senior was nominated as one fit to be entrusted with the militia in Durham. But when the Earl of Pembroke tried to induce King Charles to agree to Parliament's control of the militia for a limited time only, Charles snapped, "By God, not for an hour." A king with no army, he realized, was no king at all.

In April of 1642, when the Militia Bill was still the main topic of debate, Henry Killigrew made the sensible suggestion that members return to their home counties and find out how the people there felt. Young Vane opposed him strongly, taking "great exceptions" to this novel idea. Already Vane, like many revolutionaries, was beginning to develop a mystical attachment to the instruments by which the revolution was to be wrought; he felt that the Long Parliament was a conduit through which the Divine Wisdom was flowing into the state. It was through the Long Parliament rather than through the people that God would work to regenerate the English nation until it approximated the heavenly Jerusalem.

In April the counter-revolution began to take on strength. Especially in the outlying counties there was still much love of church and Crown and some distrust of the burgher Commons. Petitions were sent to Parliament supporting the older, traditional views of the English people. Though the Lords generally accepted such petitions, the Commons summarily rejected them as breaches of Parliamentary privilege. But as the conflict deepened, many members of Parliament were forced to decide where their allegiance ultimately lay, with Parliament or the king. Many who had supported the initial reforms had come to believe that the Commons were now acting illegally; many of them simply mistrusted the Puritan spirit; some who held their titles and lands in fee from the king feared he might declare them traitors and confiscate their estates. For whatever reasons, some eighty peers chose to follow the king, leaving only some thirty remaining with the Parliament. A few took no part in the struggle. Even some members of Commons elected to support the Royalist cause; many of these fled Westminster while others elected to stay and seek to moderate the revolutionary forces.

Though war with the king seemed imminent, Parliament continued to exert at least nominal efforts in behalf of peace. On June 1, both Houses agreed to Nineteen Propositions which they believed might serve as a basis for negotiation, propositions which contained the familiar demands for more harassment of Roman Catholics and for reform of the English church. But there were new and harsher demands also: Parliament asked for control of the highest military and civil offices, control of all fortresses, and the promise of a foreign policy which would support the Protestant cause in Europe. Proposition Ten demanded

> That such members of either House of Parliament as have, during the present Parliament, been put out of any place and office, may either be restored to that place and office, or otherwise have satisfaction for the same. . . .

Under this clause young Vane and others like him could be restored to office or at least compensated.

The harshest demand, perhaps, was that Parliament be allowed to name "delinquents" who would be excluded from amnesty and subject to trial and punishment; on the other side, the Royalists were asking similar powers. If the king agreed, it would have meant the sacrifice of a dozen more Straffords, and whatever his conscience might permit, it could not permit that. Yet a civil war, as Thomas Hobbes said, cannot end by treaty without the sacrifice of those who were on both sides the sharpest; it becomes a case of "my head or thy head." The king's refusal of the Nineteen Propositions set both sides to prepare for war.

With the king were his two young nephews, sons of that Elector Palatine whom Gustav Adolf had vainly tried to restore to his kingdom. The older, Prince Rupert, was only twenty-three, a tall, bony-faced young man with dark hair and dark brows, older than his years after spending some time in the continental wars and three years in an Austrian prison. He was a quick, restless aristocrat with dash and energy, a high sense of pride in his royal blood, and a gift for military command.

On the Parliamentary side, the highest peer was the Earl of Essex, son of Elizabeth's old courtier, a ponderous, pachydermous man with heavy jowls, heavy-lidded eyes and a well-fleshed frame, who was slow in thought and slower in action. He had refused the forced loan back in 1626 and his grievance against the Stuarts went back even farther. While still a boy, he had been married to Frances Howard, a spirited, sensual, and ambitious girl who decided soon after the marriage that she preferred active and quick-witted men like Robert Kerr, the handsome new favorite of James I, who might some day rule the man who ruled the nation. Encouraged by James, she sought a divorce from Essex, and in the trial that followed, Lady Essex accused her husband of impotence; he confessed that he was so with her but not with other women. The divorce was granted. Later Essex remarried and after fathering a child who died in infancy, he found it necessary to divorce his second wife for adultery. Persuaded by experience that the brief joys of marriage could not compensate for its enduring woes, he lived afterwards in single blessedness.

Essex had some military experience on the continent, though he had not himself led an army into battle nor was he much versed in contemporary tactics. Still, since it was customary to place men of high rank in command of troops, he was appointed on July 12 to lead the army that Parliament voted to muster for the defense of both Houses of Parliament and "for the safety of the King's person." (It was a principal Parliamentary fiction that the revolutionaries were warring not on the king, whom they wished to preserve and restore, but on evil counselors who had misled him.) The army was also to preserve true religion and the laws of the kingdom, a fight in which the members, including Vane, pledged themselves to live and die with the Earl of Essex. It was one of those moments of high resolve that unite strong men in a common cause, the "good cause" as they would call it hereafter. As the astrologer William Lilly put it,

Had Essex refused to be General, our cause in all likelihood had sunk in the beginning, we having never a nobleman at that time either willing or capable of that honor and preferment, indeed scarce any to be trusted. So God raised up Essex to be the scourge for the son of that King who had so abused him.

The Cavaliers took his nobility and greatness less seriously, for they tended to believe that a nobleman who had failed to make a sufficient number of women happy was no true nobleman and probably not much of a soldier. And so the Royalists poured poetic scorn upon him. An old ballad which had done much public duty needed only a change of names to suit the new case.

> The Earl of Essex searched for his wife,
> And where do you think he found her?
> Upon the bed of Robert Kerr,
> As flat as any flounder.

John Cleveland, one of the best poets of the king's party cried out,

> Impotent Essex! Is it not a shame
> Our commonwealth, like to a Turkish dame,
> Should have an eunuch guardian? May she be
> Ravished by Charles, rather than saved by thee,
> A gelding Earl.

Clarendon was kinder. He remembered Essex as a man who neither sought preferment nor was ambitious for his name. He wished only to be "kindly looked upon, kindly spoken to, and kindly to enjoy his own fortune." No man, said Clarendon, abhored rebellion as much as the earl; though his understanding had been intoxicated by the new doctrines, in his heart Essex never ceased to be loyal to the king. The time would come when Vane would think so too. Essex was the kind of man revolutionaries use but never fully trust.

After Essex's appointment, there was considerable delay while Parliament debated his demands: he wished to be named High Constable and given the right to treat with the king. These demands young Vane opposed, for he had been annoyed by Essex's opposition to his own Root and Branch Bill; nor could he forget that Essex was a peer who, in the established order of things, owed everything to the king. In normal times, Vane's opposition to Essex might have been considered simply political, but in these tense times when everything took on larger proportions, Essex took offense.

When Parliament rejected his demands, he replied symbolically. Ordering a coffin large enough to house his substantial remains, he carefully folded upon it a winding sheet whereon he placed his family escutcheon, signifying that he would die rather than blemish his name.

As he left London to open battle with the royal forces, the cheering citizens turned out, confident that one battle would end the war. The brightly uniformed regiments with the Parliamentary colors and the motto "God with us," the martial music, the prancing horses, the smartly stepping regiments, stirred the people who waved and shouted and cheered. Essex felt none of it. His jowls sagged more heavily; he sank more deeply into his saddle; his shoulders hunched, his forehead wrinkled, his face was melancholy and grave. He was the greatest nobleman in England and he was marching off to fight his king. Already some were predicting that when it came to blows, he would not be able to deliver the fatal one. And there were "some bloodsuckers," Denzil Holles would say later, who looked on him with a jealous and dubious eye. And no one doubted that he meant, among others, young Harry Vane.

The king proclaimed Essex a rebel and traitor, whereupon Parliament proclaimed the king's followers traitors. On August 22, the king erected his standard at Nottingham, a sign for retainers to rally round their lord. In the best manner of an old tradition, he carried his ensign out of the castle and onto a field. From the top of his standard hung a flag displaying the king's arms, quartered with a hand pointing to the Crown which stood above and bore the motto "Give Caesar his due." In the high excitement of the pageant few reflected that real Caesars do not have to be given their due; they simply take it.

The Puritan Parliament responded to the king's defiant pageantry by asserting the beauty of esthetic denial. They forbade all stage plays, which spectacles of pleasure, they said, were commonly expressions of lascivious mirth and lechery. Those who frequented the theatres were recommended instead to "the profitable and seasonable consideration of repentance, reconciliation, and peace with God." It was perhaps not an exciting alternative, but the Parliament was likely right in believing that it is the earnest men who win most battles. And William Prynne found himself justified at last.

In August, just before Essex marched northward, young Vane was appointed sole Treasurer of the Navy and, in September, he was appointed to the powerful Committee of Safety. This committee, which had been formed the preceding July with Pym, Hampden, Holles, and others among its members, was to take all measures necessary, including those of finance and supply, to ensure the safety of the Parliamentary cause. To this committee the Earl of Essex would be responsible, and it could not have pleased him when young Vane was added to it. Soon they would be bitter enemies.

At about the same time, Vane was made one of the unpaid commissioners of the navy, for which in considerable measure he was now responsible. And so the young idealist who had once rejected a military career was forced by the exigencies of political life to become one of those who controlled an army and a navy with every intent that they should efficiently destroy as many Englishmen as need be until the good cause had triumphed.

The first major battle of the civil war was fought at Edgehill on October 23, 1642. Because neither army was very professional, the action was both confused and indecisive, but from it emerged a cavalry tactic new to English fields. Formerly the horse had advanced at a trot to pistol range, where pistols were discharged and holstered. Then the troopers closed, fighting from their saddles with swords. Rupert had learned and adopted the different continental tactics of Gustav Adolf. Setting his cavalry in a line three deep, he charged at full gallop, penetrating the enemy ranks before drawing pistols. Only after the pistols were discharged in the melee were swords drawn. The shock of three lines of charging horse set the enemy in confusion and disorder. So it was at Edgehill: Rupert charged the right wing, routing the Parliamentary cavalry and some of the infantry, which turned and ran through its own reserve. Denzil Holles performed most gallantly, planting himself "just in the way" and trying to rally the fleeing soldiers. The routed foot were not checked, however, until John Hampden, with his steady regiment, marched up from some miles away and with artillery support deflected Rupert's pursuing cavalry.

In the Parliamentary center, the phlegmatic Essex stood firm. When some of his men fled, he seized a pike from a soldier and himself took the lead of his own regiment. Oliver Cromwell's troop of horse remained unbroken and fought well. Finally the old

Scottish veteran, Sir William Balfour, led a cavalry charge against the king's infantry and broke them. Many were killed and many were taken prisoner on both sides. By now the confusion and disorder were so great that both armies withdrew; Essex ineptly withdrew towards Warwick, leaving no force between the king's army and London. He immediately wrote to Westminster claiming victory and at the same time urging the Parliament to arm every available man to defend the capital.

After the battle, Englishmen heard many reports and many judgments. It had been observed that King Charles had ridden around in the heat of the battle ordering mercy for the captured, and that Lord Falkland, at some personal risk, had attempted to stop the slaughter inflicted by Rupert's hot-blooded troopers. It came to be known too that the Earls of Denbigh and Dover, with the king's guard, charged against their own sons under Essex. In the bitter cold of that night, the many wounded and dying who lay on the field were stripped of their clothing by the civilian scavengers. Sir Adrian Scrope, badly injured, awoke in the darkness to find himself freezing to death, but at least the cold had stanched his bleeding. Pulling a corpse over on top of him, he spent that night in the embrace of a dead man who saved his life. The next day when observers saw this field strewn with the naked and the dead, they realized with some surprise that they could not tell who had died for the king and who for the Parliament. All were Englishmen whose lives had been forfeited to the passions of the times. And there was no turning back. As Bulstrode Whitelocke had said, whoever draws his sword against his monarch must throw away the scabbard.

During the battle, Oliver Cromwell saw that impressed young men mounted on farm nags were no match for young men of blood who were filled with the pride of honor and animated by chivalry, and he told his cousin Hampden as much. "You must get men of a spirit . . . that is likely to go on as far as gentlemen will go, or else I am sure you will be beaten still." With the insight of a military genius he saw that all the Puritans had to pit against chivalric valor was religious fervor, and he began to look for young men to whom freedom of religion was dear enough that to save it they would hurl themselves against the enemy's pikes and muskets.

On October 29 a proposal was made in the House of Lords to reopen negotiations with the king. Edmund Waller urged the

Commons to concur and was seconded by Denzil Holles in Commons and by many citizens in the City. On November 2, without slackening preparations for the defense of the City, the Commons consented to send a negotiating committee to Charles. On November 4, the Parliamentary deputation arrived at Reading only to be told that one of their number, Sir John Evelyn of Wilts, a day or so before had been proclaimed a traitor and could not be admitted to the king's presence. At Westminster, both Lords and Commons inclined to believe that this was a fiction to justify a refusal to negotiate. It appeared now that the war might neither be settled by treaty nor won in some brave, decisive battle, but that it might be protracted and deadly. Therefore Parliament voted to invite the Scots army to invade northern England and come to the aid of the good cause. From this time on, John Pym apparently placed his chief hope in that possibility. In the meantime, however, the clamors for peace must at least be allayed, and so it was decided to send a deputation from the two Houses to address the citizens at Guildhall—Lord Brook from the Peers, young Sir Henry Vane from the Commons.

On November 8, the Guildhall was filled with concerned Londoners. Having been in the field with his troops, Lord Brook was newly come to London, and he apologized for the absence of other peers who were busy about the good of the kingdom. No doubt, said Lord Brook, the citizens had heard rumors of an accommodation; no honest man, no freeman, no lover of religion could be against that, for nothing is more miserable than war. But neither House had ever thought of an accommodation "upon terms ignoble and disadvantageous." Those now marching on the city intended to swallow up religion, lives, liberty, and estates. Lord Brook then told them that the king had refused to admit Sir John Evelyn to treat. The purpose of the committee's presence in Guildhall was to assure the citizens of London that although Parliament wished peace, the king apparently did not, for while he was willing to receive petitions from the rebels in Ireland, he had refused to receive a petition from the Parliament of England.

Then, representing the Commons, young Vane arose to speak. Parliament, he said, had for a long time fought to bring the liberties and religion and welfare of the kingdom into such a condition as would satisfy all the inhabitants. But from the beginning this work had its enemies, some of them capable of the greatest malice. He then repeated the story of the rejection of Sir John Evelyn which both Houses, he said, thought a matter of "great importance." (Sir John himself had not thought so; he had modestly and earnestly requested that his rejection should not be allowed to stand in the way of peace negotiations.) Vane insisted that no servant of Parliament should be summarily refused, especially when that refusal came not from the king but from those who had "hemmed in His Majesty" with ill and even desperate counsel. These ill counselors, said Vane, will destroy "all that is near and dear to you in this Kingdom."

The members of the House of Commons, he continued, wished the citizens to know of their loyalty to His Majesty and their care for all that belongs to the people, but now, seeing that all their efforts for peace have had no effect, they ask that the citizens "join resolutely with your purses, with your endeavors, and all that lies in your power to acquit yourselves like men, to defend yourselves, to defend them that have labored in your work, in your cause, and who are willing to spend their lives and blood in your service to the utmost man." Violence and oppression, he concluded, are at the doors and we unanimously ask you to defend yourselves. He did not say that he himself would join them in taking up arms. Nevertheless it was an effective speech, gentle to the king but harsh on his counselors, and it linked the need for money to the liberties and welfare of the people.

Even after all the rhetoric, however, cries for peace were still heard. So, two days later, Pym himself went to Guildhall where he explained once more that Parliament wished to establish any peace which would secure religion and liberty. Mere words, however, could not do that. "To have printed liberties and not to have liberties in truth and realities, is but to mock the kingdom." Pym's careful but forceful words carried more conviction than the heroics of Lord Brook.

Realizing that the Parliamentary reason for refusing to treat was rather slender, Pym authorized the commissioners to wait on the king without Sir John Evelyn. Charles replied modestly and courteously, suggesting Windsor as a negotiating place. Although the House had ordered Essex to observe a truce, Charles said nothing about a cessation of hostilities, and what happened next elicited charges of bad faith from both sides. Essex and Skippon marched out of London, presumably to take up defensive positions. Rupert rather easily persuaded himself that this constituted a violation of whatever agreement there was, and he charged out of the mist with his cavalry and ran with full shock against the regiments óf Denzil Holles and Lord Brook. Holles' regiment fought bravely, as it had at Edgehill, but the Cavaliers rode the soldiers down, slashing with their swords, driving the confused remnants toward the river. Their prisoners they herded into the pinfold where stray animals were kept; then they raided the cellars, got uproariously drunk, and proceeded to pillage and sack with the random, boisterous destructiveness of young, victorious and anonymous soldiers.

Charles then advanced to Turnham Green where his army and that of Essex faced one another, both weary, unsupplied, and unpaid, neither quite ready to engage. But Charles turned and marched away, relinquishing the only chance he would ever have to seize London and victory.

In this second battle, there was less chivalry shown. When Lord Brook's regiment had fled, one young captain stood his ground. It was Honest John Lilburne, the former prisoner of the Star Chamber who had been released at Cromwell's petition. Now the Royalists proposed to hang him, for treason they said, but more likely because he was such a symbol of stout resistance. The Parliament responded by saying that if Royalists executed prisoners they would too, and so Lilburne was returned to prison which, for his impatient spirit, was torment enough.

It was inevitable that Essex, as commander of a losing army, should come under criticism. In the north and the west of England, Royalist troops were thrusting, attacking, consolidating. Essex, whose winter movements were saurian, stayed at Windsor. Henry Marten, sharp-witted, impatient, and generally unpleasant, remarked that it was "summer in Devonshire, summer in Yorkshire, and cold winter at Windsor."

The tumults in London grew worse. Some of those who had once bayed "No bishops" were now crying "Peace, Peace." They jostled and insulted members known to be favorable to the Parliamentary cause; they broke up committee meetings in the City; they did things which, such a short time ago, had been effective and applauded. But not now: the representatives of the people called for the Trained Bands to disperse their disorderly constituents.

All the world now wanted peace, said a Royalist writer, but not young Vane nor Pym nor Henry Marten nor Cromwell. They had embraced a cause which, although it had run into heavy weather, they believed was inherently strong enough to triumph. And Vane had become too engaged in passionate events to reflect upon what was happening. Much as he hated war, he had become one of the leaders of a "war party." Violence sickened him and he could never, he said, shed blood; but believing that the price of peace might be the death of the cause, he now insisted that blood be shed. Those old comrades, commitment and absurdity, were traveling together again.

9

Young Vane and the Scots Alliance (1643)

Vane soon realized that the course he had reluctantly chosen was by no means popular, for during the cold winter of 1642–1643, the agitation for peace increased. Now the London citizens were assembling spontaneously to cry "Peace!" wherever Parliamentary committees met in the city or wherever the aldermen assembled. Many of those who opposed the war party were themselves becoming violent; they would cut throats, they said, but they would have peace.

On December 20, the Lords, dominated by the peace party, sent down terms to be debated by the Commons. Vane urged that these terms should not even be considered, because he feared that if the Parliament once began to negotiate, it might grow careless of its own defense. He was answered by Sir Symonds D'Ewes, who voiced what many were feeling. Because of a war that was scarcely three months old, poverty and famine were already coming with winged feet; the whole land was in confusion; tenants would not pay rents. He feared that if the two armies clashed it might be impossible ever to achieve a peace. D'Ewes sat down amid loud applause, and the motion for peace negotiations carried.

As the debate on proposals for peace proceeded, the Parliament seemed little inclined to generosity. Episcopacy was to be wholly abolished and both armies were to be disbanded before negotiations could even begin. The king was to agree that "delinquents," that is, his own followers, should be tried according to the judgment of Parliament; the militia was to be settled in a way agreeable to both Houses.

Charles received these proposals on February 1 and returned equally impossible counterproposals; he did, however, offer to declare a cessation of hostilities during negotiations. Vane opposed this offer; only when armies were disbanded, he said, could Parliament carry on free from the threat of force. The Lords, trying to salvage something, suggested that the Commons withdraw the demand for disbandment. Impatiently, Vane countered by proposing that a new ordinance for raising money be passed; that would at least demonstrate that Parliament was firmly determined to carry on the war. Accordingly, on February 24 a general tax ordinance was passed which assessed all the counties after the manner of the old ship-money ordinance; even the ship-money lists were used. But this tax made ship money appear very moderate. Ship money had been an annual assessment, but this formidable tax was weekly. Whereas ship money had been designed to bring in only about 200,000 pounds, this one was expected to return 1,600,000 to support the costs of swollen armies and navies.

Hampden's protest against ship money somehow seemed less heroic that it once had; he was a relatively wealthy man and his ship-money taxes were only some twenty pounds a year. Of course he had acted on principle and not because of the sums involved. But still, on that same principle many London merchants might now have wished to resist and dared not. William Lilly remembered that under ship-money taxation his assessment was twenty-two shillings, no more. Now his annual payments "to the soldiery," as he put it, were twenty pounds sterling though his estate was no greater than before.

Meanwhile the House of Lords believed that it had found a successful compromise which would enable peace negotiations to proceed. They proposed a cessation of hostilities for twenty days during which time further discussions could proceed on disbandment. After passing in Commons by the narrow margin of three votes, this proposal was sent on to Oxford. The day after it arrived, Charles wrote to his queen who had recently arrived in England with arms and money.

Yesterday there were articles of a cessation brought me from London, but so unreasonable that I cannot grant them. Yet to undeceive the people, by showing it is not I, but those who have caused and fostered this rebellion that desire continuance of this war and universal distraction, I am framing articles fit for that purpose; only this, I assure thee, that the distractions of the rebels are such that so many fine designs are laid open to us we know not which first to undertake; but certainly, my first and chiefest care is and shall be to secure thee, and hasten our meeting.

Like so many of Charles' compromising letters, this one was intercepted: its duplicity disheartened the peace party and strengthened the war party who found in it one of their most useful and powerful phrases. From now on, any proposal from the king, it would be said, was another "fine design."

Even after this, the desire for peace was so strong that on March 18 both Houses empowered their commissioners to compromise on control of the garrisons and ships. Apparently realizing that the measure would pass, Vane disgustedly absented himself from the House that day, a practice that would become rather common with him. But Charles refused this conciliating gesture and so, on March 27, Parliament, despairing of peace, passed an ordinance of sequestration. Anyone who supported the king would have his lands confiscated, and the money so obtained would be used to support the government. Now a good many Royalists whose lands lay in areas controlled by the Parliament quietly deserted the king, valuing their estates above political ideology.

As a kind of emotional reprisal for the aid Queen Henrietta Maria had brought from France, the House deputed Henry Marten to arrest the Capuchin friars at Somerset House and to tear down "the idols" in the chapel. One of them, an altarpiece by Rubens, was thrown into the Thames; others were mutilated or destroyed. Naturally the French king dispatched a protest which his representative, M. de Bures, wished to present to the House. Under the legalistic quibble that the House did not know for certain that M. de Bures was indeed a legal representative of France, Vane opposed receiving the letter. His purpose was to protect Marten from the House of Lords for this act of vandalism. Marten was the most rashly outspoken of republicans and the bitterest of the king's enemies, for in August of 1642 the king had openly accused him of high treason. He was famed for his often impudent wit, for becoming drunk too easily, and for inveterate wenching. It was said, in 1639, that his wild ways were costing his father a thousand pounds a year. At about that same time the king had called him an ugly rascal and a whoremaster, and ordered him turned out of Hyde Park. And Marten had once confided to Edward Hyde that he did not think "one man wise enough to govern us all." But he was a useful ally against royalty, and so on April 14, when the House received the king's final reply to their offers, couched in terms they could not accept, it was Marten who delivered the obsequies of any hope for peace negotiations. "Let us not trouble ourselves to send an answer; but rather answer them with scorn, as being unworthy of our further regard." Vane concurred.

The next drama in which Vane was to play a role was the exposure of a Royalist plot, a confused, inefficient plot which succeeded only in strengthening Parliamentary resolve. The poet Edmund Waller had been with the king's party but, with the king's consent, had returned to Westminster. As a member of Parliament he had attached himself to the peace party, meanwhile keeping in touch with Lord Falkland who, among those close to Charles, was most ardent for peace. Waller believed that the majority of the people wanted an end to the war and that, if they could be organized, they might perhaps effect a peace.

At the same time and perhaps without informing Waller in advance, the king issued a Commission of Array which would authorize the arming of persons in London who supported him. This document was smuggled into the city by Lady Daubigny, carried in the safest place that women know. In London she had turned it over to one Chaloner, a linen draper, who in turn had given it to Waller's brother-in-law, Tomkins. It was found in his cellar. When the plot was disclosed, the frightened French lady took refuge in the house of the French ambassador, where the Commons sent Vane and John Lisle to demand her person. But the ambassador, a true Gaul, refused to yield up a woman, especially to Puritans incapable of appreciating the good things of the world.

When Waller was apprehended, he told everything he knew and some things he didn't; to the disgust of the Cavaliers and the amazement of the French, he indicted some "women of real honor," including the lady with the documented bosom. Attorney John Glyn moved that members of Parliament who held military command should be formed into a court-martial to try the case.

Vane, always very harsh in matters of treason, supported this extralegal procedure. Waller's two accomplices were tried in one day and executed two days later. Although Waller himself was only fined, his reputation among the ladies was heavily damaged which, for a Cavalier poet, may have been punishment enough.

Edward Hyde never believed that Waller was seriously connected with the king's Commission of Array; he thought that Parliament, finding the plot useful, made too much of it. Whatever the truth, this plot that never had the slightest chance of success destroyed any lingering hopes of peace. It also contributed to the general atmosphere of insecurity which on June 14 induced a strict licensing of the press in an ordinance probably worse than the one under which Laud had once reviewed all books and pamphlets. The ordinance threatened, among others, an anonymous radical who had written a tract in favor of divorce, which opened the door, it was said, to all immorality and the destruction of religion. The young poet whose unhappy married life had motivated that tract, now doubly alarmed, began to pen a defense of freedom of the press. When it was finished, he would address it to the Parliament and call it *Areopagitica*. Many other Englishmen, despairing of the taxes, the impressments, the refusal to entertain petitions which embodied opposing views, and now the licensing act, felt the truth of one man's cry, "If this be liberty, give me the old slavery."

With the Great Seal now in the hands of the Royalists, a legal question arose as to how the ordinances of Parliament should be made official. Stamping a document with a prescribed emblem was purely a formality, but it was the kind of powerful formality that had been sanctioned by long usage. Vane, with his contempt for forms, simply urged that a new seal be made; the old one held no mystical significance for him. As debate continued, Vane asked that the ordinance be so phrased that either of the two Houses could by itself authorize a new seal so that Commons alone, without either Lords or king, could legally pass ordinances binding on the nation.

Men were perceiving that young Vane was contemptuous of legal forms; he would, they said, take the shortest way. Looking back on these events, Clarendon said that Vane was "above ordinances." And so in the minds of lawyers first, and then others, although no one had yet put it into words, Vane seemed to be a political as well as a religious antinomian, in some ways the quintessential revolutionary, for he had no hindering sentiments about the past or even as yet about procedures for the future. He knew what had to be done; he knew what the result was supposed to look like. Thus his early political courses were quite remorselessly set and unwaveringly held.

Despite Vane's growing notoriety and influence he was not yet considered a major threat by the Royalists. In June of 1643, the king issued a proclamation which offered amnesty to all his opponents except for a specified few: the five members, Henry Marten, and some others, but Vane was not among them. Perhaps it was because the king whom he had once served thought he could win back a former servant; perhaps he was not yet considered important enough to be proscribed.

As the peace negotiations dwindled into demands and recriminations, the country suffered. The prisons in and about London were full of "malignants and delinquents," as the Parliament men styled their opponents. Because the prisons could not hold them all, Windsor Castle, London House, the Deanery of St. Paul's, Ely House, Lambeth House, and Winchester House were all turned into jails. England itself, it was said, might soon become a large prison as "the eyes of a bleeding and miserable nation" looked hopefully towards peace negotiators who now had no hope to give.

Both sides were feeling the carnage of the war. On the Parliamentary side, Lord Brook, the most tolerant Puritan, had been shot through the head at Lichfield. But even this loss could not compare with the disaster of John Hampden's death at Chalgrove Field.

> His purer thoughts were free
> From all corruptions: he not valued friends,
> A fair estate or self-propounded ends,
> Any preferment, or aught else above
> A quiet conscience and his nation's love.

Among the king's men, Sidney Godolphin had been killed at Saltash, struck by an aimless, unintended bullet. Falkland had loved this brother poet, wit, and gentleman who had, Clarendon said, "so large an understanding, so unrestrained a fancy in so very small a body." Northampton was killed at Hopton Heath, and at the storming of Bristol, Sir Nicholas Slanning and John Trevanion were killed. At Landsdown, Sir Bevil Grenville, equal in courage and martial strength to his Elizabethan ancestor, was struck down.

> Four of the wheels of Charles's wain,
> Grenville, Godolphin, Slanning, Trevanion slain.

In January of 1641, Lord Broghill had married the daughter of a Howard, and for his absent friend, Richard Lovelace, John Suckling had described the affair in one of the most delightful of art ballads:

> Her feet beneath her petticoat
> Like little mice stole in and out,
> As if they feared the light.
> But oh, she dances such a way!
> No sun upon an Easter day
> Is half so fine a sight.

But now the bridegroom and the poet were both dead, and because he had presented an unacceptable petition to Parliament, Lovelace was in exile. Soon the incomparable Falkland would be dead too.

His death would lead Edward Hyde to complain of an unequal fate which destroyed "persons of honor and public name" on the Royalist side while on the Puritan side only "some obscure, unheard-of colonel or officer was missing," or perhaps "some citizen's wife bewailed the loss of her husband." Seldom did Hyde betray such crass insensitivity, such lack of the decencies of heart and head. After every battle, when the human scavengers had left the field, the naked corpses lay alike vulnerable to the fierce birds and the fiercer elements. Whitelocke rightly said that gallantry and courage were common to both sides: "All were Englishmen, and pity of it was that such courage should be spent in the blood of each other"; he might have reflected that all the dead were quite simply *men* and that the tragedy was universal.

The living were enduring still other grievances. Everywhere the soldiers plundered and poached. The Parliamentary soldiers, when not fighting the king's men, fought their ideas and symbols: at Worcester they sacked the cathedral, defecating with acrobatic ingenuity on what to others were sacred places and objects; they also ripped down the "sweet-toned organ." They sacked Rochester Cathedral and destroyed its library. At Canterbury they served their God by destroying the illuminated service books, hacking the tapestries, and, with better marksmanship than they often showed in battle, shooting at the crucifixion over the South Gate. They also broke into private homes and estates of Royalist or Catholic families, demolishing paintings and windows, and even breaking open the family tombs and scattering the bones of the reposing dead in the dusty ways and trampled fields.

And they plundered the very essentials of the people's lives: both Royalist and Parliament armies raided for cattle and horses, slaughtered sheep, fowl, and game. Both sides quartered their troops in private homes, homes already overcrowded, where all the industry of the family could scarcely provide for its own. These uniformed bellies, armed and justifying their actions by appeals to the goodness of the cause, were consuming the best of everything. As Thomas May said, there were more seats of war than there were counties; every field had seen a skirmish, almost every city a siege. This war, which like others had begun in high resolve and deep commitment, had declined into brutality, sordidness, and despair. Thomas Hobbes, reflecting that 100,000 men had been killed, said bitterly that it would have been better, 100 to 1, to have slit the throats of the seditious priests who had inflamed the people. Though simplistic, his view is not without truth: the "priests" on both sides were often the most emotionally unstable, the most aggressive, the most inflamed, and the most unwilling to compromise; the luxury of satisfying the feelings aroused by their fanaticism came high.

In the summer of 1643 the Parliamentary cause was in trouble. Bristol and Exeter surrendered to Prince Rupert and Prince Maurice. The Fairfaxes were badly defeated at Adwalton Moor, and at Roundway Down, the army of the West under Waller was almost annihilated. And as the cause seemed in danger of being lost, what had been vague dissatisfaction began to crystallize into antagonism towards the Earl of Essex. Since the battle of Edgehill in the preceding October he had fought no major engagement. His reasons seemed valid enough: many of his army had deserted because Parliament had not paid them; they were untried and untrained; besides, plague had broken out in their camps. But while his complaints were real, the feeling grew that he complained too much, that he was perhaps disinclined to attack the king, that a more vigorous and energetic man might do better. Lucy Hutchinson expressed a general sentiment:

It was too apparent how much the whole Parliamentary cause had been often hazarded, how many opportunities of finishing the war had been overslipped by the Earl of Essex his army; and it was believed that he himself, with his commanders, rather endeavored to become arbiters of war and peace than conquerors for the Parliament.

It was also known that when Vane and Pym had initiated new actions against Laud, Essex had said no one believed the archbishop guilty of treason. For all these reasons there was, as the Venetian ambassador said, "a great deal of secret ill-feeling" against him.

As early as the preceding February the City had impugned Essex's conduct of the war in a petition to Parliament: Parliament had instructed him to march from Windsor to attack Reading, but he had not done so. Pym, recognizing Essex's value to the revolutionaries as both a symbol of the Old England and a protagonist of the new, tried to restrain the attacks on him and did his best to provide him supplies and money. Then in June, Hampden was killed. As a colonel in one of Essex's regiments, Hampden had exerted a great deal of influence over the earl, and he was a man of such unimpeachable integrity that it was almost impossible to indict the earl without seeming to touch him. But now that Hampden was gone, Essex was free to act in his natural, dogged, and blundering way. On July 9, he wrote a letter to Parliament, undiplomatic and naïve, but typically forthright. He complained that the Royalist infantry always retreated before him, as though this were an unfair tactic, while at the same time their cavalry struck him from all sides. (Essex's own cavalry, it had been rumored, was lacking in discipline because he was too lenient with subordinate officers.) Essex then proposed to the Parliament that terms of peace somewhat more yielding than those offered at Oxford should be sent to the king. As this suggestion was read in Commons some of the more "violent spirits" plucked their hats over their eyes and hemmed. But there was more. If Parliament was not inclined to peace, the earl said, let the king withdraw where his sacred person would be safe and let the two armies put all to the hazard and abide by the result. This new version of the old trial by combat revealed a frustrated and despairing general.

Pym quietly said that the proposal was hazardous; Vane sarcastically remarked that Essex was really telling the Parliament he would do his duty if they would negotiate first. This accusation aroused

Essex's supporters who had themselves fought in the field, and Philip Stapleton forced Vane to apologize once; others forced him to apologize again. The time had not yet come when a young revolutionary could successfully attack one of the country's great and titled men.

Essex, impatient with the confident advice of civilians who direct wars at a distance and fight battles in retrospect, heard of Vane's jibe and sent a letter to Parliament on July 13. I shall arrive on Friday, he said, and

> I shall entreat the favor that Sir Henry Vane the Younger may be an eyewitness of our actions, he being an intimate friend of mine, and who by his constant carriage in the Parliament, which hath gotten him a good reputation in all places, may be a true testimony of our actions, it being of huge advantage to keep a good correspondence between Parliament and their servants the Army.

These, as everyone recognized, were heavy sarcasms. Vane was certainly no intimate friend of Essex who, according to Clarendon, hated him above all others. Vane scarcely had a reputation for constancy nor was he well thought of in all quarters. Essex reserved his sharpest thrust for the last:

> He is, besides, a man I put so much trust in, as that, if he pleaseth, I shall go hand in hand with him to the walls of Oxford.

Everyone could see now, D'Ewes wrote, that "this was spoken in a scoffing way." There was first tittering and then general laughter. Young Vane was not there that day, but his father, who was, "looked very blank." There was no one to explain it to him.

The point of the thrust was sharp. Many Parliament men had served in the field: Haselrig, Fiennes, Stapleton, Cromwell, Hampden, Strode, and Marten, among others. Of those who had never been under fire but seemed hot for war, young Vane was most conspicuous. Essex proposed to bring him under fire, to let one of those who cried havoc taste a little of what he asked for. Now that the latent suspicions between the two men were public, their differences grew more bitter and deadly.

Worse news for Parliament was still to come. In Scotland a Royalist plot was discovered in which the Earl of Montrose was to foment an insurrection and support it with Catholic troops from Ireland. Coming as it did shortly after Waller's plot, it excited great agitation. Sir Symonds D'Ewes wrote,

> The discovery of this plot did more work upon most men than anything that had happened during these miserable calamities and civil wars of England, because it seemed now that there was a fixed resolution in the Popish party utterly to extirpate the true Protestant religion in England, Scotland and Ireland.

On the day that D'Ewes wrote these words, Parliament agreed to send a deputation of members from both houses to Scotland. Remembering both the cost of the previous Scottish army and the difficulty in getting it off English soil, Parliament was cautious about asking Scotland for more military aid. And perhaps the resolution originally intended no more than an embassage of courtesy to invite some Scottish ministers to attend the sessions of the Assembly of Divines at Westminster, which was to begin meeting on July 1 in order to settle the new forms and doctrines of the English church. But then came news of the disasters to Fairfax in the North and Waller in the West, the latter of which had occurred on July 13, just four days after Essex had written his despondent and despairing letter to the Parliament.

For some time Pym had endeavored to bring the Scots into the war. Now the disasters in the field brought others to realize that the only hope for a Parliamentary victory lay with the Scots army, and within a week orders were given for the embassage to proceed. Originally it was to consist of ten members—four from Commons, two from the Assembly, two from the City and two from the House of Lords—but neither of the Lords went, and the City declined to send anyone; finally the delegation consisted of four members of Commons and two clerical advisers, Stephen Marshall, "the archepiscopal presbyter of England," and Philip Nye, an Independent. Vane was the acknowledged head of the delegation, and he and Marshall were to act as draftsmen. "Sir Harry Vane was one of the commissioners," Clarendon wrote, "and therefore the others need not be named, since he was all in any business where others were joined with him."

Vane was an almost inevitable choice. By his betrayal of Strafford, who was as badly hated in Scotland as in England, and by his advocacy of Root and Branch, he had already endeared himself to the Scots. At the time of Strafford's trial, Robert Baillie had spoken of Vane as "a very gracious youth," and to a Scots Presbyterian the word "gracious" was deeply charged with meaning. Later, when Vane had been added to the Committee on Religion, Baillie rejoiced, for Vane, he said, was one of "our firm friends." So, when the English commissioners arrived at Leith on August 7, 1643, Baillie was designated to meet them and, although he put all their names into his diary, he commented only on Vane who, he said, was "one of the ablest and gravest" of the English nation.

Clarendon later remembered Vane as he appeared at this time.

He was indeed a man of extraordinary parts, a pleasant wit, a great understanding which pierced into and discerned the purposes of other men with wonderful sagacity, while he had himself *vultum clausum* [a closed countenance], that no man could make a guess of what he intended. He was of a temper not to be moved, and of rare dissimulation, and could comply when it was not seasonable to contradict, without losing ground by the condescension. And if he were not superior to Mr. Hampden, he was inferior to no other man in all mysterious artifices. There need no more be said of his ability than that he was chosen to cozen and deceive a whole nation which excelled in craft and cunning; which he did with notable pregnancy and dexterity.

Clarendon went on to say that Vane was astute enough to know that the only way he could prevail upon the Scots was by appearing to advance Presbyterianism, which in his heart he already despised. Through the hope they had in young Vane, said Clarendon, the Scots were persuaded to sacrifice "their peace, their interest and their faith" to the erecting of a power that would ultimately "persecute presbytery to an extirpation." The Independent party, armed with the sword of Cromwell, would indeed destroy for a time the political power of Presbyterianism in England. Clarendon's remarks were cynical, hostile, and too sweeping, but something like the same charges would be echoed by many other observers.

Vane and his committee were given some general instructions by Parliament: first, he was to explain to the Scots why England hadn't paid her past debts, never an agreeable assignment; he was also to speak of Parliament's desire and intention to reform the church; and he was to remind the Scots of the danger (revealed by the Montrose plot) that papists and malignants posed to both kingdoms. His instructions included also a strict limitation: he was to reach an agreement with Scotland which would maintain both the liberties and the religion of England.

All this was public knowledge. Privately Pym, Vane, and others knew that time was crucial. Parliament was in desperate case, seeking mutual assistance when the knife was at its throat though it had no assistance to give. Under such difficult circumstances, Vane was to secure help and to secure it speedily.

The best mind among the Scots negotiators belonged to Archibald Johnston, later Lord Wariston, a strange, intense, erratic, and capable man. Bishop Burnet, his nephew, wrote that his great energies scarcely permitted him to sleep for more than two or three hours in any twenty-four. Sometimes he would pray with his family for two hours at a time and "whatsoever thought struck his fancy during these effusions, he looked on it as an answer of prayer, and was wholly determined by it and so was out of measure zealous in it." In those long nights when he couldn't sleep, when study had become tedious, Wariston would wrestle with his God; he would experience violent tremblings, cold shudderings, actual physiological expressions of his inward agony. Sometimes he was overpowered with the sense of his own sinfulness in coveting public office; other times he thought he was among the elect. His journal is a kind of Augustinian confession of a life tormented by self-loathing and fear followed by the descent of the dews of grace. Every day and almost every hour he was conscious of the state of his soul. Reading Wariston helps one to understand why the serene and rational Emerson turned away from the New England Puritans because of their sickly, obsessive concern with self.

Vane knew that he had reached a critical moment for both his cause and himself. Laud, still confined in the Tower, was only a helpless shadow of a foe, and episcopacy itself was on the defensive; with Presbyterian aid it could be demolished. Vane was sincerely eager for an alliance with the Scots, for he believed, as did Pym, that it would assure victory to the Parliamentary cause, after which there might be a satisfactory new settlement of the church. Yet he realized that if the alliance were secured on the wrong terms he might lose to the orthodox Protestants what he intended to wrest from the Anglicans—freedom for independent and individual worship. Within a year Milton would discover that the new presbyter was merely the "old priest writ large," but Vane had learned it already from Congregationalist elders in New England. The religion Vane lived by, sensitive to the least stirring of the winged and unconfined spirit, could not survive in the nets of either episcopacy or presbyterianism.

Vane must have been a very lonely man at this moment. Had he disclosed his whisperings from the spirit to Pym or the Parliament, they certainly would not have sent him to Scotland. Pym had spoken publicly against Anabaptists and antinomians and was wary of those who professed to act by inner direction; Vane was, to be sure, bargaining for England and the Puritan party, but he would also bargain for the future of himself and the little inchoate band of the thrice-born. Later he explained to his friend and biographer George Sikes the principles he acted on. He had in his mind, Sikes said, a pattern of the earthly polity that exactly corresponded to the Heavenly Jerusalem. Presumably he had come by this information through his personal union with the Holy Spirit and his allegorical understanding of scripture. But he had learned caution; it might not be wise to reveal God's intentions all at once, prematurely, for men might misunderstand them. "His principles, light and wisdom," Sikes continued,

> were such that he found the bare mention of his utmost aims among his fellow laborers, would (in all probability) so expose him to censure from all parties and sizes of understanding, as would disable him from doing anything at all. He was therefore for small matters rather than for nothing, went step by step, their own pace, as the light of the times would permit.

Thus, because Vane could never make full disclosure of his ultimate purposes, he always found it necessary if not to dissimulate, at least to conceal something, and that constant concealment puzzled and disturbed his contemporaries. Because of it they could never quite make out what he was after; and his changes of tactics, his readiness to use whatever effective means lay to hand, led to his being called weather-Vane and Sir Harry Weathercock, or, as Anthony Wood put it, the Proteus of his time. Vane himself believed that he was not dissembling, but merely reserving full disclosure until the time was ripe for it, and that the end he sought, the Heavenly Jerusalem on earth, justified the means he was forced to use. He believed, too, that the mind of God, expressing itself in the events of the times, would eventually lead other men to his position. Meanwhile he proceeded a step at a time and not always in the same direction. It is easy to see why this emotional and mystical man developed that closed face, and why men increasingly distrusted him.

Negotiations began in an atmosphere of caution. The first Scots proposal was that their army, as declared neutrals, should march across the English border and offer to mediate. Wariston, in his nervous, forceful way, "alone did show the vanity" of this empty scheme.

Next came the question of whether the agreement between the two nations should be a covenant (a religious alliance) or a league (a political alliance). The Scots wished the former, the English the latter. Vane, remembering always the need for concluding the negotiations swiftly, proposed A Solemn League and Covenant, a compromise in which the order of the words might indicate a small victory for the English point of view.

The religious negotiations were more difficult. The Scots' demand for the abolition of episcopacy in England created no problem, for both Houses had already gone on record in favor of it. But when the Scots asked that the Presbyterian discipline, or something close to it, be imposed in England, Vane demurred, countering with a shrewd proposal of his own. Henderson, the Scots draftsman, had written that both nations should pledge themselves to preserve

the Church of Scotland in doctrine, worship, discipline and government, and the reformation of religion in the Church of England according to the example of the best reformed Churches. . . .

And Henderson, Baillie, or Wariston could readily have named the country where the best reformed churches were to be found.

Vane redrafted Henderson's proposal and added eleven words to it. Scotland and England, he wrote, would jointly pledge to preserve the Church of Scotland in doctrine, worship, discipline, and government *according to the word of God,* and the reformation of religion in the Church of England according to *the same Holy Word and* the example of the best reformed Churches.

Accept these changes, said Vane to the Scots, and we have a treaty.

The Scots negotiators understood very well the drift of Vane's proposal, but they could not well resist it, for they had before them the Scots covenant of 1638, one clause of which read:

to the which confession and form of religion we willingly agree in our consciences in all points, as unto God's undoubted truth and verity, grounded only upon His written Word.

If, as no Scot could deny, the church of Scotland was founded not upon tradition or apostolical succession but solely upon the Word of God, it would be difficult to find any reason to refuse Vane's phrasing. Further, in Pym's Grand Remonstrance which the Scots had considered an inspired document, clause 184 had asserted that

we hold it requisite that there should be throughout the whole realm a conformity to that order which the laws enjoin according to the Word of God.

And so the Scots agreed. They, too, felt the urgency of the times. Rumor had already brought word that Bristol was lost, and it was feared that the king might march to London and take the city. With good reason the Scots felt that they were acting generously and selflessly. Baillie wrote,

Surely it was a great act of faith in God and huge courage and unheard of compassion, that moved our nation to hazard their own peace, and venture their lives and all, for to save a people irrecoverably ruined both in their own and all the world's eyes.

Did Vane, then, deceive the Scots? Surely it would be truer to say that they deceived themselves. They were neither fools nor impulsively generous; they fully expected that their victorious army would enforce their interpretation of the agreement. They were not yet aware of Fairfax and Cromwell and the kind of Puritan discipline now arising in the English ranks. It is also possible that the Scots were overconfident, tainted with spiritual pride, believing that the scriptures were so consistent, clear, and Calvinistic that they would inevitably lead the English to a form of church government like their own. Vane knew otherwise. In New England he had seen interminable disputes over the meanings of scriptural passages torn out of context and fired like bullets at opponents. Many others had observed the same thing. "Sentences in scripture," said John Donne, "like hairs in horses' tails, concur in one root of beauty and strength, but being plucked out one by one, serve only for springes and snares." John Selden said it more simply: "*Scrutamini scripturas* [search ye the scriptures]: these two words have undone the world." It is doubtful that the Scots were deceived, but Vane had indeed left open a door for Independency, as would soon be seen in the Westminster Assembly when the divines would wander in devious labyrinths of scriptural disputes.

For the present, the most remarkable thing about Vane's mission was that he had concluded a difficult agreement in ten days. As soon as it was concluded, the Scots immediately called to the colors all men from sixteen to sixty and, as a courtesy, made Vane a burgess of Edinburgh. By August 26, the proposed League and Covenant had reached Westminster where it was debated, slightly altered, and adopted by September 25. That, too, was a remarkable achievement, and Vane had come home deserving gratitude and much respect; to many he was a hero.

While Vane was in Scotland, the peace party in the Lords had drawn up new propositions, which it seemed would give Charles almost everything. True, Parliamentary privileges were protected, but to Charles was conceded the royal revenue, the command of the navy, and the forts. Expelled members were to be readmitted to the Parliament while a new Assembly of Divines would attempt to settle the church. By a majority of twenty-nine, a very substantial majority at that time, the House voted to consider these proposals. Since the attitude of Essex toward these proposals would be decisive, each House dispatched an embassy seeking his support. The Lords sent the Earl of Holland to ask him to stand with his army for the peace proposals. The Commons appointed the inevitable committee, with Pym at its head, to urge Essex not to consent to what seemed to them a capitulation. After hearing the arguments for both sides,

Essex threw his influence behind Pym and cut the ground from under the peace party.

This did not end the peace efforts. The king, having heard of the favorable terms proposed by the Lords, sent for an accommodation to the House of Commons on Saturday, and a majority seemed in the mood for peace. But the managers of Parliament secured an adjournment until Monday and over the weekend they set the pulpits to work. Many of the ministers were cut to the Old Testament cloth, believers in the military triumphs of the faithful, and on the Sabbath they inflamed the people. At the same time placards were set up calling on all well-disposed persons to go to Westminster on Monday morning because 20,000 Irish Catholics were about to land in England. Some people believed this outrageous lie because it was known that Charles had sent overtures to the Irish.

So on Monday, "rabble by thousands," actually about 5,000 people, thronged around the House. Some members thereupon proposed that further consideration of the king's offer be set aside until the tumults had been stilled and members could again debate rationally and vote freely. Pym, however, would not hear of it, and the debate was carried on in the presence of an aroused and intimidating mob. This intimidation, thought Denzil Holles, was the greatest violation of the authority and freedom of a Parliament ever known and was even worse than the king's attempt on the five members.

So now it seemed that the only road to peace lay through the already blood-soaked ways of war. However, the women of London, under the impression that they had been liberated, decided to take a hand. On August 8, the day after peace had fallen victim to the pulpit, a large crowd of women with white ribbons in their hats gathered around Westminster shouting for peace. On the next day they were back in larger numbers. Rushworth, who saw things from the Parliamentary side, said these women were generally of "the meaner sort," whereas Clarendon declared them to be "wives of substantial citizens." After presenting their petitions for peace, the women pressed through Westminster Hall to the very door of the House, and some shouted that Pym, Strode, and others of the "war party" should be thrown into the Thames. The confused soldiers who were supposedly guarding the Parliament were ordered to load their muskets with powder but not ball, and fire at the women.

They fired, but the women, seeing no one hurt, cried out, "Powder, powder only," and then from their aprons or other convenient recesses they drew stones, bricks, and other blunt objects and hurled them at the soldiers. This time the soldiers, when loading their guns, added the ball and fired into the ranks of the women. At least two persons were killed and several hurt, but others only became more enraged. "Give us those traitors that were against peace," they cried. "Give us that dog, Pym." Finally a detachment of General Waller's cavalry arrived to rescue Parliament and the soldiers. The women, dauntless now, rushed at the reinforcements calling them Waller's dogs. In self-defense, as it was later explained, the soldiers began to lay about with their swords, mostly though not always with the flat edge. Sir Symonds D'Ewes, who was now becoming a collector of ironies, noted that the treatment accorded by Parliament to petitioners depended on the nature of their petitions. People who came in support of the right issues were, as in any revolution, quite welcome.

Not long after the siege of the angry women, a book came forth from a fanatical preacher named Saltmarsh in which he spoke some hitherto unspeakable words. The surest way to engage the people in this war, he said, was to convince them that they were fighting popery—as Saltmarsh, of course, belived they were. And if the king failed to grant the demands of the Parliament he should be rooted out and the royal line given to someone else. At once some members of the Commons denounced the book as scandalous and demanded that it be recalled and burned. At that point the surly Henry Marten arose. This time he had no witticism to amuse the Parliament; he said bluntly that it was better to have one family destroyed than many, and that he thought the book both wise and valiant. At last the great Parliamentary fiction had been publicly challenged and exposed: it was not the king's advisers but the king himself who must be overthrown. Pym could not ignore the challenge. Presumably he still believed in that fiction to some extent, and so he demanded that Marten be sent to the Tower. He was released a short time later, but he did not return to Parliament until 1646 when young Vane, needing the support of the king's enemies, found a way to bring him back.

Even while Vane was in Scotland, Pym was visibly ailing; he no longer had the energy to guide and direct the Parliament. The

Committee of Safety, the most important Parliamentary committee and Pym's principal instrument of action, now seemed to lack direction. It was soon realized that Pym had fallen to an enemy swifter and more inexorable than Rupert himself, a foe from whom it was useless to beg for life. He was dying of cancer.

The war went on, and on September 20, in the first major battle Essex had undertaken in eleven months, he and Rupert faced each other at Newbury. It was a hard fought, bitter, indecisive struggle in which the king, apparently because his ammunition was spent, withdrew from the field. His departure did not make Newbury a Parliamentary victory, but it was claimed as one because Parliament desperately needed hope.

It was in this battle that Lord Falkland died, and in the mode of his death he became a kind of emblem, giving form to the vague feelings of many people. When Falkland had succeeded the elder Vane as Secretary of State to Charles, he would allow no private letters to be opened, and would employ no spies; if he could not be both a gentleman and a secretary he knew which he must choose. He had become weary of war, so agonized by its inhumane and irrational brutalities that he could not sleep. He thought his heart must break if it continued. At Newbury he insisted on joining the battle, though as Secretary of State there was no reason why he should. As Whitelocke later heard,

> Being dissuaded by his friends to go into the fight, as having no call to it, and being no military officer, he said he was weary of the times and foresaw much misery to his own country and did believe he should be out of it ere night and could not be persuaded to the contrary.

On the morning of the battle, he called for a clean shirt, and being asked why, he replied that if he were slain they should not find his body in foul linen. In the heat of the fight, he noticed that his commander had pulled up before a gap in a hedge, through which intense enemy fire was pouring. And there Falkland, who was weary of both Parliamentary demagogues and Royalist fops, who was deadly weary of irrationality and folly but could see no end to them, who preferred to die rather than to kill more Englishmen or to live to see them killed, rushed the strong point alone and went down riddled with Puritan shot.

He was a man of learning, said Clarendon, who knew Greek and Latin well, a man of ineffable sweetness and delight in conversation, of simplicity and integrity of life. He was superior to the passions and affections "which attend vulgar minds," ambitious only for knowledge, and an enemy only to uncharitableness. He embodied the humanistic ethic, the kind of man which sometimes takes generations to create. But such an ethic is at war with that harsh Nature which ensures the survival of her own children whose mailed fists are linked directly to the brain. Falkland died the victim of primitive energies which the idealists had released and now could not control. It would take a strong man to cage the beast, and a strong man was waiting.

An even greater loss to the Parliament than Falkland was to the Royalists was the death of Pym on December 8. London went into deep mourning in heart as well as habit, and on December 15 the funeral was held, with Vane acting as one of the pallbearers. Then London noticed an incredible thing: no Scot attended the funeral. When asked why, Robert Baillie explained with the insensitivity of a fanatic that funerals were part of the trumpery of popery. The hatred and bitterness of the Scots in England, always latent, became open and acknowledged at Pym's funeral. Then the alliance of Scotland and England which Vane had negotiated under Pym's direction began its fatal decline.

But initially Vane would try to carry out the political pledges he had made to the Scots. For a time in Parliament he would be their best friend, seeking financial support for their armies and understanding for their difficulties. But with every day that passed, as he came to know the Presbyterians better, he would consider them the mortal enemies of the cause he thought himself called to foster and protect—the cause of liberty of conscience in religion.

10

Maelstrom (1644)

Later in his life Vane would occasionally tease some Scottish friend about the English coup in the religious settlement, but standing on the scaffold, weighing his words against that most solemn moment, he said that he had always assented to the "holy ends" of the covenant; it was only the "rigid way of prosecuting it," he said, the "oppressing unformity," that he could never approve. His conduct immediately after the negotiations were completed bears him out, for the Solemn League and Covenant dealt with matters other than religion, and Vane worked as strongly as he could to turn the spirit of negotiations into realities.

One clause of the covenant expressed an intention to form a union.

> We shall each one of us, according to our places and interest, endeavor that [the two kingdoms] may remain conjoined in a firm peace and union to all posterity. . . .

And although it was not a part of the document, Vane had agreed that Parliament would support the Scots army to the extent of 30,000 pounds per month with 100,000 to be paid in advance, an agreement that led Sir John Denham to scoff that it was

> more our money than our cause
> Their brotherly assistance draws.

When Vane returned to London, probably on October 25, 1643, he revealed that commitment, and the Commons quickly passed an ordinance for a forced loan. They then sent Vane and Marshall to acquaint the City with it and to seek voluntary contributions. On October 27, Commons Hall, the largest hall in the city, was full of citizens eager to hear about the Scots agreement. Vane spoke first. He said that England's condition was somewhat better now than when he had gone to Scotland (everyone knew of Essex's relief of Gloucester and the Battle of Newbury). The Scots, though they knew England's desperate condition very well and had received many fair offers and promises from the king, remained faithful to Parliament out of concern for religion. That was why they were willing "to break through all difficulties, and to expose themselves to all dangers, to take us by the hand, and to join cordially with us in the maintaining of this cause." As soon as the covenant was taken in England, said Vane, it would bind the two nations together, for it was already being taken in Scotland, not only by the Committee of Estates and other governmental groups, but also by the entire kingdom, on whom the severest penalties were invoked for failure to take it.

Vane then praised the incredible dispatch with which the Scots had mobilized: within forty-eight hours they were ready to march, but they were now held back for lack of money. The new allies were sensible of the "vast expenses" the city of London had incurred to maintain English armies, but they had even greater problems. After all, the "present troubles" had begun in Scotland and had created financial hardships there as early as 1638; even now the Scots were maintaining an army in Ireland at the request and desire of the Parliament.

Then Vane came to the crucial point. As representative of the Parliament, he had agreed that before the Scottish army should stand on English soil, they would be sent 100,000 pounds, and since it would cost twice that much to move their army, both nations would be sharing the cost equally. Even though it was winter, Vane felt certain that the Scots army, once in motion, would "advance very far in those northern parts." All that was needed now was the money to set them in motion.

The Scots were asking this money from England not out of greed, said Vane, but out of necessity; they were so eager to help prosecute the war that if by mortgaging their estates or even "if there were money sufficient in Scotland," they would give it for the cause. As for the forced-loan ordinance, the Parliament had provided that the burden should not again fall entirely on those who had so cheerfully contributed before; "those that are unwilling and disaffected" were now to be compelled to give. This should also encourage the well-affected to give once more, knowing that they would no longer carry the burden alone. But forced loans took time; voluntary subscriptions could raise the sum in a few days and bring into action the formidable army of Scotland led by officers who had learned their trade under Gustav Adolf.

It was a tightly structured, well-argued speech, a bit sanguine as it turned out, but not expressing hopes beyond those which the Parliament generally was feeling.

It was otherwise with Marshall's speech. He expansively stressed how willingly the Scots would carry the entire burden themselves if they could, out of sheer love for the cause; they would plunder their own kingdom to save England. Seldom have the Scots received such a tribute for cheerful giving. If London could now find a little more money, Marshall concluded, everyone would soon be sitting under his own vine or fig tree enjoying Christ's gospel of which the Royalists were seeking to deprive them. Marshall also had much to say about popery, one of the revolutionary catchwords that never lost its appeal. The combined efforts of Vane and Marshall prompted the burghers, a hard-bitten lot in financial matters, to give once more.

Nor was this the only matter in which Vane spoke out effectively for the Scots. He became a leader of the pro-Scottish forces in Parliament, continually insisting that their needs were as pressing as those of Essex. Some members affected to see in this the beginning of a conspiracy against Essex led by Vane, but it was nothing more than what he had promised in Scotland.

Vane's mission to Scotland triggered a chain of events that tumbled over one another, many of them resulting in unusual and unpredictable new directions for the revolution. At this time, with Pym now dead, Richard Baxter thought that Vane was occupying the same position of leadership in Parliament that Cromwell occupied in the field, and that Vane's management of Commons and Cromwell's rise to military power were neither fortuitous nor unrelated. Certainly he was one of the principal leaders of the state during this wild and confused period, the very maelstrom of the revolution.

In the midst of such turbulence, a man who values inwardness must find somewhere a circle of quietness: Vane found one in his family. Just one year after marriage Lady Vane had given him a daughter, Frances, and in the following year, 1642, his first son, young Henry, was born. More children would follow with the seasons.

Because he had grown so suspicious of formal religious observances—all that he had felt about New England Congregationalism having been confirmed by his observation of Scottish Presbyterianism—he preferred to worship informally at home as the spirit moved him. Even the Sabbath day, he thought, might be turned into a snare for the spirit. And he and his wife not only loved each other, but increasingly they were able to share illuminations of spirit and harmonies of mind, as he had once shared them with Anne Hutchinson, but now in far greater intimacy.

In his family services he was sometimes joined by his friends, neighbors, and servants. To this little group Vane interpreted the scriptures, not as the dead letter of the past but as a living allegory of the spirit. From the apocalyptic books, in which he delighted, he sometimes foretold the future, predicting the triumph of the thrice-born elect and the descent of the Heavenly Jerusalem. There were "sweet" occasions when the spirit of God and his glory rested upon them, when Christ was formed within them, dwelling in their hearts by faith; and from that circle of silence he emerged with new resolution and confidence.

And yet these sweet moments had their dangers, for to this little group of adoring men and women Vane became more than minister: he was master and they were disciples. Not one of them could match him in position, personality, or intellect, and apparently they never challenged his words or message. It is perilous for a man in public life to exclude his equals from full intimacy, admitting only adulators and denying himself that candid intellectual criticism of purpose and method on which public life is based. In the House of Commons Vane sat near Henry Marten and Oliver St. John. If either of them had ever joined his little circle to feel the force of his enthusiasm, to sense the vagueness of his theological formulations and the exclusiveness of his dogmatics, Marten would have jeered and St. John would have been appalled. Vane's noetic assurances could scarcely have survived the assault of such sceptical minds. Therefore he could not subject either his divinity or his ultimate political hopes to the criticism of his Parliamentary peers; he could only renew his faith in his divine vocation through these intense and private communions.

In January, 1644, moved at last to action by the imminent invasion of the Scots, King Charles summoned his anti-Parliament at Oxford. His proclamation promised amnesty to all who would join him and expressed indignation at the threatened invasion of England by a foreign power, even though he himself was then trying to bring an Irish army into England.

The announcement of the king's new Parliament and the rigid demands of the Scots in the Assembly of Divines led some of the city people who wished peace without Presbyterianism to enter into unofficial negotiations with the king about a church settlement which would leave some room for tender consciences. Apparently in connection with this scheme, Lord Lovelace (not to be confused with the poet) approached young Vane and offered a solution based on "liberty of conscience." Legally Vane should have rejected the offer and informed Parliament of it; just a year earlier he and St. John had sponsored a bill which made it high treason for anyone to enter into peace negotiations without informing both Houses or their Speakers or the Earl of Essex. Vane, however, never inclined to give the Lords much consideration, informed only the Speaker of Commons. With the assent of Haselrig and St. John and in the presence of the Scots commissioners, he asked Moses Wall, chaplain to the Earl of Warwick, to pursue the offers of peace at Oxford.

Vane assued Wall that his mission was lawful because the Speaker of the House knew about it. So, at Windsor, Moses Wall met with Lord Lovelace who took care to put nothing in writing but said that the king esteemed "Sir Henry Vane and his party to be the honestest men of them that stuck to the Parliament." If restored, he said, the king would annul any act which was against "tender consciences." While this negotiation may have seemed hopeful to the Independents, it put Vane into an uncharacteristically vulnerable position.

One of those who, under Charles' promise of amnesty, had deserted Westminster for Oxford was the Earl of Holland. But Charles was foolish enough to receive him with royal discourtesy, and the disconsolate Holland returned to Westminster only to have Vane and St. John charge him with treason. Holles and Stapleton, both moderates and friends of Essex, opposed them. Initially Parliament had refused even to consider the charges against Holland, but Vane and St. John now prepared to revive them. Before they could do so, Essex, hearing of the Lovelace negotiations, charged Vane himself with high treason. Vane's defense was ingenious, tough, and clever. He pleaded that the treason ordinance he had himself sponsored was illegal because, through the "cunning" of some peers, it had not been entered in the Lords' Journal. Even if the ordinance were valid, he said, the Speaker of the House knew of his negotiations; he failed to mention that the ordinance required that either Essex or the Speaker of the Lords should also be informed.

The fact that this legalistic defense clearly violated the intent of his own treason law might have been embarrassing had not Vane quickly played some stronger cards. Accused of a plot himself, he revealed to Parliament the existence of a new and dangerous Royalist plot which came to be known as the Brook Plot. Having "heard something," he said, he had called Sir Thomas Gardner, Solicitor St. John, and Lord Wharton to meet him in Goldsmith Hall on Thursday at 8:00 P.M. to interrogate one Riley, "a man above all suspicion, esteemed singularly religious, of so great reputation that he was a prime leader of the City Council."

But the Parliament men questioning him were surprised at his confusion and the guarded nature of his answers. The Solicitor, pacing up and down musing on this strange conduct, happened to kick a piece of paper on the floor; he kicked it again over to the fire where it started to burn. Some inner impulse then prompted him to seize this small brand from the burning, and he found it to be conspiratorial. Thereupon the Parliament men required Riley to empty his pockets, and there they found other letters which clearly revealed a conspiracy. The House, disturbed by the serious nature of the new plot and realizing that whatever technical violations Vane had been guilty of he had not intended treason, thanked him for what he had discovered and said no more about the charges against him. The House also asked that a deputation from Parliament go to Commons Hall and reveal the plot to the citizens there.

On Monday Vane appeared at the Hall along with others. The meeting was opened by the Earl of Northumberland who not only had title, like Essex, but was also one of the greatest feudal lords in England, the possessor of lands, estates, and servants. He made a brief statement and then turned the platform over to Mr. Solicitor St. John, who disclosed the plot.

This plot, he said, was more serious than Waller's. Here, under a "specious pretence of peace," the king wished to divide the City from the Parliament, the Parliament from itself, and the English from the Scots, for the plotters advocated a peace treaty "without advice or consent of our brethren of Scotland," and they even planned to embroil the two allies in a war.

How was this somewhat ambitious design to be accomplished? According to St. John, there were two "Jesuited papists," Sir Basil Brook and Colonel Read, and, in sympathy with them, a Mr. Violet of London, a goldsmith of Royalist leanings who had spent some time in jail for not contributing to the cause; there was also Mr. Riley. These latter two were "Protestant in show." Conjoined with them were the Queen and the Duchess of Buckingham (both militant Catholics whose names could be counted on to stir the emotions in Commons Hall), and Lord Digby who, since Falkland's death, had been Charles' secretary. Such an eminent collection of Catholic names made it inevitable that St. John should refer back to the Gunpowder Plot of 1605, when Catholics had once before tried to destroy the government.

Having delineated the principals, St. John turned to the plot itself, a rather simple affair, one feels, considering the ambitious nature of its ends. His Majesty was to write "a powerful and promising letter" to the Lord Mayor and to the citizens. This letter would declare the present Parliament invalid and propose peace negotiations directly between the king and the City. It would also offer safe conduct for any member of either House who wished to join his king. Then, with peace achieved in England, the Scots would be driven out, even though, as St. John reminds his audience, an article in the Solemn League and Covenant pledges that neither nation shall entertain peace without the consent of the other.

This was the design: it was too ugly, it was too black, bare-faced, to have been presented to your view, and therefore it must be masked; this hook must be baited with the sweet word *Peace*. . . .

These men . . . they cry *Peace, Peace,* that destruction might have come upon you as an armed man.

Having concluded his peroration, St. John relinquished the platform to Vane, who was to read the letters written to one another by the plotters and to comment on them.

Vane commented on the "finger of God" which, he said, was visible in the way the plot was discovered. Then he read the examination of Riley, who had remembered letters from the king, one of which said "that he had many good subjects in the City that did desire peace, and were weary of their misery."

Then Vane came to the confession of Violet, who had been drawn to the plot because the king had promised to impose an excise tax which, "if the times were quiet," that is if there were no expensive military force to maintain, could be expected to bring in about three million a year. This amount would quickly satisfy the "debts of public faith" which had been primarily borne by London merchants. Thus the king was tempting the city in the pocketbook, its most sensitive area, and many others besides Violet must have been moved by the offer.

Feeling a little uneasy, Vane paused to comment. The design, he then admitted, was plausible because it promised two things everyone wanted: peace and repayment of public debts. But he pointed out that under this proposal of an excise tax the city of London would still be paying the burden of the debt, both Parliamentary and Royalist. Besides, the king's proclamation abolishing Parliament was a mere piece of paper; he could not dissolve a legally constituted Parliament even though he would like to. And, in the last analysis, Parliament was the only guarantor of the liberties of the people.

Vane then read the king's letter which concluded,

And you shall assure all our good subjects of that our city, whose hearts are touched with any sense of duty to us, or of love to the religion and laws established, in the quiet and peaceful fruition whereof they and their ancestors have enjoyed so great happiness, that we have neither passed any act, nor made any profession or protestation for the maintenance and defence of the true Protestant religion and the liberties of the subject which we will not most strictly and religiously observe and for the which we will not be always ready to give them any security that can be desired.

Vane scornfully rejoined that though the king says he will observe any act hitherto passed, by proclaiming this Parliament no parliament he has sought to destroy the whole framework of the laws of the kingdom. On this subject Vane spoke with conviction. Parliament, he said, is a word that "ought to be sacred to the ears of all true English men and lovers of their country," yet Charles calls it a "pretended Parliament," which no man ever dared say or write "at any time heretofore in England." If the king succeeds in "disannuling" this Parliament, said Vane, England's laws, liberties, and rights will have "a being or not a being solely in His Majesty's pleasure."

Here Vane touched the heart of the issue. However the City was suffering, however much it desired peace, it had to decide whether it could rely more on Charles or on the Parliament; it had to choose between divine prerogative and elected representation. However tempted, the City was not yet ready to reverse its choice. Vane then concluded by pointing out that if Parliament sat at Oxford instead of London, trade would decay in the City. And he could assure the assembly that any Parliamentarian who defected to Oxford would have his lands and goods confiscated.

So spoke Pym's lieutenant and almost with Pym's voice, convinced now as the older man had always been that power and sovereignty should be transferred from king to Parliament. In Vane's many tackings and veerings, even when he came to be called weather-Vane, his devotion to the legally constituted Parliament never wavered. He had now defended that position against the king; he would ultimately defend it against Cromwell and the army; finally he would defend it against Charles II, and at last he would die for it.

Though Vane's part in exposing this plotting earned him further support in the City and prestige in the House, it did not at once remove him from danger. The Commons, who were becoming a little shrill about plots, had ordered the Earl of Essex to establish a standing commission for trying by martial law persons suspected of treason. Apparently acting under this authority, the earl ordered his advocate-general, Dorislaus, to take depositions from Moses Wall, from Lord Lovelace's servant, and from another chaplain. On hearing of this questioning, Vane and St. John called upon Dorislaus, insisting that the kind of interrogations he was conducting was a breach of Parliamentary privilege, the principle under which a member of Parliament could be protected from almost any charge. Essex then offered to drop his charges against Vane if the charges against Holland were dropped. Vane and St. John refusing to do this, the Parliament did it for them, voting to clear Vane and reprieve the fickle earl. So Vane was at last out of danger.

During much of December unusually heavy snowstorms had fallen throughout northern England and immobilized the Scots army. Finally on January 18, it crossed the Tweed into England. In the Solemn League and Covenant, Vane had pledged that England would move towards a union of the two countries. Now that the Scots army was moving, some political machinery was needed by which Scotland and England could begin working together. On January 30, therefore, Vane and St. John introduced an ordinance for the appointment of a permanent committee of seven peers and fourteen commoners, to be joined by the five Scots Parliamentary commissioners to form a Committee of Both Kingdoms which would replace Pym's old Committee of Safety. Constitutional historians have been excited by this proposal, for it contained the germ of the modern cabinet system, an executive committee acting for Parliament and responsible to it. It was also the first significant legal step in the ultimate union of the two nations. Again Vane was demonstrating his devotion to what he considered the spirit of his agreement with the Scots.

The Long Parliament, however, was not altogether pleased with this proposal. As originally drafted, the bill gave this committee power both "to order and direct" the war and to negotiate for peace. This so-called "omnipotent ordinance" was so unpopular in Commons that it never even came to a vote. The Lords, however, apparently without quite realizing what they were doing, approved it. Vane took note of this unusual situation: a bill approved by Lords but laid aside by Commons. Saying nothing, he drew up a new ordinance designed to appease wounded feelings and reassure the suspicious: it proposed that the Commons as a body should select the members of the committee. It further conceded that in treating with the Scots the committee should not go beyond instructions received "in charge from both Houses," and that they were to report all their activities to both Houses. In the matter of conducting the war, Vane rearranged some words without making the slightest concession: the Committee of Both Kingdoms would "advise, consult, order and direct" the course of the war. It was empowered to carry on negotiations with foreign states, but could not propose any cessation of arms or any treaty of peace with the king without the express order of Parliament.

The peace party in Commons resisted the new ordinance as strongly as they could. In heated debate one member said that if the bill was passed it would enable a few men to prolong the war at their own will and to fatten their purses at the same time. This was an outrageous insult to Vane, who immediately moved for censure. But he was voted down and this same charge against him would be heard more than once, in Parliament, the City, and the nation at large.

Although Vane lost the vote of censure, his ordinance passed, though somewhat weakened by an amendment the peace party attached which limited the duration of the committee to three months. In that form, the bill passed on February 16. To those reluctant to put a committee in charge of a war, the membership of the committee must have been reassuring, for all the major military commanders were on it: Essex, Manchester, Warwick (the Lord Admiral), and Sir William Waller. Holles, the most outspoken member of the peace party, was passed over, but that party was still well represented by Philip Stapleton, John Glyn, and others. Later it was said that Vane had managed to rig this committee (both he and his father were members), but the truth is that it was reasonably well balanced. Only the presence of the Scots, who at this time mistrusted Essex and supported Vane, gave his faction an advantage.

The Lords realized that if the committee in fact ordered and directed the war, Essex would be shorn of his discretionary power to act. As the three months allotted to the life of the committee trickled away, the Lords tried a number of Parliamentary gambits. First they tried to delete from the ordinance the word "order" and to substitute "directing and consulting." Then they tried to increase the numbers serving on the committee and to limit its life. It was a divisive struggle. The Lords kept sending down proposed ordinances which the Commons rejected until the term set for the life of the committee expired; for some days there was no legal authority to direct the armies in the field except for a confused and harassed Parliament.

What could be done? Vane remembered that the earlier ordinance though shelved by the Commons had first been passed by the Lords; if it were now revived, the Commons could vote it into law. On May 22 the Commons passed this bill, once so much disliked, by a majority of two to one, the largest majority on any vote since 1642. But even while Vane's supporters admired his efficiency, some of them shook their heads over his procedures, which were a bit too clever.

The committee came to exert a surprisingly effective control over its military leaders, even in small details; sometimes it seemed more like a general staff than a committee, and this was precisely what the supporters of Essex had feared, especially with young Vane and the Scots in control. During one meeting this committee recommended that the fleet for the Irish coasts be speeded, that the London regiments stay where they presently were, and that Colonel Weldon's regiment march to Sir William Waller's quarters in Essex. In the early days they even sent orders to Oliver Cromwell.

The committee was also active in matters of peace. In March, when Charles offered to negotiate, the reply proposed by the committee went so far as to fix a time for the king's return to Parliament, failing which the government would be settled without him. Because the Scots opposed this reply, it was rejected by the Commons, but now the idea of Charles' abdication or even his dethronement had been publicly stated. Henceforth it could be talked about as a possible solution.

Until he personally took the field in late April, Essex attended most of the sessions of the Committee of Both Kingdoms, as did Vane. While there was yet no incivility between the two, still after the charge and countercharge of treason, each knew that he had a mortal opponent. By now Essex was the leader and symbol of the "peace party" which wanted to end the war and bring the monarch back, though with some limitation of his powers. His chief supporters were Holles, Stapleton, and Glyn. Vane, on the other hand, led the "war party," which believed that Charles' powers and functions could never be effectively restricted without a military victory. As Essex became ever surer that Parliament was discriminating against him, failing to support his army as generously as it did Manchester's, Vane became increasingly convinced that Essex, insufficiently committed to the cause, was failing to conduct his campaigns with full vigor. But the two men, mutually suspicious, opposed in principles as in personality, and implacably hostile as they were, somehow managed to continue working together.

When the Scots had crossed the Tweed the Royalists had abandoned Newcastle, retiring within the walls of York where they were shortly besieged by the Scots army under Leven, the northern Parliamentary army under Fairfax, and the Eastern Association army under Manchester. While these armies were sitting before the historic city, Rupert had taken Wigan and Liverpool, the gate through which his Irish reinforcements might come. Now Rupert, whose troops plundered freely and whose tactics were imaginative and daring, was arousing so much fear that he was becoming a mental as well as a physical hazard. So on June 3 the Committee of Both Kingdoms dispatched Vane to York to induce at least one of the armies to break off the siege and confront Rupert. But the generals, unwilling to turn their backs on a powerful unreduced garrison to face a brilliant and capable adversary, held that York must fall first. Vane saw their point and justified their decision to the committee.

But beneath his open and public mission which he accomplished with his usual cool efficiency, he had a more significant secret mission to perform. Three months earlier he and others had proposed to the Parliament a settlement which excluded Charles. Apparently he now made this same revolutionary proposal to the three generals: depose the king, crown a successor (either the Elector Palatine or the Prince of Wales), and settle the government. At least this rumor was heard in London by the Venetian and French ambassadors, who believed it and reported it to their governments.

Whatever Vane asked, the three generals refused, decisively and even angrily. Manchester was so shocked that he appeared thereafter to have lost his fighting spirit. He had seen something on the horizon, now considerably larger than a man's hand, that frightened him more than the old monarchy. That something was the new men, not merely Vane but also his own lieutenant-general Oliver Cromwell and Cromwell's army of sectaries. They were enthusiastic, zealous, and so independent that they denied any religious authority over them; they conducted their own services, preached their own sermons, and prayed their own prayers. The old generals, and Manchester especially, still believed that they were freeing Charles from his evil counselors. When they thought of an England governed by the untitled, the unlearned, and the impassioned, they dug down more deeply into the trenches before York, and even more deeply into the trenches of their minds. Cromwell and Vane had too much in common not to have seen one another during Vane's visit, and shared its concealed purpose. After Manchester's angry refusal, Cromwell's hostility to that noble Lord became marked.

Even as Vane was arriving back in London on June 30, Rupert lifted the siege of York by a brilliant maneuver, causing the Parliamentary armies to fall back on Marston Moor. There, on July 2, they inflicted on the Royalists a shattering and decisive defeat. Next they took the city of York, and the North was in Parliamentary hands. The Scots believed and tried to persuade the English that Scottish infantry had won the victory, but Cromwell knew otherwise: the victory was God's will and Cromwell's cavalry had executed that will. Exultantly, triumphantly, Vane echoed Cromwell in London and in the Parliament. This might be the victory that would bring peace. Two days after the surrender of York, the three generals asked the Commiteee of Both Kingdoms to take prompt action for peace and settlement of the church, and they reiterated their resolute support of the Solemn League and Covenant and their intention of carrying on the war.

But in the meantime Essex was behaving with uncharacteristic rashness. Earlier in the spring the port of Lyme Regis in Devon had been besieged by Prince Maurice with 6,000 troops, and as it repelled attack after attack, it became a symbol of stout-hearted resistance. Now if it was to resist much longer, the town would need more soldiers. In late May, therefore, the Committee of Both Kingdoms began to urge upon Essex the needs of Lyme, pointing out that its heroism deserved succor, and that the relief of Lyme might be a key to recovering "the whole West whose affections are already very inclinable to Parliament." Essex was hearing the same thing from his own advisers, West Country men who believed what their own interests persuaded them to believe.

On June 6, both Essex and Waller were present at a Council of War, and although Waller held the principal responsibility for the West, it was decided that Essex should go to the relief of Lyme, for his army lay nearer that city and farther from the king's forces. Besides, it was composed of many professional soldiers, enlisted for general service, whereas Waller's army had been furnished by local levies, men who when they were fighting away from their home counties frequently deserted in large numbers to go back to the homes they were supposed to be defending.

On June 7, the committee learned that Essex was resolved to relieve not only Lyme but the entire West: he had marched off with his army, commanding Waller and Haselrig to remain and "watch the King." On June 11, the alarmed committee told Essex that since Waller's forces were responsible for the West, Essex should send only enough horse to relieve Lyme. They reinforced their advice with a Parliamentary resolution "that it was most convenient for Sir William Waller to go into the West." They continued to hope, however, that he had already detached a body of cavalry to raise the siege at Lyme. On the same day, the committee ordered Waller to march west.

On June 13, Parliament once again ordered Essex to return to the siege of Oxford after dispatching cavalry for the relief of Lyme. Essex replied with a defensive, angry letter. You told me, he said, to relieve the West, and I marched. He insisted that Lyme could not be relieved by a mere party, especially a party of horse. In this he seems to have been right, for Prince Maurice had an army of foot before Lyme and the ways leading into the city were steep and difficult. If the enemy should close off a pass, argued Essex, his horse would be shut up forever.

Essex also complained that Waller, despite vast levies and much money, had initiated no significant action. It was almost as if he was saying about Waller what he knew the Parliament men were saying about him. And in defiance of the committee's orders, Essex continued his march. At the approach of Essex's army, Prince Maurice abandoned the siege of Lyme and on June 16 Essex wrote triumphantly to the committee that he had relieved the city and that no body of horse alone, however strong, could have done it.

For the moment Essex was a hero, and had he now acted with his usual prudence, he would have remained one, for he had shown himself capable of daring and imaginative action. In the face of bad advice he had stubbornly adhered to sound military tactics. It is all the sadder that in this moment of triumph he over-reached himself. In the same letter to the committee in which he announced his victory, he said, "If I am not hindered, I shall quickly reduce these parts to Parliament's service." He conceived of nothing less than victory over the entire West Country, over those fierce Celts whose loyalties had always been with the older ways. He began well by summoning in quick succession Weymouth and Portland Castle.

The committee (with Vane still absent in the North) reacted intelligently. They rescinded their orders for Waller to march west and instructed him instead to follow the king. Waller fully expected Charles to retreat within the walls of Oxford and submit to siege, but instead the king drew a fresh force out of Oxford and with an army of some 10,000 marched towards the West. Now Essex was caught in a potential trap, for ahead of him he was driving a formidable Royalist army while, behind him, unhindered by the hapless Waller, the king was moving up.

In early August Essex finally faced the disaster that had been developing. At Lostwithiel he heard that three armies were marching against him; the people, far from joining him, had risen against him unanimously. His soldiers had no bread. Thoroughly alarmed, the committee raised money to be sent by sea and ordered all available troops to march westward. But Waller could not move for his recruits had not arrived and there were no mounts for his foot; there were not even enough horses to pull the artillery. He would have marched yesterday, he wrote, but could produce only one team. He knew that calumnies were being spread about him and his failure to relieve Essex, but they were false. "I am your servant," he cried out to the Committee of Both Kingdoms.

But this explanation did nothing to relieve Essex, now trapped by his own rashness. On August 31, he ordered his cavalry to break through the encircling armies. The next day Essex himself boarded ship, abandoning his infantry, under the command of Philip Skippon, to make the best terms they could for themselves. Now the Royalists taunted: why should the soldiers have sworn to live and die with Essex when he would not live and die with them?

So Essex and the peace party had been discredited in the field where Cromwell, supported by Vane and the sectaries, had been triumphant. Soon the peace party was saying that Vane and his group had destroyed Essex by conspiring to deny him aid. Such charges were to be expected, but they are rather difficult to evaluate. Many Puritans like Cromwell and Colonel Hutchinson rightly believed Essex to be a mediocre commander. Any member of the Committee of Both Kingdoms might well have felt that it was unwise to give Essex men or supplies that might be more competently used elsewhere. But charges against Vane went beyond that; it was said that he doubted the earl's loyalty. If this meant that he thought Essex was secretly in communication with the enemy, then Vane was wrong; the earl's relations with the Royalists were beyond cavil. But if the charge merely implied that Vane felt in Essex the lukewarm devotion that divides the reformer from the revolutionary, he was surely right. Essex was no zealot but a fair-minded, slow man who believed that the cause could be won through good will and the forcing or negotiating of change by degrees. As a peer with a fabled name he did not wish to see the old order overturned. But Vane, like Cromwell, was looking for men whose spirits bore witness to their zeal, men for whom the cause was everything. And it may be true that Vane undermined Essex, as Cromwell undermined Manchester, by doubting his fervor and effectiveness and spreading this doubt among a small majority of highly influential men.

The war was progressing, but the church was still unsettled: the Assembly of Divines had been meeting regularly but with few results. In those tragic times, the Assembly afforded a certain comic relief. A group of rather narrow intellectual specialists had come together to debate "the issues." Everyone wished to be heard; all believed themselves to be both morally right and intellectually significant. There was much earnestness, much tedious discourse, and little action. On one point, as Robert Baillie complained, they labored for three weeks. John Selden, one of the laymen in the Assembly, sometimes amused, sometimes annoyed, was the principal Erastian antagonist. During a long, inconclusive debate on the theological implications of Christ's descent into hell, he arose and proposed that a committee be appointed to go and investigate on the spot; after all, the revolutionaries were appointing committees for everything else.

More influential in the Assembly than the laymen were the few Independents who, without realizing it, had adopted the same tactic as the Scots. From the beginning, the Scots had realized that a Presbyterian solution for the church depended on the military successes of their army. But now, two months after all those city funds were sent north, Newcastle still had not been taken, and most of the North was held by the Royalists. "Our friends are sad, our enemies speak and write contemptuously," said Baillie; the eyes of the Scottish delegation in London could only turn "toward the Lord."

While the Scots army was immobile, the Scots in the Assembly of Divines decided to stall until their army stirred and brought their hopes alive. The Independent divines, secretly in touch with Vane and St. John, had agreed on the same policy. So the debates dragged on, the two most opposed groups unwittingly assisting each other and delaying the majority from acting. Even so, certain issues took shape. The principal question, it seemed, was formal rather than theological: what structure should the church have? The Presbyterians favored the "classical" system in which several individual congregations formed a *classis*, several *classes* a synod, and synods throughout England and the world formed the church militant, an ecclesiastical unity with powers of examination and excommunication which made it possible to preserve that unity. The Scots wished the Assembly to proclaim that such a church government was *jure divino*, established by divine law; Selden and the Erastians held that no church government was divinely constituted, that all were matters of civil law and the will of Parliament. This seeming technicality opened up a complex and agonizing question of the exercise of church authority. How much control should the church, conceived as a single entity, exercise over the individual congregation? the individual worshipper? Could a synod call a *classis* to account in matters of conduct or doctrine? Could a *classis* rebuke a congregation or order ministers and elders to conform in life or doctrine? Could the ministers suspend members of their congregations from the communion? Could a single congregation ordain a man to the ministry or must that power come from the *classis* or synod? In every instance, the Presbyterians stood for an ordered, supervised, hierarchical authority which the Independents openly and Vane secretly held to be worse than the bishops. Because of their religious intensity and their belief in a single true order, the Presbyterians had come to hate the word "toleration," conceiving it to be the root of most religious evils. But the Independents knew that liberty of conscience was indispensable to their own survival; it also coincided with the current of the future.

But there was something which should qualify our judgments of these two groups, the one seemingly so generous, the other so narrow. In the Independent mentality there was a spiritual pride which made it unsuitable to control the principal church structure of a nation. That pride can be seen in Roger Williams and others who held that a congregation must consist only of certified believers, that one must not admit to the sacrament any "ordinary professor" of Christianity, but only such as could give "certain or satisfactory signs of regeneration." Many Independent congregations had separated not for the good of mankind but rather out of a fastidious sense of their own purity. They would have excluded the very people who most needed the church. As religious liberty continued to foster the growth of the sects, this exclusiveness tended to break down, but it did not disappear. The Independent Milton's contempt for the "heads without name" should give us a more balanced view of the struggle in the Westminster Assembly. And if one wishes to see how generous in spirit a Presbyterian could be, he should read the autobiography of Richard Baxter.

In April Baillie had been terribly depressed:

> I cannot tell you what to say of the Assembly. We are almost desperate to see anything concluded for a long time. Their way is woefully tedious.

There was never an assembly like it for prolixity, he continued, except that of Trent. But from all this haggling one astounding fact emerges—the Scots never seemed to doubt for a moment that Vane and St. John were on their side. Vane, after all, had negotiated the Solemn League and Covenant; he had established the Committee of Both Kingdoms; he had kept the Scots informed of plots; he continually fed them information about the doings of Parliament.

And he had not protested when St. Paul's and Westminster Abbey had been purged of their images and organs.

From these facts, Baillie deduced too much. Sir Harry Vane, he wrote, "whatever be his judgment," (did Baillie have some tickling hunch?) does not acknowledge the Independents "and gives them no encouragement." It is one of the most staggering miscalculations in political history. Yet Baillie was vaguely apprehensive about the future. He saw sects multiplying around him: Independents tended to fall into Anabaptists; Anabaptists into Antinomians, and they into something worse if there was anything worse. Further, he knew that "the most resolute and confident men" in the English army were Independents and that their yeasty ferment was spreading now among the soldiers in the Scots army.

Then suddenly came the disasters. Credit for the victory at Marston Moor was claimed by the Independents. Essex, initially suspected by the Scots, had by his conservatism and strong sense of order become the leader of their party, but now he was hopelessly trapped in Cornwall. Presbyterian ministers who harangued the Parliament about these disasters said that Essex's army perished because religion had not been settled according to the covenant, and heretical tracts, including Milton's on divorce, were freely published.

But a still greater blow fell on the hapless heads of the Scottish ministers when they finally realized that what the Parliamentary Independents really wanted before any form of Presbytery should be established was an act of Parliament which guaranteed their toleration. Vane had betrayed them; the man who had seemed so much their friend, the stay and support of their cause in the Parliament, had secretly been opposed to them all along.

Our greatest friends, Sir Henry Vane and the Solicitor, are the main procurers of all this; and that without any regard to us, who have saved their nation and brought their two persons to the height of power now they enjoy and use to our prejudice. . . . The great thought of Cromwell and Vane is to have a liberty for all religions without any exceptions.

Now, to those inclined to see political life in terms of conspiracies, the grand lines of a devious design were taking shape. Vane had gone to Scotland to secure military aid and through his cunning had inserted the words, "according to the Word of God" in the covenant; seizing that phrase the Independents had delayed the Assembly of Divines for a year until Cromwell's army, filled with vigorous sectaries, had become too strong to be ignored or pushed aside. Then when the proposals from the Assembly finally reached Parliament, Vane and St. John had at last pulled off their masks which had deceived the entire Scots nation. In restrospect the Scots could see the whole plot.

In October, Baillie wrote home to Scotland that the Scots in London were under a cloud. The successes of the Scots rebel Montrose, the prolongation of the siege of Newcastle, the defeat of Essex—all these were bad. And then, "Sir Henry Vane, our most intime friend, joining with a new faction to procure liberty for sects; these did much afflict us for a fortnight."

Thinking sadly on "Sir Henry Vane whom we trusted most," Baillie could now recall signs of that alteration which had seemed to come with such devastating suddenness. He remembered that twice at the dinner table Vane had "prolixly, earnestly, and passionately" reasoned for "full liberty of conscience to all religions without any exceptions," and he had publicly opposed the clause that required ministers to subscribe to the covenant. He had also said on one occasion that the Scots army musters were actually less than the Scots were being paid for; if he was right, the Scots were falsifying their military records in order to receive more money from England than they were entitled to. Such things as these should have been ample warning, but the Scots had been blind.

During this time, the deep and bitter differences between Cromwell and Manchester had become public. Cromwell alleged that Manchester avoided fighting—that he no longer sought a military solution. Manchester replied sharply: Cromwell, he said, wished to abolish the nobility of England; and he himself had heard Oliver say that if necessary he would draw his sword against the Scots. He also charged that Cromwell had threatened to form a party of the sectaries in order to extort his own conditions from king and Parliament. Robert Baillie, observing this struggle, knew that if Presbyterianism were to be established in England, Cromwell must be removed from command. Soon he found some reason to think that Cromwell actually might be removed, and in all the gloom and depression, he made one joyful entry in his journal. The House of Commons, he said, "in one hour has ended all quarrels," though he tempered his optimism: "Yet it seems a dream and the bottom of it is not understood." Soon it would be understood only too well, and at the bottom of it he would find Cromwell and Harry Vane.

By this time an affectionate friendship as well as a strong alliance had developed between Oliver Cromwell, the rising military genius and political pragmatist, and Harry Vane, the political visionary of inflexible principle and subtle diplomacy. The differences between them were very great. Cromwell was a man of the sword, Vane a pacifist by temperament; Cromwell was active, with strong emotions linked directly to both heart and tongue; Vane cautious and reserved. What held them fast together was that they had shared the central Puritan experience—the despair of sin and the joy of grace. Soon they were playfully calling each other by affectionate names, the significance of which remains dark: Cromwell was dear Brother Fountain and Vane was Brother Heron. For a time their letters show a profound mutual understanding, and they worked in Parliament for the Independent cause almost as one man.

Certainly they were working together when, on December 9, Zouch Tate asserted in a speech that the forces of Parliament were being divided by "pride and covetousness." Cromwell agreed. Even the friends of Parliament were saying that since the Parliament men had military commands and seats of power, they prolonged the war to maintain themselves in power. He therefore believed that in order to disprove these charges, no members of either House should "scruple to deny themselves and their own private interests for the public good."

Finally Tate moved "that during the time of this war no member of either House shall have or execute any office or command, military or civil, granted or conferred by both or either of the Houses of Parliament, or any authority derived from both or either of the Houses." His motion was seconded by Vane who also, according to Clarendon, made a strong speech, and by others who were not Independents. Baillie thought it had ended all strife, for under its terms both Manchester and Cromwell would presumably resign their commands and there would be a separation of military command from civil government.

After the Essex party failed to alter the proposal so as to make an exception of the earl, on December 19 the proposal was sent up to the House of Lords who were highly suspicious of it. They saw that Cromwell, Haselrig, Stapleton, Holles, and others in Commons could continue to hold their commands in the army by resigning their House seats, whereas peers had no similar privilege, for a nobleman could not resign his inherited seat in Parliament. To the peers it seemed that the ordinance was not, as Baillie thought, an attempt at a fair compromise solution but a directed attack on Essex and Manchester. They were almost certainly right. Therefore they laid aside this Self-Denying Ordinance, as it was called, and it rested for a while. In the meantime a grimmer drama was being staged in Parliament, where old Laud was being baited to his death by sectarian hounds. Confined to the Tower for years, his very existence was a reproach and an embarrassment. His power was long past—but what was to be done with the tired old man? Hugh Peter had proposed in April of 1643 that he be sent to New England; at about the same time Vane and Pym had signed a warrant which allowed William Prynne to search Laud's cell, his belongings, even his pockets. Prynne knew that Laud was a traitor; every twinge of his ears told him that. If he could not find evidence of treason, it was because of the devilish cleverness of the old man in concealing it. Therefore evidence must be searched out to support the truth. To do this, Prynne suborned witnesses, manufactured evidence, made alterations in Laud's diary, and employed every other device that malice could suggest.

By now most Englishmen and even the Scots had lost interest in their former troubler. Robert Baillie wrote that Canterbury was every week before the Lords for trial, "but we have so much to do and he is a person now so contemptible that we take no notice of his process." Hugh Peter, in an exercise of Christian charity, agreed to accept Laud's library, and Prynne, still frustrated in his search for evidence, asserted that Laud had already burned the incriminating papers.

In the meantime, Laud was conducting himself with patience and dignity; he had been imprisoned for two years without a trial and he had been subjected to all the indignities that the ungenerous can heap on those they hate. Through it all he showed no fear except of the scorn and the jeers of the crowd. He apparently had long ceased to hope either for his life or reputation, but his vulnerability to the irrational and illiterate mob gave him pain. "No noise till I came to Cheapside," he had written when first taken into custody, but from thence to the Tower he had been followed and railed at by the prentices and rabble. And as the libels, ballads and cartoons circulated, he remarked sadly, "I am a tavern jest." The fastidious and now helpless old man was deeply injured because his name and his very life had become the common property of those whom he had never understood, whose privacies he had once invaded as they were now invading his. He had, he said, drunk up the cup of the scornings of the people to the very bottom.

When Prynne's attempts to find or manufacture evidence failed, due process was circumvented and Laud was attainted as Strafford had been. On January 10, 1645, he was taken on foot to Tower Hill, the fifth Archbishop in England's history to die by the violence of the state. On the scaffold, he defended himself in a brief speech, fumbling with his notes and fussing about his faulty memory; he then turned toward the block. The great press of spectators barred his way. "I did think," he said, "that I might have had room to die." Even on the scaffold two Puritan ministers plagued him with rhetorical questions, still tried to force some confession from him, until he turned from them to the executioner, a gentler man, he said; turned to the headsman who would end the strife and the public scorn, and the stroke of whose axe would begin the rehabilitation of Laud's memory and the redemption of his aims for the English church.

He forgave all the world and every one of the bitter enemies who had persecuted him—and then he died. As Laud's disciple Peter Heylyn said, the state had merely "plucked a few years from a weak old man."

At Oxford Charles heard of Laud's execution and hoped that somehow, by this senseless act, the scales of Divine Justice might be weighted against the Puritan cause, balancing his own abandonment of Strafford.

By the beginning of 1645, two parties had been polarized within the Parliament. From then on the Scots, the Earl of Essex, Holles, and their followers in Parliament and the City would be called, rather loosely, the Presbyterians; Vane, Cromwell, St. John and their followers would be known as Independents. Both terms had formerly been primarily religious designations, but more and more they were coming to have political significations. And strong in the Independent party a growing republicanism was perceptible.

For Vane, 1644 had been an unpredictable year with complex intertwinings of the fortunes of peace and war. He had ridden through the maelstrom, showing himself shrewd, clever, and dedicated, a tough revolutionary willing to employ whatever tactics the moment demanded. But he had lost public credibility, for to achieve a series of immediate goals necessary to win the war and secure toleration, he had run a very tight course. Watching his turnings and shifts, the lawyers thought he had no feeling for precedent; the Scots considered him a betrayer, the peace party a war-monger. From 1644 onward, whenever any faction suspected Independent "designs" or bad faith, it would be said that Harry Vane was at work again; he would bear the reputation of "England's Machiavel." Only to himself did he seem consistent. If to make England a field where Christ's wheat could grow he had to sacrifice the possibilities of a longer range statesmanship, if he had to lay himself open to misunderstanding and slander, so be it. He had yet to learn that no aim is so pure that it cannot be tainted by unworthy means, and that reputation is the immediate jewel of a political man's soul.

The End of the War
(1645–1646)

In November of 1644, Vane had supported, in the Committee of Both Kingdoms, the remodeling of the army, partly because Essex was sluggish and Manchester remiss, but even more because troops levied locally, unaccustomed to serving outside their home counties, tended to desert in large numbers when taken "abroad." Besides, local taxation was not producing enough money to pay local soldiers. In January of 1645, Commons agreed to create a national army of some 21,000 men to be paid from a nationally imposed taxation. The Lords used this action as an excuse to shelve the Self-Denying Ordinance because, they said, military command should not be disrupted during a difficult period of transition. On January 21, the Commons proposed that Fairfax be the new commander-in-chief, with Skippon as major-general, an office which carried command of the foot. No name was proposed for the post of lieutenant-general, which assumed command of the cavalry, a position Oliver Cromwell was highly qualified for. The proposals carried 101 to 69 with Vane and Cromwell as tellers for the affirmative.

On January 29, at the insistence of the Scots, peace negotiations were reopened with the king. Vane was chosen one of the commissioners from Parliament to meet with the Royalist commissioners at Uxbridge. Before negotiations began, both sides agreed upon three main points for discussion: religion, control of the militia, and Ireland. It was next to certain that the rigidity of the Presbyterians on all three points would preclude any agreement, but Vane thought the attempt worth making even if nothing came of it but realization by the Scots of Charles' intractability. Besides, he thought, the clamors of the people for peace would be diminished if not stilled.

The Scots commissioners demanded that Charles himself take the covenant, that he consent to the abolition of episcopacy and the Prayer Book, and that he establish Presbyterianism as the one national religion and authorize a new Directory of Worship. Charles countered by offering a modified episcopacy in which the bishops would be deprived of all coercive jurisdiction. He wished to retain a modified Book of Common Prayer, but would allow complete freedom of "ceremonies," though not of doctrine. If Vane and the other Independents had agreed to these proposals, a compromise might have been reached, but they were still suspicious of Charles and they could not yet bring themselves to consider even a modified and limited episcopacy. So Vane, the erstwhile Root and Branch man, sat silent while the Scottish and Presbyterian commissioners wrangled fruitlessly with Charles. Later Clarendon charged that the leading Independents, including Vane, had been sent as "spies" to control the negotiations so as to resist peace.

As soon as it was learned at Westminster that the king was not yielding on the issue of the church, Parliament passed the ordinance for the New Model Army with the proviso that officers above the rank of lieutenant be nominated by both Houses. As any sensible field commander would, Cromwell opposed this proviso, and he won a compromise: Fairfax would appoint the officers but the Houses should ratify the appointments. Cromwell also objected to requiring the New Model to take the covenant, sufficient evidence of the sectarian nature of the army and of his own opinion of Presbyterianism. But on this he was defeated.

In discussing the militia, the Royalist commissioners proposed that the armies on both sides be disbanded and His Majesty then be invited to return to Westminster. The day before this proposal was made, Charles had written to Henrietta Maria. "As for trusting the rebels, either by going to London or disbanding my army before a peace, do no ways fear my hazarding so cheaply or foolishly. . . ." He was a strange and difficult man, always taking back with one hand what he offered with the other, apparently unaware that he was becoming known as an incorrigible dissimulator. So the negotiations dragged on and ended where they began. But at last the

Scots, who had been so sanguine about peace, were now ready to join the Independents in prosecuting the war.

On February 25, 1645, sensing the hopelessness of the negotiations even before the commissioners returned to London, the Commons appointed a committee to draw up another Self-Denying Ordinance. Thus the Treaty of Uxbridge, though it failed, motivated two important pieces of Independent legislation: the New Model Army Ordinance and the Self-Denying Act. No wonder the Royalists suspected a plot at Uxbridge and saw Vane behind it.

Now that the New Model Army was authorized, money was needed to pay it, and until the new levies came in, there was no way but for the City to lend once more. On March 4, Parliament sent an influential committee to request the new loan: the Lord of Loudon represented the Scots, Northumberland the Lords, and Vane the Commons. Northumberland began—with unconscious humor—by reporting on the Uxbridge negotiations: "All we desired" in religion, he assured the City, was the abolition of episcopacy. He then proceeded to the most potent issue, the "cessation" the king had made with the rebels in Ireland when Parliament had wished to prosecute the war vigorously. When Northumberland had aroused all the adrenalin inherent in this issue, he asked for some 80,000 pounds to be secured by the new ordinance of taxation.

Lord Loudon, an effective speaker, followed Northumberland. With amiable candor he acknowledged that the Scots more than any others had wanted the treaty, partly because they delighted in peace and partly because they wished to silence the cavils of their enemies. Then he reaffirmed the Parliamentary fiction: His Majesty's counselors still labored to subvert religion and to introduce an arbitrary and tyrannical power, and so His Majesty had again been misled into asking impossible terms.

Vane had little to add: the Parliament, he said, was convinced that the shortest way to peace was by firm prosecution of the war. The important thing now was to put an army in the field at once. This army, he said, was even now "molding and framing," but it needed equipment and supplies.

There can no argument I know be more prevalent with you than the shortening of the war; the Houses of Parliament have been willing to end it either way, by treaty or war; but they think all treaties will be useless till they be in a posture to show themselves able to repel that opposition that can be made against them.

This speech marks a subtle inner change that has taken place in Vane and perhaps in the nation itself. His speech is crisp, tight-lipped, with conviction but without much emotional expression of it; he knows better than to overstate religious and patriotic themes at a time when war is not a glory but a repellent necessity. Into his plea for money he obtrudes no ideological fervor: the time for that is past. The cause is still unobtrusively avowed, but no one is asked to respond with feelings which the long war had exhausted and the poverty had rendered anachronistic. And never again was Vane asked to go to the City as friend and trusted member. Increasingly Presbyterian in its sympathies, the City had less and less sympathy for him and the cause.

The day before these appeals to the City, the House of Lords had reluctantly approved Fairfax's list of proposed officers despite the preponderance of Independents in it. And on March 24, the new Self-Denying Ordinance was presented to the Commons, which contained some significant differences from the former bill. First, it provided that within forty days after the ordinance became effective, members of Parliament must resign from any post conferred by the existing Parliament. But it said nothing about their subsequent re-employment. The final provision was also different. It stated that members who had been granted office before the Long Parliament met, who then were displaced by His Majesty but restored by Parliament, should continue to enjoy their places. As this was precisely Vane's situation, the new Self-Denying Ordinance did not require him to deny himself anything.

And yet he had been exercising great denial. From August 8, 1642, when he had been reappointed Treasurer of the Navy, until May 12, 1645, he had been entitled to draw over 9,000 pounds in fees; but he had, in fact, drawn just over 600 pounds. The rest was being carried in "surplusage," that is, it did not revert to any general fund but was available to him upon demand. Thus, for the first three years of the revolution, Vane had been strenuously and fastidiously exact in money matters. The 200 pounds a year he had allowed himself was the salary of a civil servant, the sum soon to be paid to Milton by Cromwell's government, and the sum allowed to

Robert Earle of Essex, his Excellence. Generall of ỹ Army, Imployed for ỹ defence of the Protestant Religion. ỹ Safety of his Ma:ties Perſon. & of ỹ Parliment. ỹ preſeruation of ỹ Lawes. Liberties. & Peace of ỹ Kingdome. & protection of his Ma:tied Subiects from violence & oppreſsion.

The slow, heavy, phlegmatic Earl of Essex led the Puritan armies, but was ultimately discredited by his own ineptitude and the hostility of Vane and other revolutionary zealots. (Radio Times Hulton Picture Library)

Ambitious and expedient, the elder Vane occupied an important place in the government of Charles I. When the Earl of Strafford was doomed, he switched his allegiance to the Puritan party, but in the fratricidal Civil War neither side trusted or liked him; he died lonely and embittered. (The National Portrait Gallery, London)

financially distressed members of Parliament. It was no more than enough to live on, and without anyone's knowing about it, Vane had taken for himself only this bare minimum. By virtue of his parsimony he was in a strong moral position which entitled him to that revolutionary fervor he had formerly displayed when exhorting the London merchants who had given once, to give again and yet again—to hold back nothing for the sake of the cause. It also gave him in Parliamentary debate that inestimable inner confidence enjoyed by a man who has carried out the duties of his office from conviction rather than from interest. As sponsor of the Self-Denying Ordinance, he was only asking the nation to do what he had been doing himself: to put aside self-interest, to forsake greed and gross advantage.

And then, at the very time when the Self-Denying Ordinance became a reality, Vane began to depart from its spirit and intent. In the month after the ordinance was passed, he began to accept his full fees as treasurer and to draw on surplusage as well. By the end of 1647, he had taken about 16,000 pounds in some two and a half years. This is the more surprising because after the Self-Denying Ordinance had passed, the Presbyterian majority, wishing no doubt to assist Vane in carrying out his own ordinance, ordered him to return one-half of his treasurer's fees in the future, but he never did so. Apparently considering this an ad hominem piece of legislation inspired by Presbyterian vindictiveness, he defied not only the intent of the ordinance but also the law of Parliament itself.

These actions indicate a major moral crisis in Vane's life. Perhaps the only fortunate revolutionaries are those who die young. Those who survive come to know the silent rust, the wingless moth of corruption and then, under the pressure of some unusual event, comes the beginning of the long inevitable walk with compromise. In 1645 there was an outcry from landed people all over England that they could not collect their rents because tenants could not pay. In ordinary times the tenants could have been replaced, but now with the military levies, with the many wounded and dead, new tenants could not be found. It is estimated that in 1645 only one-seventh of the rents came in throughout the nation. For the Vanes it was much worse. In the summer of 1645 some Scots Royalists surprised and plundered Raby, although they were soon driven away by forces raised by young Harry's brother, Sir George

Vane. Three more times in that same year the castle was taken, plundered, and retaken. Vane later estimated his losses at 16,000 pounds, the same amount that, by the end of 1647, he would take in treasurer's fees. Presumably he was repaying himself for the Royalist depredations. When he finally had to choose between revolutionary fastidiousness about money and the probable loss of Raby, the storied and towered castle made stronger demands upon him than a waning ideological fervor. On the matter of Raby, the republican in him gave way to the aristocrat. Undoubtedly he saw other revolutionaries selling offices, taking bribes, getting rich from the war. Expediency greater than one's own is never hard to find, but when he violated the spirit of the Self-Denying Ordinance, he became vulnerable and would in time smart for it.

Meanwhile, it was being said that the Self-Denying Ordinance was simply a way for the Independents to snatch power from the Presbyterians, or that it was a specious attempt to demonstrate their own integrity. In practice it did indeed remove some Presbyterian peers from command in the army, but it did little to foster self-denial among the Parliament men.

During the summer of 1645, some curious maneuvers connected with the Uxbridge peace talks came to light, illustrating the fear both parties had of separate peace negotiations. In June, a Presbyterian minister named Cranford circulated a report that Vane, St. John, Pierrepont, and Crew, all Independents, had negotiated secretly with the king. But after an investigation proved Cranford's words false and scandalous, Parliament ordered him to be imprisoned in the Tower and to pay 500 pounds to each man maligned.

Vane and the Independents counterattacked at once by trying to indict Holles and Whitelocke for treason on two charges. First, in the presence of the king they had allegedly distinguished between a war party and a peace party in the Commons, and because all actions of the House were theoretically actions of the entire body, it was scandalous to imply any division into parties. The second charge was more serious: Holles and Whitelocke were accused of helping the king write his answers to the Parliamentary proposals at Oxford in the past November. Unable at first to take the charges seriously, Whitelocke soon came to realize that if they could, the Independents would cut off his head or at least expel him from Parliament. He became sufficiently alarmed to call upon his friends for help. Among them was Lambert Osbaldeston, Vane's old headmaster, who responded by urging moderation on Vane. Like many a schoolmaster to whom ideas are only intellectual counters, Osbaldeston had become shocked to see how far some of his pupils were carrying his ideas in practice. He was now attempting to allay those angry forces of vindictiveness and disorder that in their infancy he had nourished.

The House disposed of both charges on the same day, deciding that while they had some technical truth in them, they did not amount to treason. Meanwhile, it was with sardonic pleasure that some Royalists observed the revolutionaries beginning to turn on one another. It had not come to blood this time, they said, but it would. They could wait.

On June 4, The Common Council of London asked that Cromwell be placed at the head of the new forces to be raised in the Eastern Association. All of the officers present at a Council of War not only supported this request but also petitioned that Cromwell be appointed to the vacant post of lieutenant-general. Forty days had passed since the Self-Denying Ordinance had taken effect, so Cromwell could now be legally reappointed. The Commons voted to reappoint him, and when the Lords postponed consideration, Fairfax and Cromwell simply assumed that the consent of the Commons was enough.

At the same time, in mid-June, the Parliamentary army was facing Rupert at Naseby in the crucial battle of the civil war. There Cromwell's cavalry, supported by his cousin Whalley and the Independent colonels Okey and Pride, was once more decisive. In his account of the battle to Speaker Lenthall, Cromwell expressed fully the relationship between military victories and the sectarian demand for toleration. "He that ventures his life for the liberty of his country, I wish he trust God for the liberty of his conscience, and you for the liberty he fights for." Though the Presbyterian majority in the House deleted Cromwell's sentiments from the records, the complete copy was soon in circulation, and wiser heads were realizing that a victorious army was a force to be reckoned with. While there were still pockets of Royalist resistance here and there, the war was practically over. After Naseby, it was said that Charles was hunted like a partridge on the mountains.

Nor was Charles' position helped by exposure of his private correspondence captured at Naseby, which included drafts or copies of letters to Henrietta Maria. To her he always had to seem more intransigent than he really was if he wished to avoid conjugal scoldings, but even so, these revelations of the king's private mind came as a profound shock to most of the people. In one letter he revealed that he did not recognize the Houses of Parliament at Westminster as a lawful Parliament, although such recognition had been a precondition for the negotiations at Uxbridge. Others revealed that he was negotiating for an Irish army to land in England, in partial payment for which he would abolish all laws against English Catholics. He was also negotiating for a foreign army from Lorraine to land in England and fight under his banner. Once these facts were known, no one could take his pleas for a treaty seriously.

Meanwhile, there were arising new forces that had to be reckoned with. Wherever an army had passed, Royalist or Parliamentary, soldiers had confiscated livestock and crops, and stolen whatever they could lay hands on. There was also the statistically small but emotionally potent quota of rapes and drunken brawls—all the disorders of a large army quartered on a civilian population. It was simply to protect their lands and homes against plunderers that the common people assembled a kind of army; because they were armed with scythes, rocks, an occasional musket, but mostly with clubs, they were called Clubmen. Upon one of their flags they flaunted a piece of doggerel:

> If you offer to plunder or take our cattle,
> Be assured we will give you battle.

One such group boasted that they were ready to defend themselves against either king or Parliament. After all, both Royalist and Puritan troopers behaved alike; they all had large bellies and got drunk and took unlimited license to use their weapons. To the Clubmen, the issues of the war had become irrelevant; they were "absolute neuters," they said, who would be quiet with those who were quiet, but would lay hold on all disorderly soldiers. Their concern was their own survival.

As the Clubmen were increasing in the counties, a strong populist movement was growing inside the army, inspired by John Lilburne, who was both leader and symbol of it. When Cromwell, whom he at this time reverenced, had tried and failed to prevent legislation requiring soldiers of the New Model to take the covenant, Honest John was the only officer who resigned, though many had detested the oath. Now out of work and free of military discipline, filled with a fierce energy that found its outlet in ideology and political idealism and eloquence, Lilburne began to make his name and character felt.

Like most compulsive reformers, he knew what he was against: formerly it had been Star Chamber and High Commission; now it was the payment of tithes to the church, corruption in the House of Commons, and the very existence of the House of Lords. But unlike ordinary reformers, he also knew what he believed in; for example, he wanted unrestricted freedom of the press. More important, he insisted that sovereign power resided in the people of England and was exercised solely through the House of Commons. The power of kings and nobles he accounted for by the "Norman Yoke" theory which—to oversimplify—asserted that in the good old times, the Saxons in England enjoyed their rights and liberties under a republican form of government and that the conquering Normans imposed on them the monarchical tyranny. Now the Norman yoke must be lifted from their necks and the old ways restored. However naïve the theory sounds, it had emotional power and was believed in by men of intellectual quality, including Vane and Milton. If Lilburne had merely asserted that the civil war, like such other great moments as the writing of Magna Charta, was another attempt to reclaim lost liberties, he might have carried Vane and Cromwell with him, but he went too far—he attacked Parliament itself, first the Lords and then the Commons, saying in effect that new Parliament was old king writ large. And that his faction was called the Levellers indicated the inaccurate but common belief that they wished to do away with all rank, hierarchy, and inequalities of property, so that every man might be his own priest, king, and landlord. Both Levellers and Clubmen were manifestations of the same phenomenon: the rise of a new political consciousness among the lower classes as they realized that under present laws and forms they were not receiving their share of England's good things. And though both Levellers and Clubmen were moving in directions Vane and Cromwell had pointed out, they both now thought that the leveling was going too far. Like many Independents, they were men of property and rank, and while Lilburne never favored "equalling" men's estates, some of his followers did. The successful

Puritan revolutionaries therefore resisted the new movements. Once again they found they had released forces which were no longer within their control.

As a result of the Royalist attack on Raby, the Committee of Both Kingdoms recommended that a garrison be kept there until further notice, and the elder Vane was authorized to send to London for ordnance, field pieces, 150 common muskets and 150 firelocks, all to be kept in the castle. On September 9, young Vane informed the Commons that Raby was now garrisoned, and to ensure its strength four additional pieces of small artillery were sent from the Tower.

At about the time Raby was under attack, Roger Williams was in England writing his most famous work, *The Bloody Tenet of Persecution*. In the preface to it he recorded the impression Vane had made on him during the previous autumn, pleading in Parliament against repressive measures advocated by the Westminster Assembly.

Mine own ears were glad and late witnesses of an heavenly speech of one of the most eminent of that High Assembly of Parliament. . . . 'Why should the labors of any be suppressed, if sober, though never so different? We now profess to seek God, we desire to see light.'

Vane, Milton, and Williams, all of whose religious views required a good deal of latitude, were becoming spokesmen for the growing national sentiment for toleration, strongest among the sects and the soldiers.

On September 11, the already stricken king suffered a shocking disaster when Prince Rupert, contrary to all Royalist expectations, surrendered the city of Bristol. Unable to acknowledge the realities of the war, the king lashed out at his nephew and accused him of traitorous conduct. It was evident to everyone but the king and a few die-hard Royalists that his cause was lost, although Lord Astley did not publicly concede it until the following March. When surrendering to Colonel Birch he told his men, "You have done your work, boys. You may go play, unless you fall out among yourselves." But even before Colonel Astley predicted it, the falling out had begun.

Shortly after the surrender of Bristol, the Parliament asked the

Scots to send their army south. The Scots commissioners rejoined sharply that they had not seen much of the money that Parliament had voted them, nor had the provisions of the Solemn League and Covenant been activated yet. Before they would move, they demanded that a Presbyterian church government be established and negotiations reopened with the king. At this critical juncture, as a Parliamentary observer said, Vane "showed great discretion and judgment in turning all into a fair way." Apparently he proposed that if the Scots would march to Newark, the English would meet them there with 200 barrels of gunpowder and 30,000 pounds in cash. He and others apparently agreed also that a form of Presbytery might be set up, though not with the powers the Assembly of Divines desired: the kingdom of Scotland, Vane said, should not press for that. But he wrote his father that he would like to see the Scots army return home unless it could be more serviceable; Parliament had received many complaints about the expense, disorderliness, and ineffectiveness of that army.

As Royalist counties fell one by one to Parliament, new writs of election were issued to fill the places which had been held by members loyal to Charles, but the balance of power between Presbyterian and Independent remained unaltered. Henry Marten, the bitter and witty republican who had been ejected by Pym, was now restored without an election when Vane proposed that his ejection be expunged from the Journal. Others among the new recruits were men famous for military action, such as Ireton, Fleetwood, Ludlow, and Algernon Sidney. And now that Parliament was at full strength again, they tried once more for peace.

Through December and January the peace negotiations fumbled along. The king offered various concessions regarding religion and control of the militia, and Parliament worked out counterproposals, with Vane apparently managing the negotiations for the Commons. But exposures of the king's simultaneous secret correspondences with the Irish Catholics and the King of Denmark, and the queen's "agenting" with the French clergy and the Prince of Orange caused Parliament to take an even harder line, though they did keep trying to negotiate.

During the debate on the peace propositions in December of 1645, one of the Parliamentary conditions proposed was that some of the members should be promoted. Denzil Holles was to be made a viscount; Haselrig and Stapleton were to become barons with an income of 2,000 pounds a year; and Sir Henry Vane, Sr., was to become a baron, an honor he is not likely to have won by himself. Since his son likely wished to inherit both a title and the land that went with it, he must have supported the proposal, but it died when the peace negotiations failed.

On January 15, 1646, when the king sent "a very pathetic letter" asking for peace, Vane helped draft a reply which was virtually a Parliamentary ultimatum. But the king persevered. On January 31, he suggested that religion should be as in the days of Queen Elizabeth, "having regard still to tender consciences." But Vane, thinking that this proposal was merely an attempt to detach the Independents from the rest of Parliament, urged that it be ignored. When matters of peace and war and the managing of the kingdom were settled, he said, the Independents had rather receive tranquility of conscience from the Parliament than from the king.

In January rumors circulated that four or five Independents meeting secretly were agitating to depose the king; the king and his advisers apparently believed that Vane was meeting with them. One of the king's secretaries wrote to Vane and, receiving no reply, in a few days wrote again. In these letters Charles offered once again independence of conscience in exchange for political support, and he indicated, too, his awareness that his dethronement was being discussed: "You cannot suppose the work is done, though God should suffer you to destroy the King." Vane never replied to either of these letters.

Perhaps he was too concerned about what the Presbyterian majority at Westminster was suggesting for the reform of the church. The Presbyterians had proposed a clause which would give the elders and ministers the right to exclude church members from communion. It was opposed by a coalition of Independents ("prime men, active and diligent," Baillie called them) and Erastian lawyers. They believed that this clause sanctioned arbitrary exertion of power, so they demanded that offenses meriting exclusion be listed and published. The frustrated Scots answered that Satan's wiles could never be encompassed in a list however long, nor could the corrupt heart of man be revealed in a legal document; church leaders must have discretion to name, judge, and punish offenses.

Vane replied that it was better to convince the offender of his sin and reform him than to exclude him, and that the power of exclusion was too dangerous to be entrusted to anyone but Parliament. The lawyers modified Vane's position slightly: the Presbyterians themselves should draw up the list of sins, but if some ingenious sinner managed to evade the intent of the official catalogue, he could be suspended until Parliament decided his case.

Losing their fight in Commons, the Presbyterian ministers again used their pulpits to arouse the citizens, who stormed Westminster with petitions against the proposal, but this time the Commons dismissed the protest as a breach of Parliamentary privilege. The ministers next presented a petition in which they alleged that ecclesiastical jurisdiction was vested solely in the church by divine right. The Commons calmly voided this petition too as a breach of privilege. Thus it was becoming evident that even though some form of Presbyterianism would be set up, the church would become to some degree laicized and even secularized, for Parliament was determined to retain final control. Not the law of God but the law of Commons would determine the structure of the church.

Meanwhile, financial needs continued to press upon Parliament. To meet them, a number of committees had been established, two of which were especially significant. The first was empowered to sequester estates of "delinquents," to sell them, and turn the money over to Parliament. The other was the Committee for Compounding which met at Goldsmith's Hall; the work of this committee was accelerated by a new ordinance for compounding passed in October of 1645, and for years Vane was a leading spirit on it. To "compound" meant that anyone judged "delinquent" (someone who had directly or indirectly helped the king or failed to pay Parliamentary taxes) could by paying somewhere between one-sixth and one-half of his estate be released from further judgment. In each case, the committee had to determine what was fair. Because tenants were not paying rents, many of those fined could not pay their compounding fees. Therefore, they would offer to sell part of their estates in order to retain the rest. The lands were eagerly bought up by the London merchants, by army officers, and, too frequently, by members of Parliament. Even after the war was over, the work of these two committees continued.

> But tired-out cruelty pauses for a while
> To take new breath amidst her barbarous toil.

So does not avarice, she unwearied still,
Ne'er stops her greedy hand from doing ill;
The warrior may a while his spear forsake,
But sequestrators will no respite take.

So efficiently did these committees work that it was said hyperbolically that half the real estate of the realm changed hands, an economic revolution in itself. As these sequestrations and compoundings continued, resentment and anger grew. And as the years passed, Vane became the symbol of the compounding committee, faithful, meticulous, efficient, passionless, with every chance for advantage or corruption and yet never accused of any—with one exception. In May of 1646, Vane's sister Anne married the heir of a prominent Royalist, Sir Thomas Liddell, who made his composition in that same month on what some regarded as too favorable terms. Because Vane was such a prominent member of the committee, there was talk of favoritism, but other than this, apparently not even Vane's enemies could find grounds for reproach. Nevertheless, one day Vane's work on this committee, so necessary for the survival of the army, the navy, and indeed the revolutionary government, would rebound against him, like the Strafford affair. One day he would face in Parliament many young men whose fathers' estates had been whittled down by this committee to support something called "the good cause" about which they cared not at all.

The king, meanwhile, disappointed in his overtures to the Independents and losing hope of substantial help from abroad, surrendered his person to the Scots on May 5, 1646. Baillie believed that since the Independents were a minority, they needed a military victory, and a negotiated peace would "be their quick and evident ruin." So, he concluded, "the King's being with us made them mad; but all good people are joyful of it." To many, the desertion of Charles to the Scots was indeed so maddening that they were not only willing to settle the government without him, but were even willing to put away "the whole royal race." The Scots commissioners to Parliament insisted that they had neither conspired in this surrender nor even known of it beforehand. The Independents remained sceptical of the Scots' good faith, and lost what little trust they had in the king's word.

A few days later, Vane offered an amendment to a bill which

required that upon demand of both Houses, the king should be delivered to Parliament to be disposed of as both Houses should appoint. It failed to pass, but as long as the king remained with the Scots (some eight months) there was a dangerous possibility of conflict between the two nations. In June, Parliament proclaimed "that this kingdom hath no further use for the continuation of the Scots army within the Kingdom of England," a sentiment Vane had earlier whispered to his father.

In July the Parliament finally agreed on Nineteen Propositions to be submitted to the king, and they dispatched them to Charles at Newcastle by commissioners who were instructed not to negotiate but to demand the king's assent to them all. If they did not receive that assent within ten days, they were to return home. These propositions were hardly easier for Charles to accept than the earlier ones. He was to take the covenant himself and agree to an act of Parliament which would enjoin it on all of his subjects in the three kingdoms. He must agree to "utterly abolish" episcopal church government, to give Parliament the control of the militia for twenty years, to end the cessation in Ireland, and to consent to the punishment of most of his own followers and advisers. These harshly Presbyterian terms would enforce on England the demands of the first Scottish covenant of 1638—to abolish episcopacy forever.

Faced with such impossible terms, Charles could only play for time, and he asked to be allowed to come to Westminster to discuss them. When this reply was read aloud in Parliament on August 12, the Scots also presented a letter offering to withdraw their army from England provided they received arrears of expenses, and suggesting a consultation between the two kingdoms to decide on the best way to dispose of the king. After debate on how much should be paid the Scots, a compromise of 400,000 pounds was finally agreed upon—but the money, of course, was not available and would have to be borrowed from the City.

The Presbyterian majority was pushing for the spirit as well as the form of what they considered a true church settlement. On September 2, they proposed an ordinance to suppress blasphemy and heresy. It is incredible that this piece of legislation should have been favorably considered in a Parliament which lacked a Presbyterian majority, but it was. In its final form the ordinance said that denial of doctrines relating to the Trinity or Incarnation would be punished

by death; an incorrect view of infant baptism merited life imprisonment, as did denial of other Presbyterian views. If enforced, the
ordinance would have filled the jails with the sectarians of the
Independent left, including Vane's little band of Seekers; yet it was
read twice without even a division and sent to a committee for
further study. It must have been that the conservative instincts of
the nation had been aroused by stories of sectarian excesses which, as
Baillie observed, would upset men of all faiths. And Vane found his
name associated with the extremists. John Biddle, for instance, when
jailed on charges of anti-Trinitarianism, appealed to Vane as the
man most likely to help him. His confidence in Vane's tolerance was
justified when Sir Henry sensibly moved that Biddle be either tried
or released. He was freed but soon embarrassed Vane again by pref-
acing a new heretical pamphlet with a letter to him; for this pamphlet, Biddle was tried, convicted and sentenced to death but never
executed. There were stories, too, of Anabaptists who immersed
naked women at midnight and tales, likely apocryphal, of orgies
conducted by the Family of Love. Fears that had stalked New England during the antinomian controversy were now abroad in England.

The Independents became sufficiently alarmed that in the same
month the new ordinance was debated, they made another offer to
Charles: for liberty of conscience and Parliamentary control of the
militia, they would accept a moderate episcopacy once the Scots
were gone. This proposal is much like one Vane would offer later;
he therefore undoubtedly agreed with it and may even have
originated it. Certainly by now he preferred a limited Anglicanism
to an unrestricted Presbyterianism.

Somewhere in the midst of all this dissension Vane began to be as
uneasy about the Independent left as he was about the Presbyterian
right. To speak of the rights of an abstract "people" as Lilburne was
fond of doing was all very well; but to watch that sweaty mob as it
was pulled by strings from the pulpit, from Parliament, from the
City, crying out against bishops one week and Presbyterians the
next, defaming and acclaiming the king, cheering the army and then
hissing the soldiers—all this could hardly inspire confidence. Yet
when the "people," as Lilburne's followers called themselves, were
not allowed to vote, the City had elected a mayor of royalist
sympathies. The Independent position Vane now occupied was a

very narrow one without popular support. Educated men who owned land and managed it, who were taxed for the Poor Fund, who had a real stake in the governing of the nation—these, he thought, were the men who should vote. The Levellers had an incipient enemy in Vane, and they were coming to know it. At the same time the Presbyterians heartily despised him. More pragmatic Independents, like Cromwell, could see that without popular support, the cause would more and more have to rely upon the military. There is some reason to think that Cromwell brought Vane to see this also.

In September, 1646, the Earl of Essex died without issue and his peerage was terminated. After an eloquent Presbyterian funeral sermon, he was laid to rest among the mighty dead in the Abbey Church at Westminster. An effigy of the earl clad in robes, with a coronet upon his head and the baton of command in his hand, was brought into the church and set up under a temporary monument in the east end where the communion table had once stood before the earl's party had declared it idolatrous. For many days, large crowds came to see the honors devised for the earl, whose military failures were balanced by his loyalty and devotion to the cause of Parliament. But some ten days after the earl died, a sectarian leftist named John White was privately ordered by an angel to destroy images. He entered the Abbey and mutilated the figure of William Camden, the fine old scholar and antiquarian who had taught Ben Jonson at Westminster School; then he hacked into pieces the effigy of the noble Essex. It was portentous, some thought, that an inwardly illuminated Independent sectarian had at once desecrated the grave of a gentle Anglican and the effigy of a confused Presbyterian.

In December, before any large issues had been settled, Vane asked to be allowed to surrender his navy treasurership, not to resign from it, but to sell it. Although both Houses approved, he did not really relinquish that office until four years later. Perhaps the reason was that as 1647 approached, Vane could see that the issue of toleration with the Presbyterians would require a military solution as had the earlier conflict over church reform with the Anglicans. Not so long ago, in the days of his passionate youth, the bishops seemed the ultimate enemy. But their secular lordliness and their alliance with the power of the state Vane now perceived as less dangerous than Presbyterian dogmatism. Laud had not cared so much for what people believed as he did for how they behaved; he wanted communal order in worship. But the Presbyterians, with the aid of the state and its military power, wished to open a window into men's minds and souls. If the ordinance to suppress blasphemy and heresy were to pass, there would be no room in England for John Milton or Roger Williams, for the sectarian soldiers in Cromwell's regiments, and certainly no place for young Vane. Where could he go? Not to New England certainly. Perhaps he thought at times of joining with the continental Protestants in Germany or Holland or Denmark, but he knew well enough now that the spiritual warfare was universal, that what he positively required, full liberty of conscience, was allowed nowhere. It would be as easy to win it in England as anywhere else, and in the coming struggle his naval post might prove decisive.

It is an unspeakably sad moment when successful revolutionists inwardly concede that their revolutionary aims achieved by force can only be upheld by that same force. Oliver Cromwell had already made that concession to reality and it seems likely that young Vane, always subject to impulse by the nature of his antinomian beliefs, made the same silent concession when he withdrew his request and continued to serve as Treasurer of the Navy.

12

Vane and the Army (1647)

At the beginning of 1647, the political scene was intricate and dangerous. A long, chaotic, and bitter war had been won by an army largely Independent in sympathies and supported in Parliament by an able and resolute minority including Vane and Cromwell. The city of London, which had largely financed the war, was now generally "Presbyterian" in sentiment, as was the majority in the House of Commons. Thus, even among those who originally supported the revolution, there had come about a divergence of political, economic, and religious interests. And the king had loyal supporters throughout the country—noblemen, landed men, and ordinary citizens whose hearts were swayed by the mystique of that slight, elegant figure with the distraught manner and the sad face, now darkened and chastened by loss and suffering. These Royalists mistrusted the Presbyterians and despised the Independents.

There was already distrust between the king and his Scottish hosts, for Charles had no sympathy with the covenant or with the style and tone of Scotch Calvinism—its doctrinal rigidity, canting sermons, and politicized ministry.

The soldiers, now objects of almost universal scorn, had their own bitter grievances: there were still no pensions provided for widows and orphans of the slain; there was no indemnity for soldiers for acts committed while in uniform; worst of all, the infantry were owed several weeks' and the cavalrymen several months' pay. The people, in turn, were bitter because they had not been repaid for the quarter many of them had been forced to give to the soldiers: one man boldly wrote, "no man knows what a bondage it is to be under the power of an army but they that feel it." Even the silly extravagances of a Court seemed trifles compared to the economic drain of a large standing army.

People were tired, too, of revenue committees that met behind closed doors, from whose judgments they had no appeal. They were tired of all the old taxes and outraged at the new ones, many of them illegal. They were alarmed at the excesses of the sectarians, some of whom stood up in sacred services to shout down the minister, refused to remove their hats in churches, which they called steeple houses and habitations of the devil, and justified their impulses by calling them whispers of God. Some of them denied the divinity of their Savior. No wonder there was a growing desire to see the church settled decently and safely.

A minor incident illustrated the mood of the people. When one stout yeoman purchased an ox at Smithfield, he lacked money to pay the excise tax on it. When the excise collectors, armed with Parliamentary warrants, seized the ox, a riot ensued and the casual by-passers who gathered to see what was going on took the farmer's part. They battered the collectors, burned their office, and tore up their books; and they fought over the eighty pounds or so they found in the excise office until the strongest carried it away. This incident was a straw in the wind. Armies meant taxes; if the army could be demobilized, perhaps taxes could be lowered. So the people sent a petition to Parliament. It was sympathetically received by the Presbyterian majority, which then blunderingly proposed to retain the professional cavalry but to discharge all infantry in England except what was required for garrisons. In the future, infantry would be furnished by the Trained Bands, citizens serving temporarily under officers with Presbyterian sympathies. In theory it was not a wholly bad proposal, for at least it balanced an Independent cavalry against a Presbyterian infantry.

But the Parliament was grossly unfair to those infantrymen who, having risked their lives in its cause, were now dismissed unpaid. Some members even voted to reward these men by sending them to Ireland, where plague and fever would eat them up. And the House of Lords, with the nobleman's disdain for common foot soldiers, refused to continue the assessments on which payment of the troops depended, even though payments were far in arrears.

They decreed further that except for Fairfax there should be no officer in the army above the rank of colonel: that disposed of Cromwell. Then they provided that no member of the House of Commons could hold any command whatever, and nobody who refused to take the covenant could continue to hold rank. Now a sergeant-major must swear to the Presbyterian covenant before he could swear at his troops. Cromwell quickly perceived that Parliament was jealous of the power of the army and was moving to contain it. "Never," he wrote to Fairfax, "were the spirits of men more embittered than now. Surely the devil hath but a short time." And the Commons, hearing of soldiers' threats to cut Presbyterian throats, placed a guard around Westminster.

At this juncture the Scots decided that if they were paid part of the money owed them, they would deliver the king into the hands of Parliament. In February, accordingly, the monarch was conveyed by easy stages from Newcastle to Holmby House, and along the way he was greeted by sympathetic crowds who, tired of the war, suspicious of Parliament, weary of soldiers, saw in the person of the king the magic touch that might make everything whole once again.

At the same time, Vane was again absenting himself from Parliament when things were going against him. When he thought he might win or even when the matter was in doubt he fought tenaciously and shrewdly, but when he was sure of losing he simply stayed away. He seems never to have realized that politicians sometimes make their deepest impact when supporting issues they know to be lost, that they may subtly alter psychological balances in those who observe them and thereby create a climate of support for some future issue. Vane knew that the Presbyterian majority, by its treatment of the army, was pursuing dangerous delusions, and, unable to influence that majority, he simply quit coming to the Parliament as the crisis brewed and boiled.

The army was naturally disturbed at the hostile tone of the new legislation and on March 21, a council of officers with Fairfax in the chair received a Parliamentary deputation of Presbyterians at Saffron Walden. After listening politely, they asked the deputation four hard questions: what regiments were to be kept in England? Who was to command the army in Ireland? What assurance was given for payment and subsistence of those who went to Ireland? What satisfaction could be given about arrears of pay and indemnity? On the demands implied in the last two questions, the officers were unanimous, and if the Presbyterian majority had not been obsessed with their desire to disband the Independent soldiers, they might have realized that pay was now the crucial issue. Had they given satisfaction about that, Parliament might well have had its way about the rest.

The soldiers now drew up a petition of their own, threatening in tone and violent in language. In its final—and softened—form, soldiers in any war would have approved of it: it asked for back pay and indemnity for acts committed while in uniform; exemption from impressment in any future war for the veterans of the past war; and it asked that widows and orphans of men killed in action be granted an allowance sufficient to maintain life, and that soldiers who had suffered losses while fighting for the cause might be compensated.

But this petition aroused a storm of indignation in Parliament, which considered it a new and arrogant threat to constituted authority. Cromwell himself shared this view, for now it seemed to him that soldiers were demanding concessions at gunpoint. Though he understood and perhaps sympathized, he disapproved.

Cromwell's stand outraged John Lilburne who, in spite of his resignation from the service, was still the idol of the common soldier. He could not understand his admired leader's present pusillanimity, his failure to stand behind the men who had stood behind him in battle; and in *Jonah's Cry out of the Whale's Belly*, Honest John gave Cromwell both a scolding and a way out by suggesting that, like King Charles, he was the victim of evil counselors. The soldiers could deliver themselves from the "tyrannical clutches of Holles and Stapleton" if it were not for Cromwell, who was being "led by the nose by two unworthy, covetous earthworms, Vane and St. John—I mean young Sir Henry Vane and Solicitor St. John—whose baseness I sufficiently anatomised unto thee . . . above a year ago."

There was a bite in Lilburne's words. Cromwell's most prominent feature, a large red nose, had long been a butt of humor: his fiery indignations seemed to find outlet through it, and men said that there was a glowworm continually burning in his beak. But aside from the jest, Lilburne made a serious charge: the two leading "silken Independents" had moderated Cromwell's affection for the troops. "Sir, I am jealous over you with the height of godly jealousy." Another Leveller took up the cry, accusing Lord Saye, Lord Wharton, Cromwell, Vane, St. John, Fiennes, "and the rest who now oppress the people" of having conspired in many "private councils" to enable a few Independents to "hold the reigns of government in their own hands, not for a year, but forever."

These are wild charges. But it is true that at the very time he was absenting himself from Parliament, Vane was meeting with Cromwell and other Independents to formulate plans for opposing Presbyterians and Levellers, and Lilburne's phrase "silken Independents" stuck. Now the former revolutionary comrades were divided into three factions: Presbyterians, Independents, and Levellers, and the two parties which had most in common, the Independents and Levellers, hated one another most.

The Presbyterians were so upset by the petition of the soldiers that they proposed that all the petitioners be declared traitors and Cromwell arrested. Late one night, when many Independents had left the Commons thinking nothing more would be done, Holles pushed through a manifesto proclaiming that those who continued to promote the petition should be "proceeded against as enemies of the State and disturbers of the public peace." Even Holles, who never betrayed an excess of intelligence, might have wondered who would proceed against an aroused and victorious army.

To further teach the soldiers who was in command, Parliament voted to borrow 200,000 pounds to be spent in England and Ireland, but not one penny of it was to be used to pay arrears of wages. Alarmed by the hostile reaction of the soldiers to this bill, the Lords proposed that every soldier receive six weeks' pay upon disbandment. Far from placated, the soldiers entered upon one of history's most extraordinary political gambits. Eight of the ten cavalry regiments agreed to choose for each regiment two representatives whom they called "agitators," a prophetic word which then simply meant "agents."

These agitators promptly composed a letter of grievance against Parliament (much as the Commons had once remonstrated against the king), and they rode off to London to present it. Now the Presbyterian majority in the Commons reacted with the same sense of outraged authority that Charles had once exhibited: they called the agitators to the bar and demanded to know who had written the letter. The agitators, with the poise under fire they had learned on the battlefield, replied that they were merely agents of regiments, and that those regiments would have to answer.

The thought of bringing eight good regiments to the bar gave some pause, so the members turned again to Cromwell, who agreed to go to the army and promise the soldiers an ordinance for indemnity, payment of part of the arrears, and security for the rest. After meeting with the agitators, Cromwell produced on May 16, 1647, a *Declaration of the Army*, signed by 223 commissioned officers. This document asked Parliament to acknowledge the right of soldiers to petition their generals on military matters, and it requested that their original petition be considered once more. Having offered concessions and promoted conciliation, Cromwell believed that he had accomplished what he had been sent to do.

But then occurred one of those strange turns of events that a disrupted nation may expect: the peace party in the House, who in righteous voices had continually impugned the motives and charity of the war party, themselves began to prepare for war. On April 16, Parliament authorized the Common Council of the City to select the leaders of the Trained Bands. Of course they chose Presbyterians, who at once formed a committee which, in Cromwell's absence, was given Parliamentary authority. This committee immediately cashiered any officer suspected of Independent allegiance. At the same time, some Parliamentary leaders began to negotiate secretly for the services of an army in Scotland. Immediately seeing his opportunity, Charles sent new peace proposals to the Parliament in which he agreed to accept a modified Presbytery for three years and to grant Parliament control of the militia for ten years. His principal request was that he be allowed to come to Westminster as king in order to give his royal assent to the bills embodying these proposals. On May 18 these requests were accepted by the Parliamentary Presbyterians and the Scotch commissioners as a basis for an accommodation. Thus was born an alliance between Scotland and the English Presbyterians that would lead to a second civil war.

All this was too much for the army agitators, who now demanded that the politicians who treated so lightly the liberties they had fought for be called to account. The Parliament replied by ordering the army to disband on June 1. But when the commissioners from Parliament arrived on May 31 to disband Fairfax's own regiment, they encountered mutiny. Refusing to hear them, the soldiers marched towards London, and Parliament recalled its commissioners.

In the meantime, rumors had been circulating that the Presbyterians, in conjunction with the Scots, designed to carry the king off into Scotland, but the plot was betrayed, it was said, by "a false Presbyterian father . . . . to his Independent son." This was certainly a reference to the Vanes, and it must have been young Vane who warned Cromwell of the design so that he could forestall it. Cromwell immediately instructed Cornet Joyce to proceed to Holmby and resist any attempt to carry off the king. But Joyce did more than that: he carried off the king himself. On June 2, Joyce arrived at Holmby with 500 men. The fifty troopers guarding Charles, who were wholly in sympathy with the agitators, welcomed him. whereupon he courteously requested the king to accompany him to a place unnamed. Under promise of safety to his person, Charles agreed. The next morning when he appeared, Joyce's men were drawn up in ranks. The king asked Joyce if he might see his commission. Here it is, replied Joyce, pointing to the troopers, some of whom had been at Naseby. The king, gracious as always, smiled and said that it was as fair and as well written a commission as he had ever seen, "a company of handsome, proper gentlemen," and he gave himself into custody. Thanks to Vane's urgent warning, the king was now in the hands of the army.

Now the Presbyterian party, baffled and outraged, but completely outflanked, did what it should have done weeks before: it voted to pay the soldiers full arrears and it expunged from the Journals the declaration in which soldiers who had promoted the army petition were called "enemies of the State." But the army was still not placated. On June 5, the soldiers drew up *A Solemn Engagement of the Army* which charged that the Presbyterian leaders were hostile to the army and were fomenting a new war. Before the Commons received this paper, they selected new commissioners to the army and, with whatever reservations, they appointed Vane one of them. That part of the army which was now opposing the Presbyterian Parliament was composed largely of sectarians, including many Quakers, Anabaptists, Antinomians, and inner-light men of varying persuasions who, like Vane, never attended an established church. These troopers could never understand Vane's pacifism, but in his mistrust of formal religion and in his inward, solitary seeking he seemed one of them, and so they trusted him now when almost no one else did. That, of course, was why Parliament had chosen him.

But later Holles angrily alleged that although Vane was sent to pacify the army and present a good impression of Parliament, he had really inflamed the sectarian troops and subordinated his Parliamentary obligations to the advantages of his faction. But this charge must be regarded with some scepticism. Holles had known Vane for years, had long been his chief opponent in Parliament, and had been accused by Vane of treason. He and others who appointed the new commissioners were selecting men because they thought they would be acceptable to the army, and not because they could be expected to uphold the Presbyterian position. All that could be reasonably asked of them was that they would maintain the sovereignty of Parliament and work for an accommodation. This they undoubtedly did. But when, after some negotiation, the men of Fairfax's regiment were apprised of the new and more favorable proposals from Parliament, instead of accepting them gratefully they courteously but firmly referred them to the new Council of the Army for reply. Then the entire army marched towards London.

Three of the Parliamentary commissioners then wrote a letter, probably drafted by Vane, in which they said they were forced to

> declare our own dissent to and disapprobation of the removal of the army so near London; not only for the reasons expressed by us to your Excellency the last night, but for the reasons given to us this morning, as the sense of your Excellency and the Council of War; which we do not judge as at all sufficient and warrantable for any such action.

It was signed by C. Nottingham, P. Skippon, and H. Vane, Jr.

When the City learned that Fairfax was marching towards London, the Presbyterian Militia Committee ordered out the Trained Bands on pain of death and ordered all London shops to be closed. They intended to put the City into a total mobilization, ready to resist a siege, but it is one thing to give orders and another to get them executed. In some regiments of Trained Bands only the officers appeared for duty; in others the muster was desperately thin. Except around Exchange and Cornhill no shops were closed. Meanwhile, a deputation of temperate citizens met with the Council of the Army at St. Albans and entered into amicable talks with them, after which the army responded to a request of Vane and the other commissioners that they set forth all of their demands. They embodied them in a paper called *The Declaration of the Army*, the first reasoned and deliberate attempt by the army to set forth a political program.

This document declared that the army was not a mercenary one, hired to serve an arbitrary power, but had been assembled by legal acts of Parliament in defense of the "just rights and liberties" of all the people, including Parliament itself. All authority and power, it said, were vested fundamentally in an office, but only ministerially in the persons holding that office: there is a difference between kingship and a king, between Parliament and its members. Since this theory permitted both royal ministers and members of Parliament to be called to account, the declaration asked that Parliament be purged of members who were guilty of malfeasance or corruption, or who had in any way abused power. But the purging or even the dissolution of the old Parliament would not guarantee that a new one would be better. Therefore the duration of Parliament should be shortened so that if the people have chosen badly one time they may choose wisely another. This was the beginning of what would become an overwhelming demand for a new representative, and it implied what would soon be put into words: the people are the ultimate source of political power.

Therefore the *Declaration* proposed that the House of Commons should set a date for its own dissolution, and although future Parliaments could not be dissolved without their own consent, they should still establish some maximum period beyond which they could not legally sit. Parliament must also account to the nation for the vast sums of money that it raises and spends, and the right to petition Parliament must be established. Finally, with few exceptions, there should be a general act of oblivion.

While this document was the direct work of Ireton, it unquestionably expressed the wishes not only of the army but also of people throughout the nation who thought the Long Parliament had exercised too much power for too long without sufficient public accountability. Not long ago public sentiment had demanded that the king's ministers be made accountable to the Parliament. Now the Parliament itself must be made accountable to the people.

Clearly, that instrument of revolution, the Long Parliament, was no longer sacred to the sectarian army, as it still was to Vane. On the same day that this document reached Westminster, the army preferred charges against eleven members of the House of Commons: heading the list were the two leaders of the Presbyterian faction, Vane's old enemies Holles and Stapleton; the lawyers Maynard and Glyn were also there. The heaviest charge against these members was that they had attempted to raise forces in order to throw the kingdom into another war. Thus the peace party was formally accused by the army of being warmongers. The other charges included attempting to overthrow the rights and liberties of the subjects, delaying and obstructing justice, and misrepresenting the army in order to obtain Parliamentary authority for harassing the soldiers.

The Parliament responded by desiring proof of the alleged misconduct of the eleven members. Vane would have likely agreed to their expulsion for "delinquency"—there was ample precedent for that—but neither then nor later would he ever agree to the dissolution of the Long Parliament except by its own consent and without duress. On that point, this despiser of forms was a formalist.

In the present crisis, Vane and the other commissioners met with the army almost daily. On June 23 the Army Council told the commissioners they would be willing to postpone impeachment of the eleven members were it not that their continuation in office increased the risk of war, and the next day the army formally renewed its demands for their expulsion. One need not assume, as Holles did, that these demands were the result of a plot conceived by Vane, for the army was thoroughly aroused. Three days later, on June 26, the eleven members requested a leave of absence from the House in order that they might voluntarily withdraw.

On July 6 the eleven members were formally charged in the Commons with attempting to bring in the king on their own terms, with inviting the Scots and other foreign forces to invade, and with encouraging disbanded soldiers to engage in riots and tumults around the Parliament House. The charges were not wholly without foundation.

On July 19, after several narrowly averted crises, the army presented to Vane and the other commissioners more moderate proposals which made only four requests: prisoners who had never received a lawful trial should be released; Parliament should declare against invitations to any foreign troops; the army should be paid regularly; and the London militia, recently placed under the direction of a City committee, should be returned to Parliamentary control, that is to say, to the Independents. When they heard these terms, many Presbyterians quietly gave up the struggle and permanently absented themselves from Parliament.

Now the real power in the nation was not Parliament but the army, and it remained to be seen if it could come to terms with the king as neither Presbyterian nor Independent had been able to do. Under Ireton's direction, a committee of agitators and officers drew up a document called *The Heads of the Proposals*. On August 1, this document was given to the Parliamentary commissioners, but before young Vane could present it to the House of Commons other events interposed.

While the army had been gaining ascendance, the London mob had again become conscious of its political power. Before Pym died, it had risen to harass the bishops; it had turned up to see that Strafford got "justice." Upon receipt of appropriate signals from the pulpit, the City Council, or even Parliament itself, the mob had come to Westminster in support of one issue after another until their demonstrations had become part of England's political life. Now the City was profoundly disturbed. Largely Presbyterian in sympathy, increasingly hostile to the disruptive tactics of the extreme sectarians, suspicious of the Independents and the army, sore from having suffered one defeat after another, the citizens had become angry and vindictive. A few weeks earlier, after the Independents had successfully opposed bringing the king to London, Vane had found his coach surrounded by a shouting, menacing, London mob that threatened to cut him to pieces. Once he had been possibly the most popular Parliament man in the City, as he had once been the most favored among the Scots. Now both hated him, coldly, furiously, irrationally.

The mob spirit that had threatened Vane in June now turned against Parliament itself, and when the eleven members withdrew, it erupted into flame. On July 21, the burly young apprentices, the disbanded soldiers, the watermen who plied the Thames, and other men of action met in Skinner's Hall where they drew up a *Solemn Engagement* which pledged to maintain the covenant and to restore the king if he would agree to establish Presbytery for three years and surrender control of the militia for ten.

A few days later, Parliament proposed to take the leadership of the militia away from the City, and denounced the *Solemn Engagement.* The City fathers immediately petitioned Parliament for the return of the militia. They were followed to Westminster by an aggressive, youthful crowd which surrounded the House of Lords and threatened the nine peers who were sitting there that unless they restored the militia and repealed the declaration against the *Solemn Engagement*, they would not be permitted to leave the chamber. The Lords, knowing now how the bishops had once felt, obeyed and adjourned.

Next the mob rushed to the Commons, filled the lobby, burst open the doors of the House itself and, although not entering at once, they called from the entrance for the legislation they had succeeded in getting from the Lords. They were rude boys, said Bulstrode Whitelocke, young fellows with their hats on and, in this arrogant posture, they shouted "Vote, vote." For more than six hours, the House was virtually imprisoned in its own chamber. No help came from the City, neither from the sheriff nor the Trained Bands, and so the emboldened mob pushed into the chamber; some forty or fifty of the more militant thrust their way onto the floor while a thousand more clamored outside the door, aroused and righteous, terrible with the energy and the outraged piety of the young.

In the attempt on the five members, only Charles had dared cross the threshold of the chamber; a semblance of orderly and legal proceedings had been preserved. But this was complete anarchy. At eight o'clock in the evening the weary and intimidated members passed the required legislation and voted to adjourn. But the young men had not finished. Rudely they thrust Speaker Lenthall back into his chair, as in the early days of the revolution members had once thrust the despised Speaker Finch back into the same chair. They would not let him go yet, they said. Wearily the aging Speaker—who had been given that moment of grace some years before when he had courteously yet courageously defied his sovereign and upheld the integrity of the House—found that grace does not come easily in the presence of a mob. "What question shall I put?" he asked. That the king should be invited to come to London "with honor, freedom, and safety," they replied. A voice vote was taken which allowed Colonel Ludlow to shout a loud "No," but he noticed with disgust that out of "prudential compliance," most of the members voted in the affirmative. Then the mob, still shouting and threatening, withdrew.

Though young Vane was with the army when this invasion of Parliament occurred, it must have occasioned in him some sober thoughts. Holles and other Presbyterian men of Parliament had accused him of being too lenient with the army and, in support of their views, a Presbyterian mob had threatened his life. Then only a few weeks after that traumatic episode, John Lilburne as an army spokesman had said that he would rather cut Vane's throat than Holles'. The Levellers thought Vane too cautious, too conservative; he stood in the way of the immediate gratification of their desires. There is probably no more bitterly instructive moment in the life of a revolutionary than when he finds himself at last in the middle, labeled as turncoat, apostate, and reactionary by those whose cause he has served; branded as time-serving, corrupt, and a man of blood by the conservatives. And now Vane had reached his sticking point: the lawful Parliament, the body of decent men who had freed England from one tyrant, had fallen victim to a new one, the monster of many heads and no mind. In attempting to understand Vane's political position in the years ahead, his growing conservatism, his paradoxical denial of the value of forms in religion and his meticulous adherence to them in politics, one must realize that vague and disturbing premonitions had crystallized in his mind in those days of June and July when he resisted the threat of military dictatorship on the one hand, the threat of civilian anarchy on the other, and learned that in a time of aroused national passions no one seems to want a man who stands in the middle.

When Fairfax heard about the forcing of Parliament, he wrote a strong letter saying that "the rudeness and violence of the people was an unparalleled violation of all privilege." Such things, he said, if allowed, would dissolve all government. He thereupon marched his army to Hounslow Heath. On July 30, the date on which Commons was to meet again, the two Speakers of the Houses were absent, said Clarendon, along with "Sir Henry Vane and some others who would concur with him." Actually eight peers and fifty-seven Independents absented themselves, and many, including Vane, went to Hounslow Heath where they complained to Fairfax that "they were in danger of their lives by the tumults," and appealed to the army for protection.

As Clarendon conceded, if it had been only Vane and some of his friends, known to be fanatics in religion, who had fled to the army, "they would have got no reputation nor the army been thought better for their company." But neither Speaker had previously shown any inclination towards the army and Lenthall, in fact, was believed favorable both to the king and the Episcopal church. Manchester, Speaker of the Peers, despised Cromwell (who had assaulted both his honor and his competence) and his "brutish" officers; he and Warwick were staunch Presbyterians. The truth is that no man of spirit can be forced by a mob to act against his will without a humiliation sufficiently intense to split him from his former party or his former friends. So it was now, at least with some of the deserters.

At Westminster, the Presbyterian factions and some neutrals, numbering about 140, tried to become a Parliament. They elected new Speakers, recalled the eleven members, and reconstituted the City militia under its Presbyterian leadership. This Parliament and the city of London, now allied against the army, sent the Trained Bands to man the walls of the City and imposed a general levy on the entire male population capable of bearing arms. Then with fatal arrogance they ordered General Fairfax not to approach closer than thirty miles to London. It was all very gallant, no doubt, but it remained to be seen how the people would react when confronted by disciplined troops who were marching against them as bitter enemies.

By August 3, as ideological ardor gave way to threatening reality, the City dispatched a letter to Fairfax disclaiming any desire for a new war. Fairfax replied that he intended to march against the City nevertheless and ordered that the eleven members be kept in custody until they could be tried by law. He then assembled his 20,000 foot and horse, drew them up in marching ranks, and with the two Speakers and the fugitive members, including Vane, rode along the front of the regiments. The soldiers threw their hats into the air, crying "Lords, Commons, and a free Parliament."

On August 6, the army, still accompanied by the fugitive members, marched along the road to Westminster, every soldier with a laurel in his hat. At Hyde Park, the Lord Mayor and the aldermen swallowed hard and uttered words of welcome. On that day Parliament resumed its sitting. The first item of business in the restored Commons after the speech of welcome from the chair was the long-delayed consideration of the army's *Heads of the Proposals*. Vane arose and presented this document that was to play so considerable a role in his future political life. It is a long document containing more than fifty propositions. Like other army documents, it asked for a dissolution of the Long Parliament within a year; it provided further that Parliament should be called every two years and that during the first 120 days of its sitting it could not be dissolved except by its own consent. After the 120 days it could be dissolved by the king but was, in any case, to be automatically terminated at the end of 240 days. The *Heads* also called for a more equitable apportionment of members according to the population and asked that suffrage be based largely on property.

One of the more significant innovations in the document called for a Council of State, modeled perhaps on the old Committee of Both Kingdoms, the principal duties of which would be to serve in place of the former Privy Council and to control and direct the militia. This council could make war or peace, however, only with "the advice and consent of Parliament." It was to continue in office for a term of seven years and to provide continuity in government.

Such was the document Vane presented to the Commons on the day when the army restored the Independents to their seats. Some of the political ideas he could not have agreed with, although this was not the time to say so. But the terms for the settlement of the church he could support completely. Under those terms, no one was required to take the covenant and, at the same time, episcopal power was drastically reduced.

An act to be passed to take away all coercive power, authority, and jurisdiction of bishops and all other ecclesiastical officers whatsoever, extending to any civil penalties upon any; and to repeal all laws whereby the civil magistracy hath been or is bound upon any ecclesiastical censure to proceed (ex-officio) unto any civil penalties against any persons so censured.

These provisions would not abolish Anglican bishops or Presbyterian elders but they would strip them of power; more than that, they provided for a clear separation of church and state and removed conscience from the jurisdiction of the magistrate. This is what Roger Williams had already praised Vane for advocating; it is the one thing above all others that Milton would praise him for. While this provision for a religious settlement suited the Independents generally, it can have pleased no man more than Vane, and it is not unlikely that he had a hand in formulating it. Of all the propositions on religion ever tendered to the king, from Vane's point of view this was the best. But the Presbyterians considered the proposals outrageously tolerant, providing as they did that no one could be required to come to church, to perform any religious act, or to engage in any religious duties. Vane thought these provisions would create a purer religious society; in fact they pointed to a secularized state.

One other provision would have pleased Vane: the *Heads* asked "the present unequal, troublesome, and contentious way of ministers' maintenance by tithes to be considered of, and some remedy applied." Other proposals called for extensive social and legal reforms.

Even while the House was considering these proposals, Cromwell sent them to the king, but it was unlikely that Presbyterians would ever assent to the document, and they could still command a majority. Their dominating power induced the agitators to renew their call for a purge of Parliament. This time brave Oliver was inclined to hearken. "These men," he said, "will never leave till the army pull them out by the ears." And sometime in August, suspicious that Holles and Stapleton were still influencing the Parliament too much, Cromwell said, "I know nothing to the contrary but that I am as well able to govern the kingdom as either of them."

The Independents now tried to pass an ordinance declaring the proceedings of the Parliament in the absence of the Speakers null and void. After being rejected once, it was brought forward again, and this time, after stationing a regiment of cavalry in Hyde Park, Cromwell and other officers who were also members went to the House of Commons. Leaving a party of soldiers outside the door, they called for the vote on the ordinance; to no one's surprise it passed. In the face of this new show of force, more Presbyterians withdrew from Parliament, leaving the balance of power with the Independents. Denzil Holles was convinced that the force exerted by the army against Parliament was "more horrid" than the force of the apprentices, for the latter were idle young people without design whereas the force used by the army was part of a "deep-laid plot."

Now that the army and the Independents were in control of Parliament and had agreed on the *Heads*, everything rested in the hands of the king. He found many things in that document to object to: he wanted amnesty for all his followers, and since he wished to maintain the principal Laudian reform of restoring lands and monies to the church, he could not agree to the abolition of tithes. He objected to the militia's being removed from his control, and, while he did not say so, his deepest objections must have been to the democratic innovations which would have so unsettled the accustomed patterns of his life.

After many delays and ambivalences during which he again negotiated with Scotland for an army, Charles sent a delaying reply in September. He liked the *Heads*, he said, better than the old Newcastle Propositions, and he now wished to enter into a personal treaty with Parliament during which specific articles might be discussed and modified. To this response, both Cromwell and Ireton were favorable.

But the king's reply to the *Heads* split the Independent party into two factions. The one, under Marten and Rainsborough, asked for the abolition of monarchy and voted that no more addresses should be made to Charles, that Jonah in the ship. But neither Vane nor Cromwell was yet ready for this; they had real hope for the *Heads of the Proposals* as did all the sturdy leaders of the good cause. Cromwell acted as teller for the negative which carried strongly.

The moderation of Vane and Cromwell brought them under attack from all sides. Hugh Peter, chaplain to the New Model, berated the supporters of the king as "great courtiers." John Lilburne, now languishing rather vigorously in prison, said that Cromwell had become glued in interest to four sons of Machiavelli: Vane, St. John, and the Lords Saye and Wharton, men who had never cared for the liberty of the people but only pulled down great men who stood in the way of their own preferment. Lilburne charged further that Cromwell had "used" the agitators to frighten the Presbyterians into doing what he wished and that the "precious young Sir Henry Vane" had been pleased to join in that design. Cromwell and his son-in-law Ireton, he went on to say, held the power in the army and combined with "four grand jugglers" (including Vane) in the Parliament to support and uphold the usurpations of the House of Lords. That House had placed Lilburne in prison without legal right to do so, and Cromwell was doing nothing to free him. "I clearly see Cromwell's and Vane's designs," he wrote, "which is to keep the poor people everlastingly (if they can) in bondage and slavery."

Royalist newspapers, no friends to Lilburne, were also saying that Vane and Cromwell were working together for the ruination of the country and the exaltation of themselves. It was being said, too, that the king had offered Cromwell the Garter and the vacant Earldom of Essex, and that there were members of Parliament who, by long continuation in office, had enriched themselves and gained power which they refused to relinquish. Such men were contemptuously being referred to by the Spanish title of "grandee"; according to wilder rumors these grandees had provided themselves with homes and monies in the Low Countries, where they would take refuge when they were overthrown. Now both Cromwell and Vane were popularly called grandees. But both men were really trying to find some middle ground on which to stand, a position that could be maintained in the face of both military dictatorship and civilian anarchy.

In November, Vane again showed where he stood on the matter of intellectual and spiritual freedom. Cambridge University had already been purged by Parliamentary visitors. Now Oxford's turn had come. The visitors, including the indefatigable William Prynne, were to reform the discipline and doctrine of the university in accordance with the covenant. But the covenant was not cherished at Oxford, and the entire body of the university passed a declaration against it; an action, said Clarendon, which was "a monument of learning, courage, and loyalty." And when the Visitors required the university administration to appear before a Parliamentary committee, the scholars were defended by Vane, Selden, Whitelocke, and Fiennes, none of whom cared for any kind of conformity, least of all Presbyterian. It did not go unobserved that Vane, who had negotiated the covenant, was now encouraging those who defied it.

Vane was now becoming ever more unpopular in the city of

London. In November he and three other M.P.'s were called on to rebuke the City for its unsatisfactory collection of assessments. Then on December 1, Vane persuaded the Commons to deny the City's petition that the army be removed to a safe distance. The citizens said that Vane threatened them with military intervention.

Charles, meanwhile, was alarmed by rumors that he would be assassinated, and on November 11 he fled from Hampton Court and went to the Isle of Wight, where he was seized and made a prisoner in Carisbrooke Castle. There both the Independents and the Scots offered him peace proposals. He decided that the Scots' proposals were more favorable to him, and to Vane's dismay, on December 26, in return for some concessions, he agreed to confirm the covenant by act of Parliament and to suppress heretics, blasphemy, and schism.

At the end of 1647 there were little signs which may have been more portentous for the long future of the revolution than all the political crises. Although the Puritan victors had ordered London merchants to keep their shops open on Christmas, all of them were closed. Parliament set a good example by sitting on that day, but despite ordinances to the contrary, some ministers conducted services out of the Book of Common Prayer. In Canterbury there were tumults against the Christmas ordinance, with shouts of "Up with King Charles," and equally loud shouts of "Down with Parliament and taxes." When the Mayor of Canterbury attempted to allay the tumult, he was abused "by the rude multitude," which broke his head and dragged him up and down until he escaped into a house where he was given shelter. The rioters invaded the homes of the godly, shattered their windows, abused their persons, and threw their goods into the street, all the while shouting lustily, "For God, King Charles, and Kent."

In other counties and towns there were similar riots, and, despite the presence of the army, some disturbances in London itself. This widespread rioting amply justified the caution being exercised by the grandees. The country had been taken in a new direction as far as it was willing to go. The cry was for peace and a return to the old ways which, after all the anarchy, all the blood and bitterness, seemed like a lost golden age.

13

The Death of the King
(1648–1649)

Through all the anxieties and uncertainties of the confused months after the army had captured the king, Vane's home and family continued to provide him an emotional and spiritual refuge. He had become ever more deeply bound in mutual affection with his wife, Frances, as they shared the joys of birth and the griefs of death. In twenty-two years of married life, Lady Vane would bear fourteen children, seven sons and seven daughters. Cecil, born in 1646, had died in infancy; Edward, born in 1648, would live less than a year. Eight of Vane's children would precede him to the grave. Although the dates of birth and death of some of his children have not survived, at least three of them were now living, and perhaps one or two more. The Lord took away much but gave more, and his name was blessed in the Vane household, where Sir Henry liked to think of himself as another Abraham, patriarch to his family and faithful servant of his God.

His public role, however, was more confusing and distressing now that the main battle had been won. The king was a prisoner, but what should be done with him? What could be done next to advance the cause? Early in 1648 Vane's private and public suspicions of Charles increased when the king rejected Parliament's latest proposals for peace. He remained silent on a motion to impeach Charles and settle the kingdom without him, but surely not out of compunction, for he had himself previously proposed the same. Perhaps he was only waiting to see how things would go, for when, after much debate, Commons voted 141 to 91 to make no more addresses to the king, Vane voted with the majority. At the same time, by dissolving the Committee of Both Kingdoms, Commons legally ended that experiment in joint government through an instrument which Vane had forged: they placed the affairs of state in the hands of the English members of the dissolved committee.

For some reason, at about this time, Royalist newspapers began to subject Vane to unusual vituperation. They said that he had stolen the fabulous ring of Gyges that made its wearer invisible, and that he lurked unseen behind most of Parliament's maneuvers. They also jeered at some deformity in Vane's shoulders, a new point of attack. Since Vane was only thirty-five, the rounded shoulders and stooped back must have come from too many hours hunched over a desk; they may also have been outward signs of an inner weariness.

In January some kind of break occurred between Vane and Cromwell, indicating a major disruption in the Independent party itself. It was said that Cromwell "bestowed two nights' oratory" on Vane without effect, and in February Clarendon heard that Vane had left the prevailing party, causing "great fears and suspicions." The likeliest cause of this rift was the decision on the part of Cromwell and St. John, faced with a Scottish invasion, to open negotiations with the queen and with the Prince of Wales, whom they tried to induce to take his father's place. Henry Marten, who wanted a commonwealth at once, was angry with Cromwell for what he considered a temporizing conservatism, and it may be that Vane also was now ready to exclude not only the present king but all of his family and perhaps any monarchy. Whatever the cause the rift was soon healed, for in early March a Royalist newspaper again referred to Vane as a leader of the Commons, one who thought he could "carry a kingdom on his camel's back."

Those who had lived through the riots and tumults of the first civil war watched with dismay as the same kind of violence broke out again. On April 9 several thousand apprentices "tumultuated" in the vicinity of the Mews, unfortunately at a time when Cromwell happened to be there. He immediately ordered out a regiment of his horse and charged the mob, killing two and injuring many.

This new agitation stemmed partly from the people's sympathy with Charles who, as a fallen king, was making a new impression on his people as a man of sorrows and acquainted with grief, a man reduced from three kingdoms to three rooms in Carisbrooke Castle. One poet imagined Charles meditating on his sorrows:

> For my wronged kingdom's sake, my very grief
> Doth break my heart. Until I find relief
> I'll sue to heaven mercy from God, my chief:
> Never was grief like mine.
>
> Causeless they like a bird have chased me;
> Behold, O Lord, look down from heaven and see,
> Thou that hearest prisoners' prayers, hear me!
> Never was grief like mine.

This newly acquired sympathy for the king was coincident with increasing economic distress caused by maintaining a large army. The City had tired of seeing soldiers everywhere, and of paying taxes for their clothing and supplies and salaries; the people no longer were willing "to feed those horse-leeches of the Army." The army's agitators, understandably angry, talked of taking by the sword the pay they could no longer get by persuasion.

In Wales unrest and sporadic violence turned into an armed insurrection on May 1; at once Fairfax ordered Cromwell into the field with his cavalry. The City now thought it a good time to press some of its demands. It asked that the chains, once anchored to steep posts and used to block off streets against cavalry or massed infantry, might again be put in place, that the army should remove to a safe distance, and that Phillip Skippon, whose good heart and gentle tongue everyone trusted, should be appointed to command the Trained Bands. Wishing to be placatory, Cromwell moved that these conditions be granted and Vane seconded. This concession, however, outraged the army. Sir Henry Weathercock, they said, was now acting Sir John Presbyter. But both Cromwell and Vane may be excused for minor expediencies; this was no time to take umbrage. Then on May 6, when the Commons voted not to "alter the fundamental government of the kingdom by King, Lords, and Commons," Vane joined with most of the Presbyterians and many Independents, who thought that this vote for stability might reassure the nation.

On May 8, the Parliamentary forces at St. Fagan's won their first victory of the new campaign, and May 15 was set aside as a day of thanksgiving for it. But never were the city churches so empty; not even victory endeared the military to the weary citizens. And everywhere signs of unrest continued. There was a maypole riot at Bury St. Edmunds, the maypole being not so much a present delight to the apprentices as a certain offense to the Puritans. From Surrey came petitioners to London crying out for "an old King and a new Parliament." There was a serious insurrection in Kent. A new and full-scale civil war was developing.

At this juncture the city of London demanded that peace negotiations be reopened with the king, and a sharp debate ensued in Parliament. Fairfax was informed that Vane had voted against the "honest party," that is, the Independents; but at the same time the Royalist press said that he was leading the Independent opposition to negotiations.

> Then Vane the Father, Vane the Son,
> Two devils in conjunction. . . .
> Their votes are near to seek, aye, aye,
> To all that bans His Majesty.

Thus both sides mistrusted Vane: he seemed to be voting on both sides of every issue. On questions of religion, however, he was unswerving. In this debate over renewing negotiations, the Presbyterians were demanding that Presbytery be established not merely for three years but until king, Lords, and Commons should alter it. Acting as teller against this proposal, Vane carried it by 67 to 48. Parliament was not inclined to write the Presbyterians a blank check.

In the midst of the debate came deadly news: on May 27, six ships lying in the Downs mutinied, declaring for the king and refusing to allow the sectarian Admiral Rainsborough back aboard. This mutiny plunged Vane back into naval affairs, attending naval committee meetings and reporting to Parliament belated attempts to keep the rest of the navy loyal by providing wages and supplies. On June 8, Vane and some others were dispatched to try to recover the revolted ships, fully empowered to grant indemnity if officers and crew would comply. But Vane could not persuade them. Disillusioned with the revolution and distrustful of its spokesmen, the officers sailed off to Holland to join the forces of Charles and Rupert. The

Committee of the Navy formally thanked Vane for carrying out his instructions faithfully.

With a squadron of the fleet disloyal, it seemed essential to strengthen the defenses of the Isle of Wight against any attempt to rescue the king from his prison in Carisbrooke Castle. Vane was ordered by the Commons to contribute 500 pounds for that purpose and to reimburse himself from his profits as treasurer. For this odd action there was a precedent. Back in 1641, when Lord Russell was accused of inattention to naval duties, Parliament had required him to advance a large sum to the fleet, partly because it was needed and partly to punish him. It may be that both these motives were also behind this order, whereby the Presbyterian majority was perhaps implying that Vane was partly responsible for the naval revolt. Or perhaps they merely took pleasure in extracting money from him on any pretext.

Throughout the dispersed and chaotic actions of the second civil war, the outcome was never really in doubt. Sporadic uprisings of gentry or citizens, rioting, contempt for puritanical statutes—none of these could be sustained against the organized and trained troopers of the New Model Army. If the uprisings expressed an unbearable civil frustration, there was no less intense frustration in the officers and soldiers who had to put them down, for to have lived through a war, to have won it, and then to be again subjected to hazard of life was unendurable.

By mid-July the army had ended the domestic danger, but the Scots army was poised on England's borders; the Irish confederates were threatening to invade; and the Prince of Wales, having secured a fleet in Holland, was hoping for an army to transport. Meanwhile Cromwell was marching north for a final test of strength against Leslie. That was the situation when the king again offered to treat. The Independents, made cautious by the popular uprisings, quickly agreed, provided only that the treaty be negotiated in the Isle of Wight rather than in London, where popular sentiment and Presbyterian feeling might force them into reluctant concessions.

In mid-August, Cromwell defeated the Scots at Preston; their army, he said, had withered like grass. Then, as usual in his reports to Parliament, he asserted that in his victory the hand of God had once more been made plain for all to see; he hoped therefore that Parliament would exalt and acknowledge God "and not hate his people who are as the apple of his eye." God's people, of course, were the Independent sectaries.

At about the same time Cromwell vented his pious exultation to Parliament, he also began gently chiding Vane. After the Battle of Preston, in a letter to St. John he showed his concern over his recent differences with Vane, differences which especially troubled him now that God's hand had been shown him so clearly in battle. He wrote to St. John that he was as unsatisfied with Vane's "passive and suffering principles" as Vane was with Cromwell's active ones. A few days later, he returned to the same theme.

> Remember my love to my dear brother H. Vane: I pray he make not too little, nor I too much, of outward dispensations: God preserve us all, that we, in simplicity of our spirits, may patiently attend upon them. Let us all be not careful what men will make of these actings. They, will they, nill they, shall fulfill the good pleasure of God.

Cromwell and Vane represent two of history's most persistent types: Cromwell was a man of energy and arms with all the forces of his time funneling through his body; a man who knew the fear that sits like a cap of snow on the heart before the charge of the horse, and the fierce triumph when the God of Battles shows his face; a man who knew that his own life, that vulnerable flame, had burned through cyclone and deluge and the wrath of armed men. To know such things was to know God. In contrast was Vane, leader of the war party yet a despiser of war; never elated, puzzled by the complexity of all the "signs" which history and providence whispered to more reserved men; more intellectually sophisticated than Cromwell; a man who found at last that for him there was only one haven, the haven of the soul, where, as God sent sunlight or frost, dew or drought, one knew His will. To the pragmatist it was events that mattered; to the mystic it was man's inner response to those events. The wonder was not that Vane and Cromwell finally fell out, but that for so long they had worked together in affection and harmony.

Now, assured by the seal of God on his victory, Cromwell began speaking like an Old Testament prophet. In his letter to Parliament, after praising God and pleading for his people, he uttered dire warnings: those who troubled the land should be speedily destroyed out of it. This was a warning to Charles, the Presbyterians, the Royalists, and especially the Scots, for it was towards Scotland that he was now moving, confident in both his strength and his right.

While Cromwell was marching north, Fairfax, too, enjoyed victory: he reduced the Royalist stronghold of Colchester, whereupon John Milton found occasion for both celebration and warning. In the octave of his sonnet to Fairfax, he praised him as a man of war, but in the sestet he praised peace and warned of corruption.

> O yet a nobler task awaits thy hand;
> For what can war, but endless war still breed,
> Till truth and right from violence be freed,
> And public faith cleared from the shameful brand
> Of public fraud. In vain doth valor bleed
> While avarice and rapine share the land.

These are strong words to be aimed at the Long Parliament by one of its strongest defenders, who yet realized unhappily that charges of public fraud were continually being raised against its members. Some of the Parliament men had become wealthier than the noblemen whose sequestered estates they now owned, estates sometimes acquired in transactions so private that they could not bear public scrutiny. Fairfax and Cromwell were winning the war, Milton said, but corruption and avarice were losing the peace. Vane too had been accused of benefiting personally from continuance of the war.

There was in England widespread longing for peace, but how was it to be achieved? In August, proponents of peace by treaty (who included Holles and others who had now returned to Parliament) gathered enough strength to repeal the vote of no more addresses to the king, and so cleared away the legal barrier to negotiation. But the soldiers and officers did not favor fumbling again towards a treaty. Colonel Ludlow tried to persuade Fairfax to bring his army from Colchester to London and impose a military settlement, but Fairfax remained cool, evasive, vague. Nor was Ireton willing to act yet; it would be best to let negotiations proceed until the people turned against both the king and those who still trusted him.

In Commons the dispute was hot. Thomas Scot, Vane's classmate at Westminster, said once again, "He that draws his sword upon a

King must throw away the scabbard." The answer was equally familiar and sharp: war is some people's gain. Vane argued that Charles had broken his word so often that he could not be trusted again, to which Sir Symonds D'Ewes flatly replied that the House now had no choice but to trust His Majesty,

> For . . . if you know not in what condition you are, give me leave in a word to tell you: your silver is clipped, your gold shipped; your ships all revolted; yourself contemned; your Scots friends enraged against you; and the affections of the City and kingdom quite alienated from you.

So Parliament decided to try once more to work out an agreement with Charles, this time through a commission carefully balanced for fair representation. Northumberland, Holles, and Glyn were chosen from the Presbyterians; Saye and Vane from the Independents. Then there was a country lawyer, Sir Harbottle Grimston, and young Nat Fiennes whose position no one was sure about. It was a well mixed group.

Charles, that man of grief, was aging with pathetic grace. His hair was gray now, his clothes were old, his pleasures even simpler than they had been. He loved to walk out of the castle and on to the greensward, the old parade ground known as the Barbican. There he would touch for the king's evil; occasionally he would bowl; otherwise he meditated, prayed, and read. His favorite reading was the Bible, but he also loved the poems of George Herbert, Spenser's *Faerie Queene*, and the prose works of Richard Hooker and Bishop Andrewes. He was a man of exquisite taste. Occasionally in the margin of one of these works he would write what was now his favorite motto: *Dum spiro spero*—while I breathe, I hope. He seemed also to be spending part of his time writing a book of devotion which, it was said, he had started before the battle of Naseby.

In previous negotiations it was believed that the king would have been more lenient if his advisers had permitted; this time, therefore, the king was required to treat in person; his advisers, standing behind a curtain, could hear him but might not interpose. To defend himself against hasty decisions made under pressure, the king required that no single item to which he assented would be in force until the entire treaty was signed.

As the negotiations proceeded, the king made substantial concessions, but on two matters he stood firm: he was willing to establish a Presbytery for three years and to negotiate after that, but he was unwilling to abolish episcopacy; also, while he agreed to some form of punishment for the most influential of his followers, he would not consent to their being charged with treason (he remembered Strafford), nor would he consent to their lives being taken for things done under his commission. The sticking point here for the Presbyterians was the status of the bishops, for their lands had been pledged against the debts owed to the City. Men who believed that the church would be disestablished had therefore committed funds on speculation, expecting to be well paid by exorbitant interest or else given those rich lands outright. The emotions which once lay behind Root and Branch had now been replaced by calculating self-interest. The Independents could afford to compromise, but the Presbyterians could not, for it was the City merchants, their supporters, whose money was at stake.

When the negotiations appeared to stall, Holles and Grimston threw themselves on their knees before the king, begging him to accept the Presbyterian proposals for, they said, Vane was not sincere in his alternative proposals. He was simply trying to draw out the treaty to a great length, they said; he wanted "an unbounded liberty of conscience," and to gain this he would delay until Cromwell could subjugate Scotland and the North when, backed by his victorious army, the republicans would establish a commonwealth.

Later Vane was blamed for the failure of the negotiations: Clarendon said that he was the only man who did not want a peace to be established by treaty. Bishop Burnet thought that it was not only Vane but the entire Independent faction that was temporizing.

> Sir Henry Vane, and others, who were for a change of government, had no mind to treat any more; but both city and country were so desirous of a personal treaty, that it could not be resisted. Vane, Pierpoint, and some others went to the treaty on purpose to delay matters till the King could be brought to London.

What then did Vane propose and what were his real intentions?

He proposed to the king a negotiation based on the army's *Heads of the Proposals* which Ireton had written, assisted perhaps by Vane; Vane himself had presented it to the Parliament a year before. While it did not ask for limitless liberty of conscience, it did ask for concessions to nonconformists; and to get them, the army had been willing to accept a bounded and limited episcopacy. That is what Vane now offered to the king: his intention was to gain as much toleration as he could. But of course since he had once demanded the extirpation of episcopacy, this apparent veering of the weather-vane aroused suspicion. He could not be sincere, it was said; he must be plotting with Cromwell. If so someone had neglected to inform Oliver, who was more than a little annoyed with Vane for being willing to accept episcopacy on any terms, as he said in a letter to the Governor of Carisbrooke Castle.

> But as to my brother [Heron] himself, tell him indeed I think some of my friends have advanced too far and need make an honorable retreat.

Cromwell, in the same letter, also hinted that it was high time for a new Parliament; the old had sat too long.

From September 13 until the end of November, the commissioners pleaded with the king, each in his own way and for his own ideas, and the army began to express its frustrations. In November, the Council of the Army drew up a long remonstrance to Parliament in which once again it not only asked for a new Parliament with more equitable representation, but required that any future king must be elected and must surrender any power of legislative veto. They further asked that "corrupt" members be excluded from the House, along with all "obstructors of justice," a provision which would eject Glyn, Maynard, Holles and other Presbyterians now restored to their seats. The most ominous statement was a stricture against the king: "The person of the King may and shall be proceeded against in a way of justice for the blood spilt, and other evils and mischiefs done by him."

When Parliament understandably delayed action on the extreme and intransigent remonstrance, the army demanded immediate dissolution of the House. At the same time, Fairfax marched towards London, demanding 40,000 pounds in back pay for his soldiers. On that same day, the commissioners from the Isle of Wight arrived in London amid high tensions between Parliament and the army, and on the following day, the debate on the negotiations with the king began. The main question was whether or not His Majesty's replies to the Parliamentary proposals could be considered a satisfactory basis for further negotiation. Many, including young Fiennes, thought they could.

Vane disagreed and on the second day of debate he made the most unwise and inflammatory speech of his life. Angry, frustrated, annoyed with what he considered the blindness of the Presbyterians to the intentions of the king, he emerged from his shell of caution and reserve; his closed face was animated now, his somber eyes flashed. The only record we have of the speech is from the pen of a bitter enemy who said that Vane began with "the highest insolence and provocation," telling the House that "this day they should discover who were their friends and who were their foes, who were of the King's party in the House of Commons and who were for the people." He then proceeded "with his usual grave bitterness against the person of the king," saying that after they had once voted to address him no more, they had been governed in peace, and had begun to taste the sweetness of a "republican government," when a combination of the Scots and the citizens of London "with some small contemptible insurrections in England" had led them to reverse themselves and to turn again to the king. His Majesty was now in no condition to demand anything, but he still reserved a power in himself or his posterity to exercise as tyrannical a government as he had ever done.

Now that the insurrections had been subdued and Scotland reduced, Vane continued, there was nothing wanting but their own consent and resolution "to make themselves the happiest nation and people in the world." To do this they must settle the government without the king and punish so severely those who had disturbed the peace as to terrify men from such attempts in the future. This, he said, would be especially gratifying to the army which had merited so much from the Parliament.

While Vane was speaking, exclamations from the surrounding benches grew into murmurs of dislike and outrage. Immediately there were sharp answers, one from young Fiennes who "rationally and gallantly" argued that the king's concessions were surely enough to secure religion, laws, and liberty.

According to Clement Walker's account of the scene, young Vane, a whelp of the old cur, had asserted that by this debate all could distinguish friend from foe. Then an unnamed gentleman arose and said that since Vane had prejudged and divided the House into two parts in such a bold and threatening way, he would like permission to divide it in a different way: those who were gaining and those who were losing by the war. Those who had suffered losses in the last few years wished peace; those who had gained favored war. He therefore humbly moved that the gainers should contribute to the losers so that all might be brought to equality. This speech was greeted by many signs of approval from the benches.

But not everyone had disliked Vane's speech. Colonel Ludlow said that Sir Henry had "so truly stated the matter of fact relating to the treaty and so evidently discovered the design and deceit of the King's answer, that he made it clear to us, that by it, the justice of our cause was not asserted, nor our rights secure for the future." And there came then into his mind certain words from God's law which "struck him hard." Blood was defiling the land which could not be cleansed of bloodshed except by shedding the blood of the guilty man. If Vane could have read Ludlow's thoughts, he might have moderated the tone of his speech, for he was walking on the edge of a sword. If he fell, he would fall either into betrayal of the revolution in a treaty with the king, or into a pit which contained dead men's bones.

On December 4, two days after Vane's heated speech, the soldiers moved the king from the Isle of Wight to Hurst Castle, near the mainland, where he would be more secure. On the following day the House sat through the daylight hours and most of the night discussing the dangers of the situation. On the one hand was the pressure of universal desire for peace, the newly aroused sympathy with the king, the disillusionment with Parliament. On the other there was the army, with much talk going around that it might dissolve Parliament by force.

During this crucial debate, the longest and most significant speech was made by William Prynne in support of further negotiations. As he reminded the House how the king had made one capitulation after another, he spoke also of his own sufferings, and all those old injustices came flooding back. Those sufferings, he said, were surely evidence that he was no Royalist toady, but neither was he an enemy to the army. We are all weary, he continued, of a long and costly war which some men seem to wish to spin out from generation to generation. And why did we take up arms in the first place? Was it not to banish popery, to defend the king's person and rescue him from evil counselors—was it not above all to secure the freedom of Parliament? At a cost no man could have foretold, these ends were now all accomplished, but, he said, the war goes on and on, and the land is full of schisms, of horrible blasphemies. Prynne, too, went on and on; at long last, in the dim morning hours, it was voted 140 to 104 that the king's concessions were sufficient ground for settling the peace of the kingdom, and a committee was appointed to present this information to General Fairfax.

After all, that bitter speech with which Vane had initiated the debate had failed to prevent a new negotiation, but it had exposed him to virulent counterattacks. His enemies were now openly making the often whispered charges that he opposed peace because war was making him rich. Royalist newspapers spread the taunt abroad, and Clement Walker was composing a tract in which he would reveal to the world the corruption and hypocrisy of the Parliamentary grandees. When this tract was published in the following year, Vane did not come off as badly as people might have expected and as Walker must have hoped. Walker charged that Parliament had granted 300,000 pounds to its own members, and although he did not identify individual sums, the charge was in substance true. In 1646, Denzil Holles, John Selden, and some others had been granted 5,000 pounds each for the "great losses and sufferings" they had endured in the third year of Charles' reign; the heirs of Eliot, Stroud, Heyman, and Hampden had been granted similar amounts. The Earl of Essex had been given 10,000 pounds upon his retirement, and, as Lilburne never tired of reminding the world, Cromwell was even now receiving some 2,500 pounds a year. Even Lilburne himself, though never a member, had received Parliamentary largesse in September, 1648, when he was granted 3,000 pounds for his former suffering. Vane never received such a grant.

Nor was he in Walker's long list of members who had more

recently received offices, emoluments, lands, and other private sums. Included were St. John, Prideaux, Haselrig, Pierpoint, Cromwell, and Thomas Scot. Finally Walker listed specific corruptions with the names of 101 guilty persons, and Vane was not among these either.

Up to this point he seems to have been free of corruption, a conclusion borne out by Giles Greene, for many years chairman of the Navy Committee, who, two years before Walker published his charges, testified in a pamphlet that as treasurer Vane had issued all the money spent on the navy according to the directions of the committee, and he continued, "I dare confidently affirm that he discharged with as much clearness and freedom from any corruptions as ever Treasurer did." Nor, he said, did either he or Vane or any other member of the committee ever receive a penny for any appointment they made. Though a Royalist newspaper accused Greene himself of occasionally "licking his fingers," no one believed the charge, for Greene was considered a man of complete integrity. As evidence that Greene was right about Vane, when in 1648 Sir Henry turned over to Parliament his accounts for the years 1642 to 1645, they were assigned for audit to William Prynne who, having been mutilated himself, never hesitated to mangle others. Had there been the slightest irregularity, he would have found it and published it to the world. Instead, he certified that some 640,000 pounds had been disbursed and accounted for.

But despite this formidable testimony on his behalf, Vane was not beyond suspicion. It was common knowledge that he had secured remunerative positions for his brothers; a Royalist whom his sister had married had been permitted to compound on easy terms; his father had been proposed for a baronetcy; and—more significant than all these—he had never returned half of his emoluments from the treasurer's office as Parliament had ordered him to. Though oddly enough Walker mentioned none of these, the Vane family does not go unnoticed in his exposé. One of the principal sources of corruption in Parliament that Walker did mention was the father-son, brother-brother, and other combinations of kinship that filled the Commons. These family pairs, he said, constituted couples more unclean than any of the beasts that entered the Ark, and among them he named the Vanes first. Further, Walker said, the elder Vane is the chairman of the revenue committee that collects and disburses what was once the royal revenue; though somewhat decayed, this revenue would still amount to nearly half a million pounds a year. Walker made no specific charge against the elder Vane; he simply pointed out that the shrewd old man was handling much money. Yet when the elder Vane died six years after Walker wrote, although he left a considerable estate, it was encumbered with a debt of 10,000 pounds which young Vane assumed.

But some of the charges Walker leveled against the Vanes were specific. Between them, he said, the son being "a principal publican and Treasurer," they are paid from public revenue 6,000 pounds a year. In addition they have their "private cheats." What were these? According to Walker, the Vanes bought "old sleeping pensions for trifles": people who had once been awarded pensions but who were receiving nothing because of a general lack of revenue would sell their rights to the Vanes at a heavy discount. Apparently the Vanes would then use their political influence to see that all the arrears were paid to themselves along with the current obligations. There was a subtler cheat, too, according to Walker, one a little more difficult to follow. Apparently many individuals whose estates had been sequestered, or who had compounded, found themselves unable to pay their debts in full. The Vanes would then pay what was still owing and take discount for the entire indebtedness. There is no way to check the charges of Walker, but he was a bitterly biased man to whom young Vane was "the chief secretary to the seven deadly sins."

Vane suffered, too, from complaints about his work on the Committee for Compounding, which operated in secret sessions but was believed to give out valuable information to friends so that they might know when the best lands of delinquents or of the church would be available for sale on favorable terms. Two years in the future, in October of 1650, upon surrendering his office of treasurer, Vane would be given lands worth some 1,800 pounds a year. In the same year he would request the Council of State to allow the Earl of Lindsay, banned from London as a Royalist, to come to the City to arrange a sale of his lands to "a very well-affected person." That person was Vane himself. In Lincolnshire, he bought properties including the manors of Belleau, Aby, and Swaby for some 8,500 pounds; being a landowner it was only natural that he should also become a militia commissioner, a justice of the peace, and a vice-admiral in the county.

In all of these transactions there was only one outright illegality: his failure to return half of his treasurer's profits. Of the rest one cannot be sure. Public finance at that time was not channeled into a central Exchequer, but rather ran, as Walker complains, "in so many muddy channels" that no one could really know how much had come in' and where it had gone. Naturally the suspicion developed that the Long Parliament did not dare to dissolve itself for fear that illegal dealings might be disclosed and judicial reprisals follow.

But the public suspicions, the innuendos in Parliament, even the charges of Walker, are too simplistic to be fair. It could not justly be said that those who opposed further negotiation with the king did so because of private greed. Vane and most of the other revolutionaries had not lost all purity of motive. But to Walker and to much of the public the entire Long Parliament seemed hopelessly corrupt. And indeed time and chance had happened to them all: surrounded by little nets of easy temptation many had been snared, Vane doubtless among them. Even so, he appears to have been more financially upright than most of his fellow revolutionaries.

After Parliament had voted, despite Vane's impassioned warning, to reopen negotiations with the king, the more faithful members arose next morning and, weary from loss of sleep, made their way to Westminster. On their way they observed two troops of horse before Whitehall, and in both the new and old palace yards they saw many companies of foot and horse. Vane did not join the gathering members; either he knew what was to happen and could not consent to it, or he was following his old pattern of absenting himself after losing an important battle.

The members who went found that Colonel Pride, a former drayman, had drawn up a troop of foot in the Court of Requests, on the stairs and in the lobby before the House. At the head of the stairs, Pride stood with the dwarfish Lord Grey of Groby, who held in his hand a paper of names. When members appeared whose names were on that list, Pride detained them and sent them away under guard, some to the Queen's Court, some to the Court of Wards or other places where, by order of the Council of the Army, he held them under restraint. And though the House sent sergeants to these members requesting them to take their seats, the soldiers refused to let them go.

Perhaps the touchiest moment came when William Prynne appeared. When Pride ordered him to stop, he refused and walked up another step or two until Pride seized him and jerked him down. Then Hardress Waller and other soldiers took hold of him. By what authority, said Prynne, do you do these things? There was no verbal answer, but one soldier pointed to his sword.

At three o'clock that afternoon, Hugh Peter, wearing a sword, came bustling in officiously to see the prisoners. By what authority, he was asked, do you detain us? By the authority of the sword, he replied. After he reviewed those in captivity, he ordered Rudyerd and young Fiennes released. By what authority do you release them? he was asked. By the authority of the sword, he replied.

As night drew on, the prisoners requested the captain guarding them to ask Colonel Pride to come and speak with them. When he appeared they asked him by what authority and for what cause they were detained. Pride, more cautious than Hugh Peter, told them he was too busy to reply. That evening the soldiers carried away thirty-nine members to a cellar under the Exchequer, "a common victualling house" popularly known as "Hell." There they were all thrust into the common dining room where they remained that night, most having no beds "though some were ancient, infirm, and gentlemen of honor." Seven of the oldest were offered parole if they wished to go home, but all declined because to accept the offer might be to acknowledge the authority of those who made it. For the captive members, Henry Marten had a bitter jest: since Tophet is prepared for kings, he said, it was fitting that the friends of kings should go to Hell.

The men arrested included Sir Symonds D'Ewes (who had watched with prophetic melancholy the decline of respect for laws and forms), Prynne, Sir Harbottle Grimston, and Clement Walker. Including members imprisoned and secluded, some 143 were now "purged." The intention was not to exclude them all permanently; those could return who were willing to pass a test of loyalty by disclaiming their vote made on December 5 in favor of continuing negotiations with the king. Most refused to do so and many of these did not return to Parliament until after the Restoration. In the meantime a mere fifty or sixty members were carrying on the business of the House: Henry Marten, Thomas Scot, Cromwell, Ludlow, Ireton, Mildmay, Peter Wentworth, and others. But Vane was not among them. The imprisoned members might very well have reflected that the mob had once delivered Parliament from the king's guard; the army had delivered them from the mob now, but who would deliver them from their newest deliverer?

No one would own this violent purging of Parliament. Fairfax said he had known nothing about it. Cromwell, too, had known nothing of it, but when he heard about it he immediately approved. His direction was consistent. Vane, on the other hand, seemed inconsistent. He neither approved nor protested the army's action, but he pointedly absented himself from the purged Parliament. He must have known as well as Cromwell did that the revolution could now survive only with the aid of military force; at least he knew that it stood a better chance with the sectarian army than with the intolerant Presbyterians. Yet he lent his support to the army reluctantly. Whatever the Heavenly Jerusalem he envisioned for England would be like, it certainly would not resemble a military dictatorship. Though Vane would have been glad to be rid of some of the secluded members, and though he himself had helped to weaken the civil and religious forms that bound the nation together, this act of violence went further than he had either foreseen or intended and he could not condone it. Even the visionary Vane was beginning to see that those who begin the destruction of forms cannot always prescribe where the destruction will stop. When raw human energies are aroused, encouraged, and sanctified, no one knows into what strange new channels they will eventually force their way. This time Vane could simply refuse to go along; some day he would become the helpless victim of forces he had himself unleashed.

The tattered remnant of the Long Parliament that was now functioning as the government was the mere pawn of the army, and most of the nation held it in contempt. It was no longer a people's Parliament, said John Lilburne; it was Colonel Pride's Parliament consisting of men who would do what they were told at the point of a gun. It was a mere Rump.

Very well; the army had disposed of the recalcitrant Parliament Now it was time to settle with Charles Stuart, that man of blood. H

was not ill-treated, but Hurst Castle was not Carisbrooke. Here the
king lay in rough lodgings; he could enjoy no bowling green; no
loyal subjects pressed forward to be touched. His only recreation
was to step forth from gray walls into the gray of winter, to walk
along the shingle with the gray sea on one side and mud flats on the
other. And on December 19, he was taken from Hurst to begin the
journey to London.

On December 23, the House of Commons appointed a committee
to consider how to proceed against the king by way of justice. Since
he could not be tried under the law by any existing court, a special
High Court of Justice was created by ordinance to try him. It was
an axiom of the English law (although Edward Coke had demurred)
that justice proceeded from the sovereign. Therefore, in order to try
the sovereign at all, it was necessary to establish justice upon some
other base. On January 4, 1649, the Commons therefore passed a
resolution, the substance of which had been "in the air" for some
time. The people under God are the source of all power, the
resolution said; and the House of Commons, chosen by and
representing the people, holds the supreme power by delegation.
Their acts need no concurrence from a king or a House of Peers. By
this authority, then, was constituted a court of 135 commissioners
who would serve as both judge and jury.

Many of those empaneled refused to serve on this unprecedented
tribunal: two Chief Justices, Oliver St. John and Henry Rolle,
declined; so did Lord Chief Baron Wilde of the Exchequer Court.
Algernon Sidney spoke for many when he said, "First, the King can
be tried by no court; secondly, no man can be tried by this court."
To which Cromwell replied, "I tell you we will cut off his head with
the Crown upon it."

On January 20, the trial began with 68 of the 135 judges present.
Sidney noted with some surprise that among the spectators that day
was young Harry Vane, who, although continuing to perform his
regular duties at the admiralty, had absented himself from Westminster since the day before Pride's Purge. Perhaps as a man who had
served the king and whose mother had been an intimate of the
queen, he felt some compunction deeper than most other men. Later
he would say that he opposed putting the king on trial because of
"tenderness of blood," and those words have the ring of truth. Had
it been a trial to depose or even to imprison he most likely would

have approved, but judicial murder of the sovereign was going too far. After the execution was carried out, although he came under considerable pressure to sign the Parliamentary oath of approbation of the trial and execution, he vigorously and steadfastly refused.

Descriptions have come down to us of the improvised court in Westminster Hall. There seats had been placed on a dais for the judges, and a chair, facing the judges and covered with red crimson, was placed for the king; the two galleries were filled with high-born ladies and men of privilege, but most conspicuously there were soldiers everywhere. When the ultimate form is about to be destroyed, only the military can ensure the passivity of the people. So there were Trained Bands rhythmically marching or standing at parade rest, troops of horse, militiamen, and musketeers in the streets, in the public squares, before public buildings, in barges on the river, passing in columns, filing in and filing out—soldiers fed, clothed, and armed at the people's expense. And carefully instructed soldiers were stationed inside Westminster Hall, in the lobby and on the stairs.

There was some little disturbance in the gallery. When the names of the commissioners of the High Court were being read and that of Thomas Fairfax was called, a veiled woman in the gallery cried out, "He has more wit than to be here." Later, it was determined that this was Fairfax's wife, daughter of Lord Vere, who, under Elizabeth, had been one of England's doughtiest soldiers.

Then Charles came in, dressed in black which set off the gray of his hair; around his neck hung a jeweled George on a blue ribbon, while on his black cloak rested the starkly contrasting silver star of the Garter.

The lengthy charge was read, enumerating all of Charles' crimes and ending with his impeachment "as a tyrant, traitor, murderer, and a public and implacable enemy of the Commonwealth of England." At the absurdity of this charge Charles laughed aloud. It was a true cavalier gesture, the Royalists said later; it showed his mettle and his fearlessness. But Colonel Ludlow did not think so. There had been a war in which many thousands had been slain, and to some degree Charles was responsible for it. Ludlow thought that the king's face, when he laughed, was an impudent face.

Bradshaw, the president of the court, ignored the contempt and called on the king to answer the charge "in the behalf of the

Commons assembled in Parliament and the good people of England." Once more the masked lady cried out: "It is a lie; not half,
nor a quarter of the people of England. Oliver Cromwell is a
traitor." Colonel Axtell, not a poised man at any time and a highly
excited one now, ordered his troops to fire into the gallery. The men
of the New Model ignored the order while some gentlemen in the
gallery induced Lady Fairfax to leave.

Now, with the interruption over and the charge of murderer and
traitor upon him, Charles must make his first answer in the court
before his people. He did not stammer. In his reply he seized on a
word that the members in Hell had used so frequently a few weeks
earlier: "authority." By what authority was he being tried? Until he
knew that, he could not answer. Bradshaw, knowing that this was
the central legal issue, had his answer ready. Charles, he said, was
being tried by the people of England who had elected him king.
Elected? This was a "strange point and new." Charles had been
under the impression that he had inherited his troublesome throne,
and so, once again, he asked for authority. Since the king refused to
plead, the trial could not continue, and so Charles was removed to
Cotton House by the soldiers who, as they had been instructed,
shouted "justice, justice," as he passed. But from that part of the hall
where civilians sat, there were cries of "God save the king." Hugh
Peter raised his arms to the square and cried out to whoever would
listen, "This is a most glorious beginning of the work." What had
once seemed amusing or refreshing in him was now beginning to
seem tiresome and harshly fanatical.

That night, because soldiers were stationed in his room, Charles
refused to take off his clothes or go to bed. The next day, Sunday, he
spent in meditation and prayer with Bishop Juxon. And that same
Sunday the Presbyterian pulpiteers went to work preaching fervidly
and emotionally in the king's behalf. But the commissioners did not
listen to them; they heard three appointed sermons. Joshua Sprigge,
chaplain to Fairfax, preached on the ambiguous text, "Whoso
sheddeth man's blood, by man shall his blood be shed," a text that
could be read either for or against the killing of Charles. The second
speaker was an army chaplain who spoke on the text, "Judge not
that ye be not judged," a rather strange text, some thought, for one
representing the army. The third speaker was Hugh Peter who,
following the scriptural text, "To bind their kings in chains and

their nobles in fetters of iron," made what amounted to a demand for the king's life.

On Monday, January 22, Charles was brought back to Westminster Hall and again seated before the bar. Again Bradshaw asserted the authority of the court and demanded that the king plead guilty or not guilty. Charles replied that no earthly power could question him as a delinquent and he added,

> It is not my case alone; it is the freedom and liberty of the people of England; and do you pretend what you will, I stand more for their liberties; for, if power without law may make laws, may alter the fundamental laws of the kingdom, I do not know what subject he is in England that can be sure of his life or anything that he calls his own.

It was a brilliant statement, spoken with passion but without arrogance or fear. It was as if this delicate man, all his life so careful of forms in the church or in the Court, now defended at last that form on which all other forms depend: the law itself, which is the only control or restraint on arbitrary strength. He was speaking like a king now, like a man who had found out at last what he stood for.

As Charles was being removed from the Hall that day one of the soldiers forgot his instructions and said, "God bless you, sir." The king thanked the soldier whom an officer, at the same time, struck over the head. "The punishment exceeds the offense," said the king. Later he remarked that the soldiers should not be blamed for crying out upon him; if ordered to do so, they would cry in the same fashion after their own leaders.

The king had some other things prepared to say that day had he not been hindered "against reason" from doing so. He intended to say that although he could not grant that the authority of the people of England could serve as the legal basis for a trial, suppose for the sake of argument that it could. How many people had Parliament enquired of? Had they sought popular opinion? You have not, he would have said, and you do not have it; nor do you have the people's delegated power, for the higher House is totally excluded as is a major part of Commons. Again he was right. The people's republic was simply a term devised to designate by an inoffensive phrase what was, in fact, a military state.

A third session of the court on January 23 was equally inconclusive. Every time Bradshaw found himself in a difficult position trying to assert the common law to justify an illegal proceeding, he finally had to call on the soldiers to escort the unresisting king back to his confinement. Bradshaw was learning how useful soldiers could be.

At last on January 27, Charles was brought before the court for sentence. This time Bradshaw was robed in red, an appropriate color for a judicial murder. As the king entered, the officers prodded the soldiers who set up their mechanical cries of "justice." When Charles was at last allowed to speak, he made a final and startling offer: he asked to be heard before Lords and Commons in the Painted Chamber. After some confusion in the court, he was refused. What would he have said? He had in mind, apparently, a new plan of peace for the kingdom, and later men speculated that he would have offered to abdicate in favor of his son.

Condemned to die as a traitor, Charles composed himself for that final scene which would be played out on January 30. On the night before, Thomas Herbert, Charles' most faithful retainer, dreamed that William Laud had come to the door and asked to speak with the king. After private conversation, the old archbishop kissed the royal hand and took his leave, bowing so low that he fell. Herbert, in the dream, was just helping the old man to his feet, when the king called. Charles seemed touched by the account of Herbert's dream. "It is remarkable," he said. He told Herbert that this was his second marriage day, that he hoped before night to be espoused to blessed Jesus. He then asked his retainer for a warm shirt, fearing that in the cold weather he might shiver and give cause for some to say that a dying king had trembled. "I fear not death," he said. "Death is not terrible to me. I bless my God I am prepared."

Then Bishop Juxon came in and read the morning service from the Prayer Book; by coincidence the lesson for the day dealt with the Passion of the Lord. "They led him away for envy and crucified their King." The reading set the tone and mood of Charles' mind, and there were Biblical echoes in what followed.

Charles was to be executed on a platform built outside the new Banqueting House. It seemed the safest place. Opposite it ran the blank wall of the Tiltyard; the street was broad here, about 120 feet, enough room to interpose many soldiers between the king and his people, enough to keep his subjects from hearing anything he might say. Every building that abutted on this place of execution was a part of army headquarters and, in the angle between Holbein Gate and the Banqueting House, a battery of guns had been mounted on a platform.

Waiting for the execution, Charles felt no desire to eat, but Bishop Juxon persuaded him to take a little bread, a little wine. Then he stepped out onto the scaffold. Knowing he could not be heard by his people, he nevertheless addressed himself to the little group on the scaffold who might hear the echo of the scriptures in what he said. His mind was on Strafford: "An unjust sentence that I suffered to take effect, is punished now by an unjust sentence on me." Now, faced with imminent death himself, he had forgiven all the world; especially he had forgiven his enemies. What he had most wanted, he said, was peace for his people; he also wished for their liberty and freedom which could be found only in a government of laws. Had he been willing to give way to arbitrary law, to have all laws changed by the power of the sword, he need never have come to the scaffold, "and therefore I tell you (and I pray God it be not laid to your charge) that I am the Martyr of the people."

He would die a Christian, he said, according to the profession of the church of England, "as I found it left me by my father." He had a good cause, he said, a phrase the Puritans believed their own; and he had a gracious God; he would say no more.

But perhaps already he had said too much. Among other things, in those last moments he had continued to insist that subjects had no right to share in a government, that there was nothing in governing that pertained to them. Sovereigns ruled, subjects obeyed—in that lay happiness. Surely the most tragic thing about his execution is that he died understanding so little those titanic and tragic forces that had played around his head. He could never have believed that Lilburne and Cromwell and the sectarian troopers, filled with inner light, martial zeal, and vague republican yearnings, would yet mark out the configurations of the future. Had he known that, he would have died not only resignedly but gladly.

The crowd heard none of this. They saw him tuck his gray hair under a white satin nightcap. They saw him, with the natural grace of his lithe body, place his neck on the block. In that moment, the troopers, only boys with guns and always lacking the judgment to exercise the power guns confer, drew in their stomachs and waited uneasily. Their king prayed silently for a moment; the executioner awaited the signal with his axe high, the muscles of which he was so proud rippling, tense, expectant. Then the king stretched out his arms, the axe fell, the dainty head rolled on the scaffold. The executioner ripped away the white nightcap, seized the gray, flowing hair in his great hand, held the king's head high, and cried out as he had been trained, "Behold the head of a traitor." From the soldiers there was only silence: they had neither orders nor spontaneous impulse to respond.

There was only silence; then from the people who were gathered behind the soldiers, who faced the mounted guns, who were surrounded by troopers and militia and armed sailors, there arose a moan, a low sobbing sound that rose into a long, crying wail, "such a groan," one said, "as I never heard before and desire I may never hear again." They seemed to think, these people, seeing their king's head hanging there from the fist of a hangman, that it was no doing of theirs, that it was all the work of others. And so they wailed; and then they stood around in groups, angry, hostile, abusive to the soldiers, luxuriating in self-pity and self-esteem until orders were given for two troops of horse to disperse them. Looking at the people that day, one is inclined to think that the king was right about them.

But not even the horse troopers could prevent the growth of legends about the death of the king. Many who witnessed the execution said that the man with the axe was not the professional executioner, that no ordinary subject could possibly have been forced to strike that final, sacrilegious blow. No, they said, it was some Puritan hidden by the mask, perhaps Hugh Peter who was, at the moment, the Puritan they hated most.

Nor could the soldiers prevent the clandestine sale of a little book, *The Portrait of a King*, the book which Charles had been writing before the Battle of Naseby and all through his confinement, and which now someone had edited for him and given unity of structure and tone. It was a series of the king's meditations on the major events of the civil war: the execution of Strafford, the attempt on the five members, the negotiations with the Parliament, all written in quiet tones, without defensiveness, without a hint of arrogance. And at the end of each section was a formal prayer, with Charles crying out to his God for forgiveness, for understanding, for compassion. In one year, at home and abroad, the book ran through twenty editions, then thirty, and forty. Bishop Burnet said it made the greatest impression of any book of the age, that nothing but his death could so have raised Charles' character in the public mind. Now the book combined with the martyrdom to create a sentiment that made the restoration of a king inevitable. Charles' character and his cause were elevated even further when Milton, at the bidding of the Rump, wrote a bitter, righteous reply. *Image Breaker* he called it, a monument of Puritan insensitivity to what the feeling of a moment requires.

While the king's book professed to speak of the events of the civil war, at the same time it spoke without words, in quiet, somber tones, of all the smashed windows and organs, the Virgins and Babies in stone or wood that had been shot down with troopers' guns; it spoke of the horses stabled in cathedrals, of holidays forbidden, of Christmas with no remembrance of the Christ child; of canting, four-hour sermons; of the illiterate rantings of the untaught who believed that their wild words reflected the mind of God. That book, in some mysterious way, whispered to the people of yule logs and plum puddings, of good ales in warm taverns, of maypoles and songs—and of a land where boys with guns now enabled men with swords to rule everything. The people, some of them, remembered the decorum, the dignity, the peace, the simple terse beauty of the old service. John Cleveland expressed the national mood:

> Thus 'tis a General Eclipse,
> And the whole world is al-a-mort.

It is not known whether or not Vane attended the king's execution. In any case he did not allow the passions of the moment to interfere with the business of office. On the day of the king's death, he dropped around to his office in the admiralty and signed his name to some dated papers. It was a simple act. He had performed it a thousand times. He felt no whisper of warning.

14

Vane and the Commonwealth (1649–1653)

The small junta which Parliament had now become immediately took steps to insure its own continuation in power. A day or so after the king's suffering, this Rump decreed that no member who had voted that the king had offered satisfactory terms for a settlement should be admitted to his seat until he publicly recanted. A few days later, a resolution that the House of Lords was both "useless and dangerous and ought to be abolished" was carried without a division. On the following day another unopposed resolution abolished monarchy.

With so many of the old constitutional forms torn down, it was necessary to form a new instrument of government, and it was proposed that it should be composed of a House of Commons and a Council of State, modeled on the old Committee of Both Kingdoms, with sweeping power in both foreign and domestic affairs, including the right to administer oaths and take testimony from those suspected of designs against the Commonwealth. This was simply a revival of the detested ex-officio oath of Star Chamber and High Commission.

Vane was one of the forty-one members chosen to serve on the Council of State. At first, however, he and others refused to sit because they would not take an oath expressing assent to the death of the king and to the abolition of the House of Lords. When the new council met first in February, only fourteen members were present. Since inquiry determined that the others were staying away because of the new oath, a simpler vow was substituted in which the deponent engaged to be loyal to the Commonwealth as established without king or House of Peers. Twenty-two of the forty-one council members still dissented; Vane was among them because he, like the Quakers, objected on principle to taking oaths. And so on February 22 a resolution was passed to the effect that members of the council should disregard all previous resolutions and take their seats. When the council met on the following day, Vane was there.

One of the first acts of the new council was to dismiss the Earl of Warwick (whose brother was on trial for treason) as Lord High Admiral and to put the navy directly under the Council of State, which appointed a subcommittee to oversee the fleet. Vane was the principal member of it, and except for tactical warfare, the navy now came largely under his jurisdiction and administration. He became equally powerful in many other areas of government by virtue of membership on proliferating new committees by which the business of the nation was conducted now that there was no separate executive power. Probably no man in Parliament served so assiduously and on so many interlocking committees as Vane did in the next few years. In addition to the Council of State and the Committee for the Navy, he continued to serve on the Committee for Compounding and, at some time during the brief life of the Commonwealth he also served on the Irish and Scottish Committee, on the subcommittee for Treaties and Alliances, the Committee on Trade, Plantations, and Foreign Affairs, and on many others.

The critical problem that this new government faced was of course money, and most of the methods proposed to procure it were highly offensive to the public. Surely the very worst proposal was to sell off the paintings which Charles had acquired through a lifetime of discriminating collecting. The council had them gathered together, appraised, and sold for whatever they would bring. *Peace and Plenty* by Rubens "with many figures as big as life" sold for 400 pounds; Titian's *Pope Alexander and Caesar Borgia* sold for only 100 pounds, but his *Burial of Christ* brought twenty pounds more. Raphael's cartoons of *The Acts of the Apostles* went for 300, while Titian's *Venus* "lying along, playing an organ," was appraised at only 150 pounds, though the astute merchants working for the council pushed the sum up to 165.

There were also paintings by Correggio and del Sarto, and many by Van Dyke, including *King Charles on Horseback*. Raphael's *Saint George*, a sentimental favorite in England which was not much prized abroad, sold cheaply, as did Leonardo's *St. John*, an unimpressive work, the council thought. Everything went: Dürer's paintings of his father and himself, the Van Leydens and the Palmas, the Caravaggios and Tintorettos. The council was both delighted and surprised at the willingness, even eagerness, of French, Spanish, and Italian officials to buy those works and cart them off to Paris, Vienna, Rome, and Madrid. When it was all over, the passion for beauty and the exceptional good taste of Charles had netted the Commonwealth some 50,000 pounds, enough to support the army for almost two weeks or the entire military machine of army and navy for at least seven days. The foreign purchasers, on the other hand, considered the willingness to sell these works of art certain evidence of the barbarism of the "new men."

The council concerned itself with other artifacts, too. It ordered that the statue of Charles, standing at Exchange, was to have the head taken off and an inscription added: *Exit tyrannus Regium ultimus, anno primo restitutae libertatis Angliae*, 1648. Thus, symbolically, the "Norman Yoke" was broken. Since it raised no money, this was an act of disinterested vandalism; but from time to time, it was proposed that the cathedrals of the land be dismantled and the materials sold, their great bells stilled and melted down that they might speak again more forcefully as naval guns. The lead was stripped from Lichfield Cathedral; Cromwell's horses were stabled in St. Paul's, a fitting rejoinder to Laud, some thought; Canterbury suffered from the iconoclasts; but some glimmer of good sense, or perhaps the anger of the people, kept Yorkminster and Durham, Salisbury, Canterbury, and St. Paul's standing.

The first serious challenge to the new Commonwealth came from the militant left. In February, 1649, even as the new government was being settled, Colonel Harrison and others had urged that the Fifth Monarchy, the Kingdom of Christ, should at once be established on the earth by incorporating the civil state and the church into one body. At the same time Lilburne and the Levellers were saying that the new Council of State was simply a new form of power as arbitrary as monarchy had once been. Whereupon Parliament declared Lilburne's writing seditious and ordered that he and others who thought as he did be proceeded against as traitors. Brought before the Council of State, Lilburne was asked if he was the author of the seditious pamphlet; he had earlier refused to incriminate himself before Star Chamber and he refused now before the Council of State.

Some 80,000 people signed a petition on Lilburne's behalf, and a large group of women appeared at Westminster demanding his release. This time there was no John Pym to console or placate them; they were curtly told to go home and do their dishes. The Parliamentary revolutionists were becoming tired of revolutionary tactics.

The Royalists, too, were causing difficulties. On April 18, 1649, Isaac Dorislaus, who had taken part in the prosecution of the king, was sent to the Hague as ambassador from the Commonwealth. There he aroused such savage and bitter resentment among the English Royalist emigres that one of them assassinated him. His body was returned to England amid a general Parliamentary outrage, and Vane was placed in charge of the funeral; he turned it into a military demonstration, a stern warning to the enemies of the Commonwealth at home or abroad.

On May 15, Vane was given his most intractable assignment: he with one other member was assigned the "special care" of directing a committee which was to work out a way to end the Long Parliament and hold new elections. The members of this committee quickly disagreed and debated so long that the army men began to say that they were delaying on purpose so that this Parliament would never dissolve itself.

When the new government seemed safely settled, Parliament turned to the perennial problem of Ireland. The revolutionaries could not forget Strafford's threat to bring over an Irish army and they knew that even now Prince Rupert was intriguing with the Irish. Danger seemed so imminent that they sent Cromwell at the head of an army to reduce the complexities of the Irish problem to the stark simplicity of a military solution. In September Cromwell began the devastation and the slaughter. In his marchings, he would summon a town, a castle, or a fortified place, as the half-mad Humphrey Gilbert had done in the days of Elizabeth, and if any of them refused to yield, he considered it just to slaughter the soldiers and execute the priests of Babylon (as he called the Irish clerics); civilians too fell victim to the aroused soldiers. Invoking the name of his God at every step, Cromwell outdid in ferocity all of Ireland's previous English conquerors, and those Irish who had once known "the faith of Grey," now knew the "curse of Cromwell." It was Vane's role to keep supplies moving to Ireland.

While Cromwell burned like a comet through that lost land, John Lilburne wrote a tract about him and dedicated it to him. He called it *An Impeachment of High Treason Against Oliver Cromwell and his Son-in-law, Henry Ireton*. In it, Honest John argued that while it was lawful to take arms against a tyrant, even a successful armed force must bow to the sovereignty of the people. He preferred a restoration of monarchy to the rule of the sword, and he feared that under "Saint Oliver," England would have a new king who, thanks to his standing army, would exercise unchecked power to make the people "absolute and perfect slaves."

Lilburne's imprisonment and subsequent trial was one of the pivotal events of the Commonwealth. In the teeth of Cromwell's troopers, a jury of Englishmen stoutly held that John was innocent and freed him amid general rejoicing. But the rejoicing proved somewhat premature, for the danger which both Leveller and Royalist presses posed caused the government to promulgate a new Licensing Act in the enforcement of which many distinguished men, including Clement Walker, were jailed. Milton, one wonders, wast thou living at this hour? He was indeed and was serving as Latin Secretary to the Council of State on which Vane, in Cromwell's absence, was the leading member. The word which justified such repressions was "necessity," which Milton would later call "the tyrant's plea." And it would be his Satan, the most convincing and appalling creation of his imagination, who would invoke "necessity" for political immoralities which even a demon needed to justify.

Though in October of 1649 young Vane and his Committee on a New Parliament had been ordered to meet every day and report back to Parliament by the end of the month, now, three months later, no report had been made; the troubles in Ireland and the impending trouble with Scotland seemed reason enough to avoid further disruption of domestic affairs. The committee made its report at last on January 9, 1650. Following a scheme endorsed by the army, it recommended that the new Parliament should consist of 400 members elected according to a new and more equitable apportionment. Such a proposal had the support of everyone, but a further significant recommendation did not. Vane proposed that there should not be a new general election; rather, present members of the Long Parliament and previous members who could or would qualify themselves by manifesting their loyalty should continue to sit. The remaining vacancies would then be filled or "recruited."

Vane's scheme satisfied neither the Levellers, Cromwell, his army, the Presbyterians (most of whom had been excluded), nor the Royalist sympathizers who were probably now a majority in the nation, certainly in London. Presumably it did satisfy the Independent party, but that was and always had been a precarious minority. Why then did they attempt to push through such an unpopular idea? Henry Marten tried to explain why. The Commonwealth, he said, was like the infant Moses; when Pharaoh's daughter sought a nurse for him, she found his own mother. Similarly this loyal remnant of Parliament, these republicans and Independents, were the true mother to the fair child of the Commonwealth and therefore the fittest nurses for it. Since Marten had previously joined the Levellers in demanding a new Parliament, his change of view is highly significant. The question always arises whether successful revolutionaries will relinquish the power they have gathered by the sword unless it is taken from them by the sword. Behind Marten's Biblical irrelevancies lay a hard and terrible fact: sentiment in England being what it was, there was almost no way that Vane's committee could ensure the election of persons devoted to the cause. On the contrary, it was certain that new general elections, no matter how exclusive the franchise, would devastate or even destroy the Independent party. With the return of Presbyterian influence, backed by the other Royalists, civil and religious liberty might be in for hard times and the revolutionaries themselves for harder ones. While there may have been some impurities of motive, even active self-seeking, the dilemma of the revolutionaries was acute enough to make even honest men stumble. We shall never know whether the kind of election Cromwell advocated would have been better than the partial one proposed by Vane. But at a time when many of the electorate believed that the principal reason for the Long Parliament's wish to continue itself was fear of being investigated, Vane's proposal aroused general frustration and irritation.

It is little wonder, then, that at this time Vane was despondent. Mr. Cann reported that a friend of his had gone to dinner with Vane and two other men. Vane said that Independents were in worse estate than ever before, that all the world was and would be their enemies. The Scots had abandoned them; their own army and general were not to be trusted; the whole kingdom, he said, would rise and cut their throats upon the first good occasion, and he did not know where an Independent could be safe. He also feared that when Cromwell marched the army against the Scots, the city of London would become Parliament's most dangerous enemy.

The reasons for Vane's pessimism are illuminated by a small incident. In Berkshire, five roaring lads had spent too much time in the local tavern where the more they thought about the king and the Long Parliament, the taxes and the soldiers, the more outraged and desperate they became. Finally they agreed to show their devotion to Prince Charles, whom they wished to see restored, by drinking his health in their own blood. Simultaneously, each would cut off a piece of his own buttock, fry it on a gridiron, and then eat it in a kind of primitive, drunken communion. Four of the five went through with it, and one bled so profusely that the others had to send for a surgeon whereby the whole affair was discovered and apparently regarded as sedition.

Vane's own insecurities probably led him to an overzealous concern for the safety of the government. Royalist newspapers reported that it was the two Vanes who had conceived and sponsored an act that, in February of 1650, required all Catholics, soldiers of fortune, and known or suspected Royalists to leave London within a month and not to return closer than twenty miles. The same reports said that some 30,000 people left the city, and though that was undoubtedly an exaggeration, many city people were certainly uprooted. Perhaps the Vanes were not wholly responsible but were only expressing a general sentiment; how is one to know? They were blamed for so many unpleasant things. Later in the same year Vane reported to Parliament that the Council of State was concerned because prominent Royalists abroad had left wives in England who were perpetually intriguing and causing political disaffection.

In 1650 Vane had been Treasurer of the Navy for twelve years with only one interruption. On June 27, he petitioned Parliament that he be allowed to surrender the office and receive just compensation for it. At the same time he proposed that in the future the office should be managed with less charge to the public.

Accordingly, the inevitable committee appointed to look into it recommended that in the future the Treasurer of the Navy should not retain a percentage of the monies passing through his hand but simply be given a salary of 1,000 pounds a year. It also recommended that Vane be given public lands then worth 1,200 pounds a year, which would immediately increase substantially in value.

In the same month Vane surrendered his office, Cromwell returned from Ireland to receive the thanks of the Parliament and to prepare an army for the projected invasion of Scotland where young Charles had already taken the covenant—swallowed it whole without tasting it as John Selden had once prescribed. In September of 1650 at Dunbar, Cromwell outmaneuvered and outfought the Scots whose army had been purged of some 5,000 "profane persons" who had followed Montrose or Hamilton, Cavaliers who were their best fighting men. If God was pleased at the purge, he failed to show it. When the battle of Dunbar began before dawn, Cromwell cried out, "Let God arise, let His enemies be scattered." They were, and the crowds of prisoners taken were ravaged by dysentery and fever on marches and in prison camps. Those who survived finally found themselves in New England as indentured servants; after a few years they became substantial citizens of the new Commonwealth, men of whom their descendants are inordinately proud. Harsh as this may seem, Cromwell's treatment of the Scots was lenient compared with his savage slaughterings in Ireland.

Early in the following year, 1651, Vane displayed both the liberal and punitive sides of his nature. John Fry, a member who had sniffed the winds of change, was sick of the religious controversy. While he would not with Hobbes go so far as to slit the throats of all clerics, he was vigorously anticlerical and he wrote a book in which he demonstrated that the slight differences between Catholic and Protestant were scarcely worth the blood of a nation. Many of the orthodox, believing themselves insulted, wished the work to be condemned and burned by the common hangman. But Vane vigorously defended the book, the author, and his right to publish, and he served as teller against condemnation.

Vane's more vindictive side appeared when a Royalist conspiracy was uncovered. The seething and suppressed discontent in the country was bound to break out sooner or later. When in January the extensive but badly organized plot became known, the committee appointed to examine plots immediately recommended that Parliament encourage informers by promising them a part of the estate of any conspirator they informed against. More drastically they recommended that any who disturbed the peace or conspired against the government should lose life and estate without mercy. At the same time Parliament was asked to prohibit all sports and games such as hunting or hawking matches, football games, horse races or cock fights, any activity that, by bringing people together in large numbers, might serve as a cloak for conspiracy.

Even so, plans for the uprising continued and leaders were appointed in each county; but what really frightened Parliament was the information that the conspiracy was especially strong in London and that every house there concealed arms ready for apprentices and servants to use. At a signal the armed mob was to come to Westminster to put a forcible end to the Long Parliament. It was said that the design in London was forwarded primarily by Presbyterian ministers, in correspondence with other ministers in the counties; they wished to restore the Presbyterian members ejected during Pride's Purge and then to urge both prince and Parliament to agree to the terms Charles had proposed at Newport. As fear increased many were arrested, including three Presbyterian ministers; one of these, Christopher Love, was selected to be tried by the High Court of Justice. He was undoubtedly guilty of conspiracy but there were extenuating considerations. He was only thirty, his wife was heavy with child, and he himself was immensely popular in the City. Thinking it unwise to further alienate the citizens, Parliament hesitated to execute him. The Independents, however, with Milton as their spokesman, demanded his death. These clerics, said Milton, "fill their pulpits with alarm and invective, preach disobedience and treason with open mouth, keep private fasts for the destruction of the Parliament. . . ." And Vane agreed. When it was proposed that Love's case be postponed, he was a teller against it. As petitions poured in asking that Love's life be spared, some members suggested postponing the execution, but Vane opposed that also. It was even proposed that instead of being killed, the young minister might be banished, perhaps to the deserts of New England. Vane opposed that, too, as did the Independent majority.

The controversy became so emotional that it was believed only

Cromwell could settle it, and Colonel Hammond, who had been so compassionate of his royal prisoner at Carisbrooke, wrote Cromwell urging him to spare the young man. But Vane wrote two letters urging him not to, and in August Christopher Love was executed. He died well, saying in his last moments that the men who hungered after his flesh and thirsted after his blood would only hasten his happiness and their own ruin. And though Vane had been only one of a majority, he was remembered as the man who had howled after young Love's blood.

During this agitation, Vane's brother George, who had once fought stoutly in the defense of Raby and on behalf of Parliament, was arrested and charged with Royalist sympathies. Naturally the Committee on Examinations proceeded with caution, wondering if their prisoner might have protection from the Council of State. Finally they merely discharged him under bond of 1,000 pounds. But George Vane's defection was part of a larger pattern. Many who had fought against an old king were now prepared to fight for a new one. Vane's mother had never wavered in the slightest in her devotion to Anglicanism and the frail king who had died to uphold it, but now, most of Henry's brothers were becoming disillusioned with the cause and would ultimately favor a restoration of the monarchy. In defecting, they would simply be participating in the shifting mood of the nation, but their revolutionary brother would be left ever more lonely and isolated, excluded from full intimacy with his own family, except for Frances and the children, and his little band of disciples.

At about the time of Love's execution, Parliament interrogated William Prynne about a new book he had written, no more acceptable to the army than his previous ones had been to Laud. In fact, many of the old revolutionaries were now having the same trouble under the Commonwealth as they had endured under monarchy. Nothing changed it seemed—not their outrage, their righteousness, or the quantity of their unreadable, seditious prose, nor the anger of whatever government was in power.

Meanwhile, an even more serious threat was arising abroad where economic interests were beginning to separate the English and the Dutch: there had been a general deterioration in their relations and already their navies had clashed. Then in October of 1650, when the Prince of Orange died, it seemed in England a propitious moment to try for a rapprochement. Every Protestant statesman since Gustav Adolf had hoped for a grand alliance of all Protestant states; now it was to be seen if the political and religious ties between England and Holland were strong enough to effect some kind of union.

In January of 1651 the inevitable committee—including and probably dominated by Vane—was appointed to examine the relations between the two countries, and to effect a treaty the committee sent two ambassadors to the Hague. There an agreement was reached that a basis for a new treaty might be found in an old one, the *Intercursus Magnus* of 1495, which had guaranteed free trading and shipping between the nations and promised mutual military aid, including expulsion of refugees. The Council of State directed Mr. Milton to translate that document, which he was "to have from Sir Henry Vane"; Vane, probably the instigator of the plan for union, had apparently been studying it already.

But things did not go well in Holland. The English ambassadors, not very keen about their assignment to start with, were outrageously harassed and threatened by the exiled English Royalists. Everywhere they heard shouts of "King's murderers, Cromwell's bastards, English hangmen," and so on. For the very safety of their lives the English retinue traveled the streets only in armed groups; frequently they slept in their clothes. And the Dutch government did not seem to be making much effort to suppress the violence against them: their windows were broken, their servants beaten, and St. John was fortunate to survive an attempt to assassinate him.

Nor did the Dutch immediately vouchsafe any reply to the English proposals. When a reply finally came in June, it was disappointing, for while it reasserted the desire of the Dutch for free trade and military assistance, it made no mention of expelling refugees. What the Dutch wanted was to open the colonies of both nations to both trading fleets; they wanted liberty of fishing and access to all harbors. What the English wanted was the expulsion of the English refugees as an assurance that Holland would not become a staging area for an invasion. For the Dutch this was a difficult demand: these refugees had come at the invitation of the House of Orange and having been more or less under the protection of the late prince, they were objects of compassion and romantic concern to the people as a whole. To expel the refugees might throw Holland into internal disorder. And so the attempted rapprochement failed and on June 18, shortly after the Dutch reply, the ambassadors returned to England.

In the same month, Vane, impatient with the fumblings of committee and subcommittee, proposed that the naval affairs be vested in an independent commission with enough authority to do the necessary jobs—to provide stores, magazines, and provisions for the fleet. But the bill failed and the navy was continued under the Council of State.

Meanwhile, a new threat was approaching from the North. The Scots had joined forces with the young king-in-exile to invade England and overthrow the Commonwealth. Gathering strength from Royalist volunteers as they marched south, they got as far as Worcester before Cromwell's army was in a position to oppose them. But there Cromwell shattered the Scots army and sent young Prince Charlie running for his life.

After Cromwell's victory, the Parliament turned its attention back to the Dutch. Shortly after the ambassadors had returned home, a Navigation Bill had been introduced as reprisal against the Dutch and now, on October 9, 1651, Parliament enacted it into law. It prohibited the importation of goods into England from any country in Asia, Africa, or America except in English vessels. From Europe imports must be shipped in English vessels or else in vessels whose owners were citizens of the nation in which the goods were manufactured or produced. This latter was a hard thrust, for the Dutch, a nation that thrived not on what they produced but on what they traded, would be able to transport to England only the scanty produce of their own limited acreage. The Navigation Act was not intended to be a declaration of war, but eventually proved to be just that.

Before that war actually broke out, certain matters at home needed attention. For his victories against the Scots, a grateful Parliament gave Cromwell lands worth 4,000 a year, causing Hugh Peter to cry out, "This man will be king of England yet." And when Cromwell returned to London it seemed to him that the time had come to do something about the endless Long Parliament: he instigated a resolution requiring Parliament to fix a date for its own dissolution and to call a new House; it passed by a small majority of 33 to 26.

Accordingly a bill was brought in and referred to the committee of which Vane was chairman. Supported by the officers and urged on by the general unrest in the country, Cromwell pleaded with his usual eloquence and fervor that Parliament should not throw away something it might never have again—the chance to restore public confidence.

Instead the committee debated for nearly six weeks as opposition to dissolution increased. While the committee was debating, the Fifth Monarchists produced a pamphlet which demanded that the new Parliament be elected only by the saints of the "gathered" churches. Others brought forth more elaborate proposals. Marten, Vane, and the republicans appeared to feel that if the electorate were forced to live by the new ways and new ideas for a time, they might lose their antagonism and be converted. Vane never lost the hope that with just a little more time the revolution would become established not merely by the power of the sword, but also in the recesses of the heart. But if new elections were so rigged that the Independents retained power, it would certainly require an increase in military strength to keep them there. It appeared to Vane that if a new election were held, either counter-revolution or military dictatorship would follow; and so he judged it best to retain in power the small band of faithful who had unseated a king and dismantled a church.

When Vane and his committee returned to the House, the first question put was whether a date for dissolution should be set. By a bare majority of four it was decided affirmatively. Then the actual question of whether there should or should not be an actual dissolution was put, Cromwell and St. John acting as tellers for the yeas and Vane strangely silent through it all. The yeas carried, this time by only two votes; and after four more days of debate it was decided, without a division, that the Long Parliament should be dissolved on November 3, 1654, three years in the future. Whatever chagrin Cromwell felt, he must endure; whatever impatience the people manifested must be suppressed.

Cromwell and the army had won something; Vane's scheme for recruitment was dropped and there was eventually to be a general election and a new House. But the Independents, as blind about unrest in the military as the Presbyterians had been, for the first time since Pride's Purge were at odds with the only force that could keep them in power.

In November of 1651, a new Council of State was chosen, Vane being voted a member for the third time. He continued in his many committee assignments and to these another difficult and delicate task was soon added. The Parliament knew that if it was to have any peace with Scotland, that nation must be immediately disarmed. To moderate the bitterness that might ensue, they decided to offer Scotland a plan of union with England in which the Scots would share fully in the privileges of Englishmen. Accordingly a committee was sent to Scotland to effectuate this plan. Vane and St. John were the principal civilian members, and from the military there were Salwey, Lambert, Deane, Monck, and others. Vane and St. John were to be in charge.

In Scotland the commissioners met much resistance: Royalists still supported Charles II, and Presbyterians said they could never acknowledge a government that supported toleration and subordinated the church to the state. So the commissioners proceeded with the sword and the statute. On February 7, 1652, in Edinburgh, the king's arms and the crowned unicorn were battered off Market Cross, and the crown was suspended from the gallows. The commissioners then publicly proposed that the estates of Scotsmen who had invaded England in 1648 and 1651 should be sequestered to pay the expenses of the war. Lands thus acquired by the government would be leased at low rents to the common people towards whom this appeal was directed.

On February 13, the declaration was read at Dalkeith to a deputation from the burghs and shires. At the same time a general toleration was promised including protection for those ministers who wished to follow the order of the Scottish church.

In March, Vane and Colonel Fenwick returned from Scotland and reported to the Parliament that twenty shires and thirty-five burghs had agreed to the union. On March 18 an Act for Incorporation of the two nations was brought in to Parliament, accompanied by a declaration which announced the proposed union and instructed the Scots to invest a committee with full powers to discuss and assent to the proposal. On April 21, the declaration for a union was read at Market Cross in Edinburgh, where the English soldiers shouted their approval as they had been ordered, but "the Scots showed no rejoicing at it." Nevertheless, in 1654 Cromwell finally issued the Act of Incorporation which bound the two nations;

it was based on the work done in 1651 and 1652 by Vane and the others.

While Vane was in Scotland, Roger Williams again came to England as petitioner, but he waited until Vane's return in April before presenting his petition to the Council of State. It seemed that William Coddington, one of many who had left Massachusetts under governmental disapproval because they had supported Anne and the antinomians, had obtained a charter by which the island settlement of Aquidneck became independent of the Rhode Island colony, with Coddington its governor for life. To prevent this splintering of the colony, Williams wanted the charter withdrawn. Though he did not succeed, thanks to Vane's assistance he did get something: the old charter of 1644 was to remain in force until Coddington and Williams could settle their differences. "Under God, the great anchor of our ship is Sir Henry," Williams said, and he stayed as a guest at Belleau for some time. While he was there, he dedicated one of his pamphlets to Lady Vane, whom he recognized as a leading spirit among the Seekers.

Since the passage of the Navigation Act, which both Vane and Cromwell opposed, relations between England and the Dutch had worsened. During those precarious days, Vane further enhanced his reputation for that prescience attributed to him by his biographer George Sikes, who said that Vane had "a certain foresight of particular events" and could spell out the most secret decrees of foreign councils, which "the Hollander did experience to their cost." In March, 1652, the Council of State learned that the Dutch were fitting out 150 ships to add to the 76 already in service, and in May, Blake and Van Tromp had exchanged gunfire almost by accident. The Dutch, unwilling to concede that war was inevitable, sent the aged Pauw to England with a final demand for redress, but if the response was unsatisfactory, he was to return to Holland. In July the ambassadors abruptly departed, most likely because the prescient Vane had warned the council that the Dutch were only attempting to win time while they prepared for war and the council therefore ordered them out of the country.

A few days after the Dutch ambassadors left England, Milton sent Vane a sonnet, the most famous tribute he ever received.

Vane, young in years, but in sage counsel old,
Than whom a better Senator ne'er held

The helm of Rome, when gowns not arms repelled
The fierce Epirot and the African bold,
Whether to settle peace, or to unfold
The drift of hollow states hard to be spelled,
Then to advise how war may best, upheld,
Move by her two main nerves, Iron and Gold,
In all her equipage; besides to know
Both spiritual power and civil, what each means,
What severs each, thou hast learnt, which few have done.
The bounds of either sword to thee we owe.
Therefore on thy firm hand religion leans
In peace and reckons thee her eldest son.

The first quatrain is derived from Livy, who praised the courage of the Roman senate against Pyrrhus, King of Epirus, and Hannibal in their initially victorious invasions of Italy. The analogy suggests not only that Vane was a senator after the ancient mold, but also that he stood firm in Parliament in the face of the early Royalist victories. Vane's ability "to settle peace" must indicate that Milton favored the hard line Vane had pursued through the many negotiations with the king. His ability to "unfold the drift of hollow states" refers to his detection of Dutch perfidy, whatever it was. Vane's ability to supply iron and gold refers to his work on the committees of revenue and supply, where he provided for the navy, and also for Cromwell's armies in Ireland and Scotland. But all of these, one feels, are subordinate to Vane's supreme achievement, that of freeing the religious conscience from the civil magistrates. The entire course of Vane's life substantiates Milton's praise, but it was particularly germane to recent situations in which both Milton and Vane were concerned.

For one thing, throughout England citizens were coming to deplore the spiritual anarchy of which there were ever more manifestations. Four men out of Somersetshire, who had received an immediate call from God to go and preach the gospel in Galilee, sold their estates and went to London to embark. Two fanatics named Reeves and Mugleston announced that they were the Two Witnesses foretold in the Apocalypse, and had power to shut the heavens that they should rain not, to turn the waters into blood, or to smite the earth with plagues. Perhaps the oddest incident occurred in Whitehall, where Peter Sterry, said to be a disciple of

Vane, was preaching with enthusiasm on the resurrection when a woman, far gone in ecstasy, took off her clothes and ran mother-naked into the middle of the congregation shouting, "Resurrection, I am ready for thee." Some of the congregation said they did not hear the first syllable. Such self-display was less admired then than it is now, and this case of the Naked Lady seemed to epitomize the drift towards moral anarchy invited by toleration. And new threats of doctrinal chaos appeared when in February, 1652, the Racovian Catechism containing the doctrine of the Socinian churches in Poland was published. This confession explicitly denied what were then considered the very foundations of Christianity: the doctrine of the Trinity, the immortality of the soul, the satisfaction of Christ, the existence of heaven and hell, and so on. What with free utterance of heretical doctrine and the antics of the fanatics and the increasing disorder of the Quakers, some Independents began to reconsider the implications of complete religious liberty and to seek a way to restore some kind of order.

One of these was John Owen, a graduate of Queen's College, Oxford, who had been driven into Presbyterianism by Laud, then into Independency by the intolerance of the Presbyterians. Like Roger Williams and John Milton, Owen had composed a treatise on religious liberty which had endeared him to Cromwell, for in it he had argued that although the civil magistrate was unqualified to make judgments in disputed matters of religion, it was proper for him to deal with those who disturbed the public peace in the name of religion, or who, like itinerant preachers, wandered from place to place without fixed abode, or those who spoke contemptuously of divine things. Owen believed that many of the doings of the sectarian left fell under the jurisdiction of civil magistrates, a position which Cromwell strongly endorsed, as had Governor Winthrop of Massachusetts.

Owen led fourteen other ministers in complaining to Parliament about the publication of the Racovian Catechism, and was gratified when the entire edition was ordered to be burned. Along with their protest, the ministers sent a plan for the settling of church questions under which, though there was to be an established church, dissenting groups might meet provided that they did so in places publicly known and that they informed the civil magistrate of their places of meeting. This established church would be controlled by two sets of commissioners composed of both laymen and ministers, one commission to remove unfit ministers and schoolmasters, and the other to preside over admissions to the ministry.

This plan must have alarmed Vane even though it left dissenters free to meet. The most offensive proposal in it was one which required that the saving principles and doctrines of the Christian religion were to be officially formulated, and that no one would be allowed to preach anything contrary to them. As for the proposal that anyone who sought to discover the mind of God otherwise than through the holy scriptures should be proscribed, it would go hard against the whole sectarian left, and not least against Vane's little band of Seekers. The proscription of unorthodox views on the Trinity or the immortality of the soul would not have touched Vane but would have silenced Milton. The most rigorous proposal of all was that those who forsook and despised the duties of God's worship were to be disciplined and anathematized. This seems to have been an attempt by the ministers to require attendance at their churches, something Vane could only regard with astonishment and anger. In these circumstances the sure knowledge of the limits of civil and religious authority which Milton rightly attributed to Vane would illuminate the contradictory and self-destructive nature of the plan for combining religious stability and freedom.

While all the emotional controversy aroused by the printing of the Racovian Catechism was raging, Vane showed that he was moving always in the direction of complete and universal toleration. In May of 1652 the House was debating a proposed religious settlement in Ireland, one clause of which declared that Parliament did not intend to force anyone—even Catholics—to worship contrary to conscience. When the vote on this clause was called for, Vane and Marten, seldom together on anything these days, were tellers for the affirmative and they won, but even in a Parliament that was mostly Independent, they won by a slim majority. On the issue of freedom of religion, even in a purged Parliament, Vane was still isolated.

From July 1, 1652, until the following September 9, Vane failed to appear either in the meetings of the Council of State or in the Parliament. It is possible but not likely that he was simply following his old practice of absenting himself when he was helpless to prevent decisions he considered indefensible, for though he heartily despised the Dutch war, he was unlikely to stand silent in such a crucial time for the Commonwealth. There is another plausible explanation: it was probably in this period that Cromwell sent Vane to France to negotiate some unknown matter with De Retz, the clerical voice of the Fronde, who recorded the interview in his memoirs without dating it. He said that he found Vane to be "a man of surprising capacity," though obviously he had not expected much from a sectarian revolutionary.

In July and August of 1652, while Vane was still absent, futile efforts were made to stop the Dutch war. Hugh Peter, who still had many friends and congregational brothers in Holland, persuaded the Dutch congregation which worshiped at Austin Friars to petition Parliament for a revival of peace negotiations. Cromwell said that he detested the war, would support the petition, and would do whatever he could to bring about peace. Shortly thereafter an unofficial ambassador was dispatched to The Hague, carrying a letter from Peter saying that Cromwell, Vane, Bulstrode White-locke, and others of their kind were anxious to end the fratricidal war.

The names of all these men carried weight, but the most thoroughgoing proponent of peace was Whitelocke, who had also opposed the English civil war. He was then writing a history of it in which he was making some melancholy and timely reflections about the "good old cause." When men undergo the "vast hazard" of civil war, he said, the conquered are all too often ruined and the conquerors create for themselves only more war and new troubles. Besides, he thought, military success had raised in the Puritans a haughtiness of mind and such a roaming of the imagination that everyone expected to have his own private fancies put into action and himself to be little less than a prince. To satisfy their inordinate private desires, he said, they dream some of one thing, some of another, and all are willing to employ violence to realize these dreams. Whitelocke hoped that men of discretion who read his history would learn to avoid the miseries of civil war. Even this war with the Protestant Dutch he found simply another suicidal example of faction and schism: men linked in religious brotherhood were slaughtering one another over trade differences that should be worked out under law. For Whitelocke, order under law was the essence of the whole matter.

When Vane returned to his duties with the Dutch war going still from bad to worse, he must have found the work of the Navy Committee crushing. The navy needed thirty new frigates which would cost 300,000 in addition to its routine expenditures which were now almost a million pounds a year. The revenue appointed for the navy fell far short of this: there was no more money to be squeezed from the London merchants; there were no more church lands to take; the government could scarcely add another tax to the nineteen now imposed; and so, once more, the Royalists were pilfered. A list was drawn up of some 618 people, mostly quite undistinguished and relatively harmless, guilty of nothing except being inwardly opposed to a military government that needed money. Their lands were sequestered or they were required to compound; once more they were squeezed and then squeezed again until these landed men grew uncontrollably bitter—bitter at the revolution, even more bitter at Cromwell and his henchman Vane who so efficiently and dispassionately deprived them and their heirs of the very soil out of which their families had grown and to which they had given names.

In November of 1652, for the fifth time during the short life of the Commonwealth, a new Council of State was elected with Cromwell receiving the most votes, followed by Whitelocke, St. John, Rolle, and then Vane. This election was considered a triumph for the party seeking peace with the Dutch.

But on November 30, Blake's fleet, reduced by mutiny and want of provisions, met a superior Dutch fleet under Van Tromp and was so badly defeated that only a lack of pilots, it was said, kept the Dutch from sailing up the Thames. This defeat shocked the Parliament into taking the action Vane had proposed some eighteen months earlier, and it appointed a small committee fully empowered to organize provisioning of the fleet. As head of this committee, Vane at last had freedom to give the navy the help it needed.

And it needed help most desperately. The commission first consulted personally with Admiral Blake and told him of their plans: to encourage sailors to enlist voluntarily by such inducements as higher wages and more generous provision for prize money; to supply and pay the fleet regularly; to take care of the sick and wounded. They actually persuaded Parliament to raise the taxes on the countries from 90,000 to 120,000 pounds a month and to give more of the money to the navy, less to the army. To strengthen the fleet further, they induced 1,000 men from Cromwell's and Ingoldsby's regiments to join it, and they found clothing, beds, and money for these and other new men. The commission also made the first attempt in English history to codify naval law. Early in February, 1653, Vane reported all these prodigious efforts to the House, which gave warm thanks to the commission.

According to his biographer Sikes, Vane's accomplishments seemed to the House almost incredible. And it was not to the commission but to Vane personally that Admiral Deane wrote asking assistance for the families of the dead and wounded, and supplies for the many Dutch prisoners they had taken. Since there were still not enough sailors, a new impressment act was rushed through the House. Towards the end of March, when it was rumored that the Dutch would again attack the Newcastle coal trade on which Londoners absolutely depended, Vane went down to Gravesend to help prepare a fleet of hired merchant ships. And through all this, he had to maintain a ceaseless stream of correspondence, working all day and often well into the night, his shoulders growing more rounded, his stoop more pronounced. In four months the navy was reorganized, its finances and supply regularized, its manpower replenished. Sikes probably did not exaggerate in saying that Vane was "the happy and speedy contriver of that successful fleet that did our work in a very critical season." When Vane signed his last letter as naval commissioner on April 18, 1653, he left a navy strong enough to wrest victories from Van Tromp's fleet and induced the Dutch to negotiate a peace treaty which was signed on April 5, 1654, just a year later.

While the Dutch war was absorbing the attention of Parliament, some internal forces were proving equally disturbing to the people at large. All their complaints, it seemed, stemmed from one grievance: the promised new Parliament had not been provided for. In August of 1652 the army officers had met and drawn up a petition asking reforms in the law, a settlement of religion, and the immediate election of a new Parliament. Cromwell took it upon himself to modify the demand for an immediate election so that the petition asked only that future members of Parliament be so elected as to ensure that all members would be faithful to the Commonwealth.

To consider this petition, Parliament had appointed in September,

1652, a select committee to which Cromwell and Harrison were appointed but Vane was not, obviously because he was so firmly identified with his own scheme of partial elections. In a conversation with Whitelocke, Cromwell explained the army's position.

As for members of Parliament the army begins to have a strange distaste against them and I wish there were not too much cause for it; and really their pride and ambition and self-seeking, ingrossing all places of honor and profit to themselves and their friends, and their daily breaking forth into new and violent parties and factions; their delay of business and design to perpetuate themselves and to continue the power in their own hands . . . and the scandalous lives of some of the chief of them; these things, my lord, do give much ground for people to open their mouths against them and to dislike them. . . .

Beginning to see the need for balance in the power of state, Oliver was having second thoughts about the abolished monarchy and House of Lords, and about the wisdom of putting the executive and legislative powers in the same hands. But as lawyer and judge, Whitelocke could see enormous legal impediments in the dissolution of Parliament without their consent. Both he and Cromwell, he said, acknowledged Parliament to be the supreme power, and from it they and all who served the government had their commissions and authority. How, then, could they restrain or dissolve a legally constituted authority? It was then that Cromwell, frustrated by legalities, looked at Whitelocke closely and said in a quiet voice, "What if a man should take upon him to be King?" Whatever shock Whitelocke felt he tried to conceal. Patiently he pointed out that the whole course of the war had been to establish a free state; surely a restoration of Charles II, under limitations and safeguards, would be preferable to such an assault on an ancient and awesome form. Cromwell listened thoughtfully, sullenly, silently, but his countenance and his carriage showed that he was displeased.

About this time the friendship between Cromwell and Vane was crumbling under pressures of disagreements both political and temperamental. It was becoming evident to them both that they no longer agreed about how to govern righteously: Vane's faith in the sanction of the Long Parliament was still unshaken; Cromwell was growing more and more impatient with the bumbling inefficiency of interlocked committees and commissions, and the interminable wranglings in Parliament. He saw what needed to be done, he wanted to do it, and he was becoming irritated with Vane's delaying tactics and his reluctance to support proposals for action. And Vane was beginning to recognize under Cromwell's piety an arrogant belief in his own rectitude, and under his driving efficiency a dangerous appetite for power.

When on January 13, 1653, a committee of officers met with the Council of State, it was agreed that a new Parliament should be chosen. Yet the ensuing Parliament took no action on that question. Now the officers began to press Cromwell to dissolve the faithless Parliament by force. "I am pushed on," he said, "by two parties to do that, the consideration of the issue whereof makes my hair to stand on end."

As debate on the new Parliament continued, the House agreed that, in the counties, the possession of 200 pounds in either real or personal property would entitle the owner to the franchise. In this they defeated Vane, who argued for qualification of voters based on landed property only. He and others like Arthur Haselrig were still alarmed at the egalitarian proposals of Harrison and his followers, for they were convinced that they and their class were better able to establish a commonwealth than any unstable combination of soldiers and sectarians.

As delay continued, the army petitioned that the bill be acted on at once and that first consideration be given to qualifications which would exclude improper persons from Parliament. But in addition to qualifications intended to keep out Royalists, the House added stipulations that only people of integrity who feared God and were not scandalous in their conversation should be admitted. As Vane's shrewd mind saw at once, this dangerously imprecise provision placed all power in the hands of whoever might interpret or apply it. He therefore proposed that this bill should apply only to the filling of vacancies, and that the present members be given authority to decide on the godliness and virtue of those newly elected. If the bill passed as amended, he intended to move for an adjournment of Parliament for six months in order to gain now what he was always after—a little more time for the truth to carry its own conviction into the hearts of the honest people. Again Cromwell opposed

Vane vigorously and pleaded for a general election; it was high time for a new Parliament, he said. Someone, most likely Henry Marten, replied that it was more than high time for a new general.

So Cromwell was faced with two possibilities: he could throw his weight behind Vane's scheme of recruitment or behind Harrison's plan of creating a wholly new assembly of pious and virtuous men. Smelling danger, he drew back from both proposals. He wondered if he could not find a third way that would not further weaken authority and respect for legal and political forms, the value of which he was coming to appreciate more. "If it have but the face of authority," he had said, "if it be but a hare swimming over the Thames, I will take hold of it rather than let it go." And so he wondered if Parliament might not voluntarily suspend itself and appoint a body of men with limited powers to carry on the functions of state for a limited time. He acknowledged that Vane was right about one thing: the people, at this time, could not be trusted to elect a sound Parliament. It would be, he said, a tempting of God. On this point no one disagreed. Five or six men empowered to act, he thought, might do more work in one day than the Parliament in a hundred. Besides, if they were capable and unbiased, they might be the best instruments of the people's happiness.

On April 19, the day after Vane had signed his last paper as Commissioner of the Navy, Cromwell called a meeting of Parliamentary leaders in his lodgings at Whitehall and presented his proposal. The lawyers, including Whitelocke, pointed out legal difficulties; Vane and other politicians opposed him on their own grounds; only St. John sided with him. Before the meeting ended inconclusively, Cromwell did extract a promise that the Parliamentary leaders would delay discussion and action on Vane's bill the following morning until he could consult with them again. Later, Oliver said that, at parting, "one of the chief and two or three more did tell us that they would endeavor to suspend further proceedings." It has generally been agreed that the "chief" was Vane.

In the morning Cromwell learned with shock and disbelief that Parliament was already sitting and that discussion on Vane's bill was far advanced. His first thought was that the liberties of the nation would be thrown into the hands of men who had never fought for them—men like Vane. It has never been determined precisely what young Harry's role was that morning. Whitelocke, who was there, said that no one endeavored to prevent or delay discussion of the bill. If so, Vane did not carry out what Cromwell considered a commitment.

In any event the members called for the bill, wishing to hurry it through before Cromwell could be advised. Harrison warned them of the risk and since they would not listen, he sent a messenger to Cromwell. Oliver summoned a guard of soldiers, took them to the House, and stationed them there to await his further orders. Then he entered the House alone, removed his hat, took his seat, and silently watched the proceedings until he could see that Vane's bill was going to pass. Then he leaned over and whispered to Harrison that he thought the time had come. Now Harrison, who had so aggressively proposed this action, drew back in the face of it and urged Cromwell to consider before attempting such a great and dangerous thing. Cromwell listened to the debate for another few minutes, his anger rising, his cheeks and nose reddening, his eyes glaring. At last the Speaker put the final question on the bill, and knowing it would pass and become law, Oliver arose. He was like a man in a rapture, Richard Baxter said later, as he railed at the Parliamentarians, accusing them of delays, of self-seeking, of perpetuating themselves in power. Then he put his hat on, always a dangerous gesture from Oliver. Striding up and down he said that some of the members were whoremasters (for once Henry Marten did not reply); others, he said, were drunkards; some were corrupt and scandalous to the profession of the Gospel. It was not fit, he raged, that they should sit any longer.

Peter Wentworth, himself a man of colorful language, arose to protest Cromwell's words, the more unbecoming, he said, because they came from a servant of the Parliament whom they had trusted and highly favored—a reference to the 6,500 pounds a year which Cromwell now enjoyed. Since in Cromwell's judgment Wentworth was another whoremaster, his words inflamed Oliver almost beyond endurance. "Come, come, I will put an end to your prating. You are no Parliament. I say you are no Parliament. I will put an end to your sitting."

He then ordered Harrison to call in the soldiers. The door burst open and in marched forty musketeers, their weapons at the ready. Even when Charles had attempted to arrest the five members he had not gone this far: his soldiers had stayed in the lobby. Vane, who had seen Charles violate the sanctity of Parliament now saw Brother Fountain outdo his royal enemy, and he was outraged. "This," he cried out, "is not honest; yea, it is against morality and common honesty." And Cromwell, who had tried so hard to understand this once loved and trusted friend with the visionary ideas to whom impulse and inspiration outweighed battles and facts, flushed a deeper red and shouted, "O Sir Henry Vane! Sir Henry Vane! The Lord deliver me from Sir Henry Vane!"

Old Lenthall, the Speaker who had resisted Charles but failed to resist the Presbyterian mob, thought he would try again to assert the inviolability of Parliament, and so he refused to move from his chair until Harrison stepped up with his wild, fixed eyes, and took him by the arm. Algernon Sidney, too, sat until he was compelled to rise. As the members moved confusedly towards the door, Cromwell's glance fell upon the mace, the symbol of that supreme power the House had voted itself after beheading Charles. "What shall we do with this bauble?" he asked, and in that climactic moment when everything must have seemed lost, Vane might well have thought again about the significance of forms and ritual symbols, so weak before a loaded musket, so powerful when invested by the mind with sanctity and authority. "Here," Cromwell cried to Captain Scott, "take it away."

As the members filed out, Cromwell raged on. "It's you," he shouted, "that have forced me to this, for I have sought the Lord night and day, that he would rather slay me than put me upon the doing of this work." And then he looked at Vane, singled him out, called him by name, told him that he could have prevented this, that "he was a juggler and had not so much as common honesty." The breach was open now, and Vane's friend and leader was contemptuously sweeping him aside. One day Vane would find a way to reply, but now as Cromwell raged, he dropped his eyes, set his jaw, and filed out with the others. When they were all gone, one of Cromwell's soldiers padlocked the door and the Long Parliament was no longer.

Later, Cromwell said that not a dog barked at the going out of the members. Perhaps not, but a sensitive woman had a few quiet thoughts. Dorothy Osborne wrote to a friend,

If Mr. Pym were alive again, I wonder what he would think of these proceedings and whether this would appear as great a breach of the privilege of Parliament as the demanding of the Five Members. But I shall talk treason by and by if I do not look to myself.

And so would Sir Henry Vane.

Angered by the refusal of the Long Parliament to reform itself, Cromwell and his soldiers drove the members out of the House of Commons. (Radio Times Hulton Picture Library)

The military genius of the Puritan revolution, Oliver Cromwell was Vane's close friend, sharing his ideas and ideals. But ultimately Vane's ecstatic antinomianism proved incompatible with Cromwell's belief that God acted in history to judge men and assign victories. (Radio Times Hulton Picture Library)

15

Retirement and Reflection (1653–1658)

The public reaction to the expulsion of the Long Parliament was at first relief and approval. Not many went so far as to say with Colonel Harrison that the Parliamentarians had been keeping Christ and the Saints from ruling, but most would have agreed with Milton that by an artful procrastination intended to further selfish interests rather than public good, "a few overbearing individuals" had disappointed, gulled, and dominated the people. To Milton, Vane himself must by now have appeared such a man. His mystical devotion to the Long Parliament, which he considered the only remnant of true governmental authority, had distanced him from many of his former friends.

A few days after he had padlocked the House, Cromwell chose a new council, comfortably filled with good military men who had served him and the cause in battle. Among them there was a strong flavor of the Fifth Monarchy, and listening to their counsels, Cromwell decided not to trust to elections, but to nominate a new Parliament—the Barebones Parliament, so named because a leather merchant called Praise-God Barebones was among its new members.

To this nominated Parliament Vane was invited, the flame having departed from Cromwell's heart and the wrath from his nostrils. Vane was, said Roger Williams, "daily missed and courted for his assistance." An intercepted letter to an English Royalist in Holland confirmed his report. Notwithstanding the affronts he had lately received, the writer understood, Vane had been invited to the Parliament by a letter from the Council of State. If the writer understood Vane's answer rightly, it was a sarcastic refusal: the reign of the Saints would undoubtedly begin now, Vane said, but he would willingly defer his share in it until he arrived in heaven. However, the writer continued, Vane had come up to London and like Tiberius, he would probably "upon entreaty accept a share in the Empire."

But he did not. The man who had been willing to accept almost any expedient to keep the revolution alive simply could not assent to Cromwell's present aims or views. Cromwell believed that unless firm decisive action were taken, the cause was lost, and he considered the Long Parliament, now apathetic and corrupt, incapable of taking that action. Vane wanted time: he still sought a little further extension of life for the Long Parliament, hoping either that the millennial rule of the Saints would come or that the old cause might win back the hearts of the people.

So he remained in retirement at his Belleau estate in Lincolnshire with his wife and children. Frances was then a girl of twelve and Henry only a year younger. Albinia, Anne, and Thomas were younger still, and his wife was even then great with a new son, Christopher, who would be born just a month after the Long Parliament had been turned out.

Sir Henry continued to gather around him his wife, children, and his little band of Seekers for a reading of the "outer word," for prayer and refreshings of the spirit. He also began to lecture in the homes or private halls of others, and soon, according to Richard Baxter, a little informal sect of "Vanists" arose for whom Sir Henry was oracle, hope, and promise.

Such religious exercises, however, were ancillary to Sir Henry's main effort in these days: he was writing a theological treatise which would at last disclose fully the ideas he had been making public only piecemeal and in part; along the way he would also explain and comment on recent events of the English revolution. *A Retired Man's Meditations* was printed in April, 1655, just two years after it was begun. It is an interesting but difficult book, so esoteric that it aroused feeling only because it touched on questions then being decided in the dust and heat of the arena.

For things were not going well with Cromwell and his Barebones Parliament which Clarendon somewhat unfairly described as "a pack of weak, senseless fellows, fit only to bring the name and reputation of the Parliament lower than it was." Chosen for virtue and godliness, the membership included few lawyers or men of affairs, too few to be heard above the din of prayers, exhortations, and citations of scripture. In the six months they were able to endure one another, they brought first amazement and then mirth to the people, Clarendon said; for many generations they placed a heavy burden of proof on those who wanted men of God to manage civil governments.

On December 12, in a maneuver filled with intrigue and threats of force, the Barebones Parliament dissolved itself and handed back to Oliver the power it had received from him. A few vocal Saints refused to leave the House with the others, saying that they had been "called of God to that place and they apprehended their said call as chiefly for the promoting the interest of Jesus Christ." But they were driven out by soldiers with guns, sustaining no injury except to their pride. Many of them were Fifth Monarchy men whose swords had once belonged to Cromwell but whose hearts had always been faithful to King Jesus. The question now was whether they would withdraw from Cromwell the loyalty of the sword.

On the following Sunday a group of these aggressively righteous men met at Blackfriars to listen to two of their ministers, Christopher Feake and Vavasour Powell, both specialists in apocalyptic prophecy. Their text was the Book of Daniel, with all its murky forebodings. In the seventh chapter of that book there are many formidable beasts, like the creatures of a nightmare, one of which had ten horns. Among the ten horns grew up a little horn which in turn plucked up three of the other horns. The little horn had eyes like a man and a mouth that spoke "great things." Millenarian preachers had been making a great deal of this passage for a long time. It had once been confidently proclaimed that William the Conqueror was the Little Horn until Charles I came along with his feisty little archbishop and his Court of High Commission. Then the faithful interpreters of the Word humbled themselves, acknowledged their error, and proclaimed Charles the Little Horn. But that was another time.

Now Mr. Feake, called by the spirit to open the meeting, pointed out that all the horns were kings and that the Little Horn differed from the others in that he was much stronger. Also the Little Horn had eyes, which was to say that he had spies in every corner of the land, an assertion that may have disconcerted Cromwell's spy who was sitting there taking mental notes. The Little Horn also had a great mouth, Feake said, warming happily to his subject, and this large mouth would speak great words in defiance of God and his Saints. Further, he would make war with the faithful and apparently prevail against them, but soon the Fifth Monarchy would come, and then the Little Horn's dominion would be broken by the Saints, who would take upon themselves the government of the whole earth.

All of this might be interpreted as spiritual warfare, or as some kind of general prophecy couched in the battle imagery of the Old Testament, but Feake, fully aroused, went further and ventured on recent political affairs, at least so Cromwell was informed:

Some would have the late King Charles to be meant by this little horn, but as I said at first, I'll name nobody. God will make it clear shortly to his people who is meant here.

Then Powell arose, a Welshman filled with bardic spirit and chagrin at the dissolution of the Nominated Parliament of which he had prophesied great things: from his pulpit in Whitehall only six months earlier he had said that very soon now law would stream down like a mighty river. He had not meant military law. Mr. Powell took as his text Daniel 11: 20–21 which asserts, safely enough in any age, that there shall stand up a "raiser of taxes"; this mulcter of the public shall, in a few days, be destroyed and there shall arise in his place a "vile person" who shall obtain the kingdom by flatterings. This vile man would have great swordsmen and armies by his side. Then, as Cromwell's spy listened to all this Celtic wrath, Powell cried out, overcome by the spirit, "Let us go home and pray and say, Lord wilt thou have Oliver Cromwell or Jesus Christ to reign over us?"

This might have been treated with silent amusement or with the considerable toleration Cromwell was willing to allow Protestants more or less of his own kind, had it not been that in the assemblies of the Fifth Monarchy there were always troopers who bore muskets by which apocalyptic prophecies might be brought to pass. So Feake and Powell were arrested and Colonel Harrison, the principal Fifth Monarchist in the army, was deprived of his commission.

A less violent but equally discouraged reaction to the dissolution came from moderates like Bulstrode Whitelocke, who wondered if a settled and orderly way of life would ever be possible in England again. Now family stood against family, parents against children "and nothing in the hearts and minds of men but overturn, overturn, overturn."

After the Nominated Parliament was dissolved, Oliver and the officers produced an Instrument of Government which abandoned the position, adopted for the execution of Charles, that Parliament was the supreme authority. The Instrument proposed that supreme authority should reside in a Lord Protector of the Commonwealth, the first of whom should be Oliver Cromwell; in the future, the office should be elective rather than hereditary. He would be both supported and checked by a Parliament and an independent Council of State, irremovable except during sessions of Parliament. All his appointments to high office were to be cleared either by the council or the Parliament. And so the lineaments of an older and despised government became visible in the form of the new one, because men were seeing the need for a system of checks and balances, some ways of restraining power without calling in the sword.

In the summer of 1654, young Vane took time off from his private meditations and his books to run for the first Protectorate Parliament. Early in August, his brother, William Vane, wrote to say that Haselrig had been chosen for this Parliament against his will and could not decide whether or not to serve. Also, he reported, it was rumored in London that Vane had been returned from Lincolnshire. This was not true, though his father was successfully returned from the county of Kent.

From the very beginning, the new Parliament, which met on September 3, 1654, seemed destined for further overturnings. Too many of its members wished a "free" Parliament again, if that term still had any meaning, and in this they were joined by the City, by the Levellers, by the perennially plotting Royalists, and by segments of the army. Most troublesome of all at this time was the rapid growth in numbers and militancy of the Quakers. Not only had they promoted a disturbance in County Derby in June, but they seemed to be troubling the land everywhere. Entering houses of public worship they would interrupt the minister, shouting "Come down, thou deceiver, thou hireling, thou dog!" And in church as well as before the magistrates they stubbornly left their hats on, a discourtesy justified in theory by the belief that man should uncover only before his God, and in the scriptures by the fact that the three Hebrew children kept their hats on before the King of Babylon and even in the fiery furnace.

The Quaker agitation came to be symbolized for the government by a madman who called himself Theauro-John. Pitching a tent in Lambeth and living in it for a time, he one day lighted a bonfire into which he first threw a Bible because, he said, it was letters and not life. Then he threw into the flames a saddle, a sword, and a pistol, shouting to the crowd around him that these were now the gods of England. From his tent in the wilderness of Lambeth, this new Elias proceeded to Westminster, where he began laying about him with his sword. When subdued and questioned, he said that he had been inspired by the Holy Spirit to kill every man who sat in the House.

There were rumblings from other "fanatics," too. Colonel Harrison allegedly promised that he would present a petition calling on the members of Parliament to rise against tyranny, and he boasted that he would raise 20,000 armed men to support them. Like many fanatics, he greatly overestimated the public zeal for his private cause, but he was dangerous enough to be arrested for sedition.

While all this was happening, Oliver and the Parliament were wrangling with great heat and mutual discontent over an issue that had earlier sundered the Long Parliament from Charles: his uncircumscribed control of the military. Parliament was now seeking to check Cromwell's control, but he was convinced that there had been more "dissettlement and division, discontent and dissatisfaction," not to mention conspiracies and uprisings, during the five months that Parliament had been sitting than during many previous years. There was far too much unrest now for Oliver to entrust the armed forces to other hands than his own, and rather than do so, he dissolved the Parliament in January, 1655. Like Charles, he had found it simpler to rule without a Parliament.

A year later, the sectarians were still annoying the government. In February, 1656, Henry Cromwell wrote from Ireland to his father's Secretary of State, John Thurloe, saying that he believed "the most considerable enemy" in Ireland was now the Quakers, whose meetings in County Cork were attracting many troopers and most of the high-ranking officers. The principles and practices of these men, he thought, were not consistent with civil government and certainly not with the discipline of an army. "Their counterfeited simplicity," he said, only rendered them the more dangerous. Sir Henry Vane, he continued, and other men "who are as rotten in their principles," knew how to make good use of Quakers, Fifth Monarchy Men, and other fanatics to carry on their political designs. In fact, he had heard that Sir Henry Vane was going up and down among these people in England endeavoring to shake their allegiance to the present government. Unless Vane is prevented, he warned Thurloe, "he will be a sad scourge to England." Such was the atmosphere into which Vane's first book had emerged from the press in April, 1655.

The first readers of Vane's book, who must have been looking with sharp eyes for sedition, were disappointed, for their first problem was to understand what in the world Vane was trying to say. Bishop Burnet said that he had read his works and had also heard him preach and pray frequently,

> but with so peculiar a darkness, that though I have sometimes taken pains to see if I could find out his meaning in his works, yet I could never reach it: and since many others have said the same, it may be reasonable to believe that he hid somewhat that was a necessary key to the rest.

Richard Baxter agreed. Vane's doctrines, he said, "were so cloudily formed and expressed that few could understand them, and therefore he had but few disciples." David Hume's spartan, incisive mind was to be downright offended by Vane's writings: they were, he said, "absolutely unintelligible." Only Vane's loyal disciple George Sikes asserted that except for the scriptures, no book ever "cleared" so much truth as the writings of Sir Henry.

But Vane's opponents are nearer the truth. His political writings have an almost mathematical structure in which he usually makes two or three lucid points with no excess of emotion but much factual support. It is with wonderment, therefore, that one turns to the religious *Meditations*. It is as if an organist with cold and stumbling fingers in a wintry church were playing an imperfectly remembered fugue. Themes appear, waver, and disappear uncompleted, only to re-emerge again and yet again. The treatise is further complicated because Vane believed the scriptures to be true both literally and symbolically. They must, therefore, be read through inspiration. The full truth of each passage, expressing as it does both itself and something beyond itself, both inner and outer Word, is comprehended only when the interpreter feels within himself a harmony, an ecstasy of illumination. Unfortunately Vane shifts back and forth between literal and symbolic meanings without any indication to the reader. Besides, his writing is infected with theological jargon, a spate of words and phrases that belong to the esoteric discourse of a cult but are used as though they were the common property of all readers. And Vane shows no sense of Biblical history, of people, times, or places. All of the Bible, from martial songs and high prophecy to the weary cynicism of the late writers, he treats as a single texture which, under the veil of words, contains the unified hidden glory of the Divine Mind. Nevertheless, to a sufficiently patient reader, Vane's meanings are available.

A reader is impressed first by a surprising orthodoxy. While in this highly sensitive time the orthodox might have caviled at his view of the Trinity as a unity and simplicity of essence with three properties (they would have preferred "three persons") Vane seems serenely assured of his own orthodoxy and he gently chides the anti-Trinitarians not for obstinacy but for blindness. Also he holds the standard doctrine of creation out of nothing, *ex nihilo*. In both these points he parted from his one-time friend Milton, who was heretical.

Perhaps his most surprising statement is that God, in his secret counsels before the creation, predetermined *by name* those angels and men who would taste his mercy and love notwithstanding all they could do to make themselves unworthy, and that He similarly identified the vessels of wrath. Neither group could do anything by their lives or actions to change this decree.

Not in New England, not even in the Synod of Dort, could a more orthodox Calvinistic expression be found. But Vane does not hold to this position consistently. Determinists, of course, always have trouble remembering that everything is determined, that human effort and will count for nothing; even the most obtuse Calvinist minister must at times feel some futility in exhorting to righteousness those whose fates are already decided. But the discrepancy in Vane's work is greater than this. His thinking is pervaded by a spirit of voluntarism which constantly assumes that men in a state of grace may fall and that Satan's wiles are real, not nominal. At times he even maintains that the nonelect are not really predetermined at all, for they have free will. Augustine too had said that fallen man was free to do evil but not to do good, and by this dubious, even shabby, device, he thought he had relieved his God of some unpleasant responsibilities. Vane, however, means more than this, for he asserts that God does not shut the door on the nonelect; rather, "all may be led to repentance." By "all," he means men of all nations, kindreds, and tongues, irrespective of whether they know the scriptures or not; indeed Vane's friends reported him as leaning towards universal salvation. Others said that like Origen and unlike Milton he believed that even the devils would be saved. When faced with these irreconcilable inconsistencies, one feels that Vane might have profited by a few more weeks in a formal academy.

But these matters are ancillary to his main theme which deals with the first and second comings of Christ. Though these are both literal events, it is their symbolism that engrosses Vane's mind. At first, Adam was created with a free will by means of which alone he could never have achieved salvation. Had he remained faithful, he would have received a further effusion of the spirit that would have translated him from a "wavering state" to eternal glory. But through his uncertain free will and the temptations of Satan he fell, bringing upon himself and all mankind a state of hopeless moral blindness. Then Christ came in the flesh, and in this first appearance he restored man's fallen estate to some degree. But, in addition, to some individuals, regardless of the time or place of their birth, Christ may also make a first appearance in the spirit. Men who receive Christ spiritually in his first appearance to them are called out of the world, relieved from the burden of the law, and even sanctified or made holy. They experience a real and actual change of heart, their souls are quickened and enlightened, their bodies washed with pure water; they partake of the Holy Spirit. No longer heathen, they may become great spiritual men, possessing the highest spiritual gifts, which gain for them the reputation and visibility of saints.

In Puritan theology generally, there were only two categories of persons, the old Adam and the new man in Christ. The effusion of grace resulting in a new life was considered final and irresistible as the three-personed God battered the stony heart until it broke. Then a new heart and a new will were created in the believer who, most thought, was irrevocably saved, will he or nil he. On this crucial point, Vane cannot agree. He rather holds that the first appearance of Christ in the heart merely restores man to the condition of the first Adam in the garden of delight before the fall. For men in the political arena, the first covenant offers particular dangers for in it men tend to be guided by the "books of the creature" and by God's outward manifestations; men of the first covenant are given to searching out God's providences in whatever actually happens, and so to find false reassurances of their often evil actions. Brother Heron and Brother Fountain had already engaged in some discussions about that. Perhaps Vane is reminding him.

But men need not remain under the first covenant; in fact, if they do they will "die." If they make use of the light they have, if they move from outer to inner dispensations, they are led forward to a quickening and saving of their souls. This sounds voluntaristic, and it is. To these worthy ones Christ appears a second time; he makes a second spiritual coming even before his second coming in the flesh. When this second new birth occurs in the soul, man no longer has a merely conditional promise of salvation, but, wholly relieved of the "slippery tenure" of the first covenant, he is everlastingly justified: absolutely and at once he is freed from all sins, "past, present, and to come." Now he experiences the same union with Christ that Christ has with his Father, conversing inside the veil with God as a friend speaks to a friend. Beyond the visible powers of this world, those eternally justified see the pattern of the ministry of Christ and his angels, the pattern which earthly governments should follow. And as the times of Christ draw near, those who have this enlarged insight "shall show themselves to be his servants, taking vengeance in flames of fire upon all ungodly men." Is this a suggestion of earthly violence, or is it merely the Biblical imagery of battle? Is he speaking literally or symbolically? And is it the lower or the higher meaning that an angry or suspicious reader would then have perceived?

Vane is sensitive to charges that men of his persuasion, who hold for a kind of divine union of man with God, have proclaimed themselves to be deified. And in fact some had made that claim, amid general cries of outrage. So he insists in homely language that men of the second covenant are not "godded with God nor Christed with Christ"; they remain creatures, but creatures of the highest and most blessed sort, judges of all things, but to be judged by no man. And he utters a cautionary word to those who have experienced the second coming. There is, he said, a counterfeit spiritual seed which intrudes itself into the spiritual society of true believers: some who appear to be true heirs of Christ go over to Satan and persecute the Saints. The verified spiritual seed, one feels by now, is a very small number indeed. Vane actually says at one point that in all the world they consist of the traditional 144,000—but one can never be sure that he is speaking literally.

It is not only the orthodox whom Vane considers men of the slippery first covenant, but also the Quakers, the Ranters, the Familists, and sectarians in general who know only the first coming. And though the spiritually second-born are few, they are widely scattered: men of both the first and second covenants, he says, may be found in all of the churches where they grow up together like tares and wheat. The true spiritual seed may also be found among the Gentiles, the non-Christian. Everywhere and always men must be judged individually and not by their affiliation.

The conclusions he next drew must have infuriated most Englishmen. Not only does he allow salvation to outsiders, but he denies it to most of the apparently redeemed. The devil, he says, takes little thought for those who have experienced neither the first nor the second spiritual coming, for they are his without reaching. With those of the second coming he can do nothing, for they are eternally beyond his grasp. His real opportunities therefore lie among men who, having experienced the first coming, feel assured in their blessedness. As king of this world, the devil gives them success, power, and tyranny, while the true seed are persecuted and hounded even to death. When Vane speaks of their lot, he cannot keep out the tone of bitterness. Those who have merely the perfection of the first Adam, pretending to saintship in their seats of magistracy and power, enforcing their personal will by warrant of the scriptures, the outer word devoid of inner illumination, make themselves absolute arbiters of religious controversies. With the formal Bible in one hand, the sword in the other, they determine what are heresies and blasphemies, and trample under their feet the spiritual seed. Such men have "a fixed, implacable rage and enmity" against the "chaste spouse of Christ."

How, then, will divine justice reassert itself? In his answers, Vane again does not hold to a single, consistent view. One of his theories is that the children of darkness and the children of the first covenant will destroy one another. But not satisfied with this simplistic proposition, he undertakes an analysis of the very nature of government. Any form of government whatever may be lawful and innocent, he says, but some kind of government there must be, for it is foolish to believe that even in a sinless state men would have no need of government. The good order and right dispensation they were created in can be maintained only through the discipline of the magistrate; disorder and danger, to which men are subject in their mutable (even though sinless) state, must be prevented. This strong belief in the necessity of some government may be the key to Vane's later tolerance of Lambert's farcical rule after the dissolution of the Rump Parliament.

So God ordained that magistracy should be exercised over the "outer man" in righteousness and fear of the Lord. Subjection to the magistrate, however, should not be irrational but rational and voluntary, and the rule of the magistracy must never intrude into Christ's inward government or his rule in the human conscience. Especially nothing must be done to hinder "the breaking of higher discoveries" upon the people. Consequently, the more illuminated the conscience and judgment of the magistrate in natural judgment and right, the better qualified he is to rule, but also—an ominous reminder to Cromwell—the more accountable he is to God and man if he defaults.

During the thousand years of millennial reign, the Saints shall bring forth on earth a magistracy that exactly mirrors the pattern of the Heavenly Jerusalem, but before that day there will be great distress. In those evil times, the spiritual seed—who are the Two Witnesses spoken of in the Apocalypse—will at last begin to testify and then the Earthly Jerusalem (the men of the first covenant) will join with the Gentiles in opposing the true seed. But this mixture of iron and clay will be shattered into pieces with a rod of iron.

How then shall the Saints overcome? Vane is again unwilling to commit himself to a single solution. When earthly patterns of government depart from the heavenly one, spirits and thrones, angels and invisible powers work secretly to bring them down. The Saints therefore should eschew militant action and "sit down in faith and patience to see this promise accomplished by the immediate power and hand of Christ." At the same time they should themselves use "all lawful means and endeavors" to bring the earthly rule as near as possible to the primitive pattern. God has already brought the work to birth; a true magistracy lies on the anvil, waiting to be hammered out, waiting for a new society to be established "in a free and natural way of common consent to the uniting of all good men as one man." With whatever help the Saints may receive from the inner light or outward dispensations, they should build towards the day and seek to hasten it.

Some ambiguity arises because Vane again employs Biblical language without advising the reader whether it is literal or symbolic. Kings, he said, shall ultimately be forced to conform "whether they will or no" to the righteous kingdom of Christ, who will bind them in chains. Every knee will bow and every tongue confess "either voluntarily or by compulsion." There apparently must be no forcing of conscience until Christ comes but there will be a good deal of it afterwards. The enlightened consciences, however, will be fully informed by God's will and for them freedom will no longer be relevant.

An ominous note is struck when Vane describes the battle of Gideon and his little band against the mighty hosts of Israel's enemies. In this battle, he says, because

> there was not only the sword of the Lord, but the sword of Gideon, it doth seem to intimate, that the sword and power of magistracy, as well civil as military, shall not be so quite taken out of the hands of God's people in the last and worst of days . . . but that in the midst of the little remnant of God's faithful ones, there shall be found such a holding of that sword in their hands, as was with Gideon and his three hundred.

What did it mean? That the Saints would have a civil and military force to be used in some Christian fashion and for some Christian purpose as Cromwell had used it in Ireland? One cannot be sure what Vane meant, but one can imagine what Fifth Monarchy troopers would think he meant.

The *Meditations* conclude with a paean to the Thousand Year Reign towards which Vane's soul yearns. Then the Father will authorize Christ to execute judgment, and Christ will delegate his authority to the true seed who will be the only Potentates, each one Lord of Lords and King of Kings. They shall have the power of the sword, their decrees shall be binding in heaven and earth, and they will rule the nations with a rod of iron, breaking in pieces the stubborn and rebellious.

At last, after so many years of partial concealment, all of Vane's views were on record, and what he had always feared indeed happened. He was mocked and jeered at and—he would say—misunderstood. Some thought that his book threatened the Protectorate and exhibited delusions of grandeur. Clarendon jibed that Vane thought he should be King of Jerusalem, and other mocking men said that Vane wished to rule the world but otherwise was without ambition. What all feared was that under the guise of preparing the earth for Christ, Vane should conspire for Oliver's demise.

One man who read the *Meditations* wrote a critical review to a friend. He now suspects most those who most cry for liberty in matters of religion. The trouble with the cry for liberty of conscience, as this writer sees it, is that no matter how greatly men disturb the state, when they are brought before the magistrate and cry "liberty," the state is supposed to be powerless. The things of government and conscience are so "complex and interwoven" that none can really separate them. Indeed, anything the majority wishes to do nowadays is against someone's conscience and liberty, and so the state is paralyzed. Vane is always speaking of those who have an "inner warrant" for their actions, but suppose someone else had a different inner warrant? Whom do you believe, who is to judge? In conclusion, the writer observes that Vane speaks eloquently of a great silence in heaven in the two years since the Long Parliament was dissolved, and he wishes that Vane would emulate heaven.

There is more to object to in Vane's first religious work. It not only lacks grace and lucidity, but is entirely humorless. And it lacks humility. He betrays no feeling of personal responsibility for the anarchic cruelties of the holy civil war, no realization that Vane himself might at times have been partly or altogether wrong. The cause was right, sanctioned by God and history, and adhering to the cause, he was also right. Had he, like his mother, been a devoted reader of the Prayer Book, he might have known another mood.

Almighty and most merciful father, we have erred and strayed from thy ways like lost sheep. We have followed too much the devices and desires of our own hearts. We have offended against thy holy laws. We have left undone those things which we ought to have done; and we have done those things which we ought not to have done and there is no health in us.

But there is also something to praise in the *Meditations*. At its best it discloses a public man whose life has not been entirely engrossed in estates and power, in armies and legislation and committees, but rather a man who has also looked into himself, though with less than clear-eyed wisdom. Above all it reveals a public man who has lived with some consciousness of the immanent Divine, and he has been touched with some ecstasy that he cannot quite express. But it is always a little frightening when a man of public trust and power fully displays his inner life, for then we realize what fragile pillars uphold our social fabric.

A month after Vane's treatise was published, his father died, terminating a strangely uneasy and ambivalent relationship. After Charles had ejected both father and son from office for their part in the condemnation of Strafford, they became political allies, after a fashion. But though old Sir Henry had no future with the Royalists, he was an uneasy Parliamentarian, and he followed his son's lead only with reluctance and reservations. The rather obtuse career diplomat never really understood the maneuverings of his son, for he could not comprehend the kind of inner religious direction that through all his tackings and veerings kept him headed towards the single goal of a free religious society. Not that the old man was a fool, but his intelligence ran in the rather narrow channels of practicality and self-interest; intellectual subtlety and spiritual sensitivity were not much in his range. But though their differences about church and doctrine were irreconcilable, they learned to live with them, and some stubborn affection or at least family loyalty held them together over the years. After all, the old man had done his fumbling best to initiate his maverick son into the ways of courtly success, and he was generous to him with lands and manors;

the not ungrateful son had done what little he could to advance his father with the new men in the new order of power. Even though they could not quite understand or approve each other, they had not quite broken apart. To be sure, it was rumored at the time of old Sir Henry's death that had he lived longer, he would have deprived his son of at least part of his inheritance. Indeed, Roger Williams wrote that Vane's father had "cast him off," and Clarendon thought that the father detested the son. At any rate, Harry did not accede to his father's wish that he be executor of the estate, but he did assume his father's debts, which amounted to 10,000 pounds.

Legends quickly grew up around the old man's death. Two days before he died, it was said, he came to a bookbinder asking for a copy of Strafford's trial. He read the account "as long as he was able to read." Because he was the "malicious contriver" of this murder, his dying recollections drove him into a fury in which he took leave of this world. To die in such a discomposed way was, in Puritan lore, an almost sure sign of damnation, and the writer of this tale piously concluded that while he wished no man's damnation, he did hope to see God's justice magnified.

According to another story, when Vane was told by his physician that he was approaching death, he sent for his household chaplain to ask what he thought about the Strafford affair. The chaplain replied that it was damnable. Vane then asked his opinion of the king's death; the chaplain thought that was even more damnable. Sir Henry then accused the cleric of having previously given him quite different opinions, whereupon the chaplain went to his chamber and "fairly hanged himself." When his body was found Sir Henry observed that one had gone to the devil, and another would soon follow. He died the next day. Memories of the part the Vanes had played in the death of Strafford died hard, as young Henry would one day bitterly know.

Along with whatever grief Vane may have felt for his father, he had pressing problems. In the autumn of 1655 he suffered the first of a series of harassments: the government challenged his right to Teesdale Forest in Durham. In August of 1655, he traveled to Raby Castle and found that the garrison stationed there for its defense at his request in civil war days was still occupying it. In a cordial letter to Secretary Thurloe, he asked that both soldiers and arms be removed. On September 4, the council ordered a representative to go north and effect their removal, and to separate what belonged to Vane from what belonged to the state. On September 14, Vane wrote to Thurloe that he must bring his wife to London "to lay down her great belly" if weather and ways permitted, and he hoped that the arms removed from Raby would be paid for with expedition and that the soldiers would leave shortly, for he wished to make the castle into a fit residence for himself and his family.

When Thurloe replied, his letter apparently included some friendly advances from Cromwell written in his own hand. Vane's stiffly courteous reply did not mention Cromwell by name, but it was both placatory and reproachful.

> I desire not to be insensible of the civility intended me [in your letter] by the first hand which accordingly I desire you to represent in the fittest manner you please from one who upon those primitive grounds of public spiritedness and sincere love to our country and the godly party in it, am still the same as ever both in true friendship to his person and in unchangeable fidelity to the cause so solemnly engaged by us.

All this time Cromwell's troubles were increasing. Disillusioned with the commonwealth forms of government and troubled by the increase of disorder, he had decided in the autumn of 1655 to divide England into districts and place each one under a major-general backed by troopers. The principal task of these new commissars was to suppress tumults, to put down insurrections, and to make the highways safe—all admirable ends. Somewhat less admirable were instructions to watch the disaffected, to promote more efficient collection of taxes, to secure idlers and send them out of the land. Believing that the revolution could scarcely be justified unless it produced a more virtuous England than had been possible under Charles and Laud, Cromwell instructed his generals to prohibit drunkenness, swearing, and moral offenses; they were to close many alehouses and taverns and regulate the rest more strictly. They were to put down all profaning of the Sabbath. Accustomed to carrying out the orders of Old Ironsides, the generals soon filled the jails with horsethieves, beggars, and wandering rogues. The lawyers, the country gentlemen, all of the less-than-godly men who make up the bulk of any population watched these oppressions with unhappy incredulity. Their aims appeared to be those of Laud's Court of High Commission; the methods seemed to be even worse. Many thought that they had seen it all before.

On August 28 Cromwell ordered strict enforcement of the licensing law: in the future no newspaper could appear without a license from Thurloe. From that day, only two newspapers were printed, both edited by the same man in the same interests—those of government. Then to make assurance double sure John Rogers and Christopher Feake were incarcerated in Carisbrooke Castle; Ludlow and Lilburne were also sent to prison, as were George Fox and John Biddle and many other Quakers, Royalists, and Fifth Monarchy men. Now Oliver had complete control of the army; there was no Parliament to check him; the presses had been suppressed. Liberty, such a heady word a few years ago, was scarcely to be found in England. What Cromwell offered instead was the adventure of a renewed war with Spain, that outworn rag of Elizabethan foreign policy.

Beset by all these troubles, Oliver could do no less than "wait upon the Lord," as he had learned to say in Scotland. He therefore issued a proclamation on March 14, 1656, setting forth a day of fast and humiliation "that the Lord would pardon the iniquities both of magistrate and people . . . wherein the magistrate desires first to take shame to himself and find out his provocations." By seeking the Lord, England might find out the Achan for whose transgressions the Lord was troubling the land.

This opportunity to speak out seemed to Vane a providence of God, an outer dispensation which might hasten the day of the Lord. So once again he began to write, and on May 12 he published a work designed to bring the nation together in a godly government and heal its wounds. It was called *A Healing Question.*

It was a work about the realities of politics, devoid of that cloudy mysticism and murky style which had made *Meditations* so nearly unreadable. Though the sentences are lengthy and the syntax intricate, the sense is clear and the ideas are molded into a structure. Vane begins on an optimistic (and perhaps unrealistic) note: the cause is the same now as when blood and treasure were first spent for it, and the persons engaged in the cause are not really changed in heart or spirit. Nor was the war a mistake or a waste, for by it the people's inherent right to be governed by national councils and successive representatives of their own election and setting-up was sealed and sanctioned by the right of conquest. At the death of the king it was thought that this right had been permanently secured, but of late there had been "a great interruption."

But military strength alone, says Vane, could never have liberated England; such strength had to be joined with "the nature and goodness of·the cause" which consisted in two things—civil justice and freedom of conscience. He then introduces what, for the modern reader who assumes that all civil rights are rooted in the right to vote, is a gnawing worm in the letter and spirit of his noble political utterances. The right to govern, that is, political franchise, belongs, he says, to "the whole party of honest men adhering to this cause." By that statement he excludes from voting and from expression of their "natural rights" all Royalists, Catholics, Irishmen, Scotsmen, most Presbyterians, Fifth Monarchists, Quakers, Ranters, and other sects. Had Vane been a university don in quiet times he surely would have asserted what the logic of his general position called for, that the franchise was the natural right of all men; but he was in a de facto situation where to maintain the Commonwealth and avert a relapse into Royalism he had to calculate to a fraction of an inch the practical results of any theory. For he was providing a rationale for action in the specific crisis of Cromwell's impatient assumption of power. He knew that any great extension of the franchise beyond current practice would ruin the cause and would almost certainly prohibit the free exercise of the religion he was so deeply committed to. A larger man, or a man under less stringent immediate pressures, might still have enunciated more universal principles and suffered the shipwreck of his immediate hopes while awaiting the ultimate justification of history. But Vane was expecting soon the second literal coming of Christ in the flesh, and he was fighting a desperate rearguard action to keep power in the hands of the Saints, as he defined them, until Jesus came with his rod of iron.

Those basic rights specifically recaptured in *Magna Charta* had once belonged naturally to all men, but the Norman conquerors had superimposed a tyrannic rule that was planted on the root of a private and selfish interest. And the government of Charles I was derived from that conquest. As Vane had taught in the *Meditations*, such governments, opposed by the invisible powers, must wither and degenerate. But degenerate though Charles' government was, it had managed to seize by force of arms those rights and that freedom which belonged "to the whole body of the people." The purpose of the revolution initiated and won by the Long Parliament was to restore to "the people" the rights usurped by the Norman conqueror and his heirs. But now, Vane implies, Cromwell's government is a regression to the Norman tyranny.

Vane's statement about the rights owed to "the whole body of the people" seems to contradict his proposed limitation of the franchise and, as the *Meditations* show, consistency is not Vane's virtue. Yet his restriction of the vote to adherents of the cause is not so violently inconsistent as it sounds, for Vane draws a distinction between participating in governmental process on the one hand and on the other, enjoying such natural rights as security in person and property, freedom from seizure and imprisonment without due process, freedom to come and go, and liberty of conscience which are assured to all men by any responsible government. He is distrustful of majority rule partly because he knows the majority is now against him, but also because he has seen how ruthlessly minorities were handled by the political majorities of his time. While willing to secure most of the civil rights and all of the religious liberties of every man, he thought that only a spiritual elite should create the constitution and administer it until the populace were better instructed in their own ultimate interests.

When Vane turns from his analysis of political liberty to the question of religious liberty, the modern reader is reassured, for here Vane asserts an absolutely universal natural right and freedom. In all nations Christ is "sole Lord and Ruler in and over the conscience." In matters of religion no man is to be brought before a magistrate.

This fundamental freedom of conscience is so important that Vane thinks it cannot be left to the ordinary processes of government, but should be embodied and enshrined in a written constitution which, not being subject to amendment, would be a permanent restraint on the supreme authority. Vane reminds his readers of the spiritual tyrannies of the immediate past: first there was Laud with his bishop and courts; then the "persecuting presbyteries"; and now, he fears, this same spirit will arise in the next group of clergy, whatever its faith, that can get the ear of the magistrate. Even now, he believes, there is much limitation of religious freedom, although it may be owing to the officiousness of subordinate ministers rather than to "any clear purpose or design of the chief in power."

In theory, Cromwell would agree with Vane about religious liberty: he continually said that all men might think what they would if they did not disturb the peace of the state. The trouble is that some beliefs, such as those of the Fifth Monarchists, when passionately uttered may incite action that does disturb the state. The problem facing a magistrate is whether these utterances and the actions likely to follow from them constitute a "clear and present danger." It finally comes down to human judgments made by thousands of minor officials, and these, in turn, frequently reflect the climate of the times, the degree of security or fear felt by a majority of the people.

The call for a constitution that would take precedence over the executive (a call that has endeared Vane to earlier American historians) was not new. For some time the Levellers and other minority groups mistrustful of any executive power had been asking for a new and immutable charter such as they fancied *Magna Charta* to have been. The weakness of their demand lay in a mistrust so profound that they wanted a document which not even future generations could change. Such a constitution would have created that worst of tyrannies, the rigorous control of the present and future by the past.

In the preceding years, Vane continues, when everything else had failed, in the absence of a constitution the proponents of the cause had, as an "utmost and last reserve," fallen back on military power. So successful had this proved that now honest men, combined with the army, possessed boundless might. It was therefore requisite that they themselves should set just bounds and due limits to that power. This could be done by establishing a "supreme judicature" (and for Vane this could only be the House of Commons or some equivalent), to which the army should be completely subject. This subjection should not create jealousy or fear because the adherents to the cause and the army had over-ridingly strong interests in common. When the "good" people find that the military power is theirs, that they are no longer slaves to it, then they will realize the need for continuing at one with the army and will adequately and cheerfully maintain it.

Similarly, the army will find that by submitting to the supreme judicature they will lose no power, but rather will become one with the entire party of "honest men." Thus Vane sees the political ideal, like the religious one, as a voluntary association in which unity and harmony are felt by the members.

Unlike many others who, weary of seeing ubiquitous uniforms and paying taxes to support them, thought that the very existence of a large military presence was a danger to civil polity, Vane held that in and with the army, under God, stood the welfare and safety of the whole cause. In a metaphor from *Meditations*, the army was the sword of Gideon and at present was in the hands "of an honest and wise general, and sober faithful officers, embodied with the rest of the party of honest men."

Finally Vane arrives at a climactic and dangerous point. The present magistrate (he refuses to use the word Protector) has asked where the offense in the nation lies. It lies in this: the whole body of honest men fought for rights and liberties, especially for the supreme right of creating a government under which their liberties could be secured. But now the shaping of a new government is delayed and delayed under the plea—which indeed has some truth in it—that the people are not ready to create and administer such a government. Some people even suspect a conscious design to deny them their rights completely. Is it impossible, Vane asks, to bring in true freedom among "so refined a party of men"? If so, why was this not thought of before so much blood and treasure were spilled? "Surely such a thing as this was judged real and practicable, not imaginary and notional."

If there is a design to deny the party of honest men their rights, "such an unrighteous, unkind, and deceitful dealing with brethren" may be beyond the reach of human judicature, but it will be punished by God "when he ariseth out of his place to do right to the oppressed." If self-interest and private gain should again supersede concern for the common good and welfare of the people, it will mean, says Vane, that the same tyrannical and anti-Christian principles that we punished in our predecessors have sprung up again among us.

"Who is Achan?" Cromwell had rashly asked. The Bible told how Achan saw among the forbidden spoils of war a Babylonish garment, apparently the rich robe of a priest; he also found 200 shekels of silver and a wedge of gold. Because he took these, contrary to the express order of the Lord, covetously and secretly hiding them under the floor of his tent, the Lord visited his displeasure upon all Israel until Achan's transgression was discovered and punished. Vane of course regarded this event as historical, but it also had a symbolic significance: Achan, instead of bringing the fruit and gain of conquest into the Lord's treasury, had converted it to his own use and so brought trouble to his whole people. Vane needed to say no more; the correspondence was clear. Oliver himself was the Achan of these troubled times. Vane surely realized that Oliver could not be expected to consider this discovery less than seditious.

What is to be done now to restore harmony and order? That is the healing question. It is one of the major ironies of Vane's life that a man who so valued harmony should have lived in almost continual discord. For harmony was the key to his ideal in both religion and politics. Just as the soul of man should feel "a most delightful harmony, welfare, and correspondency" when living in the presence of God, so members of a civil polity should feel when living under a righteous government. But the political harmony which Vane wishes for can never exist under the government of the sword; it can only be established "in the whole body of the people that have adhered to this cause."

If this harmony exists, the particular form of government, as Vane had said in *Meditations,* was indifferent, and now he affirms that whether the supreme power is vested in a single person or some few persons, it may be capable of administering a righteous government so long as it acts with "free consent." But when men of the sword engross the rule unto themselves and hold it in such a way that only the sword can take it from them, the result is anarchy and that is the first step towards tyranny. But if the men of the sword acknowledge that sovereignty lies in "the people" (properly defined), if they establish a supreme judicature by free choice and consent of those qualified to vote, then, Vane believed, justice and harmony will follow.

Once government by consent has been established, Vane suggests, it might be well to appoint a Council of State, something like the old Committee of Both Kingdoms, but with its members appointed for life, subject to removal only by Parliament. The function of such a council would be to maintain domestic peace, conduct foreign affairs, and to carry on the government in intervals of the Parliament to which it is subject. Vane has now come to feel that it might be best to place that branch of government which executes laws in a distinct office from the legislative power, to which it should remain subject. Such an executive power, invested in either a committee or a single person, would not be inconsistent with a free state.

This was Vane's concession to Cromwell, an implicit promise that if the Long Parliament or something like it were restored, the general would likely retain the executive power; in fact, he says that "the very persons now in power" can begin the work. Perhaps they should first call a convention "of faithful, honest, and discerning men," chosen by those who have the right to vote, not unlike the American constitutional convention of the later eighteenth century. After debate, this convention would establish the new form of government. If the sword would then voluntarily subject itself, "how suddenly might harmony, righteousness, love, peace, and safety unto the whole body follow hereupon, as the happy fruit of such a settlement." And the expected end of this work would be the bringing in of Christ as the chief ruler.

A constitution to guarantee religious freedom, a constitutional convention to decide on a form of government which must include a legislature and might include a Council of State or a single head of state—all this echoes pleasantly in the mind of the American reader. It is small wonder that President Eliot chose this essay as part of the *Harvard Classics*, works which all his young gentlemen surely ought to know. Read out of its context, it may appear to be a more significant document in the exploration and advocacy of political and religious freedom than it really is; for all its concern for the rights and liberties of all men, it excludes three-quarters of the nation from significant participation in the political process. And perhaps in its time necessarily, for as one writer asserted in 1656, if the nation were polled, nineteen out of every twenty would simply ask for their old government back. The strength of Vane's document in our time lies in its opposition to military dictatorship which, he says, of all governments breeds the most suspicion and hatred and is most incapable of bringing harmony to the civil polity. The treatise also supports an unconditional religious toleration and, whatever else it may do, manifests the personal courage of Vane.

Within a month of the issuance of *A Healing Question*, it was contributing to serious political tensions. When in late June of 1656 it was known that, against his better judgment but at the insistence of the army, Oliver would issue writs for a new Parliament, both Commonwealth men and Fifth Monarchists began to hold meetings to consider their roles in relation to it. It occurred to them that in seeking a rapprochement, they might use Vane's tract as a basis for joint action. Both were willing to revolt, but the Commonwealth men wanted first a semblance of legality, perhaps to bring together some forty members of the old Long Parliament, mostly Independents like Vane, and proceed from there. But the Fifth Monarchists wanted immediate military action in which they fully expected and counted on assistance from the sword of God. The *Healing Question* did not bring any agreement to their meetings. Thurloe, however, got wind of the plotting and arrested the Commonwealth men, although he released them after questioning; Thomas Venner, the leader of the militant Saints, went into hiding. More and more it seemed to Cromwell and the nation at large that wherever there was tumult from the sectarian left, Vane was somehow the stirrer of it.

In June, Thurloe wrote to Henry Cromwell in Ireland complaining of the trouble being caused by Fifth Monarchists and Levellers who, he said, were holding meetings "to put us into blood." By Levellers, he said, he meant those who wished a republic. Then he spoke of Vane's new writings which, he thought, proposed a new form of government, "plainly laying aside the present one." At its first coming out the book was applauded, but on second thoughts it was being rejected as impracticable, "and, in truth, aiming at setting up the Long Parliament again." Thurloe concluded in a rather puzzled manner by saying that men were judging that Vane must have "some very good hopes that he shows so much courage."

In addition to local plots and disturbances, the government learned that Colonel Sexby, soon to print a book called *Killing No Murder* (to encourage some fanatic to assassinate Oliver), was stirring up trouble abroad. It seemed a good time to round up disaffected persons who might be safer in jail or under bond.

Therefore, on July 29, 1656, the Council of State ordered Vane, Bradshaw, Ludlow, and Colonel Rich to appear before them. All obediently appeared as directed except Vane; instead he replied that in a few days he would set forth towards his house in the Strand, but his coach not being fit for such a long journey on such short notice, he would have to appoint another one to meet him halfway. Such complicated arrangements took time, said the man who was once the most efficient committee man of Parliament.

After arriving in London on August 20, over a week after he was ordered to appear, Vane blandly wrote to the clerk of the council. Parliament, he said, had previously declared it against the laws and liberties of England for any person not in the special service of the king to be ordered to appear merely at royal pleasure. He now wished to claim the same privilege and liberty. The summons sent to him contained no reasons for requiring his appearance; it was an expression of "mere will and pleasure." However, he had been at his house in Charing Cross since the previous Thursday and, in the interests of innocent and peaceable deportment, he was now ready to appear if sent for. He had, though, pressing family obligations which, by reason of his father's debts, were heavy upon him and would soon require his attendance in other parts of the nation.

The council required him to appear the next day; whether Cromwell was present or not is uncertain. Vane was told that his work was thought to be seditious, and he was ordered to post bond of 5,000 pounds "to do nothing to the prejudice of the present government and the peace of the Commonwealth"; if he refused, he would be committed. Sir Henry went home and wrote a reply which he addressed to the clerk but intended for posterity. The *Healing Question* was a witness, he said (and those who had read his *Meditations* would feel the overtones in the word), a witness which asserted the spirit, the principles, the justice of the cause for which the late war had been fought. That a work of such a healing nature should be deemed seditious was simply one more example of how those in power were now treading in the footsteps of the late king. The present governors themselves had requested free and open answers to the problems the nation was now facing. He had sent his candid response to the council and waited for a full month with no reply and no prohibition to print. His work had been put through the press in the usual way and had the usual warrant for coming forth; only now it was deemed seditious. He will not be careful in this matter, Vane says, echoing the words of the three Hebrew children before the King of Babylon, and therefore he must decline to post bond inasmuch as that would "blemish and render suspect" his innocence and the justice of the "good cause" for which he suffers. If need be, he will undergo imprisonment, but he cannot acknowledge the lawfulness of the order which requires it. Meanwhile he will use the little time of liberty left him in visiting his relatives in Kent; he can easily be found there. In not more than a week he will return to his house in the Strand.

The council did not intercept him, but after he had visited Kent he was taken into custody and driven along the road that Charles had ridden to Portsmouth. There he took ship for the Isle of Wight and imprisonment in Carisbrooke Castle where Charles had meditated on the vanity of earthly things and the fragility of human power, and where, in 1650, the Princess Elizabeth had died. Here the Fifth Monarchists Rogers and Feake were still secluded from the world of men whom their words inflamed, and Vane, now a Witness, joined them. But the warrant which committed him commanded the governor of the Isle to allow Vane to speak with no one except in the presence of an officer.

Vane's mother, desolated by the death of her husband and even more by the contempt in which he had been held, was grieved now at the strange turning that saw her son imprisoned by the friends with whom he had destroyed the blessed king and the peaceful ways. She turned again to the Book of Prayer. *"O God,"* she read to herself, half aloud, *"who sparest when we deserve punishment, and in thy wrath rememberest mercy, we humbly beseech thee, of thy goodness to comfort and succour all prisoners, especially those who are condemned to die; give them a right understanding of themselves and of thy promises."*

Others felt less compassionate. Thurloe wrote in September that there were now "divers new malignants," applying to Vane a term that he himself had so often applied to others. An intercepted letter from some Royalist at the Hague said that the imprisonment of Vane neither deserved nor found much compassion. The Royalists hated him for the original quarrel; the people of Holland hated him because he could do them no more good and because he got some money when the Prince of Orange married the princess royal.

Though the charges of corruption have gone unsupported, the writer was correct in saying that Vane was now widely hated.

In September, while Vane was undergoing questioning and arrest, the election proved that the old revolutionaries were falling out of favor. Bradshaw was not returned, nor Ludlow nor Vane, who had been rejected by all three of the places where he had stood. Once the darling of the Scots, the City, and the Independents, he could not win an election in his home county where, as heartily as they wished Cromwell out, they did not wish his principal critic in.

When Cromwell addressed the new Parliament, he knew that some members resented the exile of Sir Henry and the imprisonment of other old revolutionaries, and so he told the House that at another time he would explain the motives which had impelled him. But a suitable occasion never came.

Meanwhile, at Carisbrooke, Vane was composing a letter to Cromwell which he would later publish to the world. Everything in that letter echoes the *Meditations*. In these latter days, he tells the Protector, the Lord is trying his people not only by sinful and profane men, but also by "equals and friends that have gone into the House of God in company, and taken sweet counsel together. . . ." Even these friends now have come to hate their brethren and cast them out under the pretense of glorifying God.

Vane recalls when Cromwell, after successfully engaging Hamilton's army, had written to St. John that he should tell "Brother Vane (for so you thought fit to call me) that you were as much unsatisfied with his passive and suffering principles, as he was with your active." Vane is still dissatisfied with Cromwell's active principles, which have now become "self-establishing," and he is willing that the Lord should judge between them. Though the names of truth and righteousness remain in the land, Vane says, they are now empty words out of which the spirit has gone, and it is by the spirit of a government that the governor must be judged. When governors make themselves more than they should be, they become sinners and must expect to fall. The only authority Cromwell and the army hold was derived from the legislative authority of the people; it is Cromwell's honor, duty, and safety to use this derived power lawfully. But to use it unlawfully, as the late king did, is to destroy something which worldly gains can never compensate for.

Yes, you are strong, Vane tells Cromwell, but you trust to the sword which is but flesh; your heart is lifted up, but unless you quickly repent, lifted up to your own destruction. If you are now aiming at a temporal as well as a spiritual throne, as you appear to be, the Lord will soon "lay it open as before the sun, that none of the webs you are weaving will prove garments to cover your nakedness." To the suffering Saints, to the anointed ones, not only this nation but the ruling powers of the whole world will very soon yield subjection as they bring forth a new heaven and a new earth.

Take then in good part before it is too late, this faithful warning and following advice of an ancient friend [who] is now thought fit to be used and dealt with as an enemy.

He finally exhorts Cromwell not to "exercise public scorn and triumph" over the precious Saints, but to recognize that his true interest lies with them. Otherwise God, in whose hands Cromwell's breath is, will suddenly arise and tear him to pieces, and there will be none to deliver him (again those echoes of the Book of Daniel). Cromwell and his kind live in pleasure on the earth, nourishing themselves as in a day of slaughter while in their hearts they have killed the just one, but "behold the Judge standeth at the door." At this strange medley of justification, anger, and eschatology, Cromwell and others could only shake their heads. It seemed the work of a mind dizzied by the strong wine of apocalypticism.

Despite his defiance, Vane was released on December 31, 1656, along with Feake and Rogers. From Carisbrooke he went immediately to Raby Castle to rejoin his wife and children, only to suffer more harassment there. According to both Ludlow and Burton, Cromwell began exerting pressures on Brother Heron. He privately encouraged some army men to take possession of certain forest walks belonging to Sir Henry near his castle; at the same time, he ordered the attorney-general to present a bill in Exchequer against Vane on the pretense that the title to a great part of his estate was imperfect. This bill would supposedly make Vane expose his title to the "craft of lawyers," which would find flaws in it. At the same time Vane was privately informed that he would be freed from these legal harassments "if he would comply with the present authority." He made no gesture of compliance.

Meanwhile, the political twistings and turnings continued. In January of 1657 there was a serious plot to assassinate Cromwell, and in March, by an alarmingly strong vote, the House passed a petition requesting the Protector to exercise the name, style, and office of a king. This offer, even though refused by Oliver, presented the Fifth Monarchy men with an acute crisis. According to Holy Writ, the Beast was to reign for forty-two months; Oliver had dismissed the Barebones Parliament in December of 1653, which meant that according to prophecy his reign should end in June of 1657. But rather than allow the Beast to become king, Oliver would have to be slain; the time for debate was over. Consequently, April 7, 1657, was set as the date for an insurrection in Epping Forest, chosen as a rendezvous because there were no troops in that vicinity. Thomas Venner was the leader of this new uprising and both John Rogers and Colonel Harrison were implicated. The angry Saints flaunted a standard and a public seal on which was a lion couchant with the motto "Who shall rouse him up?" Although there is no evidence to connect Vane with the plot, once again it was widely bruited that he had inspired it.

Parliament was adjourned in June, not to meet again until January 20, 1658. Before the adjournment Cromwell was reinstalled as Lord Protector in Westminster Hall. There he sat under a rich cloth of state upon a rich chair of state; he was vested with a robe of purple velvet lined with ermine and given a Bible richly gilt and embossed while the Speaker of the House girt a sword about him and delivered into his hands a scepter of massy gold. It was simply a coronation by another name, Cromwell's enemies said. But his friends thought not. A king, they pointed out, sat on a raised throne, Cromwell on a raised chair of state; the king was called Your Majesty, Cromwell Your Highness; at coronations people shouted, "God save the King," but here they shouted "God save the Lord Protector." Surely these were substantial differences.

But the installation aside, there were alarmingly discernible differences between this Cromwell and the one whose troopers had, in the name of the Lord of Hosts, desecrated the cathedrals. When Cromwell's daughter married, the ceremony was performed by a minister of the Church of England according to the Prayer Book which Oliver had once considered "a monstrous idol." Further,

Cromwell now intended to establish a House of Lords, only it was to be called merely a Second House. He conferred knighthoods and even hereditary peerages, and after one marriage ceremony he was actually seen dancing as if he were some papist. Worse than any of these things, he told Bishop Wilkins that no temporal government could remain secure without a national church, and he thought that for England episcopacy was likely the best form. Yet once with Vane he had been all for Root and Branch.

There were subtler changes, too, and even more portentous ones. In the recent Parliament, Lord Cochrane had said something about "an evil man" who read his sermons instead of extemporizing them, which in Presbyterian and Independent lore was a mark of the Beast. The response was not righteous horror, but loud, raucous laughter such as men laugh when they hear something silly which they once thought sacred. And in Cromwell's second Parliament, Wariston would note despondently that when a member supported an argument on the floor of the House by citing passages of scripture, other members actually hissed. Apparently people were becoming weary of public piety and even coming to think that religion was too often a cover for self-seeking ambition.

On January 20, 1658, Oliver's Parliament reassembled. Cromwell was now in poor health and, after making a short speech, he gave the rostrum to young Fiennes who said things that somehow underscored the deep changes men were feeling beneath all the overturnings. Those who stir up trouble in a nation, said young Nat, seldom attain the ends they profess or desire; nearly always something happens, perhaps something tragic, which is wholly contrary to their fervent hopes and expectations. Usually the result is greater mischief and confusion than before. Those that set a house on fire, he said, when the flame has broken out cannot say that it shall go so far and no farther. The fire will take its own way.

Then in what was surely a reference to Vane as well as others, Fiennes spoke of some of "our ancient friends" who have now become more difficult than enemies, open or secret. This is particularly hard, he said, because we love them so much. And to "those of our friends" who content themselves with the privacy of country retirement while the Commonwealth suffers, he asked, "Why abidest thou among the sheepfolds?" Some day, he said, we shall indeed see Christ on the throne of these lands, not in a literal and carnal way "which hath so much intoxicated the brains and minds of many in these our days, but in spirit and truth."

Some time in 1658, George Fox came to visit Vane at Raby. Perhaps he had read Vane's *Meditations*; perhaps he had only heard that Vane consigned most Quakers to the first covenant. Either way, he and Vane quarreled. Friends that were with him, said Fox, "stranged to see his darkness and impatience." Fox himself, perhaps without realizing the pun, perceived that Harry "was vain and high and proud and conceited, and that the Lord would blast him." Vane knew, of course, that men of the second covenant, such as himself, were not to be judged by men of the first covenant, but Fox judged him nevertheless. He told Vane that though he had formerly known something, he was not the man that he once was.

The revolution was not what it had once been either. Cromwell died on his lucky day, September 3, the day of Dunbar, the day of Worcester; and however chaotic things had become, without his strong, unifying personality they would become still worse. "After Cromwell's death," wrote Philip Warwick, "as if God would pour out shame upon this nation, such a spirit of giddiness appears that our government seems to have a twisting of the guts."

The truth is that the revolution was over: the lawyers knew it—Glyn and Maynard, Whitelocke and St. John—and they began to slide in new directions; the peers knew it, and the Presbyterians, the Catholics, and the apprentices. Everyone knew it except the godly troopers and Hugh Peter and Colonel Harrison, Colonel Ludlow, Arthur Haselrig—and Sir Henry Vane.

Vane's mother, confused and apprehensive, opened her Prayer Book once more and read,

> Grant Lord, we beseech thee, that the course of this world may be so peaceably ordered by thy governance, that thy congregation may joyfully serve thee in all godly quietness through Jesus Christ our Lord.

And many who did not read the Prayer Book were thinking and hoping that too.

16

The Cave of the Winds (Richard's Parliament: January 27–April 22, 1659)

On his deathbed, Oliver Cromwell, according to the most reliable story, designated his eldest son Richard as his successor, and on September 3, 1658, with hardly a susurrus of strife, the change of Protectors took place. There was some undergraduate protest at Oxford and another fulmination from the Fifth Monarchists, but, as Thurloe remarked, "There is not a dog that wags his tongue, so great a calm are we in."

Cromwell had ruled as a king, backed by a devoted and disciplined army; like a king he had passed on his power to an heir apparent, as if this were the natural order of things. His ritual obsequies were so long drawn out that his corpse, though enbalmed and shrouded in sheet lead, demanded an earthen shroud and was interred on November 10. Even after that, the mourning crowds at Whitehall passed through three chambers draped in black and ornamented with escutcheons, to reach the room in which Cromwell's wax effigy was now standing erect, clad in velvet and ermine; by its side was the gilt sword of power, and in its hands the scepter and orb, once the symbols of kingly authority.

The funeral procession, which set out for Westminster Abbey on the morning of November 23, was magnificent, expensive, and ill-organized. Crowds of mourners jammed the streets to walk ahead of the hearse when the procession, delayed by some arguments about precedence among the representatives of foreign powers, started from Somerset House. It passed through streets packed with people and lined with infantry clad in new red-and-black coats, handsome and still unpaid for; behind the hearse marched the official distinguished mourners, clad in black cloth rationed out according to their importance and rank. It was dusk before they reached the Abbey where those holding tickets were allowed to crowd in to see what they could in the blackening shadows as the effigy was placed in the mortuary chapel with no further ceremony than some solemn trumpet fanfares. "Much noise, much tumult, much expense," wrote Abraham Cowley, "much magnificence, much vain-glory; briefly, a great show, and yet after all this, but an ill sight." Cromwell's funeral had been even more expensive than that of old King James, but this time there were no Crown jewels which could be pawned to pay expenses.

At once the new Protector felt the old pinch: he could not rule without money, and therefore he needed to call a Parliament at once. Even with money it is doubtful that Richard could have ruled long. Not quite thirty-two years of age, he had happily lived the amiable, easy-going life of a country gentleman until his father had thrust him into Parliament and onto committees, grooming him for the role of heir apparent. How Oliver, so realistic about the exercise of power and so shrewd a judge of men, could have believed that Richard could keep together a Commonwealth which he himself had held only by his iron will and military force, one can only guess. His brother, Henry, efficient and aggressive, was surely a more likely choice except for the dynastic tradition that rule passes to the eldest living son. Richard enjoyed the vigorous rural pursuits of hawking, hunting, and horse-racing whereas administering an estate and counting costs so insufficiently engaged his attention that he plunged into debt. To please his father he had served as captain in the Lifeguards for a time, but that was ten years ago, and though he had been appointed commander of a regiment of horse, and just lately inherited two more regiments from his father, commands that were largely honorary, the military life was not congenial and he never acquired the skill of command. In a stable state, he would have made a fine figurehead of a monarch for he was handsome and courteous, free from fanaticism, with a grace of manner suitable for officiating at public ceremonies. What he lacked was the decisive ruthlessness to keep a tense state from exploding.

Once the funeral was over, Richard began to plan for the new Parliament; he was, he knew, inviting trouble; he had no reason to expect that his first Parliament would be any more tractable than his father's last. But money was desperately needed to pay the army rank and file who were growing mutinous because their pay was so far in arrears. Perhaps he hoped, also, that Parliament would protect him from the pressure the army was already exerting. The officers were ostensibly his principal supporters, but having served a military genius, they were resentful at being commanded by a mere civilian. They were trying to take control of the army from him and their leaders, Generals Fleetwood and Desborough (Richard's uncle-in-law and brother-in-law), were urging the new Protector to appoint Fleetwood commander-in-chief of the military. The officers had been holding weekly meetings and had already forced a number of concessions from Richard, and the controlling weapon which had kept his father in power, the military force, was slipping from his hand. Pressed from all sides, Richard and his Privy Council arranged on December 3, 1658, for an immediate Parliamentary election.

The Court party, as Richard's supporters were somewhat ironically known, did its best to pack the House of Commons. The Commonwealth was then legally based on the *Petition and Advice*, the work of the second Protectorate Parliament. Introduced and debated through the early months of 1657 it had originally called for Oliver to assume the "name, style, title and dignity of King," along with the right to appoint his successor. It established a "second House" of Parliament, attempted to establish a national church and a dogmatic creed and called for a new apportionment in the electing of the House of Commons. After much struggle with himself and much impassioned advice from others, Oliver had decided to refuse the Crown but to accept the rest of the new constitution.

But in their dire need to return a favorable Commons, Richard's council decided to ignore the election reforms and to return to the older system whereby the more easily controllable—or corruptible —small boroughs would regain representation at the expense of the cities. The second House would stand as the *Petition* had constituted it, a combination of the Protector's Council and the Lords whom Oliver had appointed or created.

This election drew Sir Henry Vane back into public life and Parliamentary power for a year, a crucial year in which he would have his last chance to lead England towards the Heavenly Jerusalem of his theories and visions. He had been effectively rusticated for almost six years, but now he hoped to revive the "good cause" which he believed Oliver had betrayed, and he hoped to establish it once and for all on a firm legal and constitutional base. A strong Parliament under a weak Protector might at least create a true commonwealth and a home for the spiritual seed.

Because Vane had been one of the opponents of Oliver and "single person" rule, the government wished to keep him out and almost succeeded. At Hull and at Bristol, it was said, he had received a majority of votes but the sheriffs refused to return him. He was, however, elected and returned from Whitchurch in Hampshire.

The upper House in the new Parliament was divided about equally between the Cromwellians (the dynastic party), and the party of the officers who wished to control the army and make it independent of the Protector. The latter were soon to be known as the Wallingford House group from the name of Fleetwood's residence in which the cabal of officers generally met.

In Commons a considerable number of members of the old Long Parliament were returned but even so the House was made up of about half new and inexperienced men, many of them young, with their principles and allegiances still unformed. Groups and alliances were fluid and no group seemed to command a clear majority about anything of consequence. Following the pattern of Oliver's Parliaments, there were in Commons twenty-five members from Wales, thirty from Ireland and thirty-one from Scotland; how they would line up was yet to be known. The Cromwellians probably had some kind of majority, however. Defending the *Petition and Advice* and the Protectorate of Richard, they were led by Secretary of State John Thurloe. The Wallingford House faction in Commons was led by General Lambert whom Oliver had cashiered in July of 1657 for disaffection. While the Royalists had to remain under cover, there were a number of them waiting to throw their votes in any particular dispute on the side most likely to increase the possibility of the restoration of Charles Stuart.

Of all the minority groups, the most coherent and committed were the Commonwealth men or Republicans. The old revolutionaries, Vane and Haselrig, were their leaders, along with members who had formerly opposed Oliver on the *Petition and Advice*. It has been generally agreed that the principal characteristic of the Republicans, in this Parliament, was retrospection, for the issues they now raised were the same ones Pym and the Long Parliament had raised almost twenty years before. Then it had been asked how far the royal prerogative extended; now it was being asked how much power the "single person" should have. Then it had been contended that Parliament should control the militia, but recently the Protector had controlled it. After the execution of the king the Long Parliament had declared that the House of Lords was abolished, but now there was a second House; the old revolutionaries had swept away the established church, but now a new establishment had been proposed. With Oliver dead, it seemed to the Republicans that they must fight for these principles once more, that they must explain to the new men what the civil war had meant. It was inevitable that not only in their viewpoint but also in their language there should be a certain harking back to the old times of peril, hope, and high excitement. The spirit as well as the ideals of the revolution must be revived and passed on.

But during the time Vane had been out of power, those who had participated in government had become used to a whole set of new ideas, new terms, new ways of thinking. Insensibly, without painfully reminding themselves, they had tacitly agreed to return to some of the old ways in practice if not always in name. For them the revolution was a memory to be defended; for Vane it was still a goal to be achieved. He didn't quite realize that in the two decades since those first euphoric days, the center had not held, time had sickened, and experience had modified the reasonable expectations which one could hold for the "good cause." There is something poignantly outmoded about the man who only six years earlier wielded more power than any man in England save Cromwell himself.

Even so, as the session went on Vane became the most influential leader of the Republicans; never, perhaps, were his talents more shrewdly employed, or his Parliamentary tactics and speeches quite so distinguished, but despite his skill and his inextinguishable hope and faith, his efforts were all wasted on an already lost cause in a Parliament that was weak and confused.

Richard opened the Parliament by addressing a joint session at which he spoke with affecting simplicity and dignity of his father's death and his own determination to rule wisely; only hindsight would perceive the irony of his suspiration that "you will in all your debates maintain and conserve love and unity among yourselves, that therein you may be the pattern of the nation, who have sent you up in peace, and with their prayers, that the spirit of wisdom and peace may be among you." Or the irony of the confidence with which he quoted the *Petition and Advice*, the "corner-stone of this building," to the effect that Parliaments were the great council of the Chief Magistrate in whose advice both he and the three nations might be most safe and happy. Richard surely did not realize that he was taking as axiomatic what was to be a bitter point of contention: whether the function of a Parliament was to advise and consent or to initiate and control.

There had been some difficulty that morning in getting the oath of loyalty to the Protector administered to all the members before they were allowed to enter; this reluctance to swear fidelity boded ill for Richard's success. To avoid taking the oath, some, like Edmund Ludlow and Sir Henry Vane, came in late or stayed away; both these men managed to sit as members without ever having taken it.

The proceedings of this Parliament were recorded in more detail than those of any other in which Vane sat. They demand attention for that reason; not only Vane's procedural maneuvers and his remarks in the heated interchanges, but also a number of substantial and significant speeches are sufficiently recorded to convey a sense of Vane's impromptu style as well as the vigor and clarity with which he expressed his ideas. His speeches are often more eloquent and persuasive than speeches he had formally published earlier. Although this was a futile and footling Parliament which never argued an issue to its conclusion, which failed to produce a single significant act, and though the debates were random and dispersed—sometimes as funny as if Dickens had written them—Vane argued for his political theories with a single-minded consistency and persistently tried to embody them in law. Never was he more persuasive and never did he persuade so few.

He had stated his theories in *A Healing Question* where he had argued that the elected representatives should formulate a constitution which, when agreed upon, was inviolable and would establish the elected legislative body as superior to both the executive officer and the militia. Civil liberty and freedom of conscience, he insisted, could be assured only by a written constitution which embodied the central political truth that all power is derived from the people and exercised by their elected representatives. He was still defining his terms in a highly restricted way, attempting to insure the rule of people who, at least roughly, shared his own views.

At this time the nearest thing to a written constitution was the *Petition and Advice*, which Vane detested for several reasons: because it empowered the Protector to designate his own successor whereas Vane would have him chosen by Parliament; because Lords were appointed by the Protector and both had veto power over Commons; and because the Protector controlled the military. In Richard's Parliament, the drift of Vane's arguments, even when they were devious, was always towards establishing and maintaining Commons as the source of all power; he opposed or attempted to revise any proposal that even by implication surrendered power to the Protector or the other House. With Haselrig he especially tried again and again to transfer control of the military, including appointments and dismissals, to Commons.

Although God was somewhat less in Vane's mouth than in Haselrig's during this Parliament, Sir Henry's motives were more profoundly religious. And, passionate millenarian though he was, his preoccupation with the perfecting of the present civil government set him far apart from the violent Fifth Monarchy men; he conceived it as his mission to prepare the world for the second coming not by destroying Antichrist, but by carrying on "this blessed cause . . . in its progress to its desired and expected end of bringing in Christ, the desire of all nations, as the chief Ruler among us." He did not wish to burn off the wicked like stubble but rather to prepare the soil for the growth of God's kingdom.

In meetings which Republicans held at Vane's house in Charing Cross, Haselrig and Vane probably plotted together to block the moves of the Protector and the army and to establish a free commonwealth. Certainly they shared basic beliefs and purposes however much they differed in temperament and method. Both were inclined to nostalgia, to a liberal remembrance of the past, but Haselrig was voluble, long-winded, easily blown up to rhetorical heights on gusts of emotion. Vane had acquired caution and self-control; speaking in a quiet and orderly way, he cut through verbiage and emotion to fundamental issues, a man as Clarendon said, of "very ready, sharp, and weighty expression." In this Parliament he was at the height of his form intellectually and forensically and he expended his best energies earnestly, gallantly, and hopelessly.

After Richard's speech, the Commons met and chose as Speaker Chaloner Chute, an elderly lawyer who, as tradition required, protested that he was not fit for the office. His protests were easily over-ridden and he made a happy beginning: "You called me to this place for directions, so that I must not give ill examples by troubling you with a long speech. I never knew much said in long speeches. I never loved them." While his brevity was a constant virtue, he was otherwise not a strong chairman nor happy under heavy responsibility, of which he was soon apprised. Haselrig took advantage of a minor squabble to remind Chute that he was now "the greatest man in England," and should not lower the dignity of Parliament by taking instruction from an inferior court. Twice Haselrig repeated his Republican sentiment: Chute was the greatest man in England, and this implied that Commons was greater than Protector or army.

These and other preliminaries were abruptly ended when Secretary Thurloe, quite unintentionally, loosed the waters of strife. He brought in "An Act of Recognition of His Highness's right and title to be Protector and Chief Magistrate . . ." After all, Richard had succeeded to his father's position and taken the government upon his shoulders with "general consent and approbation" as the bill stated; for Parliament to ratify this happening would seem a perfunctory courtesy, a ritualistic acceptance of an accomplished fact. Unfortunately the act went a little further: it asked the Parliament to declare that Richard was the *lawful* chief magistrate and that, accordingly, the people should be commanded to obey him. The word *lawful* opened the whole question of the legality of Oliver's Protectorate, of his Parliaments, and of the *Petition and Advice*; asking this Parliament to enact and declare implied that it was within its jurisdiction to refuse to enact, and that is precisely what the Republicans intended to do.

While the first reading of the bill elicited little comment, the second reading, on February 7, found Haselrig ready. Forsaking Speaker Chute's admirable example, he launched into a wandering, emotional three-hour speech in which he recounted the history of English government from the Norman conquest, which first abrogated English natural rights, through the civil war, the execution of the king and the dismissal of the Long Parliament, and the Protectorate of Oliver. In all of his wanderings in this wilderness of words he did not forget his main point. The right of government, he said, is with the people. If any established power is taken away the right reverts to the people. When the king and Lords were abolished the right lay solely with the Long Parliament which was the representative of the people. But the Long Parliament had been forcibly and illegally dissolved; power then should have reverted to the people but had not.

His speech was the thunder before the deluge. One member after another arose to express their outrage at Pride's Purge or the ejection of the Long Parliament. Some wished no single person as ruler; others wished to abolish the other House; still others would have recalled the old House of Lords, and some, perhaps most, wished to return to the old pattern of king, Lords, and Commons but with new assignments of power and privilege. Captain Baynes wished to found the government entirely on property which now, he said, is generally "with the people." Not until late on the afternoon of the second day did Vane speak and then only to recommend an adjournment to permit more thought before a vote was taken. There is still much to be said to the whole matter, said Vane, before a question is put.

The third day began with an interruption: there were some petitioners at the door, all with "honest, old faces." Vane was willing to hear them: "The people were never denied to petition," he said, and some wanted to hear the fine old fellows at once. Others, like Sir Walter Earle, wanted to get on with the Bill of Recognition: "I have no skill in physiognomy," he grumbled. "It matters not to me that they are old faces," and so the petition was postponed and debate on the Protector resumed.

Round and round the arguments went until many wanted to refer the bill to a committee for further investigation; every phrase was analyzed and discussed until it was proposed to put off the whole matter and turn to the plight of the army, now forty weeks without pay. Why not turn to the urgent business for which the Parliament had been called, some asked, instead of this endless wrangling about phrases? When there was danger that the bill might be approved out of sheer fatigue and impatience, Vane interposed with his first major speech. It was again late in the afternoon when he tried to clear away irrelevancies and focus upon what was to him the one burning issue, the issue of where the source of power lay.

Take all the time needed, he urged his colleagues, for they should decide with greater unity if the reasons and judgments of all men were heard. As for Vane himself, he perceived that there were disagreements even about what the present state of government was, some still holding it to be in king, Lords, and Commons, believing still that old foundations, purged of evil, were firm enough to build on. But God, said Sir Henry, had dissolved that government beginning in 1640, and as he thought of those heady days he talked of what had happened and of his own role in it, of the attempt to bring the king's advisers to justice, of the struggle for the militia, of the progressive hardening of the king's heart, of the failure of the Lords to help when the Scots invaded, or to bring the king to justice. When the House of Commons had reviewed the full extent of the king's delinquency, they finally realized that monarchy itself must be abolished; they finally realized that the origin of all just power was in the people and was reserved wholly to the Commons who represented them.

Vane remembered how he agonized at the trial of the king, how he absented himself for six weeks from his seat in Commons "out of tenderness of blood." Now, he said to his colleagues, if you do not accept the fact that the just power lies in you, you draw guilt upon the whole nation. It then becomes a question of whether the king's death was justice or murder. Vane, for his own part, was certain that, after the king's death, the little remnant of the great Parliament remained the representative of the nation, comprehending all government in itself. "It seemed plain to me, that all offices had their rise from the people, and that all should be accountable to them. If this be monstrous, then it is monstrous to be safe and rational, and to bear your own good."

He acknowledged the breaks in continuity. Some governments had been dissolved and others created, but that did not mean England must now return to the old government; instead the Parliament should rebuild and they should not "be underbuilders to supreme Stuart." No, when the Long Parliament was dissolved, its right was not lost, only its possession of that right; its powers persisted even though the Parliament itself was vacated.

Such a claim was a legal fiction but it was needed to provide a kind of apostolic succession of the Parliaments and Vane therefore insisted on its validity; he was clinging to a form with all the tenacity of a William Laud urging the unbroken succession of bishops.

The Long Parliament, Vane reminded the new men, had decreed that it could not be dissolved against its own will; therefore its power and right never ceased to exist de jure. Cromwell had disbanded that Parliament but he could not destroy it. The Royalists, of course, were maintaining a parallel fiction that the moment Charles I died, his son was de jure King Charles II, and continued to be even though he was kept from possession of his right. Vane was later to be caught between the rival claims of these two successions: he staked his life on the unbroken continuance of the people's authority in Parliament, and lost it to Charles' continuing mystical kinghood in absentia.

Now Vane argued that the *Petition and Advice* was the work of a coerced Parliament and was, in any case, only a temporary expedient, not intended to create a permanent government. Therefore it must be completely and decisively rejected, for this bill to acknowledge the Protector "huddles up in wholesale what you have fought against and is hasted on lest you should see it." By asking for a recognition of Richard, Vane points out, the bill implies that there is no one presently in possession, for it asks recognition of right and title, not of Richard's person.

Now, Vane concluded, the new government must be on an unshaken foundation. If you resort to the old government, he warned, you may not be many steps from the old family and "they will be too hard for you." Therefore, if Parliament wished Richard, they should take him not as the son of a conqueror but rather as a son by adoption.

And so both the leaders of the revolution had spoken, Vane more concisely and cogently, but both he and Haselrig had invoked the "cause," had justified old actions and their part in them, had tried to recapture the passion of faded times. Both were ideologues attempting to communicate their vision of the holy community to young and impatient men who wanted to get on with the business of life, with settlements of marriages or estates, with the problem of taxes and trade. On this occasion, Vane's point was lost in a barrage of rhetoric from all sides, but as time went on it became clearer that everything the new men wanted was summed up in the word *settlement:* settlement of the militia and the church and the succession and the election. Appeals to principle and impassioned recollections aroused in them no answering passion, and so they defeated Vane and the revolutionaries; they recognized the Protector and then adjourned, each to find his way home in the biting cold and the gloom of night.

While the Protector was now recognized, it was still to be settled which powers he should enjoy and which remained with the people or their representatives. This was the theme of the next day's debate which was suddenly interrupted when charges of blasphemy and atheism were leveled at Mr. Neville, himself a member. Immediately the House fell to arguing about whether bringing such charges against a member violated Parliamentary privilege, about the proper form for such charges, about the relative priority of blasphemy and atheism in the lexicon of crime, and the difficulty of defining blasphemy. Vane had heard it all before, had known all the emotion that could be aroused by such vague charges, and how easily members could be led to censure the human conscience as it struggled to know and define its own beliefs. He arose again to speak. Jesus himself was accused of blasphemy, Sir Henry said, because his enemies could not find any other accusation that would stick. He thought the House should return to the agenda and, after several hours more of pious oratory, it did. The charges "fell asleep" and were forgotten. It was a small triumph and one of the few Vane would enjoy in this Parliament.

On February 17, a letter from His Highness recommending that the Commons start to work on military finances only stirred up a dispute about Parliamentary privilege: did the Protector have the right to address them directly and urge them to act? To be sure there was a war on with Spain, and England's interests were involved in the Swedish-Danish naval war in the Sound, all of which led Secretary Thurloe to insist that something had to be done at once. But the huge sums of money needed seemed to stupefy the debaters: some moved postponement, others wished to go back to debating the merits of the *Petition and Advice.* Vane, still worried about fundamentals, asked that first things be done first. The main question now was the extent of the powers of the chief magistrate.

Should he have the negative voice, that is, veto power over acts of Parliament? Should he control the militia? Vane thought not. The chief magistrate should be given power to do everything that was good and nothing hurtful. His task should be to carry out the will of Parliament and nothing else. While this seemed to be a clear enough statement to be put to a vote, Colonel Birch wished first to settle whether or not there would be a second House. The next day Vane was still trying to make clear that the question of the magistrate's veto power was separate from and antecedent to the question of a second House, but again he was defeated. It was resolved to dispose of the question of the other House first.

But that was no easier to agree upon, for soon the confused members saw that what they decided about the second House was contingent upon the status of the *Petition and Advice*. Was it an inviolable constitution? If so, were they a valid Parliament inasmuch as they had been elected by apportionment procedures it had abolished? Did the *Petition* conceive of the other House as an upper House? If so could the lower House impose any limits or restraints on it? The opinions veered between Mr. Drake's that "we have no commission to meddle with the constitution from those that sent us here," to Vane's insistence that "the power is yours." Once again nothing could be decided because everything seemed antecedent to everything else and behind all questions were interlocked dubieties.

Through all this confusion, Vane consistently worked in two ways: he would let debate exhaust itself, and then he would attempt to isolate and simplify key questions which might be settled one after the other. But the leaderless members still got tangled up trying to decide whether to set up a House and then bound it, or to set bounds and then create a House within them. Colonel Birch darkened counsel by suggesting that they should limit the power of the people themselves by setting a House of Peers over them, and Mr. Onslow thought that the Commons should also be bound while they were about it. Finally the members voted to recognize a second House, another defeat for the old revolutionaries.

On Monday, February 21, Secretary Thurloe explained the history and present condition of the naval war in the Sound between Sweden and Denmark, and reported that His Highness was preparing a fleet to stand ready to protect England's interests if necessary. He was merely informing the Parliament, he said, so that they might advise the government. Sir Henry Vane, who had a reputation in such matters, at once suspected a "design." He asked searching questions about the grounds of the war and as usual, his mind went back to former times. I think back to the old Parliament, he said, and I remember that when such reports as this came from the king we never looked upon them the same day; we always had a suspicion of a hidden Court design to engage us in a rash undertaking before we knew fully what we were doing. Now, said Sir Henry, it appears to be the same thing again. He proposed a delay of forty-eight hours to permit closer scrutiny.

What Vane really feared was that if Commons routinely ratified this "report," they would be dispatching a stand-by fleet into the Sound, and the consequences might be very serious. If Richard and Thurloe had entered into a secret agreement with the Swedes against the Dutch, as he had heard, Parliament would be committed to supporting it blindly. Thurloe denied any such agreement, but Sir Henry, who refused to identify his informant, was not convinced; he remembered his youthful days in Vienna when the government had entered into secret understandings which even the English ambassador had not known about. But more urgent was the danger of stationing a neutral fleet in a position where it might inadvertently become involved in an "incident" which would precipitate an undeclared war that Parliament would be obliged to finance and conduct.

Predictably the voice of the military asserted the peace-making powers of force. If a war was feared said they, there was "no other way under heaven to prevent that war than by sending this fleet into the Sound."

Vane was hardly less concerned with the question of who would control this fleet, Parliament or the chief magistrate. Unless that question was settled first, Parliament might set a precedent that would give away its rights. Of course England must have a powerful and well-manned navy, he argued, but does it need this additional fleet now? And where will Parliament find that million pounds which Thurloe so casually mentioned? If by avoiding these questions they passed them on to the Protector and council, they would surrender control of the commanders at sea and in principle might also surrender the entire military.

As debate continued, Vane became more and more convinced

that whether there was a secret agreement or not, the government's pressure for sudden action was really a screen to cover an attempt not only to control the militia but to maintain the initiatives of war and peace. "The greatest pinch of this debate," he said, "is whether you will have a war or no." And the whole affair, he feared, was being managed "to support the interest of a single person," perhaps even a foreign power, but not the interests of the people of England. So he made four recommendations that he believed would establish the right kind of precedents. The Parliament should firmly assert its control of all the military forces, and then refer the present matter of the fleet to Parliamentary commissioners for a prompt decision. The Parliament's policy should be to approve, by interview if necessary, all proposed officers. And they should appoint a committee to advise about the disposition of the whole question of military power in the best public interest.

If Vane's recommendations had been accepted, the Parliament, with the military under its power, could have still expedited the action of the navy. Instead the members channeled discussion back to the old dispute about whether the *Petition and Advice* was the constitution that should determine the governmental power and structure. The Court party argued strongly on this point; time passed, candles were brought in, and it was on towards midnight before the question was passed: His Highness was empowered to put to sea "a considerable navy for the safety of this Commonwealth, and the preservation of the trade and commerce thereof." So the Republicans lost again to the pragmatic interests of the House; they were granted a weak and ineffectual reservation: "saving the interest of this House in the militia and in making peace and war."

When this matter had been settled, debate circled for several days around the matter of the other House, how it should be constituted, and whether or not Commons should transact with it as they had to in order to accomplish anything. The practical suggestion was advanced that Commons should transact with the present upper House without concern as to whether or not it was rightly constituted, should deal with it de facto without committing themselves de jure. The most passionately held theoretical view was that the old hereditary peers, rejected in 1648, should replace this appointive House before any business be done. Some were willing to regard the *Petition and Advice* as a constitution that validated the

House presently sitting, called, as it had been, by writ. But the implications of these incompatible theories were significant; they all smelled of Royalism and might lead to Restoration. If the rights of the old peers still lived, so did the right of the king. Colonel Terrill wanted the old Lords to be restored to "their ancient right to sit, and then lay bounds to their powers"; it is the right of the Parliament, he argued, to re-establish the old House of Lords as much as it was the Long Parliament's to take it away. Thereupon Mr. Fowell explicitly demonstrated why crypto-Royalists supported the Protectorate. "The Protector," he said, "is the King of England to all intents and purposes whatever. . . . Since the Conquest we have had but one King—the King never dies."

Vane was on his feet, flushed with anger. "I cannot bear what is spoken," he said. "There is a law still in force, declaring it to be treason for any man to declare or proclaim any person to be King of England." Mr. Fowell promptly interpreted his remarks out of the shadow of treason and the debate swirled about with much impassioned defense of principle and some dry reminders that urgent business stayed undone. When the debate was hopelessly lost, Vane arose again to emphasize the central issue—where the power lay. Commons had the power, he said, and they should use it.

> If you consider how things are left, upon the death of the late Protector, by that *Petition and Advice*, I am sure, unless you shut your eyes, you may see that you are the undoubted legislative power of the nation; even by that constitution by which you are called and the Protector himself proclaimed. . . . I understand not that objection that we are sinew-shrunk and manacled, and cannot proceed; that we can effect nothing, unless we transact with these men. You have as much power to make a House of Lords with the concurrence of the Protector, as the last Parliament had. I thought you would have gone to clear the rights and liberties of the people. . . . It is but using the just power.

However, no such action was taken, and those who guessed that the cause was lost began to refer to it as the "good *old* cause"; soon even the revolutionaries were using that phrase.

During the next week Vane made no speeches, but he listened as the arguments meandered back to the *Petition and Advice* and among questions concerning whether or not the Commons should transact any business with the "other House." If they did, they would be recognizing its status and power; if they did not, affairs of state would be paralyzed. At length Mr. Boyle cried out in dismay, "There is no unity amongst us. When one moves, another crosses presently." Indeed underlying resentments were now surfacing, and the strongest of them was against the military. Bitter memories rankled of Pride's Purge, of the swordsmen who had enforced Cromwell's dissolution of the Long Parliament in 1653, and many were unwilling to acknowledge a second House in which some twenty officers now sat, in addition to the Lieutenant of the Tower and naval commanders. This opposition, in turn, brought ominous hints that a vote against the present Lords might bring the sword out of its scabbard again.

"These words of force cannot be endured," cried Sir Arthur Haselrig, and the angry debate continued until candles were brought and the doors were shut against members who wanted to leave; and then the discussion became even more shrill and minatory. Mr. Hungerford said that the army was to be feared even in the event of a positive vote in their favor. Sir George Booth cynically suggested that it was futile to think of limiting a body which was dominated by military officers. "A sword," he said, "cannot be bounded."

Mr. Higgons, weary of quarreling, moved to transact with the second House whereupon General Ludlow peremptorily moved not to transact with them for, said he, some of those gentlemen had been guilty of all the breaches upon the liberty of the people. God, he said, confidently, would blast them. Thurloe made alarming predictions about the results of a refusal to transact: such essential laws as the law of indemnity would be voided; the constitution would be abrogated; anarchy or the tyranny of rule by a clever few could supervene. If the vote were negative, he said, he feared the consequences.

In this mood of anger and anxiety, Vane at last rose to speak. As usual, he began in a low key, apologizing for troubling the members so late in the evening. Then, with increasing intensity, he insisted once more that this House had the power and the right which they should not relinquish through delay, but should use without fear. Future liberties, he said, depended on this decision about the second

House. If Commons voted against that House then all power resided with them; if they voted for it, "I dare say then, all the power is gone hence." The powers of both king and Lords had been "melted down into this house." The representative body, he said again, never dies. If that was true the old Long Parliament still lived and so by implication the Protector and the second House were usurpers. I cannot think, he said, how you could vote in the affirmative.

Vane concluded with a peroration that had never failed in the old revolutionary days. To the warnings of violent consequences if Commons voted against the second House, Vane replied that God is almighty. Would the members not trust Him with the consequences? True, he continued, the Parliament might for a little be driven into the wilderness, but if their motives were pure, God would bring them back. "He is a wiser workman than to reject His own work."

Vane here enunciated a belief from which he would take courage in the coming years of humiliations and defeats, a belief that his reverses were an exile in the wilderness, a journey into the deserts, made under the design and direction of God who would thereby accomplish His own purposes and at last vindicate Sir Henry.

But his appeal to mystical idealism did not impress the lawyers. Sergeant Maynard, his bitter antagonist, after reminding the House that there was "a necessity of transacting," attacked Vane's major assumption. We should never suffer all power to be devolved into a Parliament, he said, for they would then have a sword which God had never put into their hands. He was expressing the powerful idea which Vane himself would later accept, that concentration of all power in any branch of government is dangerous to the people's liberties, which will always survive best in a situation which pragmatically offers a chance for public disagreements to work themselves out short of violence. It is best when men of power set jealous watch over one another.

The session limped on. Four members fell ill and were permitted to leave. Mr. Sadler had taken an hour to move adjournment and would still have been talking if he had not been taken down. Then Mr. Knightley, one of those permitted to depart, returned with a distressing account of how he had been stopped outside by a group of soldiers who said that if the vote were negative the Parliament would be dissolved. He had instinctively fallen back on his

Parliamentary privilege, but the soldiers, unimpressed, had looked with "an ill face" upon him.

When Knightley finished, Vane immediately moved adjournment. "It seems," he said, "one member was stopped in going out; we may see if soldiers do stop us all tomorrow, as we come in." The threat of another military coup was heavy in the air. However, the soldiers did not stop the members the next morning, and after desultory debate, the simple resolution passed "that this House will transact with the persons now sitting in the other House, as a House of Parliament." Again a compromise rider was proposed that "it is not hereby intended to exclude such Peers as have been faithful to the Parliament from their privilege of being duly summoned to be members of that House."

So Vane and the Republicans had lost again and on a major issue. They had lost, however, by a small margin and so now they alleged that the Scottish and Irish members, nominated by the Protector and voting his wishes, had been the decisive factor.

Since the Scots knew that they would fare better under Charles Stuart, who owed them a great deal, than with the Republicans and Independents, they were easily swayed towards the Royalist cause. At the same time, Vane found it unendurable that these Scots, not even elected and therefore not honest representatives, should be able to prevent the Parliament from creating a godly commonwealth, that they should rather reinforce the Protectorate and even underbuild supreme Stuart. Accordingly he did not follow his usual pattern of waiting for debate to exhaust itself before interposing with a major speech; this time he entered the debate on the first day. On March 9, the issues had already got lost in the question of whether the Irish and Scots should be dealt with separately or together and whether the Scots should leave when their own rights were being discussed. In a minor squabble about a point of order, two men claiming the floor, Vane interposed not in his usual quiet understatement but in a note of high exasperation. If he understood anything of order, he said, the whole House had been out of order from the beginning. Until the qualification of members was cleared, nothing should have been done except the choosing of a Speaker. In the last Parliament, he said, there was a question of keeping out the members who would not approve the *Petition and Advice*; now it was a matter of taking in enough nonmembers to confirm it. In this admission of appointed members from Scotland and Ireland he saw the same packing of Parliament, the same rigging of a majority by adding or ejecting members, as had preceded other drastic changes in government. This Parliament had been drifting that way all along, by transacting with another House that had no legal base, and now preparing to function with a membership not legally constituted. The Parliament had subverted its own foundation. If the Scots do not withdraw while this issue is being discussed, he warned, they will provide a solid negative. By the Protector's appointment, sixty votes had been imposed upon the House, and Vane concluded by asking the House to vote against seating nonelected members.

Mr. Neville supported Vane: "When the question comes, they must withdraw; for if persons concerned may vote in their own cause, then it is as broad as it is long." Vane then arose to demand that the Scots withdraw even before the question, for "they will never suffer themselves to be brought to the question. They will keep off all questions." It was decided, however, at least to hear the Scots before they withdrew, and so the talk went on for days. Vane kept trying to focus the debate on the issues of right and law, not on the question of whether or not to admit specific members. Scotland is united with England, he granted, and the Scots are entitled to be represented in the House. That was not the question; the question was rather whether the right was derived according to the law. Could the chief magistrate appoint members to an elected representative body? That was the real issue.

For another week the question was sporadically argued. On the 18th of March a Mr. Bulkeley spoke at some length on behalf of the Scottish members, lauding the advantages of the union with Scotland, a nation, he said, with the greatest face of religion of any Protestant nation. While he had not been there himself, a gentleman had told him that there was not one church in Scotland where the word of God was not taught. And their representatives were being opposed on a mere "formality of distribution"; there was "only an excrementitious part wanting, as hair, or nails, or such a like formality."

Vane arose to reply. Without denying that the Scots had great virtues and the union of the two kingdoms great advantages, he insisted that the vital issue was one of law—how many Scottish representatives had a legal right to sit and how were they to be selected, by appointment or by election. These had been appointed. And if the "single person" can legally send thirty from Scotland this time he can send a hundred another time and control the Parliament altogether. We must, he said again as he had said a hundred times, we must lay foundations, and lay them now. "There is no remedy, but to do that by law, which cannot possibly be done without it. . . . I hope you will not call it an excrementitious formality: that is the very essence and being of your privilege." Vane, who had once been above forms, was no longer a political antinomian.

On March 21, Vane was urging that the question be worded so as to inquire first not whether these Scots should continue to sit but rather whether they had a right to sit in the first place. But the Speaker put neither question; the members were asked instead to decide whether the Scots should withdraw before their case was voted on. The Republicans lost the preliminary skirmish and the Scots stayed. Then the question was put whether the members from Scotland "should continue to sit as members during the present parliament," and it passed in the affirmative. Thus Vane lost on the main issue because, as Ludlow said, a question of right was turned into a question of convenience.

In the heat of the debate, a careless phrase stirred up disproportionate resentment. Mr. Boscawen, although a staunch defender of the old covenant, looked upon the Act of Union as a "national sin." That union, he said, having been made by the fag end of the Long Parliament, had no legal footing, and Scotland would not stay bound by it. As prime architect of that act, Vane must have been startled at the charge that he had acted illegally. Then, shortly after, another member insultingly said that all the laws made "in the fag-end of the Long Parliament" were invalid, and he accused Sir Arthur Haselrig of endeavoring to "make himself and Sir Henry Vane the great Hogen Mogen, to rule the Commonwealth." Sir Arthur took it hard and wished that he might be hanged rather than be so reproached after he had "acted so highly." Word of the contretemps spread abroad and stirred alarm and resentment in the army. "I doubt," commented Burton, "it may breed ill blood; for every man that acted begins to say, 'What did I do in that fag-end of a Parliament, and how shall I be indemnified but by my sword? We will not give the cause away.' " Never, says Burton, did two words work such an alteration in one day in the face of affairs, and he wondered what the consequences might be.

Although the phrase was soon forgotten, men continued to wonder about what would happen to those who had acted for the good old cause in that rump of a Parliament if the Stuarts were returned to power and decided to hold them accountable. Sir Henry Vane was one of those who would find out.

The Court party, despite their ineptness and the energetic tactics of the Republicans, was winning because the large uncommitted middle could be drawn to support the status quo, and the crypto-Royalists felt safer with the courtiers than with the Republicans. But the Court party was thrown on the defensive by a series of incidents that laid bare egregious examples of arbitrary and tyrannical actions on the part of Oliver, who had bolstered his regime by imprisoning apparently dangerous characters without benefit of trial or even formal charges. Like other dictators he had discovered that the courts were an impediment to efficiency. Once when a judge had freed one of his prisoners, Cromwell took occasion to assemble him and other justices for a lecture. But what about the law? they asked. What about Magna Charta? Magna farta, replied Cromwell, your authority comes from me. He then dismissed them with a warning not to let the lawyers prate what it did not become judges to hear. Old King James had never said it so effectively.

If new presbyter had turned out to be only old priest writ large, it also appeared that the new Protector might have been only old king writ polysyllabic, and it was difficult to be righteous about the wickedness of the Stuarts when faced with the similar wickedness of the godly Protector.

Men like Vane, who had come to see at last that the only bulwark against personal tyranny was the strong, clear process of the law, were outraged by petitions that came to Parliament from men who had been illegally imprisoned. The grievance of the first petitioner, John Portman, had been reported on February 26 by the Grand Committee of the House for Grievances and Courts of Justice. According to their report, his imprisonment was unjust and illegal, and they recommended that he be discharged without any fees or cost. Portman, along with others, had been thrown into prison by order of a letter from Oliver ("you shall have a warrant after you have done," it read); he was suspected of involvement in the rising of the Fifth Monarchists in 1657 and, apparently forgotten, had remained in prison long after the others had been released.

Mr. Jessop was not sure that Portman should be released, for Mr. Jessop himself had recently come into possession of a book of cipher, confiscated from Fifth Monarchy men, and he had decoded parts of it in which he found the names of God and Portman occurring with about the same frequency, along with a plot to take up arms. Vane replied with generosity and good sense that Parliament did not have the whole case before them, but that to be moved by a dubious interpretation of an unidentified book in cipher was ridiculous and dangerous. If men were convicted on such evidence, he said, few would escape. "Let us do what may show we bear the bodies of Englishmen, and not of slaves." His speech crystallized the sentiment. Mr. Onslow stated that "though the crime were true, no law gives the chief magistrate power to commit any man of his own accord." The report of the Committee was then accepted and Portman was released.

Even more damaging to the image of the Protector was the case of Colonel Robert Overton, a prisoner for four years on the Isle of Jersey. When he presented himself to the Parliament on March 11, Vane recommended postponement over the weekend for Overton was too ill to stand at the bar. When he did appear on March 16, the warrant for his arrest was read. It was an instruction from Oliver dated January, 1655, to the Governor of Jersey to receive into his charge the bodies of Overton and others, and detain them securely until further orders, orders which were never received. Invited to have his say, Overton simply acknowledged it as a great mercy that after four years of imprisonment, following on fourteen years of service to the Parliament, he should be brought to the bar of that honorable House; he then asked to hear what the charges were against him so that he might answer them. He spoke without rancor in a subdued tone of fatigue and pain; he wished he might "have been torn in pieces by wild horses, than have endured this great torment. That had been but for a moment." And he humbly submitted his life and cause to the justice of the House.

After this exemplary forbearance no one could refuse mercy and justice. There was some question whether or not this had been a military arrest which did not require the more careful procedures of civil charges, but the strong consensus was that Overton's detention was a piece of high-handed tyranny which provided additional reason for this Parliament to set bounds to the power of any single person who might act as chief magistrate. Vane, as usual, stressed the ethical and legal points and directed the debate towards a conclusion. Parliament, he said, should not be accessory to continuing Overton in prison for another moment. Not only should they free him, they should also grant him reparation, for the warrant was unjust and illegal and should be so declared. It was so resolved and Vane then successfully moved that the case of Sir Thomas Armstrong, detained under the same warrant, should also be investigated.

But the horrors of the new tyranny got most fully aired by a petition from some seventy people, Royalists suspected of complicity in an uprising at Salisbury in 1654, who had been kept in prison without charges or trial for a year, and then "on a sudden (without the least provocation), snatched out of prison," driven through town by horse guards and, without even a chance to say farewell to their families, hurried on to Plymouth where they were herded on shipboard, locked up below deck with the horses, and after a delay of two weeks transported in the tropic heat to Barbados. There the master sold them as slaves. Without discrimination, they were all—old men of seventy, divines, officers, gentlemen—put to work grinding at the sugar mills, minding the furnaces, and digging. They were undernourished, and lodged in worse sties than hogs in England; and they were bought and sold, or attached for their masters' debts, and whipped at their masters' pleasure. On behalf of all these sufferers, the petitioners humbly remonstrated, and begged the Parlimant to examine by what arbitrary power free people should have been enslaved, and on what grounds they should be imprisoned and punished. They brought the atrocity near to the consciences of the members of Parliament by requesting that they take a course to curb unlimited power so that neither the members themselves nor other Englishmen might ever "come into this miserable place of torment."

But the petitioners were Cavaliers and that word still roused latent fears. Secretary Thurloe thought the petition out of order; it was, he said, a conspiracy of the Royalist party, and Colonel Birch agreed. Vane did not. It was not a Cavalierish business he thought, but a matter of the liberty of free-born people who were put under hatches, who saw no light during an entire voyage, and who were then sold for a hundred pounds. He was glad, Vane continued, that the Parliament had a sense and loathing of the tyranny of the late king and of all that tread in his steps to impose on liberty and property. Such persons as tread in Charles Stuart's steps, he repeated, whoever they may be, deserved the indignation of the members. He then reminded his listeners that such oppressions, if unchecked, might set a precedent by which England's best men could be subjected to the same arbitrary treatment. Government should be established upon a foundation of sound and just law which would limit the power of the executive to do such things to anyone, Cavalier or roundhead. Nevertheless, the petition was shuffled aside and never acted upon; but at least the petitioners were not imprisoned afresh for bringing in the petition, as some members recommended.

For two months now this futile Parliament had been arguing, and despite the organization and single-mindedness of the radical Republicans and the numerical strength of the Court party, nothing of importance had been settled. Vane had maneuvered skillfully and spoken with poise and self-control but he had won no major issue and now his patience was at the ragged edge. When on March 28 the discussion returned to the still unfinished business of the other House, he became snappish. He knew that the vote on peers would go against him, and so he was fighting a rearguard action. To the proposition that Commons should transact with the peers during the present Parliament Vane wished to add "and no longer." If this were not done, he said, the Parliament would have settled another fundamental constitutional question piecemeal, on the basis of expediency rather than principle. Once again, by failing to lay the proper foundation it was strengthening the government of the single person and whittling away the rights of the people. Already, he cried, Parliament had failed to protect the people's rights in the matters of the militia and the negative voice; already appointed members had been seated; the Parliament had not had the least care for the people and if they did not accept his amendment he was afraid that Commons would bind itself hand and foot and be unable thereafter to do anything for the common good. But the members, as Vane remarked, were weary of the debate; they were also a little weary of him although he never perceived it; and the resolution passed without his limiting phrase. Again he had lost.

The next day the debate dropped to new pettiness; if Commons were to transact with peers, would they stand bareheaded before these newly minted Lords? No politician, deeply committed, can lose on so many significant issues and remain unperturbed, and this issue exasperated Vane beyond endurance. Once again, he said that the important thing was the foundation, the constitution, which had not yet even been discussed. All the Parliament had done, in every instance, was surrender to expediencies, or in Vane's phrase, they had gone upon "prudential conclusions."

To hear all the works of this Parliament called prudential outraged Vane's enemies, who promptly attacked. Mr. Grove shouted, "I move that Sir Henry Vane be called to the bar for saying, you go upon prudentials. It is an arraigning of all your votes, and be a person never so great, I believe it would not be borne abroad; and why you should bear it here, I know not, be he never so wise."

"I second that he be called to the bar," said Mr. Bulkley. "Be he never so wise or great, it will not be borne. . . . I would have him called to the bar."

And Vane would doubtless have been summoned to defend himself at the bar and perhaps disciplined for impugning the integrity of the House (a Royalist spy gleefully reported that he was in danger of the Tower), had not Haselrig interposed, praying that the House might be "preserved from heats, and answer one another with reason." The two old revolutionaries could still understand and support one another. These are difficult and ambiguous times, Haselrig continued, when the status of the House itself is partly legal, partly prudential. "Our enemies are watchful. We ought not to quarrel with one another." And for once Sir Arthur's customary injection of his personal feelings into the debate touched the right tone for the moment:

I thank God, it is otherwise with me than when I came to the Long Parliament first. I could not then endure anybody that

differed from me in judgment; but I am now come to that spirit,
through the fear of God, and more discretion than I had then. We
must bear with one another in meekness.

Mr. Knightley quickly picked up the cue. "I move that heats be
forborne, and that you bear with one another." And though a new
bill was introduced, Sir Henry Vane spoke no more that day.

He continued to have little to say until the second reading of a bill
to limit all laws of excise and customs to a certain number of years
(yet to be determined) after the death of the present Protector. This
appeared to be a move to force re-examination of these imposts, but
since they were to remain unaltered during the Protector's lifetime,
it appeared to Vane rather an indefinite prolongation of dubiously
valid taxes; he remembered how, in 1643, Pym had proposed that
despised excise tax and how D'Ewes and others had argued that it
was against the liberties of the subject. Necessity had interposed
then and principles had been sacrificed to the exigencies of war. But
now there was no such exigency and Vane could speak his mind.

All you have done these two months is to settle all power without
you, but nothing is done for the people. In former Parliaments,
the grievances of the people were always heard first. This will
make the people that sent you, think you came not to do their
business, but the business of the single person.

I never knew the like, to settle this for life. It is to settle it to
perpetuation; for you can do no less for one than for another. I
wonder who dare levy the excise upon any law now in force,
unless you settle it by this law.

If the settlement be to settle tyranny and slavery, I hope you
will not give money to maintain it.

The old revolutionary with the dying cause was querulous now
and he had again overstepped in a phrase. The Protector's
sergeant-at-law, John Maynard, was ready to call him to account. "I
except the words, dare levy it. Who dare not levy it if there be a
law? For any judge to have done as much as has been said, I know
what you would do with him. . . . I look upon this bill as a redress
rather than an imposition." Maynard had a point: nothing had been
done to finance the present government, and the Protector could not

administer with air. But the animus in his speech is unmistakable; he remembered with all the clarity that bitterness provides how Vane had supported the suppression of the "Presbyterians," how he had "destroyed" Essex. As assistant to Charles II's attorney general he would soon indulge his deep grievances at Vane's trial. It is one more evidence that as Vane hewed to the line of the good old cause in this Parliament, he was making enemies among all parties, and standing more and more alone.

He was not alone, however, in being distressed at the failure of this Parliament to achieve anything but wrangling; in frustration the members agreed to call on God by appointing a day of fasting and humiliation to bring them together in harmony. A committee drafted a declaration and reported it to the House on Saturday, April 2; immediately the excise was forgotten as a new imbroglio developed. Vane energetically opposed the title and some of the clauses of the declaration. Since he was on the committee that had composed it, he must already have been voted down many times. He objected to the title because it was so phrased, he thought, as to imply unlimited recognition of both the Protector and the "other House," and the constitutionality of the *Petition and Advice*. In this, he was going over tediously familiar ground. But he also thought that the declaration involved coercion of the conscience, for ministers were required to read it from the pulpit, even the Scots. "Be careful how you oblige the Church of Scotland," Vane said. "I plead for liberty of conscience for Scotland, as well as for England. The Covenant was to care for the liberty of both alike." He was alluding, apparently, to those saving words he had inserted in it so many years ago. Most serious of all in this declaration, Vane thought, was a clause which sounded like an invitation to persecute and suppress the profaneness and heretical thought that were alleged to be widespread and unchecked. "That which makes these abominations worse," the clause read,

> and gives us the more cause to be humbled by them, is the too much remissness and connivance of the civil magistrates; to whom belong the care of maintaining God's public worship, honor, and purity of doctrine, as well as of punishing all sins against the second table, in permitting the growth of these abominations by suffering persons, under the abuse of liberty of conscience, to

disturb public ordinances, and to publish their corrupt principles and practises, to the seducing and infecting of others.

Vane was stunned. This clause was an invitation to the civil power to take over the control of matters of doctrine and spirit from the churches themselves. Even in the theocracy of Massachusetts, the magistrates dealt only with Mrs. Hutchinson's civil disturbances, leaving the church to discipline her for false doctrine. Even though he had changed his mind over the years about many things, Vane could never relinquish the principle which over-rode all others: that the conscience of man was not to be coerced, that the civil power must never restrict belief or enforce observance.

This clause, he thought, handed over one more power, the ultimate power, to the chief magistrate. "This imposition upon conscience is, I fear, the setting up of that which you always cried out against, and disowned for your cause." He probably saw now how hopelessly isolated he was, that there was nothing left for him but the wilderness; but if he witnessed truly, there would be shades and refreshments in that weary land, and so he cried out. "This is giving away your cause. All is lost. It is coercing the conscience."

Perhaps God heard but men did not; and though Vane spoke again, spoke very high, as Burton recorded in his *Diary*, the title was passed and then the declaration itself. Vane's last statements were no longer intended to influence voters; they were witnessings from one who had fought for the good old cause from the beginning and who would die with and for it at last. "You give away all at once, and may go home and say we have done for the single person's and others' turns, and nothing for the people."

Two and a half months had passed and still nothing had been done to relieve the financial straits of the government or to settle the principles of taxation, or even to find money for the outrageously neglected soldiers. The committee to examine finances did not report until April 7, and then they presented a picture of such huge debts and deficits and such crying needs that the Parliament was bewildered into more wrangling. They had approved sending a fleet into the Sound, but now they could not see where to find the money to pay for it. Times were hard and business bad. "It is a bad time to set up with a debt of two million and a half," said Vane. "A rot has got amongst the merchants. They break every day, ten at a time."

The whole financial picture, he believed, must be clarified by a Grand Committee that could recommend consistent and coordinated actions. And for once he agreed with Secretary Thurloe: the army must be relieved immediately. The first thing now, he said, is to "ascertain the three months pay to the army, till you can debate this fully. Be sure of that; else you may be in destruction before you are aware." But the army and navy remained unpaid.

The army, which was the seat of real power, had been patiently watching while the Parliament's incompetence seemed to grow with practice, while undercurrents of antimilitarism swelled to the surface in insulting tirades and even attacks on individual officers for actions they had performed under orders. Now the officers of the army prepared to defend themselves by exercising their power in political action.

Even the New Model Army had never been free of faction, and now there were three principal groups: the Commonwealth men, the adherents of the Protectorate, and the Wallingford House cabal, still headed by Generals Fleetwood and Desborough. As it became certain that Richard Cromwell could not command obedience and would not surrender his place as commander in chief, that Parliament was not only failing to find funds for the military but was fundamentally hostile to it, this cabal began maneuvering for power. First they sought out Ludlow, then Vane and Haselrig who were willing, for the common good, to sanction the meeting of a council of officers. This council devised a *Humble Representation and Petition* which was a rather vague challenge to Protector and Parliament, strong on grievances, weak on plans for specific action, but urging a revival of "the good old Cause." His Highness received it on April 6 and sent it on to the Parliament; the Commons acknowledged receiving it and put it aside, but they were sufficiently alarmed that they tried at once to check the army, one faction demanding that all officers swear that the king's execution was just, another asking that the officers swear allegiance to Richard. The officers then increased their pressures on both Richard and the Parliament. On April 18, evidently fearing that the army might turn upon them, the Commons voted two drastic resolutions: one forbade officers to hold meetings during a Parliamentary term without express permission of both Houses and the Protector; the other denied command to any man who refused to swear not to interfere with the free meetings of Parliament. Although Vane for years had opposed the military, he now spoke against these resolutions, for he thought it unwise to offend the military before Parliament had established its control of the militia, and perhaps also he thought this a dangerous time to offend the officers whose support was increasingly necessary to the good old cause. Without the military to oppose it, the movement for a restoration of the Stuarts would likely be irresistible. Parliament was anxious lest the soldiers should once more turn upon the House and eject some members or even that His Highness might dissolve it. Some thought that he had the power to do so, but Vane argued that he had not. Nobody knew for sure who had power to do what until the test came. And it came soon.

The Protector could see that he was being deserted not only by the Wallingford House officers, but also by the rank and file; there were rumbles of resentment that a man who had never seen combat should command a seasoned army. The showdown came on Thursday, April 21, when Fleetwood called a general rendezvous of the army at St. James, at the same time as Richard called one at Whitehall. Regardless of orders by officers loyal to Richard, men defected in large numbers to gather under Fleetwood's banner. The portents were unambiguous. That night General Desborough, a little more than kin and less than kind, gave Richard an ultimatum: the officers would protect and support him if he would dissolve Parliament; if not, they would dissolve it forcibly themselves and let him find what refuge and help he could. He held out against persuasions and threats for many hours, but in the middle of the night he signed the order of dissolution and became Tumbledown Dick. The day before, the Commons had been tardily and muddle-headedly debating about control of the militia, knowing that the militia was already out of control; it was said that on the morning of the twenty-second, before the order of dissolution was delivered, they had declared it treason to use force against a Parliament. Before being summoned by the Protector they called in absent members and locked the doors. It was later reported that Vane managed to address the chair in one last speech in which he passed judgment upon Oliver, inveighed against Richard, and praised the victory of English liberty won by the people's representatives. It may be true.

He and Haselrig had maneuvered cleverly and Vane had spoken often and well for the good old cause, for his obsessive dream of a holy commonwealth, but his only successes had been negative: he had often baffled or enraged the court spokesmen, discredited and weakened the Protectorate, and hastened its end. But, unknowing and ironically, he had also helped to create a climate in which the Stuart monarchy looked comparatively efficient and stable; he had brought a little closer what he dreaded most: the return of Charles.

The main achievement of this Parliament had been to shake chaos into an adumbration of form: parties were taking clearer shape and battle lines were forming. Soon Vane would assume more powerful and effective administrative functions, though too late for any hope of success; and Richard would quietly disappear. When he abdicated, his debts were paid and he was generously pensioned off to live a long, placid, and contented life as a landscape water-colorist, far from all alarms. He was not much missed personally but his function was, and a power vacuum was created.

Though the generals immediately cleared the army of the most rabid Cromwellian officers, they did not succeed in unifying it, nor could they conceive a satisfactory mode of governing the three kingdoms. To maintain the everyday business of the economic, legal, and diplomatic life of a country it was necessary to have some responsible administrative implements.

By May 5 an agreement was reached to recall that portion of the Long Parliament that had still been sitting when Oliver Cromwell ended it in 1653, and reinstate it with instructions to frame a new constitution of government. This was what Vane wanted; this was what Richard's Parliament had denied him. At last it seemed that the first instrument of revolution would be restored, and he would have one final chance to establish a legal and constitutional base on which the good old cause might forever rest.

17

The Rump Sits Again
(May 7–October 13, 1659)

When the call for the surviving members of the old Rump to assemble at Westminster had been answered on May 7, it was found that there were four less than a quorum; from the debtor's prison two men were thereupon released and from the law courts were drafted two more. A Royalist pamphlet listed the members: among others there were hare-brained Haselrig and leveling Ludlow; that chaste cock-sparrow, Henry Marten; Colonel Ayre, whose name filled his head; and "single-hearted, preaching Sir Henry Vane now become old Sir Harry." Speaker Lenthall, physically feeble and even more doddering of mind, led the procession of forty-two members to the House of Commons, marching double file, for all the world, said the Royalists, like animals entering the ark. However, they did not enter into any such secure refuge. After suitable humility and prayer, the Parliament uttered a declaration in harmony with the petition the army had submitted, promising to establish a free commonwealth without "a single person," to continue the reformation of government, and to ensure that the ministry and magistracy would be filled by godly men.

In comparison to Richard's Parliament, this one was experienced, efficient, and even somewhat unified—Colonel Pride had seen to that long ago. But though the members liked to refer to themselves as "the Representative," they were even less representative of the people of the three nations than Richard's Parliament had been. Although the Long Parliament had once been elected according to the best procedures of its time, its complexion had been altered by time and mortality even before Pride hacked most of it away, leaving what was contemptuously called the Rump. It had become still more the organ of a faction when Cromwell had dissolved it. Now of that real fag end of a Parliament, some 200 were living; there were about ninety survivors of that junta which Cromwell had dissolved. Of those only some forty had come forward and most of them had long been out of touch with their constituencies. Although an effort was made to enlarge the membership, attendance at any one meeting was never more than eighty, and it was usually much less. What the Rump did have was the mystique of authority; since the Long Parliament had decreed it could not be dissolved without its own consent and since that consent had never been given, Cromwell had only dispersed the Parliament, not destroyed it. And it must be said in favor of the Rumpers that they did not think of themselves as governing in perpetuity, for they set a date in 1660 after which, the new constitution being completed, new elections would be held. But meanwhile they refused to enlarge their body by receiving any of those members whom Colonel Pride had excluded as unsuitable, and many of those who claimed the right to sit were barred from entering the House on the grounds that they had not sat since 1648 and had not sworn to support the Commonwealth. Notable among those barred were Sir George Booth, who then turned active Royalist, and the fearless, earless, William Prynne who, if he could not guide the Parliament from within, kept it alert with a swarm of gadfly satirical pamphlets.

The first necessary business was to set up an executive, and therefore a Committee of Safety was appointed to handle urgent matters until the larger Council of State could be selected. This committee, constituted with the strong Republican nucleus of Vane, Haselrig, and Ludlow, was given power to keep the peace and exact obedience from all officers, soldiers, and ministers of justice, but it was strictly limited to sit for only eight days. The committee took immediate measures for stability: on the seventh day they decreed that no one could hold a place of trust except those who gave testimony of their "love to all the people of God," and of their loyalty to the Commonwealth. On May 11, the committee ordered a month's pay for enough auxiliary troops to ensure peace within the nation. They also gave orders that in any attempted disturbance, disaffected persons should be seized and secured along with their horses and arms. One result of this firm grasp on order was that the uprisings of Royalists and disaffected army men which many feared (and some predicted) did not occur. The new regime of the old Rump began with as little disturbance as Richard Cromwell's had.

The Committee of Safety sat a few days beyond its appointed life and was replaced on May 19 with a Council of State composed of twenty-one members of Parliament, and ten others. The triad of Republican leaders, Vane, Ludlow, and Haselrig, again led all others in the vote and for a time dominated the council. Of the ten nonmembers, one was to be a Scotsman and, through Vane's influence, his old friend and enemy Archibald Johnston of Wariston was chosen, even though he had opposed the return of the Rump. For Vane observed that in the House of Peers Wariston had also opposed the recognition of Richard; besides, Vane had outmaneuvered that inexorably serious and egotistical Presbyterian in drafting the covenant and perhaps he could get round him again. And he did. Wariston was so flattered to be recommended by Vane that he pulled over his eyes the wool of his own self-esteem, and when Vane later opposed him, he at first could hardly believe that Sir Henry was serious.

Even though many conflicting interests were represented on the council, it turned out to be an efficient as well as a hard-working body, and it gave scope to Vane's administrative powers as the self-defeating talk-fest of Richard's Parliament never had. Even Clarendon conceded Vane to be "much the wisest man" of the Republicans. At the very time when millenarian worms were aerating his brain, he was at his shrewd and sensible best as practical politician and administrator. He shared with Haselrig and Wariston the honor of chairing the council most frequently, and it was he who prepared and submitted many of the definitive reports on the navy about which his knowledge was exhaustive. Also, he served on many of the sensitive committees such as the committee to approve and appoint officers of the army and navy, and the committee to manage domestic and foreign intelligence, a sort of "secret service" committee especially concerned with detecting Royalist plots. He was also given the management of foreign affairs and according to the French ambassador he was "the principal minister in the present government" which now aimed principally to consolidate its internal affairs and to live on good terms with all neighboring states.

While the foreign policy of the Rump was prudent and generally successful, as soon as attention shifted to domestic affairs, its surface harmony began to crack: the godly Commonwealth which all agreed to institute was easier to approve than to construct, for each faction conceived it differently. The Republicans broke apart over three principal issues: the relation of civil to military powers, the nature and limits of popular representation, and the relations of civil power to individual consciences in religion, which in practice meant setting the limits of toleration. And through all of the problems additional friction was generated by the impossibility of raising the necessary money without levying and collecting more taxes. A Royalist spy wrote that "the whole year's tax is suddenly to be levied, which probably will open the eyes as well as the purses of the stupid nation." And, as often happens, decisions that appeared most conducive to harmony turned out to be the most disruptive.

One of these was the Act of Indemnity and Pardon presented on May 23. The need for it was real: whenever a new government assumes power after turmoil, it must wipe out guilt for acts performed in the confusion of conflict, lest men fearing reprisals should be driven to new violence and thus perpetuate vengeance and countervengeance. But the provisions of this act were so ambiguous that it aroused much opposition. It granted pardon for all acts, however illegal or contrary to the interests of the Commonwealth, that were performed under demonstrable sanction of the Protector or a reputed Parliament. The army saw this as dubious indemnification for soldiers, since demonstrable sanction was in almost every case open to interpretation; the question of paying arrears in salaries and allowances was also to be judged by Parliament. So many things were left open to interpretation that Lambert bitterly protested that the bill left the army at the mercy of the Parliament, and he could not see why the Parliament should not, with equal justice, be rather at the mercy of the army.

The army soon realized that the instrument it had placed in power refused to be in any way subservient to it, but was rather asserting its total control over all things military, as Vane had argued it ought to do, both in his *Healing Question* and his Parliamentary debates. He was one of the commission of seven men who appointed officers in the army; that commission was appointed on May 13 and made its first appointments on that same day, as Vane would one day have occasion to remember. By the end of the month the new

Council of State of the Rump had reorganized the military high command, with Fleetwood as commander in chief of the armies of England and Scotland, and John Lawson as Vice Admiral and Commander of the Fleet. But these commanders were denied the usual power to appoint, remove, and discipline the officers under their command. Even the disciplinary functions of the courts martial were arrogated to Parliament, and all appointments and promotions were to be made by that seven-man commission, on which Fleetwood and other officers sat as well as Vane.

Vane thus found himself in an uncomfortable dilemma between conflicting imperatives. He had opposed the military in Pride's Purge and had courageously broken with Oliver over the military dictatorship which he despised. But the Rump, as everyone knew, sat at the pleasure of the officers without whose support the cause was lost. For the good of the cause, Vane knew that the military must be subservient to the representative of the people, and he found himself at once exercising the Parliament's control over the army and trying to keep that control from becoming so aggressive and arrogant as to press the officers to revolt. Never had he walked a narrower and more dangerous edge.

He began to break with his old ally, Haselrig, who could not understand that the Rump could not exist without the army now that the Republicans were a divided and diminishing minority in a country that, weary of turnings and overturnings, was sentimentally hankering after the good old days of the monarchy. Vane therefore opposed or softened bills that were obnoxious to the army; perhaps if he could hold this mercurial alliance together for a while, he could complete the constitution which would provide the stable foundation for the new Commonwealth. Haselrig, dogmatically assured, quarreled with Vane and refused to make any concessions to the army, even the harmless one of tact.

For example, a bill was brought in requiring soldiers to abjure Charles Stuart and swear fidelity to the Commonwealth without a "single person" or a House of Lords. Vane opposed it; Haselrig favored it. The issue bred great heats and divisions in the House, said Wariston, and the argument lasted a week. Some members jeered at Haselrig and Vane, saying that honest men might come into their own when the thieves fell out. Now even these two long and ardent allies in the good old cause were becoming open enemies.

Vane and Haselrig had also disagreed furiously over how representation was to be defined in the new constitution. On this point Sir Henry was being pushed into unfortunate positions by political realities. Through his lifetime, he had gradually narrowed his definition of "the People"; now he was saying that only those should be allowed to vote for the constitutional convention who were adherents of the good old cause, who believed in a commonwealth, and he was rapidly reducing the numbers of the latter to those who were "truly" godly. He was trying to equate the electorate and the spiritual seed. Haselrig held more closely to the egalitarianism of the Levellers and so on this issue Vane quarrelled with him, with Sir Henry Neville and others, over whether *melior au major pars* should govern.

As Vane became disillusioned about the intrinsic wisdom of the people at large, so he was also coming to understand the possible tyranny of a single House; he seemed now to be exploring sympathetically the idea of a small and choice elective body like a senate to balance and check the Commons. He was becoming less certain of what would actually work and, without surrendering his fundamental principles as theory, was more receptive to temporary expedients as alternatives to total defeat.

Vane's Royalist enemies thought his views both muddled and arrogant. Letters received by the exiled Charles' Secretary of State, Sir Edward Nicholas, biased as they are, nevertheless express the growing hostility towards Vane before which he was later to stand isolated and defenseless. Nicholas heard on June 17 that

> some of the grandees are for a general comprehensive state of all men of all religions; but Sir Henry Vane is still for the gifted men alone, and those only such as his own holiness shall deem so.

On June 24, another writer put it even more harshly:

> Sir Henry Vane looks upon the nation as unacquainted with its own good and unfit to be trusted with power, lest they abuse it to their own and his ruin, and therefore he would have some few refined spirits (and those of his own nomination) sit at helm of State together with the Council till the people be made familiar with a Republic and in love with it, that is till he ceases to be. . . .

Vane's difficulties during this year stemmed in part from his attempts to reconcile stubborn day-to-day political changes with his Republican political theories on the one hand, and on the other with his religious convictions, which had become more chiliastic as the Rule of the Saints grew imminent. Even the mildest of millenarians knew from the scriptures that on the great day all but the elect would be rejected if not summarily destroyed, and although Vane never assented to the Fifth Monarchy idea that military violence was the right way to prepare for the Prince of Peace, he apparently feared that time was running too short for the slow process he had advocated in *Healing Question* by which, through meekness and fear of the Lord, the "great body" might again be set in harmony and tune. Consequently there was now a certain irritability and hastiness of temper, an uncharacteristic contentiousness which alienated many of his old friends and allies.

In planning for the new constitution, the one issue on which Vane remained consistent was that of toleration. Again he parted company with Haselrig and contended sharply with Laird Wariston. His lifetime repugnance for religious forms, formulas, and hierarchical organizations reinforced his belief that the civil magistracy had no right to control any matter of conscience or spirit; as a millenarian he also knew that a holy commonwealth of Saints, ready to receive the Lord Jesus and fit to be ruled by him, could never be developed within an enforced state church or even alongside it; that the commonwealth must be worked out voluntarily by spiritual saints guided by the inner light, whose efforts would move harmoniously together in the right direction. Wariston still believed that the Presbyterian church was the only channel of God's grace and instrument of His will, and was still striving to make that church the establishment in both England and Scotland as he had intended when he helped frame the covenant. He still thought the Scots had been cheated when Vane inserted his pestilential phrase in that otherwise decent document, and now, as Vane continually opposed him on matters of religious toleration, he feared that he might be outwitted again. In July he heard that Vane had made some changes in the draft of a new Bill of Union, on which they had worked together, before he submitted it to the House. "I fear *latet anguis in herba* [a snake lurks in the grass]," he confided to his diary, and dramatized to himself his own ingenuousness: "Pity my simplicity preyed upon by subtilty of others. In dealing with nimble, witty, untender men diffidence is necessary to a statesman." But perhaps men so smugly confident as to believe that the Word of God casts no broader shadow than the Presbyterian synod get cheated at their own invitation. The debates on these issues were hot, and all the desire for the foundation stone of a constitution produced no way to achieve one.

Meanwhile the reciprocal sniping of army and Parliament continued until the Parliament realized that they needed the army—and at once. The committee to manage intelligence received evidence that the Royalists were laying an elaborate plot, involving coordinated uprisings in several large cities, to bring the king over from the continent, hide him, and after disposing of Parliament by a military coup, restore the monarchy. A council of Royalist leaders known as the "Sealed Knot" had been functioning since 1654; it had realized that any premature and unsuccessful uprising would set back Charles' cause rather than advance it, and when the Rump was restored they held the activists closely in check. Now, preparing to take advantage of the divisions in Parliament and the army, they were carefully estimating strengths, gathering arms, and scheduling simultaneous seizures of key cities. Through the instrumentality of spies, their plans were being betrayed to the Council of State as fast as they were made. In the face of this serious challenge, the army and the Parliament and the factions within both Parliament and army for a time composed their differences and made thorough preparations to oppose the plot. Near at hand they took precautions against uprisings in the city of London, and they assigned officers to prepare troops and lead them to the centers of projected rebellion. Late in July, many of the ringleaders were arrested before they could strike and it looked as if the rebellion might be scotched. Sir George Booth, however, went ahead with his insurrection in Cheshire as planned. Apparently there was a general failure of communications, for the council seemed to have been surprised by Booth's initial success and Booth seemed unaware of the general collapse of the rebellion. Charles and his party, learning of the debacle, had turned back before they could even embark for England.

Booth set his plans in motion on July 31, first issuing two of his three propaganda broadsides appealing for volunteers to fight for a free Parliament. The Royalists were now the crusaders for a free Parliament—but then ironies had long ceased to astound anyone. A free Parliament, it was almost certain, would declare for the king. Booth marched with the Earl of Egerton to Chester, whose citizens were friendly, and took over the city; Sir Thomas Middleton marched his army from Wales and joined Booth and they soon controlled all of Cheshire. The startled Parliament took hasty and drastic measures to oppose him. On August 5, John Lambert was given extraordinary powers as commander in chief to direct military operations in the six northern counties, to summon aid as he thought necessary, and to empower men he considered loyal to raise more troops; General Desborough was dispatched to the western counties, and Admiral Lawson to block Charles by sea. Close to home, in order to control the dominantly Royalist London which threatened an uprising to meet the royal invader, Parliament ordered three regiments of volunteers to be recruited. On August 10, one of them was assigned to Sir Henry Vane: he was ordered to recruit and equip the men and to select the officers. Sir Henry was understandably reluctant to accept a commission as colonel, for although he had long recognized that armies were essential arms of government, he had never desired any part in one himself, and had tried to hold himself aloof from violence. In this crisis, however, he had reasons for accepting it; for one thing, he knew that in these sick days the hallowed instrument of revolution existed only on sufferance of the army. Besides, it was not the military junta that was appointing him, but the Parliament, which was thereby exercising that control over the militia which he always insisted it should have. Finally, he was assured that the commission would be only honorary and titular, and on this understanding he accepted it. Booth was extending his conquests in Cheshire unchecked, and Vane set about recruiting promptly.

Since he had never spent a day in the field, Vane must have been appointed because of his power to attract volunteers among the religious extremists; indeed, volunteers were invited to name their own officers and it was a group of the sectarian left who named Vane. Reporting to the royal government-in-exile, Secretary Nicholas of course put the worst face on the facts:

> The rebels fortify their impious cause by arming madmen. They are raising in London three regiments of Quakers,

Anabaptists, and Brownists, called congregational men, to be
under Sir Henry Vane, Major Skippon, and White, a former
Quaker from New England.

In accepting this military commission, however, Vane was
putting himself in an ambiguous and embarrassing position in which
his conscience drew some pretty fine lines: he stood as commander
of the regiment, but he steadfastly refused to issue any orders, even
when his subordinate officers pressed him to do so. And he laid
himself open to the contempt and hostility of his enemies, who
would soon charge that he was actually waging war against the
rightful king. Fortunately, it turned out that his conscience was
spared the crucial test of being ordered to lead men into battle to
kill.

Meanwhile, Lambert had marched northward rapidly and after
receiving reinforcements, advanced to meet Booth near Northwick
on the eighteenth of August. There Booth's casually organized and
inadequately equipped men were defeated by Lambert's veterans,
with very few casualties. Booth escaped disguised as a woman and
was not captured until the twenty-fourth, when he was betrayed by
his whiskers. A barber summoned to an inn to shave some of Booth's
comrades became suspicious when they tried to purchase one of his
razors; the insufficiently feminized commander was arrested and
brought back to London to face imprisonment and a good deal of
lewd lampooning.

Meanwhile, on August 15 Parliament ordered that two companies
be added to Vane's foot regiment, that the work be done quickly,
and that blank commissions be prepared for the officers he would
select. But on the same day news reached Westminster that
disturbances in some counties had been checked, and that a
conspiracy of London apprentices had been exposed and prevented.
After news came that Booth had been defeated, Vane was appointed
to a committee to consider raising and ordering militia to ensure the
continued security of the state. Once Booth was safely confined in
the Tower and the emergency was over, Vane was selected, along
with Haselrig and Salwey, to interrogate the defeated officer and
report what they learned. Vane had once been very harsh on
traitors, but the Rump was lenient now, and they soon allowed
Booth to be released on bail. He was never punished for his

insurrection, and later the restored King Charles rewarded him with 10,000 pounds and a baronetcy.

During the emergency, the association of Vane's name with the Fifth Monarchists was embarrassingly revived. Two months earlier a letter from London had told of 5,000 Fifth Monarchy men who met in Sussex and dispersed after eight hours of debate. According to the writer, Harrison was to be their general and Vane their chancellor. Under this formidable leadership, they had decided to prepare for the coming of Christ with fire and sword. "We daily expect a massacre," says the writer. Actually his letter had no better source of information than a broadsheet which said that the Fifth Monarchy was ready to fire London, that Sir Henry Vane was "chief in the design." Beware Tuesday next, it concluded; "we say beware." Since that time the Fifth Monarchists had made something of a nuisance of themselves with petitions and declarations, especially demanding the abolition of tithes. The Parliament, however, could not see a better or even another way to maintain the ministry, which needed money however godly it was. Under pressure of the Royalist threat, the Fifth Monarchy men joined in the common effort; many of them enlisted in Vane's volunteer regiment and remained in it until it was dissolved. However much Vane tried to dissociate himself from the violent wing of the movement, his enemies were convinced to the last that he was playing the hypocrite, secretly fomenting their plots and planning to lead the great insurrection they were believed to be preparing. Vane was probably glad to have the fierce, godly men supporting the cause, but the hate and fear they inspired in the Royalists were bound to touch him.

Once the Royalist threat was past, Parliament turned again to settling the government, and on September 8, appointed a committee to work out the form. But all efforts came to nothing, as unsympathetic Royalists perceived, watching as they were for any change in the political tides. Secretary Nicholas had reported in July that Vane was "the giddy head of the confused sectaries," and had "talked himself to jealousies and contempt in the House. He is outvoted by the Presbyterian members and sometimes for no other reason but he shall take notice he is outvoted." By September Nicholas was shrewdly predicting that Parliament would end soon and Charles be welcomed back; Vane and Haselrig had fallen out and both, he said, were now accused of being papists. (It was becoming fashionable to charge the men of inner light with papistry because they held that a man speaking under the influence of the spirit was "infallible.") One thing was certain: the confusion was deepening.

> Those that now rule in Westminster are so very contradictory in their opinions concerning the government which they are endeavoring to settle that it will be impossible for them to agree upon anything. So if His Majesty can procure any considerable assistance in this juncture, he may easily effect his business.

And soon after, Nicholas came even closer to the mark: "The Parliament is in a very unstable condition. Most think it will be shortly dissolved, or at least purged by Lambert and the army."

And now the struggle between Parliament and the army, held in abeyance during Booth's rebellion, came to a head, for though the victorious Lambert was voted a generous gift, the members denied him the permanent rank of major-general which he believed he had earned. His response was to delay in the North and consolidate his strength. His officers met at Derby and drew up a new petition. In order to secure the civil and religious liberties of the nation, it asked for punitive action against neutrals as well as against active supporters of Booth. It requested further that appointments to the rank of general be made permanent, a move which would deny Parliament its most effective means of controlling the army. Lambert was now the most powerful officer in England, so powerful that many feared that he was plotting to realize his once disappointed ambition to become Lord Protector. To quiet such suspicions and to unify the army against Parliament and reduce faction in it, his officers were willing to name as commander in chief not Lambert, but Fleetwood, with Lambert as his second-in-command, Desborough in charge of horse, and Monk of foot. While appearing to relinquish power, Lambert was actually increasing it, for though Fleetwood had been valiant in battle, he was an emotional, unstable man whom Lambert could easily manipulate; yet with his conspicuous godliness, Fleetwood was very "popular with all the praying part of the army" and at the same time enjoyed the confidence of Parliament. His integrity was unquestioned, but he could not be depended on for decisive action in a crisis, for under pressure he was prone to dissolve into prayer. During the hectic weeks to follow, he became more and more an unhappy figurehead as Lambert quietly exercised the power.

But the man who was soon to occupy the key position in this quadrumvirate and open the door to the king was George Monk, commander of the army in Scotland. Like Lambert, he was a superb soldier and a shrewd manipulator, quite unburdened by religion and unblinded by the inner light. Both were thorough realists who enjoyed the trust and loyalty of their troops, and both were strong Commonwealthsmen. But Monk was no doctrinaire, nor was he given to making public pronouncements that would hamper his freedom of decision: he made his decisions day by day as changing situations required. But though his intentions were mysterious and his actions inconsistent and surprising, he did not get a reputation like Vane's for slyness and dissimulation. Perhaps his taciturnity and directness of manner belied subtlety—"a dull, heavy man," Samuel Pepys thought him.

Lambert tried to get Monk's support for his petition but Monk held aloof and refused to approve it. While Lambert, newly arrived in London, was still rounding up signatures, Fleetwood showed the petition to Haselrig who erupted in anger and wanted to send Lambert to the Tower. The House was more temperate; it failed to pass a motion to denounce the petition, but the members resolved that it would endanger the Commonwealth to increase the number of general officers, and decided that further debate should be secret. Feelings went on smoldering.

Meanwhile, the House was disbanding many of the regiments that had been mustered against Booth, though for some reason they left Vane's regiment untouched. The constitution was still unsettled; they were snagged on the question of religion, in which Vane was opposed by both Haselrig and Wariston. The latter, being strong for "ordinances," was, he said, at his wit's end and could not tell what to wish, for Haselrig's faction was more for ordinances and against Quakers, but less for godly men. Vane, on the other hand, was strong for godly men but despised ordinances. And at the Wallingford House meetings, Wariston said, Haselrig was still "asserting the absolute powers of Parliament," while the officers refused to be subjected to any arbitrary government and Fleetwood was prayerfully "urging them to sleep upon the whole business." By October 4, Vane and Salwey were still trying to persuade the Parliament to "comply with the current," and not to break with the army for that, said Wariston, "would be their ruin." Haselrig was talking abusively and the officers were ready to call him to account for "accusing the Airmy wrongously." Beneath all the bickering, Wariston perceived that the bottom of the question was whether the military or civil power should be supreme and whether political power should reside in "the sprite of the nation" or only in some select party.

The first of these questions broke out into the open the next day when Desborough brought a new petition from the officers, humbly phrased in its preamble, but defiant in its thrust and assertive of military rights. Vane tried to temper the fury of the ensuing debates until Parliament heard, on October 11, that Lambert and his fellows were trying to suborn officers who were loyal to Parliament to sign the petition and bring pressure on their men to sign it also. With extraordinary speed, the House then passed an act that voided all "patents, grants, acts and ordinances," passed by Parliament since April 19, 1653, which had not been specifically approved by the present Parliament. At the same time they declared it treasonous to levy, collect, or receive any money contribution whatsoever without their express consent. This drastic act not only invalidated previous appointments and traditional rights of the army, but cut off any powers it had of collecting money.

On the next day, October 12, the question came to a crisis. One of Lambert's letters, signed by him and eight other officers and not intended for the eyes of Parliament, was brought into the House and read aloud. At this clear evidence, the members dropped even the appearance of conciliation: they cashiered all nine of the officers and vested control of the army in a commission of seven men, including Fleetwood but none of the nine dismissed officers. They then ordered three loyal regiments of horse to stand guard in Westminster.

Lambert retaliated with equal speed and firmness; he decided to kick the Rump out. By the next morning he and the other eight cashiered officers had assembled their regiments and blockaded the Houses of Parliament by land and by water. They invited the Parliamentary horse guard to defect and join them, and many did;

Colonel Okey's whole regiment deserted to Lambert, leaving only two diminished but faithful regiments guarding the House. The two forces drew up facing each other, "even to push of pike," but neither side attacked, and thus they stood all day. When Speaker Lenthall came to open the session, his coach was courteously turned back, and no member of Parliament was allowed through the blockade. For hours the two opposing forces heckled each other, argued back and forth, and exchanged deserters, with the greater flow of men going to Lambert's side. At nightfall when word came that the Council of State had ordered all troops back to quarters, both sides dispersed joyfully, for "God in mercy kept them from engaging, so that no blood was spilt." And a euphemism was coined for the occasion: Lambert, it was said, had successfully "interrupted" the Parliament.

The Council of State continued to sit until the twenty-fifth, settling unfinished and routine business, but the Parliament was dead and the ruler of England was now Lambert's army. And Sir Henry Vane had to choose between defunct authority and unauthorized power.

18

The Army's Interruption
(October 13–December 26, 1659)

The "insolent usurpation" by the army, according to Lucy Hutchinson, so changed the hearts of the people that now the whole nation began to set their eyes on the king. The army officers, she believed, were ruling arbitrarily from Wallingford House "to the joy of all enemies of Parliament," and to the amazement and shock of all men that had "any honest interest." And during this usurpation, when all men were feverishly devising new governments, some honorable members of former Parliaments, "I know not through what fatality of the times," fell in with the officers and assisted them in their arbitrary rule.

One of those honorable members was Sir Henry Vane, for whom the army's interruption precipitated the decisive moral crisis of his last years, forcing him into an intolerable dilemma. Three times now he had opposed the army when it had violated Parliament by force: he had initially refused to sit in Pride's purified Parliament; he had withdrawn from public life after Cromwell had forcibly terminated the Long Parliament in 1653; and when Desborough had forced Richard Cromwell to dissolve his Parliament he had execrated the action. But now, it appeared, he had thrown in his lot with Lambert, who had violated Parliament as illegally and arbitrarily as Cromwell once had. As a result, Vane was now more terribly—and sadly—isolated then ever before. Through the years he had successively lost the friendship of the Scots, of the City, of Cromwell and the men who had supported Cromwell's government; but he had always stood fast for the Long Parliament, at least that part of it which was allowed to sit. Now the members of the ejected Rump, too, despised him with an irrational hatred, for they thought he had conspired with the military in the overthrow of that sacred instrument of the revolution.

But to say that Vane threw his support to the army is much too simple. He still believed that Parliament held authority as the sanctioned representative body, but he also realized that the pathetic handful that had constituted the Rump were splintered and the factions mutually destructive. Without the support of the army that had put them in power, Vane knew they could not have survived for a day. Too, his former ally, Haselrig, now classified as a Presbyterian-Independent, led a Presbyterian majority which was trying, Vane believed, to suppress freedom of conscience. And so the army endeavored "to keep fair" with him and with Ludlow and Salwey by making "large protestations" which undoubtedly included freedom for the sects. Clarendon, too, believed that this new Presbyterian ascendancy was the thing that made Vane "less troubled at the violence that was used (though he would never advise it)" and willing to work with those who might provide a "hinge to hang the government upon." Further, as Vane saw it, he had tried to prevent the Parliament from committing suicide by passing vindictive acts against the army, but such men as the "rigid and inflexible" Haselrig had not listened. The interruption, therefore, was in some degree the Parliament's fault, for they had forced the issue and dared the officers to act. Lambert's retaliation, though strong, was nonetheless understandable.

Now Vane faced the final dilemma: the Rump would have none of him and he could not in good conscience act as agent of the army. He could once again retire to the country to write and preach, but he felt with deep conviction that if he did the cause would be finally and completely lost; he, too, was aware of the great swell of sentiment for Charles Stuart.

So rather than surrender to an earthly king when the coming of the heavenly one was so near, Vane decided, in the confusion of the present anarchy, to try to sustain the ghost of a representative authority. He was willing to listen, to half-believe, when the officers promised to maintain military rule only long enough to formulate a constitution, that elusive foundation stone which would embody freedom of worship; then arrangements would be made for a new election and whatever Parliament was returned would be guided and bounded at last by an inviolable document. Towards these ends Vane was willing to work, and so, in the last and final irony, he found himself collaborating with the military dictatorship which he had always so roundly despised.

He felt obliged to carry out his duties as Commissioner of the Navy just as if Parliament were in session, for the Parliament had nominated him to the office; similarly, as long as the Rump's Council of State continued to meet, he met with it. When the army set up an interim government in the form of a Committee of Safety around a nucleus of ten officers and ten civilians, Vane was nominated. Unlike Ludlow, he did not refuse outright to serve on it, but along with Major Salwey, he placed himself in the ambiguous position of meeting with them but not acting with them. At his trial he would explain his relationship with the army administration. He had occasion, he said,

> to be daily conversant with the members of the *Committee of Safety* (whereof my self, with others that would not accept, were named) yet I perfectly kept myself disinterested from all those actings of the Army, as to any consent or approbation of mine (however in many things by way of discourse, I did not decline converse with them) holding it my duty to penetrate as far as I could into their true Intentions and Actions, but resolving within myself to hold true to my Parliamentary trust, in all things wherein the Parliament appeared to me to act for the safety and good of the Kingdom; however I was mis-interpreted and judged by them, as one that rather favored some of the Army and their power.

This statement is corroborated by a contemporary report that though he and Salwey met with the Committee of Safety they were signing nothing. Vane had chosen to attempt to rescue the good old cause at the moment of its death through the only existing instruments of government. He seems to have undertaken his new role in a sanguine mood: he told Salwey and Wariston that he looked upon the present dispensation "as an introduction to the glorious appearance of the Kingdom of God, and so calling much for faith and expectation of its approach." Wariston took a characteristically gloomier and more realistic view; to him "it looks judgmentlyk to the nation for their provocation."

Vane's opponents and enemies saw it all very differently. Bulstrode Whitelocke, like Vane, was asked by the officers to serve on the Committee of Safety. Although he was most dubious, he was persuaded when Desborough told him that Vane and Salwey were on it and that they designed to overthrow magistracy, ministry, and the law. Whitelocke continues,

> I knew the purpose of Vane and others to be the lessening of the power of the laws and so to change them and the magistracy, ministry, and government of the nation, as might be of dangerous consequence to the peace and rights of my country.

Vane seemed to his enemies to be proposing a highly restrictive form of Republican theocracy. They were perceiving at last that behind all of his many designs and maneuvers through the years there had been one constant purpose: to bring about the rule of the spiritual seed; to take the government from the twice-born and give it to the thrice-born who, in a few years, would be Christ's ministers in the Heavenly Jerusalem that earth was to become.

Whitelocke's revelations also point up the fact that the officers were playing a double game or perhaps were merely furthering their own factions. Whichever it was, they sent different men and different messages to Vane and Whitelocke. They promised their civilian front what they had to in order to retain their services and their names. And, too, even some of the officers still believed that they were about to build a holy commonwealth.

Enemies less moderate than Whitelocke thought Vane was hypocritically conspiring to elevate himself to power through Lambert, whom he would use as his puppet. There was some basis for this belief for Vane was planning to marry his son to Lambert's daughter, a union his enemies considered dynastic in intent. The preparations for a festive wedding were interrupted by the downfall of the two fathers.

But rather than plotting for personal power, Vane seems to have been making a last, desperate attempt to create a commonwealth fit to receive King Jesus; his only course now was to conciliate and compromise, to act as ambassador between factions, to rally what pitifully little support there was left. But this course of action only evoked suspicion and raised memories of all the other designs he had been a part of over the past twenty years. So Haselrig believed he had betrayed the Parliament; the army distrusted him because he placated the Parliamentary party and refused to act with the officers; both Presbyterians and Royalists considered him to be the greatest single enemy. Because he was opposed to tithes, the clergy assailed him; because he advocated reform and regulation of law and its practice, the lawyers mistrusted and despised him. In fact, representatives of lawyers and clergymen made a secret treaty with the Wallingford House party, one term of which was that they "were not to hearken any longer to the advice of Sir Henry Vane." Nevertheless Vane continued to function in a hopeless situation, refusing to let himself altogether lose the final hope that through him God's will might yet somehow be done.

An opportunity to which he could respond without qualms offered itself early in November when he was appointed to the commission for the establishment of a constitution; he was one of the subcommittee of six who were to draft a model of government to submit to the larger commission, though, as Bordeaux reported to Cardinal Mazarin, he did not "publicly engage in other matters of state." The subcommittee were under pledge to establish a form that would "best suit and comport with a free state and commonwealth, without a single person, kingship, or House of Peers." But from there on thought was free.

In this age of proliferating utopias, all the theorists, sound or cranky, renewed their hopes that their model governments, or at least some of their pet provisions, might be adopted. The best known and most important of these theorists was Sir James Harrington, who had sketched out his ideal government in a utopian romance, *Oceana*, in 1656; more recently he had published polemical pamphlets about it. His plan held that since the base of government was economic, voting should be restricted by property qualifications. Elections would be conducted by ballot, and members of the two Houses of Parliament would be so rotated that one-third would be replaced at each election, thus ensuring continuity in the body while obviating self-perpetuation. Vane, who had been appointed to a committee to determine the qualification of the members of the new Parliament, seriously considered Harrington's rather intricate system, and approved a good deal of it, especially its godly basis. In a public letter to Harrington, he wrote,

Where (as you all along most deservedly have regard unto) the Foundation of Government shall be laid so firm and deep as in the Word of God, bottomed upon that Corner-Stone, the Lord Jesus, there is a heavenly balance to be met with, which keeps all even.

But he could not share Harrington's trust in the people at large, corrupted by the sin of Adam, unable to subjugate their self-seeking impulses to the will of God. Vane therefore argued that for the present, voting for the legislatures should be restricted not to property holders but to men of assured godliness and fidelity to the cause of a commonwealth until

the depraved, corrupted and self-interested will of man, in the great body which we call the people, being once left to its own free motion, shall be prevailed with to espouse their true public interest.

None, therefore, should be allowed

the exercise of the right and privilege of a free citizen, for a season, but either such as are free-born, in respect of their holy and righteous principles . . . or else who, by their tried affection and faithfulness to common right and public freedom, have deserved to be trusted with the keeping or bearing their own arms in the public defense.

Vane now seemed ready to experiment with forms of government provided they followed the pattern of the Heavenly Polity and were administered by the elect.

For more than a month Vane argued tenaciously in the commission where he was, said Whitelocke, "hard to be satisfied, but did much stick to his own apprehensions." Whitelocke was referring to the millenarianism that lay beneath Vane's practical ideas of government and made him a spokesman for the large contingent of "enthusiasts" in the army. He was not inflexible on most things but on the matter of liberty of conscience he would yield no ground. In the model that he himself submitted, he established it forever:

. . . the supreme power delegated is not entrusted to the people's trustees to erect in matters of faith or worship so as to exercise compulsion therein.

Though moderates like Whitelocke, who wanted an established church with limited freedom of conscience, resisted toleration of Quakers and other sectaries, Vane's strongest antagonist was still the Laird of Wariston, unwilling to yield an inch short of a Presbyterian establishment, without any concession to such nonsense as freedom of conscience, which he regarded as Satan's open door to heresy and disorder. When he first saw Vane's draft, he "disliked the foundation of it and toleration in it"; Vane, he thought, was excluding God from government when he refused to accept the Scottish covenant.

> I saw their design to overturn the ministry and ordinances of Jesus Christ. . . . All this day I was keeped in continual debates with [Vane] and Major Salloway about the business of toleration and magistrate seclusion from meddling in religious matters.

And when Wariston read the compromise draft, intended to bring both sides into the agreement, he wrote

> the Lord be blissed that we could not agree on halfing papers which would provoke God. . . . I declared I thought I was bound to contend to death and resist to blood and go to the stake in this business, wherein they thought I was so warm and urged me to moderation. . . .

Wariston counterproposed the articles of the Edinburgh covenant but Vane and the others would not hear of that. After a month of this Gallic stubbornness, Vane and Salwey apparently released some frustration in badgering Wariston: they taunted him, he said, with Vane's putting in the Solemn League and Covenant "according to the Word of God."

Weeks passed and no constitution could be agreed upon. The officers were still trying to ensure the loyalty of their civilian front by giving them commissions and commands. Early in November a regiment of horse was ordered added to Vane's regiment of foot and Whitelocke was also assigned a regiment of horse. But such moves as these did not arrest the drift into chaos. The army and the interrupted Parliament became so bitterly estranged that Haselrig and Morley betook themselves to Portsmouth where the mayor and a body of soldiers faithful to the Rump might form the nucleus of a counterforce. Meanwhile Lambert gave up any last hope that General Monk and his army in Scotland would rally to his support. On hearing of the interruption of Parliament, Monk purged his army: those whom Parliament had promoted or appointed he cashiered; those whom Parliament had fired he reinstated. Then he sent off letters to Fleetwood, Lambert, and the Speaker of the House committing his forces to maintain the powers and prerogatives of the Rump against any rebellion in the army. Then he played a waiting game until circumstances gave him control of the balance of power.

Lambert, meanwhile, marching north to prevent Monk and his army from invading England, reached Newcastle on November 23, where he began the rituals of negotiation as both he and Monk busily sought the support of the populace and those soldiers and officers who were trying to remain neutral in this division of the army against itself. While Lambert was immobilized in the North and the constitutional committee was still haggling, the Wallingford House junto was being pressed from all sides.

On December 3, Haselrig had induced Portsmouth and its garrison to declare publicly for the Rump; the regiments thereupon dispatched to subdue them defected and joined them instead. The junto was being threatened by sea as well, for Vice Admiral Lawson was sailing his fleet from the Sound towards the Downs, reportedly to defend the Rump against insurgency. The city of London was writhing with dissensions. Sensitive to threats to their commercial prosperity and independence, exasperated at the confusions at Westminister, their mood, like that of the country, was darkening, and rumblings of protest and rebellion were heard. The citizens were not quite sure what they wanted although the slogan of a "free Parliament" seemed to arouse the most response, probably because it was a safe way of asking for the king back, but they were ready to put an end to the frustration of conflicts and reversals in government. Not that they were unified; both Royalists and fanatics of the Fifth Monarchy were proselytizing and stirring up contrary resentments and hopes. The Royalists especially, guided by an effective spy system from Brussels, were listening for the rustle and murmur of dissatisfaction, knowing that unless some positive and effective government grasped the situation firmly, the people would be ready to call the king back from his travels, not so much because they loved the Stuarts as because they longed for some known and reliable rule. Besides, the soldiers, when they trespassed in the limits of the city proper to suppress disorder, stood for all the repression the citizens hated. In retrospect, the "tyranny" of Charles the Martyr seemed benign and gentle.

Two days after the defection of Portsmouth, violence burst out in London. Reluctance to pay some unpopular taxes had hardened into refusal to pay them; some soldiers trying to collect them with the moral assistance of muskets had been roughed up. The Committee of Safety had retaliated indirectly by banning the circulation of petitions in the City. December 5 began ominously: shops were shuttered up as the mayor had ordered, but people were milling about the streets, jeering at the patrolling soldiers, a group of whom were beginning to post the proclamation forbidding the signing of petitions when some apprentices began to hurl tiles and chunks of ice at them from the rooftops. When reinforcements of horse and foot soldiers arrived, they were pelted with stones. Finally, the soldiers fired into the crowd, killing at least two apprentices and wounding more of them, and the crowd sullenly dispersed. The next day the mayor and aldermen tried to placate the Council of Officers and clear themselves of responsibility for the disturbances.

Despite the ban, more petitions were circulated and minor disturbances were frequent. The army maintained strict guard in the City and was believed to be accumulating "guns, bombs, and other artificial fires." Naturally, the citizens feared that the army was planning to subdue the City by force, and tensions increased. On December 13, the "Remonstrance of London" was circulated and signed, it was said, by 23,500 persons. It was no humble petition but a bitter summation of wrongs. Never was John Pym more aggrieved at his king than the Londoners were now with Pym's revolution, and they went one step beyond what Pym had taught them. To their Remonstrance they appended a defiant ultimatum. Their councils, the signers said, had been "affronted by armed troops," and citizens "knocked on the head at their own doors like dogs, for not so much as barking." On Monday their unarmed friends had been murdered, and now they were all to be burned on purpose, for quantities of "fireballs have been laid in St. Paul's and Gresham College." For all these grievances, said the citizens,

> we do engage our selves in the presence of Almighty God, with our lives and fortunes, to defend the rights and liberties of the City of London.

Unconditionally they demanded that all military companies not belonging to the City's own guard withdraw within twelve hours or be dealt with as conspirators.

The Committee of Safety also received a strong petition from the mayor and the aldermen, expressing fears of the consequences of the events of December 5, when mercenary soldiers "did murder, slay, and wound many" of them to prevent peaceful petitioning. Nothing, they asserted, could make the City and its people safe except a force strong enough to defend both the City and the Committee of Safety, and finally obtain "that universally desired Free Parliament."

Under fire from both citizens and government of London, who distrusted each other but agreed on the issue of a free Parliament, the Committee of Safety also received a written demand from Lawson that they recall the Rump. The committee frantically tried to shore up the ruins. To quiet the City, they took two actions. First, they agreed to issue writs for election of a new and free Parliament to meet on January 24. They also published seven unalterable "fundamentals of government" on which they would stake their very lives, and as an interim measure appointed twenty-one "conservators of liberty" to see that these fundamentals were preserved. Vane was one of these, but he had little confidence that the emergency measures would stave off Royalism. The army had lately forestalled an armed attempt to capture the Tower of London, but just barely, and Lawson's fleet was still menacing. If anyone could deflect Lawson's course or persuade him to support Lambert, it would be Vane, for not only did the two share millenarian enthusiasm, but Vane had been instrumental in assigning Lawson to his command and might appeal to old friendship and indebtedness alike. Accordingly, though he was distempered with a great cold, on December 17 he went with Salwey to Lawson's flagship. There they found two emissaries of the interrupted Rump who were determined to hold Lawson on his declared course. In a long and searching debate, Vane argued that only the army could now prevent the restoration of monarchy and save the good old cause. But Lawson, though he did not absolutely close off the possibility of future negotiations, remained unpersuaded and Vane had to return and report that he had failed to touch the Admiral.

Meanwhile, London was rife with conspiracies and rumors of conspiracies by apprentices, sectarians, Fifth Monarchists, and Royalists; the troops stationed to keep order were shot at by snipers, and some were quietly knifed in by-lanes. Alarmed most of all by the Royalist threat, the Committee of Safety ordered all persons who had ever borne arms for the Stuarts in any war, as well as all popish priests and Jesuits, to depart from the confines of London and Westminster by noon of the seventeenth, under penalty of treason; searches were authorized and rewards offered for the discovery of delinquents. Nonetheless, instead of vacating London, Royalists from near and far secretly assembled at ten places of rendezvous, ready for insurrection. But their design being betrayed, the assembling groups of horse and foot were surprised and overwhelmed by the army on the evening of December 18. Though many escaped over walls and in boats, at least twenty-one gentlemen of name were arrested, along with uncounted common persons, and stores of arms were confiscated. The army had defused the rebellion again, but just barely.

But the citizens of London interpreted the searching of houses for concealed Royalists and this military incursion into their liberties as an attack on the independence and safety of the City. Their "Final Protest and Sense of the City" was an intransigent ultimatum, accusing the army of using the threat of danger from the king's party as an excuse for subjugating the London citizens; their houses, they complained, "must be searched and disarmed, and their throats cut, to preserve the City." Finally they declared that they would oppose all violence which was not warranted by the letter of the law, and were ready to fight. The common soldiers, who do not make decisions, they would spare; for those who led them, no quarter. Thus chaotic and tense was the condition of the City when Vane reported his failure to engage Lawson's loyalty.

On December 20, the day on which a new Common Council was

to be elected in London, Vane was sent on a routine mission which was to figure in later charges against him. The unrest of citizens and apprentices was undiminished, and the tide of Royalist feeling had not been turned back by the suppression of their uprising. Vane was therefore summoned to a meeting of the Committee of the Militia in Southwark to see that the troops were in good order, ready for any emergency. While he was there, he was asked to review the regiment of foot which had borne his name since Booth's insurrection. He graciously rode past, looking them over and showing himself to them, and after a few words of commendation and appreciation for the respect they showed him, Vane dismissed them and asked the lieutenant to give them from him something to drink "as might be fitting upon such an occasion." The lieutenant paid five pounds for the drinks and Sir Henry reimbursed him. But he would pay more than that at his trial, when he would be accused of leading troops to repress manifestations of the king's cause, thereby keeping him out of his rightful kingdom.

The next day, on top of news that the troops had defected at Portsmouth, Vane gave the Council of Officers another piece of bad news: the newly elected Common Council of London was packed with "malignants." Monk's strengthened army was threatening to march south, and Fairfax was ready to join him; Haselrig and Morley were prepared to march up from Portsmouth; the Irish army (though news had not yet come through) was supporting the Rump, and the City, crying for a new, free Parliament, was on the verge of rebellion. Besides, the disillusioned soldiers were ready to mutiny against the army itself. And for Vane nothing was left but the negative action of opposing both Rump and king.

But now the great ground-swell of sentiment for Charles Stuart was rising high, and many began to think that behind Monk's apparently adamant loyalty to Parliament was a secret desire to bring back the king. Desirable or not, his return seemed to many the only alternative to anarchy. Even Whitelocke accepted it as inevitable and thought it would be better to ride the wave of destiny than to be overwhelmed and drowned in it. Accordingly, on December 22, he sought out Fleetwood, who as commanding general had power to act, and importuned him to seize one of his viable alternatives: either to conciliate the City, rally the army, declare for a free Parliament, seize the Tower, and defeat the

Rumpers in the field if necessary; or else to send an envoy to treat with Charles before Monk's representatives could make a deal with him. Whitelocke said that he himself was willing to accompany Fleetwood to the Tower and help rally the army, or else to cross the channel as an instructed envoy to Charles.

Poor Fleetwood was at first paralyzed. Clearly, he was not the man to "ride the whirlwind and direct the storm" of a military coup, for he had lost his self-assurance. When he had been asked to go to the disaffected troops to prevent their mutiny and confirm their morale, he had fallen to his knees in prayer "and could hardly be prevailed to go to them." And when he did muster courage to exhort them, he kept dropping to his knees and calling them to join him in prayer. And when, about this time, his friends had tried to incite him to act quickly lest they should all be destroyed, he had wept and answered disconsolately that "God had spit in his face, and would not hear him." So Fleetwood gave in to Whitelocke's impassioned and cogent pleadings and authorized him to make an offer to Charles at Breda, so that the king—if he must return—would return on their terms and owe them gratitude. But as Whitelocke, armed with the authorization to treat with Charles, strode through the anteroom, he met Vane and two officers entering. When Fleetwood called him to wait, Whitelocke had a disheartening suspicion of what would happen, and sure enough, within a quarter of an hour, Vane and his friends passed through with "knowing smiles," and Fleetwood rushed from his chamber crying to Whitelocke, "I cannot do it! I cannot do it!" Almost in tears he explained that Vane had reminded him of his promise to Lambert that he would make no decisive move without Lambert's concurrence—and Lambert was far away in the North. Whitelocke desperately remonstrated: he would ruin himself and his friends unless he took some definite action at once. Fleetwood could only reply, "I cannot help it." Vane had known that Fleetwood could not resist an appeal to his personal loyalty and good faith, and thereby Sir Henry had won a postponement of the Restoration. But this was his last victory, and it was a dismal and hollow one, for within a few days he would give up both Parliament and the army for lost, and with them any real hope for the cause.

Fleetwood was finished too. The next day the Council of Officers capitulated; they approved the return of the Rump and dissolved themselves. The following day, Fleetwood's own soldiers deserted him for the Rump, and he was a general without an army, his removal from office now a mere formality. And with Haselrig's Portsmouth army approaching London and the City rising against the junto, the Parliament party took new heart. Old Speaker Lenthall and the Council of State, having boldly ordered the army to rendezvous, met with the Mayor of London, seized command of the Tower, and demanded from Fleetwood the keys to the Parliament House. And on the morning after Christmas, all the members of the Rump who could be rounded up assembled at Whitehall. Old Lenthall, who had once been carried bodily out of the House, chair and all, and later escorted out with a soldier at each elbow, and two months ago shut out, now grasped the mace of authority and again proudly led the members in a triumphant procession past cheering crowds and jubilant soldiers to Westminister Hall. For a second time, the Rump of the Long Parliament, now shriveled to about forty-nine members, was haunched upon the seat of power, and it had an immediate score to settle with Sir Henry Vane.

19

The Rump Roasted (December 26, 1659– August 28, 1660)

The first business of the Rump was to appoint a new Council of State headed by Arthur Haselrig; Vane was not considered. The members then busied themselves thanking and rewarding those who had remained faithful during the interruption, especially General Monk: they voted unqualified approval of all he had done, and invited him to march south with his troops. They had learned at last that without military backing they were helpless; their reinstatement was not so much a victory for the rights of the people over military tyranny as it was a triumph of Monk and Lawson over Fleetwood and Lambert. As for those who had betrayed the Rump by working with the Wallingford House officers, they censured and rebuked them, but were not ungenerous with indemnities. Still, there had to be some scapegoats.

Vane sensed that he was *persona non grata* and he and Salwey stayed away from the House. The grim Laird of Wariston, apparently quite unconscious that he was himself a stench in the nostrils of the Parliament, confided to his diary his somber delight at seeing his enemies smitten by God. Since Fleetwood had betrayed his friends by siding with Vane and Salwey about toleration, he wrote, "His failing to God and men prognosticated to me sad things against him and the ruin of his family," and he told Fleetwood with evident satisfaction that "his enemies threatened they would not leave one hair of the Protector's family behind." A few days later, observing that Vane and Salwey had not appeared at the House, he recorded the rumor that an impeachment was being drawn up against Vane and that Haselrig refused to come in until Sir Henry went out. If that be true, he gloated, it "was the just hand of God against that man whose politic, deceitful, double false ways had ruined all the ordinances of God, and it will be no grief to good people to see him put out of power. . . . And he had drawn on Major Salloway unto the same guilty design and conspiracy for vast toleration and against the ordinances." When Wariston himself was ejected shortly afterwards, he was the better content, he said, because Vane had already been ousted.

The Rump did not act against Vane immediately, leaving him rather to stand ringed by enemies. He certainly knew that all was lost, that House, City, and army were all tacitly looking towards the king; yet with his fanatic strain of stubborn hope, he waited and watched, not yet willing either to surrender or to flee. The French historian Guizot later pondered this strange spectacle of the old revolutionary who held on when almost all others had given up. "It is a peculiarity of subtle and chimerical minds," he wrote, "to believe that success is always possible."

And Vane refused to abase himself as some of his party were already doing; whatever mistakes he had made, he had served the cause to the best of his ability. On that he would stand. This proud self-possession exasperated Wariston to whom Vane's very existence was now offensive. He told his diary that his wife had heard Fleetwood, in prayer (still or again), "give glory to God and take shame to himself in a spiritual way; and that Desborow had written to the Speaker a very Christian letter showing how he had been blinded and now his eyes were open." But Sir Henry jeered at such abasement, Wariston said, and told the Laird that he shortly expected to hear him doing the same. The noble Scot, who always hoped that God would do for him what the law would not allow him to do for himself, prayed that Vane would be smitten. His wish was prophetic, but he would have small satisfaction in its fulfillment for by that time he would have become a hunted man, broken in body, mind, and spirit, escaping only for a little while his bitter and humiliating death at the end of a rope.

On January 9, 1660, the Rump abruptly summoned Vane. The doors were ordered closed, and when he was seated in his usual place, several members rose to protest his actions since the "late interruption of the Parliament." They had just lately been alarmed by a warrant in the name of the now defunct Committee of Safety that had been intercepted along with a letter in cipher they had not yet been able to decode; not knowing what it said, they feared the worst. The warrant itself was an order to furnish post horses for Sir Henry Vane and Major Richard Salwey and their servants; it appeared to be a plot to smuggle them out of London. Also put in evidence was a series of orders from the Commission of the Admiralty signed by Vane in October and November, documentary proofs that he had exercised official functions during the interregnum without the Rump's specific authorization. He arose in his place and answered the several charges, defending himself, according to Whitelocke, lucidly and ingeniously on the grounds that his Parliamentary appointment to the Admiralty Commission had remained valid. Nevertheless, the members resolved that Vane should be "discharged from being a member of this Parliament," and he was ordered to repair forthwith to his house at Raby in Durham County and to remain there during the pleasure of the Parliament. Next Lambert, Desborough, and other absent officers were ordered to repair at once to whichever of their respective houses was farthest from London; in fact all officers who had been "against the Parliament" were ordered out of London to their country homes. The following week, to preclude any chance that Vane might defend himself by force, Parliament ordered that his regiment of foot be disbanded, that their arms be returned to the Tower of London, "and that the Council of State do take care that they be disbanded."

Despite orders, Vane did not leave London. Saying he was too ill to travel, he stayed on at his home in Charing Cross still cherishing the frail hope that his fortunes might turn. Haselrig, emotionally mercurial as usual, had wept after he had succeeded in getting his long-time friend expelled, and with Lawson's support, tried to have Vane reinstated. The Royalists, however, still feared too much Vane's mysterious powers of conspiracy and his influence with the extreme sectarians. On February 6, Vane was still in London when, because of his sickness, Parliament granted a week's further delay in his departure for Raby. But Monk, who had marched into London on February 3, learned of Vane's presence there and was told by spies that Haselrig and Colonel Rich had been seen going into Sir Henry's house. He demanded Vane's immediate departure and on the thirteenth, the Rump ordered its sergeant-at-arms to escort

Vane to his "House called Bellew" in Lincolnshire. A little later, Lady Vane, who was proving to be no hand-wringer in all these crises, had learned with indignation that General Monk's animus towards Vane was inspired by Mrs. Monk, an ardent Presbyterian who was reported as saying she would go on her knees to His Majesty and beg that Sir Henry, Lambert, and Ludlow might "die without mercy."

Haselrig wrote a letter to Monk, begging him not to believe rumors and vowing undying loyalty to Monk and the Commonwealth; he denied having seen Vane or Lambert and vowed to have no discourse with them or with anyone about them "for what I do shall be above board." The note of panic sounds clearly, for after his triumphant return with the Rump, Haselrig was beginning to feel the earth shaking under his feet.

From Belleau, Vane went on to Raby and stayed there until he could move to his secluded house in Hampstead near London in which he could reside inconspicuously out of the view of his enemies. Some of his old colleagues had taken alarm at his ejection from the House, and either had fled the country or had stayed away. Vane surely understood his own danger after Monk began dominating Parliament and attacking the "fanatics," but he awaited the unfolding of time with a quiet, fatalistic calm. From his old custom of penetrating into men's "hidden" motives, he refused to take Monk's expressions of devotion to Parliament and Commonwealth at face value. "Unless I am much mistaken," he said, "Monk still has several masks to pull off." And in his farewell to Ludlow, he read the omens clearly and resignedly: "For what concerns myself, I have all possible satisfaction of mind as to those actions which God has enabled me to do for the Commonwealth; and I hope the same God will fortify me in my sufferings, how hard soever they may be, so that I may bear a faithful testimony to his cause."

While Vane was still in London, General Monk had his crucial confrontation with the Rump, which was determined to assert Parliament's power over the military with the same bull-headed intransigence that had provoked Lambert's interruption. The occasion was an apparent mutiny in the City, which was already turning against the Rump. Citizens had petitioned the Common Council not to deal with any person or accept any tax not authorized by a "full and free Parliament, as being the rightful representatives of the people, by whom every individual doth consent." Justifiably touchy about their pretensions to being representative, the Rump interpreted this as a repudiation of their authority and a refusal to pay taxes. Besides, the City was known to be a nest of Royalist conspiracy, so it must be disciplined at once. By forcing Monk to do it, they would discipline him at the same time. They accordingly ordered him to enter the City with his troops, arrest some councilors, and destroy the barriers that the City had erected as defenses: to unhinge the gates, wedge open the portcullises, and take down the posts and chains. Much against his will, Monk marched into the City and commenced the demolition, despite bitter protests from his officers and men.

Convinced that if London were not now baited further, the City Council would pass the desired tax levy, Monk suspended operations, asking at the same time that Parliament release the arrested councilors. But with its acquired talent for forcing an issue out of control, Parliament ordered him not merely to dismantle the defenses but to destroy them completely. It was a command and he grimly obeyed it, but he did so amid the fury of the citizens and the indignation of his men at being "employed to oppress their best friends." That night he called his officers together and accepted Parliament's challenge. Next morning these officers dispatched a letter of grievance which began by reminding the Rump that it owed its present reinstatement to this army, and ended by demanding that since they were not truly representative of the people, the Parliament should at once fill out the vacancies in their body. Monk would for the present time quarter his forces in London. The Rump responded with a stiffly formal statement that they really did intend to issue writs of recruitment; it was received coldly by Monk and angrily by others. The finger was writing on the wall but the Rump could not read; they retaliated against Monk by elevating the praying, tearful Fleetwood over him as commander in chief, and unanimously and pointedly excluded Monk from the board of five military commissioners. Hearing of this, Monk apologized to the mayor and council for the violence he had so unwillingly wrought in London and sent an order to Parliament to fill its vacancies at once, to issue writs for a new and free Parliament that week, and to dissolve itself by May 6. He also complained—among other things—that he and his men had been rendered odious in the city by the dishonorable work they were compelled to, that Vane and Lambert had still not left London, and that the Rump had not ejected the "fanatics" who had acted with the "late tyrannical Committee of Safety."

Hatred had grown so intense that anything now seemed legitimate. Some citizen, presumably a Royalist, forged a letter purporting to be from Desborough in Wales to a friend in London, saying that a conspiracy had been formed to "secure the General and the Parliament." The Fifth Monarchist congregation in London had agreed; now all that was needed was a leader. "Sir Henry Vane seems born for such a time as this is; he will come up to head us." Soon an army would be marching towards London and the City bands would have to draw out to meet them. "Then you have your opportunity," the writer said, and added, "We hope you received the arms and ammunition we sent." While Vane promptly denied any knowledge of this imaginary plot, over a short course truth cannot overtake a lie and so the fear and hatred of Sir Henry grew.

The Rump was indeed done for, and as the word spread though the City on the afternoon of February 11, the long simmering hatreds started boiling over in wild rejoicings and celebrations. Wherever Monk's soldiers passed, the townspeople cried out, "God bless you," and lavished drink and money on them. Whoever had dubbed that legislative remnant a rump had supplied a word and symbol to rejoice the hearts of the citizens. For days, Pepys had observed, boys had been laughing and calling out in the streets, "Kiss my parliament!" and as evening came on, it occurred to someone that the thing to do with a rump was to roast it. As all the churchbells burst into clamorous sound, great bonfires roared in the streets, the flames rising so high that "some balconies began to be kindled," and on the fires, spitted on "little gibbets," were roasted great haunches of beef and mutton, or any other piece of meat that could be trimmed to look like a rump. By the light of the bonfires, men drank healths to the king "even on their knees." Samuel Pepys saw it all as he strolled home from the Star Tavern. "But the common joy that was everywhere to be seen!" he exclaimed.

I could at one view tell thirty-one fires, and all along burning, and roasting and drinking for rumps. There being rumps tied upon sticks and carried up and down. . . . On Ludgate Hill there was one turning of the spit that had a rump tied upon it, and another basting of it. Indeed it was past imagination, both the greatness and the suddenness of it. At one end of the street you would think there was a whole land of fire, and so hot that we were fain to keep still on the further side merely for heat.

And the fires and feastings spread clear to Salisbury.

Through all this ribald celebration old Speaker Lenthall had to make his way home from the House where he had sat very late, only to find "his men beaten and his windows broke," and before his gates a great bonfire over which a "rump in a chair" was being roasted: "Never so many rumps roasted as were that night." In the general hilarity, not all were happy. An army captain grumbled, "What ado here's made to bring home a bastard," but his comrades reported him for saying it.

In the days following, the printing presses of London spewed forth a spate of satirical verses against the Rump, and poetasters reveled in stercoraceous wit in ballads with such titles as "Arsy Versey." Vane and Haselrig, "two saints of the devil's last edition," and John Lambert were the butts of most of it, but old Lenthall came in for his share; he is like a great fart, one wrote, "for both do stink, and both we know, are Speakers of the Rump sure." Even before Vane had been expelled, "A New Year's Gift for the Rump" paid him a tribute:

> But never was such a worm as Vane;
> When the State scoured last, it voided him then,
> Yet now he's crept into the Rump again,
> Which nobody can deny.

And after his expulsion, a Royalist rhymer glanced at the vicissitudes of the Parliament:

> Old Oliver's nose had taken in snuff
> When it sat long ago, some unsavoury puffe;
> Then up went the Rump, and was firkt to the quick;
> But it settled in spite of the teeth of poor Dick.

> Then the Knight of the Pestle, King Lambert and Vane,
> With a scepter of iron did over it reign:
> But the Rump soon re-settled, and to their disgrace,
> Like excrements voided them out of the place.

"The Rump Dock't" was both nicer spoken and more foreboding:

> That knave in grain
> Sir Harry Vane
> His case than most men's is sadder;
> There is little hope
> He can scape the rope,
> For the Rump turned him o'er the ladder.

The obvious pun on his name was repeated to the point of tedium. One satirist queried "whether Sir Henry Vaine ought not to be transposed Vaine Sir Henry," and one ballad bears the title "Vanity of Vanities, or Sir Harry Vane's Picture" and makes much of the devious tactics of this "hocus pocus juggling knight" who would rule as "anointed King of Saints."

> This holy saint hath pray'd till he wept,
> Prophesied and divin'd while he slept,
> But fell in a turd when aside he stept.

The author recalls the elder Vane, too; "The Devil ne'er see such two Sir Harry's," who both "betrayed their masters." After blaming Vane for the death of Charles and assigning him the reward of both Cain and Judas, the author concludes with the old pun once again:

> Should he sit where he did with his mischievous brain,
> Or if any his counsels behind do remain,
> The house may be called the *Labor in Vain*,
> Which nobody can deny.

Several satirists harked back to the time when the two Vanes, in collusion as the Royalists wrongly believed, provided the decisive testimony to condemn Strafford; one revived the old story that the elder Vane had died in torments of conscience about his part in Strafford's death and suggested that the younger Vane too must be haunted by it in his adversity, perhaps even to suicide. "The Rump Roughly Handled" concludes,

> Like grub from sheep's tail since the Rump doth him throw,
> He'll creep to some placket of sanctification,
> And come forth a flesh-fly next summer, and blow
> New maggot's in's church, of more whimsical fashion.

> Methinks in his eyes the waters do gather,

As if the Lord Strafford's dust troubled his sight;
Perhaps he repents, and intends (like his father)
Ev'n in his own garter to do his ghost right.

Perhaps the silliest of the recurrent accusations is that Vane was not only a crypto-Catholic, but was working with the Jesuits to hand England over to the pope.

Sir Harry Vane, God bless us,
To Popery he would press us,
And for the Devil's dinner he, the Roman way would dress us.

And in a parody of an accounting of the disbursements of the Committee of Safety, after a series of such items as 500 pounds for Vane to buy Fortunatus' cap, 15 for a scrivener to write out his contract with Lambert, and 1,000 for him to pay "inciters, promoters, and instigators," the list concludes with 3,000 pounds to raise a regiment of Anabaptists and 20,000 pounds "as a present to the Pope by the said Sir Harry, for several and sundry courtesies done him by his Holiness." That this strong antinomian, this Root and Branch man, this suspected Fifth Monarchist should be accused of papistry is perhaps only another example of Vane's persistent reputation for subtlety, or in rougher terms, hypocrisy and deviousness, so that now he was attacked from all sides with contradictory accusations. He was called Anabaptist, Fifth Monarchist, papist, Jesuit, and sometimes hypocrite whose religion was only a cover for self-aggrandizement and greed for power. One of the anonymous satirists captured the essence of this indiscriminate mistrust in a rather heavy-handed but apt "Fanatic Prayer, by Sir H. V. Divinity Professor of Raby Castle," which purports to be a public prayer addressed to Lucifer. "Fit us," he begs,

in our several callings for those services unto which thou hast reserved us—Give us the tenderness and sincerity of the Olivers; the religion of the Harry's; the patience of Lambert. . . . the compunction of Haselrig. . . . These are thy faithful servants, Lucifer, and they deserve their wages. Like bats, they can both fly and creep; comply with all humors; change parties and opinion oftener than their shirts, and bewail their wanderings. Ah, be a gracious devil to those people. Cast an Egyptian darkness over the whole nation, lest they discover the delusion; and find, that to be great and rich is what we fight and snivel for.

One of the liveliest of the satires was entitled "Don Juan Lamberto, or a Comical History of the late Times, by Montelion the Knight of the Oracle." It is in the form of a chivalric romance and Vane is one of the leading figures in it under the name of Sir Vane the Knight of the Mysterious Allegories, a mischief maker from childhood. One of the principal objects of satire is the proposed marriage between the houses of Vane and Lambert.

Even though Vane had been, as one balladeer put it, "shit out of the Rump" and sent to house arrest, his unpopularity did not diminish. More than once in his political life he had been unpopular but now, as one observer said, "he lay under the most catholic prejudice of any man I know." Wariston, still lurking gloomily about London, was unable to shake from his mind the memories of Vane and Salwey, how they had been so pleased with themselves before they went to treat with Lawson, how sure they had been that they had "keeped themselves free" enough to reconcile both parties, and how they kept teasing Wariston about "how they had drolled and cajoled us in Scotland" when Vane put in the covenant those fatal words which had made and cast all loose. He prayed that the Lord would humble them "for He knew with what simplicity of heart we walked in that business of the Covenant which the other made loose that it might only serve as a politic engine for a time and then [be] laid aside; and I thought their pride in the overreaching others would meet with an overreach and a downfall." Earlier he had prophesied that Parliament itself would be taken down by General Monk, hungry for power and unchecked by any religion.

He was right. After the Roasting of the Rump, Monk had the upper hand, and the Parliament had to do his bidding. On February 21, he frustrated their attempt to select additional members when he arbitrarily reinstated members whom Colonel Pride had secluded; that gave him a secure majority in the House, seventy-three secluded members to eighteen Rumpers. Now dominated by Presbyterians and Royalists, the House quickly showed its temper. They appointed Monk commander in chief of all the land forces of the three kingdoms and Joint Admiral of the Navy. They enlarged their numbers further by rescinding all resolutions passed since 1648 that had disqualified members, and from the oath of loyalty to the Commonwealth they deleted the clause excluding a "single person" as governor. And when Monk ordered the election of a "free"

Parliament, the drift towards restoration was unmistakable even though Monk was still asserting the army's loyalty to the representative of the people.

Between the final dissolution of the Rump on March 16 and the presentation of the King's letters to the newly elected "Convention" Parliament on May 1, Monk retained his Commonwealth mask, behind which he was appraising the temper of the country. This strong, slow-spoken, bluff man was moving cautiously to make sure that England was ready to accept the restoration before coming into the open as its leader. Once he pulled the mask off, events moved with a rush. Charles sent letters from Breda to the Speakers of both Houses, along with a cordial, conciliatory declaration, largely drafted by Edward Hyde, which promised pardon for nearly all who would request it within forty days and would pledge loyalty to Charles. Its tone was warm, kindly, moderate. Response was quick: Parliament proclaimed Charles II king and after a short delay to organize the celebration and the pageantry, without which one could not decently welcome a king, Charles and his brothers landed at Dover on May 25. In the exuberant reception by the fleet and the people of Dover, he accepted from the mayor a Bible ("which he took and said it was the thing that he loved above all things in the world") and charmed everyone with his gracious affability and ease. On May 29, his birthday, he triumphantly entered London and proceeded through streets crowded with shouting soldiers and gorgeously attired citizens, the houses hung with tapestries, the streets strewn with flowers, the mayor and aldermen in full panoply of office, the fountains flowing with wine, and all manner of music filling the air.

Almost immediately petitions flooded into Whitehall. Haselrig was among the first; he had never been in the field, he said, since 1644, and he had nothing to do with the king's death. Supporting the Commonwealth only to avoid bloodshed and opposed to Cromwell's usurpation, he had joined Monk in the overthrow of Lambert. He now rejoiced in His Majesty's restoration and promised exemplary obedience.

Lambert followed Haselrig's expedient example and wrote the king that he was satisfied with the present government and was resolved to spend the rest of his life in peace. Nicholas Love, one of the "pretended judges" of the late king, maintained that he had refused to sign the death warrant even when he was "menaced." Among all these petitions there was none from Sir Henry Vane; neither did he make any attempt to escape. Rather, he continued living quietly at his house in Hampstead, busied with his family worship and his meditations on the sickened times. He waited in a stubborn hope, not quite extinguished by his often sharp sense of political reality, to find out what God—and the king—had in store for him. He found out on July 1 when he was arrested at Hampstead by the king's order, on a vague charge of conspiring with the military against the king. Around the fact of his arrest legend has drawn arabesques. The more conventionally romantic story has him caught while trying to escape disguised as a cart driver; but the more likely story, the one more in harmony with his deportment in his last years, says that he was walking at sunset in the elm-shaded avenue approaching his house when the troops marched up to take him. He stepped forward and courteously asked what they wished of him, displaying the same calm acceptance with which Charles had once faced the troopers. He was taken to the Tower of London, and held prisoner, as Laud had been, for two years without trial; never would he know freedom again except for the ultimate liberation.

Parliament had turned at once to the most urgent business—an act of pardon and indemnity. Any realist would know that pardon could not be simple, total, and universal; Charles' amnesty was generous and he was not a particularly vindictive man, but the Declaration of Breda itself had hinted that the regicides directly responsible for the beheading of his father should be punished, and many of the Cavalier noblemen were far more vengeful than the king himself. Parliament had begun to work on the "Bill of General Pardon, Indemnity and Oblivion" on May 9; it was still being hammered out when the king reached London, and did not go to the House of Lords for concurrence until July 11, ten days after Vane had been imprisoned in the Tower.

It was easy for the Parliament to decide that the regicides should be excluded from the pardon, but much discussion was required to define just what constituted a regicide for purposes of the act; it was even more difficult to decide which regicides should be excepted totally and which only for penalties short of death. At first it was decided that only seven of the judges would need to suffer death, but as the members weighed and compared cases, they became more zealous for punishment. Prynne, with his keen nose for offense and his lust for revenge, searched busily through the trial records and brought in a list of persons who, having sat in once or twice during the trial, deserved, he said, the same punishment as the signers of the warrant: he saw no shadings between total guilt and innocence.

It was decided also that there should be selected twenty citizens who were not implicated in the death of the king but were worthy of punishment by virtue of their civil and military actions during the Commonwealth, the Protectorate, and the anarchy. One member moved that someone should "die for the Kingdom as well as for the King," and suggested Sir Henry Vane as a suitable candidate. But the other members were more merciful; the twenty citizens should be excepted for all "pains, penalties and forefeitures (not extending to life) as shall be thought fit to be inflicted on [them] by another act, intended to be hereafter passed for that purpose." Sir Henry Vane, on June 11, was excepted from pardon in this category; powerless though he now was, he was still feared as dangerous to the state. But at least his life seemed safe.

His old friend Hugh Peter, whose brash, abrasive personality always stirred powerful antipathies, was first hauled in on the irresponsible gossip that he had been one of the masked executioners, indeed the very one that struck off the king's head. No one could produce evidence that he was concerned in the death of the king at all except for inciting the soldiers to cry "justice" at the trial, and approving the king's execution in his sermons. Nevertheless, he was popularly believed to be somehow responsible, and after such bitter enemies as Prynne had finished, he was, life and all, wholly excepted from pardon.

At last the Commons hammered out a bill and sent it to the Lords, who, in a mood much more vindictive than that of Commons, added names and increased penalties. After more than two weeks, the king came to the House and strongly urged the Lords to end the anguished uncertainty of the kingdom and pass an act that would carry out the promises of his declaration by excepting from pardon only "those who were immediately guilty of that murder." Instead the Lords added a proviso that the act should "not extend to the pardoning or to give any other benefit whatsoever unto Sir Henry Vane, Sir Arthur Haselrig, John Lambert, and Daniel Axtell, or any of them; but that they, and every one of them are, and shall be out of this present Act, wholly excepted, and foreprized." The Commons, more merciful, voted it down with a firm negative.

Vane's fate now depended on the conferences of the committees of the two Houses. The Lords were all for executions, arguing that "if it be just to take away their estates, it is as just to take away their lives." As for Vane, Lambert, Haselrig, and Axtell, "they should stand excepted for life." The spokesman for the Lords granted that they were not to be punished as murderers, but reminded the Commons that the king himself, whose wisdom, of course, they all venerated, had thought fit to commit them to the Tower. Further, in public letters His Majesty had asked for action to be taken against any persons dangerous to the safety of the nation, and surely the king regarded these four as dangerous. If they were deserving of mercy, the king, who was the fountain of mercy, would surely extend it to them in due time. The Lords thought that mercy was the prerogative of the king while the Parliament should concern itself with justice.

In the next conference, the Commons tried again to save these four, and Vane's lifelong antagonist, Denzil Holles, decently took his side. But Hyde was obdurate, and grouped Vane and Haselrig in a strong though vague indictment, suggestive of the profound distrust the Royalists felt for "fanatics." The two delinquents, he said, had been secured and confined by the Parliament; then, after the king had come in, they both had ignored Parliamentary censure and returned to town "never applying themselves to the King, but lurked up and down, without giving any account of themselves"; their Lordships, he said, looked on them as persons of mischievous activity. Hyde concluded by suggesting the compromise the Commons ultimately accepted; he intimated that if they would except these four, the Lords would be willing to join in a petition to the king that "mercy might be showed them and that his severity might not extend to their lives."

In the final compromise, not passed until the end of August when Vane had been in prison almost two months, Axtell was sacrificed; Haselrig was excepted for all but life and, within a year, would die in the Tower; Vane and Lambert were wholly excepted "with expectation of a further address on their behalf." The wording of the further address was agreed upon: as humble suitors to His Majesty, the Commons petitioned that if Vane and Lambert should be attainted "yet the execution, as to their lives, may be remitted." With the concurrence of Lords, the petition was presented to His Majesty, and the fountain of mercy graciously granted the request. Yet when he had first heard that Vane was in custody in the Tower, he had offered "to lay a wager [he] should not escape," and when he heard that Vane was excepted from the act he had "openly expressed his joy." The quality of mercy, it appeared, was still somewhat uncertain.

20

The Furies (August, 1660–January, 1662)

Having lain in prison now almost two months, Vane knew more or less what was before him. After some indeterminate time, he would be haled from the Tower to face political charges that would jeopardize his freedom and even his life. He would undoubtedly be found guilty of whatever he was charged with, and even if the king honored his promise—and like Strafford Vane knew better than to put his trust in princes—he could expect to spend the rest of his life mewed up, to see his estate confiscated and his wife and children impoverished. Like old Archbishop Laud whom he had once oppressed, like the oppressed Cavaliers whom he had tried to liberate in Richard's Parliament, he would long lie uncharged, untried, apparently forgotten. And then a blow fell, far worse than anything his enemies could have devised. His oldest son, eighteen-year-old Henry, a fugitive in Denmark, died there. The boy who was to inherit the estates, comfort and support his mother, and clear the family's wounded name would do none of these things now; he had fallen victim to the inscrutable designs of a Providence which seemed either not to know or else not to care about the torments Sir Henry Vane was already suffering. It was too late now for him to raise questions about Providence and his private arrangements with it; patiently he bowed his head to this and every other stroke. For some sixteen months in the Tower and then some six months in the Scilly Isles, he fought his lonely way to resignation and serenity.

The sounds from outside his prison were ominous. Just after he had received the ambivalent news of his condemnation and pardon, the vultures gathered to devour his estates, and the king quite illegally authorized three men to take possession of estates which were not yet forfeit, but which, presumably, he expected soon to be. As Vane later complained, his rents from Raby Castle were withheld, and when he tried by legal means to recover the monies due him, the Commons very nearly voted sequestration of his estates before he had even been arraigned. There were many who took a peculiar delight in depriving of his estate the man who had helped to deprive so many others. In fact Vane was convinced, probably with justice, that among those who coveted his properties there had been a conspiracy to persuade Parliament to except him from the Act of Pardon. Fortunately for his descendants, since he was the only one of his family to stand opposed to the restoration of the king, his sons and his wife's family managed to keep much of the estate from being dispersed. His father-in-law, for example, successfully kept the estates in Lincolnshire from devolving to the Crown by maintaining that though they were held in Vane's name, Sir Henry had purchased and held them only in trust for his late mother-in-law. But now he was deprived of his rightful income, lacking even the money necessary to maintain himself in prison, let alone to pay his mounting debts.

Meanwhile, he heard that preparations were going ahead to speed the trials of the regicides. On October 9, the indictment of treason against twenty-nine persons was presented to a grand jury which found it a true bill. Chief Baron Bridgman laid firm legal foundations by specifying that for the purpose of these trials, treason should be defined by a statute of Edward III as "compassing and imagining the death of Our Lord the King." Only in the case of treason against the life of the king himself could mere intent legally constitute treason, with overt acts merely providing outer evidence of the essential inner crime of "imagining and compassing," a situation based on what he called the ultimate law of England—the absolute authority of kings and the duty of passive obedience of subjects. Evidently the crime could be proved only by overt acts, including words; but just as evidently, it is a charge almost impossible to disprove in the face of gossip, hearsay, and circumstantial evidence of all kinds. Some of the regicides were as helpless against it as Vane would be later.

On Wednesday the tenth, the accused were arraigned in batches, and forced to plead guilty or not guilty in form, without being allowed to explain or qualify, or to ask advice of counsel. For in a trial for treason the accused was customarily denied legal counsel, and was not even allowed to know precisely what he was being accused of until he heard the charges in open court. Major General Thomas Harrison, a man of Fifth Monarchist faith who had, with Lambert, been one of Cromwell's gallant commanders, was second to be arraigned. Though he entertained no hope, for he openly gloried in his part in the death of Charles and his utter devotion to the godly cause, he fought stubbornly. Refusing to be silenced by the court, he aired fundamental questions about the legality of the civil wars and both the legality and jurisdiction of these retaliatory trials. He at least got it on record that he had been jailed for three months, been given no warning of his trial, and allowed no access to counsel before he was forced, like the others, to plead according to the set ritual. He pled "not guilty," and to the question of how he would be tried, he reluctantly gave the proper answer, "By God and by my country,"—though not before he had qualified it with "in your own way." Later, when Hugh Peter was arraigned, he said, "Not for ten thousand worlds would I say I am guilty: I am not guilty." And he insisted on saying that he would be tried "by the Word of God," until he was jeered into repeating the set formula.

Once all had entered their pleas, the trials began. On the next day, Thursday the eleventh, Harrison was tried, and after hearing the evidence that he had commanded the troop that escorted the king to his trial, that he had attended the trial faithfully and had been one of the sentencing judges and signers of the death warrant, he spoke up not in defense but in proud justification. What he was accused of, he said, "was not a thing done in a corner." Because of the confusion engendered by the civil war, he had not always been able to follow his conscience as he wished. "Maybe I might be a little mistaken; but I did it all according to the best of my understanding, desiring to make the revealed will of God in his holy scriptures as a guide to me." And he formulated the defense common to all those now indicted and later to Vane, too: "I humbly conceive that what was done was done in the name of the Parliament of England . . . by their power and authority." After being frequently interrupted and sometimes shouted down by his judges, he was pronounced guilty and sentenced at once to the full barbarity of the penalty for high treason:

The judgment of this court is, and the court doth award, that you be led to the place from whence you came, and from thence to be drawn upon an hurdle to the place of execution; and there you shall be hanged by the neck and being alive shall be cut down, and your body shall be opened, your heart and bowels plucked out, and your privy members cut off and thrown into the fire before your eyes; then your head to be stricken off from your body and your body to be divided into four quarters, and head and quarters to be disposed of at the pleasure of the King's Majesty, and the Lord have mercy upon your soul.

As Harrison was being drawn to the scaffold, one citizen cried out, "And now where is your good old cause?" The courageous Harrison pointed to his breast: "Here it is. And I am going to seal it with my blood." Pepys, who had seen King Charles die, watched Harrison now and blithely observed that he seemed "as cheerful as any man could do in that condition." Others wondered at his ecstatic countenance as he was dragged on the hurdle, a rope around his neck, and as he spoke the last words of an assured and triumphant martyr. "Take notice," he said,

That, for being instrumental in that cause and interest of the Son of God . . . I am brought to this place to suffer death this day. . . . I do not lay down my life by constraint, but willingly; for if I had been minded to have run away I might have had many opportunities; but being so clear in the thing, I durst not turn my back nor step a foot out of the way, by reason I had been engaged in the service of so glorious and great a God.

Though his spirit accepted death gladly, his warrior's body did not: as the hangman sliced open his abdomen for the disemboweling, his reflexes aimed a fist at the hangman's face, one last blow for the good cause. When his head and heart were held up to view, the people shouted a shout of joy, an ugly sound from those who had never dared taunt the veteran before.

On the day of Harrison's execution Hugh Peter was tried. Charged principally with his petty and loud-mouthed vindictiveness about the king's death and knowing he was already convicted, for once he had little to say: he had always stood for religion and law, he said, had cared for the poor, and done many good things for members of the king's party. The good he had done was irrelevant, the court replied; only his evil deeds were at issue. He received the same savage sentence that was even then being carried out on Harrison.

In this bloody and furious week of concurrent trials and executions, twenty-nine men were convicted and ten executed with full savagery. The fountain of mercy spared one man the quartering and generously gave the butchered quarters of another to his family for burial instead of displaying them over the city gates. But it was for Hugh Peter, who had least to do with the sentencing of the king, that the most exquisite niceties of cruelty were reserved. Peter was like Charles I in that nothing now except his death could have raised his character. Before he died, he wrote his daughter that he now realized that others had always known him better than he knew himself. He was a chastened and enlightened man, more thoughtful than he had ever been.

He and John Cook suffered on the same morning, aptly enough at Charing Cross where Peter had once torn down the ancient cross as a mischievous piece of superstition "as old as popery itself." Cook was dragged to the place of execution with the severed head of his friend Harrison facing him on the sledge. He died calmly, convinced that as a lawyer he had always been faithful to the law, that he was now suffering for once having demanded justice on the king. Peter, perhaps the most hated man in England for the moment, was jeered at and reviled by the mob, and while the hangman was drawing and quartering Cook, he was gripped by the arms and forced to watch. The hangman, turning to him, rubbing his dripping hands before Peter's face, asked, "How like you this work, Mr. Peter?" The stentorian voice was quiet now and assured: "I am not terrified at it, and you may do your worst."

Of the twenty-nine men convicted of treason, the capital sentences of all but ten were suspended, but from time to time one or more of them was taken from prison and carted through the streets with halters around their necks. Compared with the massive "liquidations" that recent history has taught us to expect, the capital reprisals were moderate. But they were sufficient, and it is unfortunate that the temperate mood exhibited by the Convention Parliament could not last. It was, said Charles, when he dismissed it on December 29, the Healing and Blessed Parliament. Certainly the next one was to be more repressive and punitive.

The rising tide of loyalty and affection for the king was the obverse of a growing fear and suspicion of Republicans and nonconformist "fanatics"; the bill for the attainder of "persons guilty of the horrid murder of his late Sacred Majesty King Charles I" expressed both impulses, and at the same time supplied the government with some additional revenue, for the estates of attainted persons reverted to the Crown. That is why the dead as well as the living, including those who were hiding on the continent, were attainted by name.

England was becoming subject to a psycopathic fear of conspiracy, and it was hard to tell whether the people had greater dread of a Catholic uprising to conquer England for the pope, or of a sectarian, fanatic conspiracy to kill the king and impose the rule of the rabid Saints. Until this obsessive terror worked itself off years later in the exposure of the grim and bloody farce of the Popish Plot, it could always be easily invoked for repressive acts against Catholics and Independents alike; for the present it was the militant dissenters who were most feared. The fact that the numerous dissenting sects, although proscribed, were still meeting secretly and talking in the fire-and-destruction imagery of the Old Testament, seemed to verify the rumors of a great hidden network of bloody-minded insurrection. While much of this was hysteria based on rumor and fear, or on forgeries like the Desborough letter, some extremists really were hoarding arms and planning a day of wrath. The first rumblings of real trouble were heard in December, 1660, when one of the plotters, garrulous in his cups, told a friend of a great enterprise then in hand to pull Charles from his throne, kill Monk, and settle a free state where "the Saints must reign." Although houses were searched and some arrests made, the ringleaders were missed. Soon a few desperate Fifth Monarchists sallied forth to destroy the Beast, led by Thomas Venner, the New England wine-cooper who had disturbed Oliver's government in 1657. At dusk on Sunday, January 6, 1661, Venner and his congregation, having elevated their spirits in an ecstatic meeting at their conventicle in Swan Alley, swarmed down the street and broke into St. Paul's cathedral. A casual passer-by, challenged by the sentry outside, declared for King Charles. "I am for King Jesus!"

responded the sentry and shot him dead. After one enthusiastic murder, there was no turning back. Although the mayor hastily summoned the Trained Bands, they were unable to prevent the men of the word and the sword from retreating into the suburbs. At Beech Lane they were opposed by a lone, courageous constable whom they shot dead. The whole City was now roused and the rebels retreated into Ken Wood, Highgate. The next morning rumors flew and the number of dead grew with the telling; security precautions were tightened, and that evening Samuel Pepys and his wife, returning home from the theatre, were "in many places strictly examined, more than in the worst of times, there being great fears of the Fanatics rising again." Nothing more was seen of Venner and his antic band until on Wednesday morning they again burst furiously into the City, battling through the streets in wild confusion. The City was paralyzed with fear: the shops were shut, the Trained Bands rushing to and fro, and the citizens hardly venturing out unless like Pepys they were armed with sword and pistol, "with no good courage at all," he said, but that he might not seem to be afeared.

After two of the vengeful Saints had been killed and Venner himself wounded, the rebels broke into three groups which spread the battle widely through the streets of London as they sought to escape. One group of ten trapped themselves in the attic room of the Blue Anchor Inn, where they were shot at through openings made in the roof. Two survived to surrender; they would have done so sooner, they said, but that their fellows threatened to shoot them. The dispersed and confused fighting continued all day and through the night: the savage Saints had been promised by Venner that if they fought valiantly enough King Jesus himself would join them. When the Dukes of York and Albemarle arrived the next morning with their troops of horse and foot guards, the rebels had already been captured or killed. In the broad light of day London could scarcely believe that a band of only some fifty inspired and desperate men had thrown the entire City into panic and had inflicted such heavy casualties on large, trained forces.

The government was jolted into prompt and merciless action. All twenty of the captives were brought to trial on charges of murder and high treason, some of them, like Venner, so badly wounded that they could not stand up to be arraigned. Venner insisted that not he but King Jesus had led the insurrection which, in any event, could not be treasonous because Charles was not yet crowned. Venner and sixteen others were convicted of treason. He and his lieutenant, Roger Hodgkin, underwent the barbaric ritual just two days after the verdict; the others were hanged on the following Monday. They could not complain of the law's delay.

Public satisfaction at this prompt, adequate punishment was apparently increased when the anniversary of the martyrdom of Charles, January 30, was celebrated with solemn fasting and prayer and the sweetness of delayed vengeance: the "arch-traitor Cromwell and two of his choicest instruments, Bradshaw and Ireton," were haled out of their graves and dragged on sledges, through a shouting and cursing crowd, to Tyburn. There the bodies were removed from their coffins and, in their shrouds, were hanged by the neck until sundown, when their heads were chopped off to be impaled over Westminster Hall, and their "loathsome trunks thrown into a deep hole under the gallows." Secretary Nicholas was pleased; they had, he commented, "finished the tragedy of their lives in a comic scene . . . a wonderful example of justice."

Venner's insurrection was short, violent, quickly subdued and punished, but its consequences were terrible: England's fear of conspiring dissenters had now been vindicated. That so small a number of fanatics could destroy so much only showed how catastrophic would be the rebellion of the whole dissenting crew with its hidden web of communication and supply and its apocalyptic sense of mission. Now dissenters everywhere must suffer, and Charles' initial hope, which was to widen toleration to include the sectarians and the Catholics, was sure to be disappointed. Venner had been captured on January 9 and on the tenth there was issued from Whitehall a proclamation "restraining all seditious meetings and conventicles under pretense of religious worship, and forbidding any meetings for worship except in parochial churches or chapels." Nonconformism was being equated with disloyalty. Quakers and Baptists were singled out, for both had been popularly, though unjustly, identified with Fifth Monarchists, and the gentle Quakers had already been persecuted both in England and America with particular animus. On the day when the last of the rebels was hanged, George Fox and others signed a declaration from those "harmless and innocent people of God, called Quakers" to clear them from the charges of plotting and fighting mentioned in the proclamation.

Now authorities were hunting fanatics all over England. On the day of Fox's appeal, a Quaker's house was searched in Hull and allegedly seditious papers were found, by which it appeared that meetings were being held and intelligence being received from all over the kingdom, along with contributions "to carry on their horrid designs, under the pretense of religion." In Bristol, the Trained Bands were alerted against Quakers and Anabaptists who were meeting contrary to the proclamation. Fifth Monarchists were reported meeting in Picadilly and the Anabaptists were said to be expecting reinforcements from France. Desborough, so rumor went, had sold land but was not traveling as he had intended, while at Newgate Fifth Monarchy men were praying "for all righteous blood, from Abel to Righteous Axtell and Harrison, to be called to account."

On January 23, three men were brought before the justice at Burwell to answer for their dangerous utterances. One reported that 300,000 men had been ready to take over the government, but had desisted because they were not sure God had authorized them to shed blood; another 40,000 had gathered and likewise dispersed "about Trinity last." But most damning was a statement by Thomas Taylor, known to have visited Sir Henry Vane in the Tower: he would be happy, he said, "to maintain a government of which Sir Henry was high constable." Not long after, Thomas Hall published an antimillenarian book of scriptural exegesis featuring a confutation of Sir Henry Vane's views, published years before in *A Retired Man's Meditations*. Though he had found it cloudy and nebulous stuff, he nevertheless itemized the arguments and one by one demolished "these high-flown notions." His conclusion is minatory: "It will be the wisdom of those in authority, speedily to suppress such real fanatical opinions; else *hae nugae feria fient*. These trifles may become troubles."

So the longer Vane waited for the disposition of his case, the less propitious became the climate for a dispassionate trial. At the opening of the vindictive Cavalier Parliament on May 8, 1661, its tone was set by the Lord Chancellor when he argued from Venner's "most desperate and prodigious Rebellion" to an all-pervading conspiracy:

Let no man undervalue the treason because of the contemptible-ness of the number engaged in it. No man knows the number, but the multitude of intercepted letters from and to all the counties of England, in which the time was set down wherein the *Work of the Lord* was to be done; by the desperate carriage of the traitors themselves, and their bragging of their friends, we may conclude the combination reached very far.

Whether or not he was here glancing at Vane, as some have thought, the list of early actions of the new Parliament reads like a retraction and confutation of Vane's principles and the accomplish-ments of his cause. The Parliament seemed to think it could obliterate all the governmental and religious changes that had been made since the wars broke out and reinstate the old forms of government as if the civil wars had never been. First, the king was protected in his primacy by an act declaring it treason to express any doctrine casting doubt on the royal rights, or justifying taking arms against him. Penalties were established against any who hinted that the king favored papists, or denied that the Long Parliament had been dissolved, or maintained that a Parliament without a king had any legislative powers whatever. The bishops were restored to their seats in the House of Lords as spiritual peers, and control of all military forces was vested wholly in the Crown. The subversive activity of petitioning Parliament was impeded by limiting the permitted number of signatures to ten. And all mayors and other officials of corporate towns were obliged to swear stringent oaths of loyalty and nonresistance to the Crown, to take Communion in the Anglican way, and to deny the Solemn League and Covenant, which had already been publicly burned by the common hangman. The new royalism was made more binding than the old.

And as for religion and liberty of conscience, a synod and a Parliamentary Convocation were at work revising the Prayer Book and planning to enforce uniformity of worship in both doctrines and liturgies. This slow and exacerbating discussion was in progress during Vane's confinement, and the direction of its course was becoming increasingly clear as latitudinarians and Puritans lost point after point. The new Prayer Book was accepted by Parliament in April, 1662. By this time the Act of Conformity was ready for the royal assent: it imposed the Prayer Book on all assemblies of worship, and required all ecclesiastics, including schoolmasters, to repudiate the Solemn League and Covenant, to deny all right to take arms against a king, and to promise to follow the legally established liturgy of the Church of England. Vane was still waiting in prison when the king signed the act on May 19, 1662, and would have been dead only about two months when, fittingly enough on St. Bartholomew's Day, August 24, the spiritual massacre took place, and some 2,000 ministers who would not sacrifice conscience to status and security were dispossessed and went underground to preach or worship in poverty, danger, and honesty.

In this thickening atmosphere of zeal against the zealots, Vane was not forgotten. After Venner's death, the Fifth Monarchists were quiet but not silent, and on July 23, 1661, information was lodged with Parliament that "the fanatics make mention of Lambert and Sir Henry Vane in their meetings; and have great hopes to disturb the public peace, if they could procure their escape." And the Commons ordered the attorney general to prepare the evidence and proceed against them capitally. Instead, in October, 1661, they were transported to more isolated and rigorous imprisonment on the Channel Islands, Lambert to Guernsey, and Vane to Scilly, where they could communicate neither with each other nor with such influential Fifth Monarchists as Rogers and Feake, whom Vane had come to know during his incarceration on the Isle of Wight. On these islands, Father Giavorina reported to the Venetian Senate, they were "under good guard, at a great distance from each other . . . and with no paper, pens, or ink they can only plot with themselves. Wise men think that they have been sent so far off that they may be put out of the way without noise or notice." In this he was wrong, for they were left unharmed, though the vengeance-minded Commons became impatient; on November 22, they asked the king to have them brought back to the Tower "in order to their trial." The Venetian envoy reported that Parliament was suppressing many "turbulent spirits" at this time and was very displeased with the removal of Vane and other sectaries to adjacent islands and wanted them brought back to pay for their crimes with their lives. "This," he concluded, "will be a good example for the numerous fanatics who survive in the country, especially as they are leaders of the sects and of the false doctrines which dominate England."

But Charles played a waiting game, perhaps out of mercy, and perhaps out of a desire to damp the fires of intolerance and persecution which were damaging to his image as benevolent healer of breaches. He answered that he would do as they asked, and blandly thanked them for giving him so much latitude to arrest suspected persons by authority of the phrase, "and others." But in January of 1662, the Commons had to remind him to "take account of what hath been done in the executions of his Majesty's commands therein." The king acknowledged their message, and said he "would take present care about it." But when on February 19 some of Vane's tenants at Raby and Barnard Castles brought in petitions, the Commons were reminded that still nothing had been done, and again they humbly moved His Majesty to order Vane and Lambert to be brought back for trial as well as to hear the tenants' petitions. His Majesty again graciously acceded to their desires, but Vane and Lambert remained enisled until April, when the arrest and execution of three fugitive regicides renewed the pious appetite for the rigors of justice.

If the Lords and the new House of Commons had had their way, Vane would have been safely dead long ago. As it was, he was left for two long years in which to possess his soul in patience and await Christ's kingdom in the only way God had left him, by suffering his martyrdom in patience and faith.

21

A Summing Up (1660–1662)

After years of frenetic activity in government, now in his close confinement Vane was thrown back upon the resources of his own mind. For a time he was incommunicado, denied even materials for writing. His wife Frances was at length granted leave to visit him in the Tower, but it was later necessary for her to petition the king himself for renewal of the privilege and for permission for him "to take the air of the Tower with his keeper, on account of his ill health." When he was sent to Scilly in November, 1661, he was confined on the ship for several weeks before sailing, during which time his wife, busy as ever on his behalf, persuaded Secretary Nichols to allow him two servants and a maid; but with all the comfort of attendance, he was nonetheless isolated from the outside world. The king was so confident of Sir Francis Godolphin's strictness in watching over Sir Henry that in December he authorized some relaxation: Sir Henry was to be allowed "freedom of ink and paper, provided Sir Francis or his deputy peruse and seal all he writes" (there was no requirement that Sir Francis understand all he perused). Vane could also be allowed to "converse with unsuspected persons," but only in the presence of an officer; and at Sir Francis' discretion, he might be allowed to walk in the open air, if accompanied by some trusted deputy. In such insulation and with no expectation of anything but death or endless imprisonment, he faced his past and came to terms with it.

In the temporal world of politics he had failed. The cause to which he had devoted his life since God first overwhelmed his spirit, a people's commonwealth fit to receive its true ruler, now lay about him in ruins, its champions martyred, jailed, or in hiding. Now that the only comfort he could find was his purity of motive and the only glimmering of hope the promise of Christ's imminent return, he found grace to develop resignation and serenity, and he wrote a final testament to witness for him after his voice was stilled.

He first had to confront the failure of the "good old cause" and his part in it. When he had written *A Healing Question* he was not only stating a theory of government but offering a plan of immediate action to salvage the cause after betrayal. Now, in *The Cause of the People of England Stated*, he reiterated his fundamental theory, for he still thought it was sound; but he found need to change his emphasis, and to explain and justify the civil wars. He maintained as always that the source of all law and political power is God, in whose will lies the perfect justice to which men owe absolute obedience. The terrestrial law and rule are derived from the divine natural law, and demand obedience insofar as they imitate God in dispensing justice and right to the subjects. By a sort of social contract, the people depute the power which God has vested in them to some kind of established government to which they owe obedience so long as the government rules justly for the good and welfare of the governed, duly respecting their liberties. But implanted within every man is a conscience to guide him in moral matters, and reason to guide him in political judgments: "the original impressions of just laws are in man's nature and very constitution of being." That is why Vane insists on the right of civil disobedience: man is not obligated to obey any law or edict that violates natural rights as defined by his conscience, and if a ruler governs by his personal will for improper ends, the people may not only withhold their obedience but may take back the powers they have granted, resorting if necessary to war.

The traditional government of England had been tripartite, with king as executive, Lords as judicial, and Commons as legislative powers; all should operate for the good of the governed in accordance with the justice of natural law. But England had lived through the anomalous situation of a split in the triad, irremediably widened when the king, along with many of the Lords, declared war on the Parliament. Never had a greater burden been placed on the individual conscience, for each man then had to choose between conflicting loyalties, and decide which of two powers was more right. Vane had no doubts: when the king was arbitrarily restricting the rights and liberties of the people, the Commons, the elected representative of the people, were empowered to act as government de facto. And when the keepers of liberty put the issue to battle, appealing the question to God just as in trial by combat in feudal days, God had decided the issue in favor of the people; then their delegates held power both by natural right and by the right of conquest. Even though many or even most of the members of Commons voluntarily withdrew or were "for just cause" excluded, a lawful quorum of the people's representative was obliged to transact the affairs of state.

On this justification of the Long Parliament as the only valid government during its long term rested the foundation of Vane's justification of his own actions as its agent. During this time of violence and confusion, when right and wrong became increasingly perplexed, he had dutifully remained active in the offices to which the people had assigned him, and tried to act for the common welfare and safety, even though he may have been forced to act contrary to the rights of king or Lords. In order to protect the liberty conveyed to it by the people, the Parliament had declared that it could not be dissolved without its own consent; consequently, even the Rump remained a lawfully constituted body. Whatever he had done as a member of that body, however "tortuous and erroneous," was neither illegal nor criminal. Certainly acting under instructions from the only lawful existing government cannot be treason.

And yet Vane realized sorely that in those chaotic times many mistakes had been made and that he had made some of them. He acknowledged that a time had come when the revolution itself tried to compel men to do things contrary to right reason, conscience, and even common sense—to disobey God, as some felt. Then men had a right to resist Parliament even as they might resist a monarch. And when he had been impelled to do so, he seemed to be turning against his own party and his own friends. Yet, most of the time, he had simply done his duty as he saw it, though he now realized that he may not always have seen it clearly. His final judgment on himself is simply that he had tried conscientiously. And so he ought to be "affirmed one that hath done his duty, even the next best that was left to him, or possible for him to do, in such a dark stormy season, and such difficult circumstances." He was neither groveling nor boasting.

Vane was now less dogmatic about political forms than he had once been. Disillusioned about the possibility of creating on this earth a pure theocracy in which form and spirit are one, mirroring exactly the Heavenly Jerusalem, he maintained that the realms of the spirit and the magistracy must be wholly separated, and that the only valid form of government was the people's elected representative, the Commons; he had rejected both Lords and "single person," whatever he might be called. But now, as in his youth, he was not sure that the precise form mattered so long as men governed according to the spirit of true justice: it was not so much the form the administration took as "the thing administered, wherein the good or evil of government doth consist." Perhaps even the restored, limited Stuart monarchy would not be beyond redemption.

But what of the good old cause, the very essence of which had been the preservation of the liberties of the people? Even though it had been defeated, he could not consider it wholly discredited. Yet God had passed a judgment on the revolution, for when triumphant, the revolutionaries had tragically over-reached; not content with deposing the king as they had every right to do, they had illegally killed him. And then the revolution somehow had reshaped itself in the very image of the tyranny it had existed to oppose. If God had declared for the cause in the victories of the civil war, He must also have declared against it when he allowed Cromwell to convert the Commonwealth into a Protectorate, and the Protectorate to be replaced by a corrupted Rump which collapsed into anarchy. This could only have happened because God willed it so, whether He was punishing the errors of the revolutionaries, however well meant, or because he was withdrawing behind the cloud of His Majesty for a time to work out His will later in some unexpected way. And if God had withdrawn His fostering hand from the cause, He had also withdrawn it from His loving servant, Sir Henry Vane. And yet since Vane was sure he had not knowingly betrayed his Lord, but had done his best, like Job he would maintain his ways before an inscrutable God. Perplexed and dubious, Vane refused to give way to despair, but searched for explanation and comfort in prophetic scripture.

If the Saints could no longer labor to construct the ideal

magistracy to receive Christ, but could hasten His coming only by patient endurance, Vane would re-examine what he had said in *A Retired Man's Meditations* about the nature of individual rebirth, the influx of the Holy Spirit, and the wondrous day of Christ's coming in glory.

It is pleasant to imagine Sir Francis Godolphin, having dutifully read *The Cause of the People* and found it both lucid and harmless, befuddling his brain as he threaded his way through the mazes of the *Two Treatises* in search of sedition. For in *An Epistle General to the Mystical Body of Christ* and *The Face of the Times*, Sir Henry was no less subtle, devious, and mistily allegorical than he had been in the *Meditations*. If anything, he is more apocalyptic.

Vane had previously divided the recipients of the Holy Ghost into the twice-born and the thrice-born or truly elect. Now he subdivided the truly elect into a lower order who have only a single portion of the Holy Ghost, and a higher order who enjoy a double portion. Both these orders dwell in the Heavenly Jerusalem and both consist of "new men" whose calling and election are sure; both orders are so "anointed and impressed with the name of God that it excludes all possibility of falsehood, deceit, or uncertainty" (Vane was certain that whatever his enemies thought, his shifts of position were neither changes of goal nor evil dissimulation). The lower order are only like the angels, whereas the higher order—the elect of the elect—consists of a select number of Christ's "choice favorites and friends that he redeems from amongst all other men" and makes His equals. These happy few experience what St. Paul felt when he was caught up into the third heaven; they behold divine beauty in its original; there they are free with an ineffable freedom, confirmed in effortless obedience to God's will. To these friends, Christ comes in familiarity and intimacy of a husband, and His coming brings love, ecstasy, and delight for they are the Lamb's wife.

Vane was still obsessed with the allegorization of the cryptic books of scripture: though he had not forgotten the Book of Daniel, he had now become enchanted with the shifting opalescent symbolism of the Book of Revelation, especially chapters 11 through 14, with their reaping sickles, burning fires, and vials of wrath. There are two prophetical allegories therein that struck him as apposite to the tribulations of the Saints. God has Two Witnesses, we are told, who shall prophesy in sackcloth for 1,260 days, after which the Beast shall ascend from the bottomless pit, make war upon them, and slay them. And the dead bodies of the Two Witnesses shall lie in the streets for three and a half days, and then arise. Mystically parallel to this prophecy and reinforcing it is another in which a woman, clothed with the sun, standing upon the moon, and having on her head a crown of twelve stars, bears a man-child who will rule the nations. This child will be caught up to heaven, but the woman must flee into the wilderness where she shall stay for 1,260 days.

Vane was teased by these numbers, as Sir Isaac Newton would be, into computations of the day of Christ's coming, which he, as one of the super-elect, so longingly anticipated. He had once hoped to live to see that day in the flesh, though he had always been too cautious to appoint a date so near in the future that if he were wrong he would be publicly confounded. But now with the hour of his own death nearing, he perceived that the death of the world was also at hand. The church had been in the wilderness almost 1,260 years. The exact year of the end could not be determined, but the heathenish Roman Empire, Vane figured, continued till "somewhat more" than 400 years after Christ, and with the fall of the Roman Empire, the woman—that is, the spiritual part of the church—was sent into the wilderness for 1,260 years. By adding 1,260 and 400 (more or less, depending on when God dated the fall of Rome) one arrives at the year 166(?). Vane, whether hazarding a guess or under the guidance of some inner impulse, concluded that the years of wrath and oppression of the true seed by the serpent should last for 1,666 years after Christ's birth. Then the Witnesses must die and lie in the streets for three and a half years, and then Christ will come. By Vane's calculations the end must come somewhere around 1670, not very long after he would probably die.

The times of tribulations were certainly at hand, and even now, Vane saw, the Two Witnesses were being persecuted. These Two Witnesses are not two individual men, but the two main orders of the spiritual seed who have testified and will testify until the end, and who are now in disrepute—silenced, pursued, imprisoned. And perhaps the bitterest of Vane's discoveries in the dark allegories was that in these last days, the sharpest and most determined enemies of the Witnesses were the reformed churches, who hated and rejected the spiritual seed. This one-time Root and Branch man, who had hated Catholicism and would have destroyed Anglicanism because its root grew in the papal garden, had learned the harsh truth that it was after all the churches of the Reformation, propounders of the Word and self-styled witnesses of God, who were the most intractable enemies of his own inward religion. And he recognized that this universal war between the serpent and the woman's seed had not only flamed in England but was now raging in America, "the last piece of ground this quarrel is to be fought out in." He had been right in placing Mistress Anne among the true witnesses.

So at that very moment the weapons of God's anger were ready; His full vials of wrath were to be poured out by heavenly militia upon the Beast and his worshipers. For a man naturally mild and now almost at peace with himself, Vane perhaps dwells too long and lovingly on the destruction of Christ's enemies, and his; though who was he to emasculate the words of John the Revelator? The peculiar ambivalence of the man expresses itself again in his dual treatment of scripture as at once factual reality and abstract allegory, and he may have relieved some of his latent hostilities and frustrations in contemplating the destruction of his enemies by the distant hand of God. He must surely have needed some catharsis. But if he felt uneasy at the holocaust by fire, he could make peace with his conscience by allegorizing it: God "shall kindle a fire of conviction and self-judging in the conscience of the wicked." On that awful day there will be both a burning of the flesh and an even more frightful burning of the conscience. But Vane had never agreed with the Fifth Monarchists that true believers should anticipate God's work by destroying the wicked with firearm and sword; it is enough that the Saints should set in order the little kingdoms of their own minds and souls.

Though Vane understood that in his suffering he was fulfilling prophecy, it was lonely enough to live as a solitary and helpless witness to the cause even without the fear that God had rejected His Saints when He had retired, inscrutable, behind the brazen heavens. But by searching further in the scriptures, Vane found not only understanding but also the solace and reassurance he needed. In the second book of Chronicles Vane read the story of Jehoshaphat who, when the Israelites were being attacked by the powerful Moabites and Ammonites, cried out to the Lord for help. The spirit of the Lord descended and spoke through the mouth of Jahaziel, telling the

Israelites, "Be not afraid . . . for the battle is not yours, but God's," and instructing them not to fight, but simply to stand still. They stood aside while their enemies destroyed each other in the valley, leaving the Israelites to gather the spoils of victory.

And in the prophecies of Joel, he read that in the last days God would gather all the Gentile nations and bring them into the Valley of Jehoshaphat. Combining these two passages, Vane understood why the Saints were prevented by the Lord from continuing the good fight; in these last days they do not need to do battle, but only to stand quiet and trust the Lord, and after their enemies have demolished each other, Christ will return and rule the world with His Saints. And so he knew that God had not averted His face in anger but rather in order to tell the Saints that they had done what they could, and that He now willed them to retire inward to a life in Christ, in retreat from the "noise and diversions of the sinful and unquiet world." And by the end of his long durance, Vane had brought himself to such a docile acceptance of God's will that his restlessness and questioning and dread were all stilled, and he enjoyed a serenity of mind such as he had never known before. "They also serve who only stand and wait," his friend Milton had once written when his own usefulness seemed at an end; now Vane was content to serve God by doing nothing but remaining constant, trusting in the Lord though He might slay him. If he, like Christ, was to be slain for the people, it would be his honor to imitate his Lord in giving up his life gladly.

Tranquillity of mind glows quietly in all Vane said and wrote and did in his last months. As he prepared to die, he wrote a series of short meditations on some of the central human experiences: the meaning and value of life, of friendship, of enemies, of government, and especially of death. In these little Baconian essays, Vane is at his most appealing as a writer—easy and simple in style, and in manner forthright, candid, and free from contentiousness. Friendship, that "complication or enfolding of two souls in one," is one of the best things life offers. Concerning enemies, we must take care "not to meditate revenge," but to take heed that when we are offended, "we do nothing unworthy or unbecoming us"; then we can "gain and conquer by dying." After all, a man should not "ill resent anything that shall happen to him," for truly we "can receive no evil but of ourselves." As for life, one must know when to "hold and preserve" it, when to "loose or give it up, for a good death is far better and more eligible than an ill life." Not that he contemns death either; as it is the last of man's acts, so it is the most difficult, and only in the light of his death can a man judge rightly of his life: "Life is measured by the end." But the right time to die is only when "to live is rather a burden than a blessing, and there is more ill in life than good." Vane had surely reached that time, and he had come to it partly by the "cross accidents" issuing from the contests of government. And he now thinks that the best way for a man to deal with such accidents is not to resist or escape, but to take them

> at their worst, let them prove what they will, though to the loss of life and all that's dear to him in the world.
>
> To resolve within himself to bear them sweetly and patiently, and peaceably to attend whatever shall happen, without tormenting himself about it, or losing the calmness and serenity of his mind in going about to hinder or prevent it. He that takes the first course, labors to escape; he that takes the latter is content rather to suffer. This many times proves the better bargain.

This was the bargain Vane had made, and he kept it without regret.

Of Vane's letters to his wife from the Isles of Scilly only the one dated March 7, 1662, survives, and it is the most intimate and personal of his utterances, despite the long gospel message that fills most of it. Or perhaps because of it, for in his opening sentence Vane asserts that he and his wife have together received and professed the "christian principles which God of His grace hath afforded you and me"—that nowhere were they closer together than in their sharing the light and seeking out more divine truth. "My dear heart," he wrote out of his loneliness, "the wind yet continuing contrary, makes me desirous to be as much in converse with thee (having the opportunity) as the providence of God will permit." And he tries to strengthen himself to meet what is to come while he helps her to the comfort of resignation. He is, after all, no different from other of God's servants in suffering these sharp trials, and through such suffering God can bring forth his Kingdom within them: "This dark night and black shade, which God hath drawn over his work in the midst of us, may be (for ought we know) the ground color to some beautiful piece that he is exposing to the light." Meanwhile, he will patiently wait until God opens the prison doors, probably by his death. And why should his enemies envy his lying buried and quiet in his grave of a prison? He has taken up a sanctuary in God; he is a Pilgrim in the world, solitary and withdrawn, longing only to be dissolved and to be with Christ. "They that press so earnestly to carry on my trial, do little know what presence of God may be afforded me in it and issue out of it." He desires to be faithful to whatever God calls upon him to endure, and if he is to give public testimony and witness, he will be "nothing terrified."

Whatever happens, he tells Lady Vane, they must be ready; "if we are stripped of all we have, the earth is still the Lord's and the fulness thereof. . . . There is nothing more destructive to us in every way than the uncertainty we are in." And if perpetual imprisonment is to be his lot, he hopes to meet it with true inward contentment.

> I know nothing that remains unto us, but like a tossed ship in a storm, to let ourselves be tossed and driven with the winds, till he that can make these storms to cease, and bring us into a safe haven, do work out our deliverance for us. I doubt not but you will accordingly endeavor to prepare for the worst.

In asking his wife to prepare for the worst, Vane was only asking her to do what he had done already. He had now stopped fighting and planning; there had been an end to conspiracies and designs, to both hope and fear. Resigned to the will of God, he will rejoice whether the prison doors open to life or to death. Christ, the captain of his salvation, drank deepest of the bitter cup; when it is handed to him, Vane will not blench. Thus he spoke to his wife, but the ultimate test was yet to come—would the act redeem the word?

Not much longer did he endure that destructive uncertainty, for in mid-April he was suddenly shipped back to England to wait in the Tower for his trial. There he completed a work entitled *A Pilgrimage into the Land of Promise*, "a serious search and prospect into life eternal." As the man who knew that he was about to die looked across the boundary into that promised land, he saw not his personal journey but only the eternal truths he had so often put into words before: it is not the resurrection of the body that matters, but rebirth of the spirit during life when the Holy Ghost makes all new; it is the second birth, not the first, that gives man his ultimate peace and security. Putting aside his personal fears and hopes and memories, in the *Pilgrimage* Vane made his final statement of his lifelong antinomianism.

During all these months of postponements and evasions of Parliament's instructions to bring Vane back for trial, it had seemed that he might finally be forgotten and left to languish peacefully in prison. Why was the government suddenly galvanzied into action in April of 1662? The grotesque fears that the "fanatics" would again burst out in conspiratorial violence miraculously inspired by Vane from his cell, had neither diminished nor lately been stirred up afresh. Of course, hatred for the man responsible for the death of Strafford was still strong, as was the generalized fear of Sir Henry's deviousness. And since the Cavalier Parliament had first met, the climate of intolerance and vindictiveness had darkened. But apparently what prompted the government to bring Sir Henry back from limbo was the capture of three regicides who had escaped to the continent. Colonel Okey, Sir John Barkstead, and Miles Corbet were enjoying a pipe and a cup of beer by the fireside at Barkstead's lodgings in Delft when Sir George Downing, the English ambassador, arrested them and shipped them off to England before the Dutch could deny extradition. Since all three had been previously attainted, it was only necessary to identify them before sentencing them. On April 19, all three were dragged on hurdles from the Tower to Tyburn, looking, Pepys said, "very cheerful." They endured their rough ride nonchalantly, Barkstead munching on some food, Okey eating an orange, and Corbet calmly reading a book. All three went to their gruesome deaths with fortitude, and in their death speeches, all three reaffirmed that their cause had been good and the king's death justified; they asserted that they had acted with neither malice nor self-interest, having spent their fortunes and bought no bishop's or king's lands. Predictably the solemn confidence and freedom from rancor with which they conducted themselves stirred popular sympathy for them, and turned it further away from Downing, who, having got his start in Okey's regiment, was widely "noticed as a most unnatural villain."

But since Okey, though maintaining the justice of his cause had exhorted his listeners "to submit quietly to the present government," the king in his gracious mercy allowed his family to inter his head and quarters in Christian burial. But the next day the king heard that they were about to abuse his clemency by holding a solemn funeral attended by a "great concourse of people." Fearing that it would turn into a political demonstration, Charles demanded that the family inter the remains quietly within the confines of the Tower. And he ordered that "the names of those who have designed the said solemnity and tumultuous concourse be inquired into." Evidently clemency had its dangers.

Just three days after the execution, Sir Henry Vane was delivered into the hands of Sir John Robinson, Governor of the Tower, to be kept in close custody; on the same day John Lambert was also delivered from Guernsey. Now that the Royalists, after an interval, had again tasted the blood of the revolutionaries, they were hungry for more, and orders were given to prepare the case against Vane and Lambert.

Vane was not permitted to be present when he was indicted for high treason before the Middlesex Grand Jury, which—not without bullying—returned a true bill against him and set his arraignment for Monday, June 2, at the Court of the King's Bench in Westminster. Now Vane knew: the charge, treason; the trial, soon; help in preparing to meet the charges, none; he was denied access to his business advisers and solicitors. All alone, then, he sat down to prove that his actions against Charles I had not been treasonous.

22

Due Process of Law (1662)

Now that he had withdrawn from all conflict and effort in the Valley of Jehoshaphat, why did Vane decide to fight his case to the last breath? Not to save his life, surely; he knew that he was a man who had to be got rid of, and he had seen what chances a man has when the magistracy considers him dangerous and his very existence intolerable. What good was a legal defense to Strafford once Vane himself had revealed the frightening document? When the Commons could not reach Strafford by laws, they sidestepped and passed a bill of attainder. Harmless old Laud had to be disposed of, and when the law could not convict him, Parliament circumvented it again. Charles himself went to the block without even pleading "not guilty," though no one had satisfactorily answered his charge that the court lacked jurisdiction; when sanction failed, determination and force prevailed. Vane must have known that even if all the laws of England could be mustered on his side, he would yet die the death. Nevertheless, he would fight.

Though it is doubtful that he even much wanted to save his life, he did want to enact fully the role in which God had cast him. If he was to die a martyr's death, he must make it manifest that it was for the cause that he was dying and that the cause was God's. And he perceived that his case was the case of the people of England, for if by corrupt legalities he could be legally killed for authorized actions, no man in England would be safe: the shelter of the Act of Indemnity would be shattered by legal processes that violated right reason, common sense, and the justice that speaks through man's conscience. He could and must shine forth in court and on scaffold as martyr and witness, as spokesman for the people of England and for the cause, which must not leave to posterity a wounded name.

Vane therefore prepared a defense against the charges he expected to meet, charges of treasonously levying war against Charles I. Considering that he was not a lawyer, he showed much legal acumen throughout his ordeal, and he now worked out a remarkably full, acute, and legally ingenious defense of his actions in the civil war as a member of the Long Parliament. About the death of Charles he prepared no defense; he had never been accused of regicide. His fundamental defense throughout his trial was that in all his actions he was the agent of a sovereign Parliament which after voting that it could be dissolved only by its own consent remained sovereign as long as it met.

It was not Parliament but the king who declared a war, first by bringing force to arrest the five members and then by mustering an army in the North and formally raising his standard. In declaring war against Parliament, the king was also declaring war against the people of England; he was also breaking his coronation oath and violating the sacred mandate of rule. Once the tripartite power was divided, the only competent judge left was Parliament, which then had the right to adjudicate not only about taxes but in all cases "of common good and necessity of the kingdom." In such circumstances, what could constitute treason? A principle had been established in the case of Sir John Hotham that it was treason to attack the king only when he was acting in his just and right authority; to oppose his personal and his unjust commands was not treason, for that was not levying war against his laws and authority but was actually defending them against his person. Treason then could not be committed against the king as a person but only when he was discharging his trust as a king.

As he prepared his defense, Vane pressed this point further. True treason is directed against the nation, and if to defend the land and the people's liberties demands attacking the king, then one must attack him. And the statute providing that "none that shall attend on the King and do him true service shall be attainted, or forfeit anything" is meaningless unless it also applies, in the words of the statute, to serving "the king for the time being in his wars." And a "king for the time being" is "whoever is for the present allowed and received by the Parliament in behalf of the kingdom." Consequently, whenever there is question about who is rightly in power, those who follow the judgment of Parliament ought to be "secure and free from all account and penalties."

But this is a knotty point and Vane emphasizes that it was a time "of such difficulty and unusualness" as made it impossible for a subject to know his duty "by any known law or certain rule extant." He insists that in such an ambiguous situation one should be safe in relying upon the "judgment and reason of the sovereignty of Parliament."

Armed with this written defense broad enough to cover whatever form the indictment might take, Vane went to be arraigned at the King's Bench on Monday, June 2, 1662. Standing at the bar, he heard the indictment read aloud in English. It was not very long, only two paragraphs, but it was intricately phrased and would have to be answered with precision. Besides, its contents were shockingly unexpected. Taken aback, Sir Henry asked and was permitted to hear it read again. But then, when he begged to hear it read in Latin, the language in which it would stand in the record, the court flatly refused. Serjeant Keeling, who was waspish all through the trial, said that though the record was in Latin, "the agitation of a cause in Court ought to be in English." But Vane listened intently to the second reading in English so that he could fix the phrases and the charges in his memory. And he listened incredulously too—it was as he had heard the first time: he was not charged with treason against Charles I at all, but only against Charles II, who had been in exile, unable to set foot in England from before his father's death until his restoration. Much of his prepared defense was beside the point, and his vindication of the Long Parliament terminated with the death of the king; he would have to plan a new defense.

The indictment charged, in the usual intimidating and grandiose phrases,

that you as a false traitor against his most excellent Majesty King Charles the second, your supreme and natural Lord, not having the fear of God before your eyes, and withdrawing that your duty and allegiance, which a true subject ought to have and bear to our said Liege and Sovereign Lord, [on the] thirteenth of May, in the eleventh year of our said sovereign Lord the King [1659] did compass and imagine the death of our said sovereign Lord the

King, and the ancient frame of government of this realm, totally to subvert and keep out our said sovereign Lord from the exercise of his regal government; together with other false traitors, to the jurors unknown, did traitorously and maliciously assemble and sit together, and then and there consulted to bring the King unto destruction, and to hold him out from the exercise of his regal authority, and there usurped the government, and appointed officers, to wit colonels and captains of a certain army, raised against the King. . . .

And the better to effect this, the twentieth of December in the same eleventh year, with a multitude, to the number of a thousand persons, to the jurors unknown, in warlike manner assembled, and arrayed with guns, trumpets, drums, etc., did levy war against the peace. . . .

The charge of "compassing and imagining" the death of the king was customary, but only two overt acts were cited and both of them in 1659. What were these violent and treasonable acts? Vane remembered the dates: on May 13 he had first sat on the committee empowered by the recently revived Rump to appoint officers in the army. That was all. And on December 20? Yes, he had reviewed the regiment which bore his name, and finding them in good order had bought them drinks. On both days he was acting on authority of the Rump. But in both these incidents he had acted with others equally responsible or guilty, and they were said to be "unknown to the jury." Of course. Since they all stood pardoned by the Act of Indemnity from which he had been excepted, the fiction that they were unknown was inevitable, for to name them along with Vane would be to incriminate them, contrary to the act. He was singled out to bear the guilt of acts in which many had participated. But since by defending himself he would also defend and perhaps clear the name of the people of England, he gathered his thoughts and struck back, countering legalism with legalism, as well as with principles of justice and law.

He first took exception to the indictment as insufficient: it did not clearly specify places, and the actions specified were too petty to amount to war, and their hostility to the king was not proved. He also challenged the jurisdiction of this court over things done in the name of the "sovereign court of Parliament"—a phrase at which the court took great offense. And for that matter, no witnesses had actually identified the present Sir Henry Vane as the one who was excluded from the act. This niggling evasion worked no better than had Henry Marten's objection that he could not be the man mentioned in his indictment because his name was there spelled with an "i," but it did annoy the court; king's counsel warned Vane that if they were to pursue this question and he lost, it would be too late for him to plead "not guilty." His exceptions to the indictment the court ignored.

But before he would plead, Vane undertook to disclose the bias and injustice of the process he had undergone. Not only had he been imprisoned for two years without being charged or even examined, but his rent and goods had been illegally seized and sequestered, and men had petitioned to purchase his estates just as if he had already been attainted. In fact, he said, his case had already been prejudged by the Lords when they insisted on excepting him for life against the will of the Commons, who were his proper judges; he had finally been the victim of a compromise to save the bill from defeat. And his present judges, being peers, were members of that body which had judged him unworthy of pardon. Now by making him stand trial for the whole cause, they were in effect adjudging the whole English people morally guilty, and despite legal pardon the moral evil would remain on the record. And how fair could a trial be, he asked, when the prosecution had two years to search out evidence and witnesses, while the defendant would have only four days? And the Parliament too had been prejudged when its actions were all voided, and its orders, votes, and resolutions forbidden to be produced even for the defendant's aid.

Vane concluded with a burst of eloquence, reminding the court that if this unique case of his was to be carried thus arbitrarily, it would be better for the prisoner to be destroyed by some special command without any form of law at all than to go through a process of justice. He now proudly stood before them, he said, not only as a man clothed in the privilege of the sovereign court of Parliament (he continued to use the offensive phrase), but as a Christian, resigned to the will of God.

The court did not listen to this prepared statement without brusque interruptions, nor was it willing to grant Vane legal counsel, despite his plea that since he was not a lawyer he would need advice upon some peculiar if not unique and unprecedented legal questions. The court rested upon the old precedent that putative traitors should not be allowed counsel, though the judges graciously promised that they would themselves provide whatever legal clarifications he might need. Accepting this small comfort as the best he could draw from them, Vane pleaded "not guilty" and was returned to the Tower unaware that most of the overt acts to be cited against him were yet to be revealed.

On the morning of Friday, June 6, Sir Henry Vane stood at the bar while from a panel of forty-eight freeholders of Middlesex County a jury of twelve men was selected. It was a packed jury, composed almost entirely of known Royalists, and although Vane was allowed peremptory challenges, he complained that since he knew none of the men, any challenge would be random and without reason. In fact, he later charged that only the night before, the king's counsel, learning that six men of a panel were moderate and disinterested, required the sheriff to "unsummon" that panel and draw a completely new one. And one of the new panel who, having been overheard speaking favorably of Vane, could rightly have been challenged by the Crown, was not even called, though he waited all the time out in the hall. Worst of all, in the bustle and confusion, Vane was not able to hear the judges hastily swear in the foreman, William Roberts, or one Sir Christopher Abdy; consequently, he had no opportunity to challenge them.

On the King's Bench sat four judges: Chief Justice Forster, Justice Mallet, Justice Twisden, and Justice Windham, and arrayed against Vane were six high-powered lawyers: Sir Geoffry Palmer, the king's attorney general, Sir Heneage Finch, Sir William Wild, Serjeant Keeling—and Vane's revolutionary allies and Parliamentary opponents, Sir John Glyn and Sir John Maynard. The latter two had prepared the cases against both Strafford and Laud, and their participation in all these prosecutions gave rise to some doggerel:

> Did not the lawyers Glyn and Maynard
> To make good subjects traitors strain hard?

Attorney General Palmer presented the Crown's case to the jury. Since the "intentions of the heart are secret," he began, imagining and intending the death of the king must be manifested by overt acts, and the prisoner had sat with others in several councils, encroached upon the government, levied forces, appointed officers, and at last levied open war at the head of a regiment. Proof of any one of these acts was sufficient to condemn him, but levying war at the head of a regiment was the crowning act which, it proved, proved all the others. However, of all his treasonous acts, said Palmer, the prosecution would restrict itself to those against his present Majesty. He then enumerated particulars unmentioned in the indictment, beginning with a warrant to officers of the navy to issue supplies for ships guarding the Narrow Seas; it was signed by Vane on January 30, 1649, the very day of the late king's murder, and the first day therefore of the reign of Charles II. Two witnesses identified the handwriting as Vane's. Then Palmer submitted entries in the *Journal* of the House of Commons which mentioned Vane's name (when he had spoken or acted as teller) to prove his membership in Commons; these entries also proved that he had presented reports to Parliament from the new Council of State and therefore must have been a member of it; witnesses testified that although they had not actually seen him sitting in the council, they had seen him enter the room and leave it when meetings were finished. Among reports from this and the succeeding Council of State was one that included the council's oath to preserve all proceedings in secrecy (the shadow of Strafford falling across him again). The treasonous nature of the Council of State was proved by the instructions Parliament had given it to suppress every person pretending to the title of king, by virtue of connection with the House of Stuart, or "any single person whatsoever." Sir Henry had not only sat on this council but had at times chaired it and signed warrants for the issue of firelocks and drums to Commonwealth regiments, and for provisions for the Commonwealth fleet.

Then, skipping from 1653 to 1659, Mr. Attorney General detailed evidence that Sir Henry had levied war. As a member of the Rump's Committee of Safety he had conferred with foreign ambassadors and appointed officers in the army whose names were in the record; he had signed warrants for swords and other supplies for "his regiment"; he had once proposed a new model of government which excluded any earthly king and assigned all power to the people and their representatives. And there were witnesses to prove that Sir Henry had been at Southwark at the review of troops,

including "his regiment," and had given Captain Linn five pounds
to provide them drinks.

During this long speech and the testimonies of many witnesses,
Vane had not been allowed to speak. When the Crown had finished,
he was instructed that he must now go through his entire case at
once, after which the king's counsel would have the last word in
rebuttal and in summary to the jury. Faced with this host of new
specific charges, Vane maneuvered for time. First he tried to lay his
legal foundation: treason, he said, can be perpetrated only against a
king in possession and actually reigning, whereas the indictment
itself assumed an interregnum. But the court interrupted him to rule
that he must first make out his case in order of the facts before
standing on a matter of law, for *in facto jus oritur*—the law arises
from fact; and they enjoined him to produce his witnesses "if he had
any." Vane asked the court for warrants to summon witnesses and
time to assemble them, but he was curtly told that since the jury
"were to be kept without meat, drink, fire, or candle, till their
verdict was delivered in," his request could not be granted. Sir
Henry then punningly compared this jury to the forty "Jewry-
men" who swore not to eat or drink until they had killed Paul.

The highly theoretical defense he had written was of little use, for
when he tried to read from it he was continually interrupted and
forced back to the specific charges. We do not know how much of it
he managed to utter, but he delivered the main substance in spite of
confusions and interruptions, and during this long and grueling
ordeal, he improvised a frequently brilliant defense which was also
an attack on legal rigor and injustice. At first he tried to stand on
Parliamentary privilege which would exempt him from trial by a
lesser court, but the court peremptorily ordered, "If the things
charged were done, justify them; if not, excuse them."

So he returned to the facts of the charges, but to legalism he again
opposed legalisms, to quibble, quibbles. As regarded the first
warrant, he thought that since his signature had on occasion been
counterfeited, sometimes for large sums, this one might have been
forged, and he produced two witnesses who opined that the
handwriting was not his. Nonsense, said Justice Windham; men
might forge a signature for money, but no one would do so merely
to "set ships to sea," and he instructed the jury to consider that. But
no witnesses saw him signing these warrants, Vane insisted, nor did

During the final, chaotic months of the interregnum, General Monk became a man of destiny. Seconded by his loyal troops, he opposed the rebellion of the officers who had "interrupted" the Rump Parliament. But, when a few months later he ordered the arrogant and incompetent Rump to dissolve itself, he precipitated a crisis of government and negotiated the restoration of Charles II. Miniature by Isaac Oliver. (Radio Times Hulton Picture Library)

John Maynard, a formidable lawyer, successfully prosecuted the Earl of Strafford for treason with young Vane as chief witness, and then, after the Restoration, prosecuted Vane himself on the same capital charge. Artist of portrait is unknown. (The National Portrait Gallery, London)

Carisbrooke Castle, a stronghold on the Isle of Wight, was a convenient place to isolate dangerous political prisoners. Here Charles I was imprisoned for over a year before his trial and death. And here his antagonist Sir Harry Vane was also confined before he was returned to the Tower of London for trial and execution. (Radio Times Hulton Picture Library)

any witnesses see him sit in the Council of State; and he was actually absent from the House from December 6 to February 2, the period of the king's trial and death. What is more, when he returned to the House he had refused to act in either the House or the Council of State so long as he had to take the oath approving the death of the king. Nor did he seek a place in the council, but was elected without his knowledge or consent.

But it was futile, Vane knew, to deal with these Parliamentary activities one at a time. Whatever the technical inadequacy of the witnesses, he certainly had functioned in these committees and councils—it was public knowledge. All of these charges would stand or fall by his central legal contention that the actions charged against him had been performed on the authority of a legitimate Parliament, and therefore could not be called in question by a lesser court. In all the changes of government, which as he said were "not done in a corner," he had been neither an initiator nor a principal actor, nor had he done anything that could not be charged against countless others who had taken part in the government after the death of Charles.

And so the whole argument was reduced once again to questions of law, and he again begged for legal counsel to advise him on them: Could a whole Parliament be impeached of high treason? Could any person acting by authority of Parliament commit treason? Could a lower court call Parliament's authority into question? Could a king de jure who is out of possession of his kingdom have treason committed again him? Could his own alleged actions in Southwark be accepted as evidence before a Middlesex Jury?

Finch quickly disposed of that last question: yes, any overt act anywhere can prove "imagining the death of the King" in Middlesex. Vane must immediately call any witnesses he had, he was told, for once the Crown began its formal reply to him, he must henceforth be silent. Then the Crown made a concession: they would stipulate that his acts were performed in the name of the Council of State, and that the council derived its authority from "what he called a Parliament."

But this seeming concession proved to be a trap with two springs, and Vane saw neither of the snares. If you so stipulate, he said, you must prove that I acted in any other Council of State after the Parliament was turned out. The Crown was ready: a warrant was produced dated November 3, 1659, after Lambert's "interruption"; it was signed by Vane as Secretary of the Navy, by authority of the Committee of Safety, and was an order to dispatch arms northward to Lambert who was marching to oppose Monk. This act obviously was performed in the absence of a Parliament, but Vane held that the office of Secretary of the Navy to which the Rump had appointed him was necessarily continued, and in that office he still acted by Parliamentary authority.

All he could now do was to prove that he had not levied war with his regiment. As for the business of the regiment, he said, it was

an employment, which I can in truth affirm, mine own inclinations, nature, and breeding little fitted me for, and which was intended only as honorary and titular, with relation to volunteers who, by their application to the Council of State, in time of great commotions, did propound their own officers, and (without any seeking of mine, or my considering any farther of it than as the use of my name) did (among others) nominate me for a Colonel, which the Council of State approved . . . and Parliament confirmed.

He had two witnesses to attest that he had refused to issue orders to the regiment even when officers requested him to do so. And the Crown had no witnesses to the contrary, even though it was said that Monk had tried unsuccessfully to pressure or bribe Captain Linn into testifying that Vane had ordered him and the regiment to fight Sir George Booth. "Be not afraid to speak," Linn reported Monk's emissary as saying, "I warrant you, we shall hang Sir Henry Vane, for he is a rogue."

Sir Henry's defense completed, Solicitor Finch had the last word, and a long, trenchant, hectoring word it was. First, he released the second spring of his trap, answering Vane's legal questions in such a way as to demolish the Parliamentary authority on which they had stipulated that his acts depended. What Vane called a Parliament was ended by the death of the king, said Finch, for that Parliament had been called by his warrants, and his warrants automatically expired at his death; Parliament's own act to perpetuate itself had no force. Besides, having been forcibly reduced in numbers, it was not even representative. It is absurd to say, he continued, that acts of the

Parliament of Charles I could be his acts in the reign of Charles II, for it was not possible for one king to impose a Parliament on his successor who must call his own. And yes, even a valid Parliament could commit treason if it departed from the allegiance sworn at the first meeting. And what is more, a king, even though he is out of possession, can indeed have treason committed against him. Here Solicitor Finch was arguing double-tongued, for he maintained that Charles II, against whom treason could be committed while he was out of possession, was never out of possession, a position that, as Vane pointed out, contradicted the indictment, where it was said that Vane had conspired to keep Charles "from the exercise of his regal government." If he had always exercised his regal authority, the charge was meaningless. It was Vane's most telling point in law, but the other four judges chimed in to buttress Finch's arguments and tear apart Vane's defense. Said Justice Twisden, the question is not whether Parliament can commit treason, but rather whether a few members, shutting out their fellows and usurping the government, were not traitors; and he asserted dogmatically that Charles II was king de facto as well as de jure the moment his father died. Thus did the judges keep their promise to give Sir Henry counsel about his legal questions. After all their strenuous arguing, what they really demonstrated was that the questions did remain ambiguous, and that when political power is divided against itself there is no unassailable way to determine whom it is right to obey.

Finch made his final summation of the facts with many "impertinent flashes of wit and declamatory flourishes of rhetoric," exaggerating and misrepresenting the prisoner's alleged crimes, and he concluded with a "large and bitter invective" in which he said openly that Vane "must be made a public sacrifice." Sir Henry believed he should have the right to make some reply: "Paul was not so served," he wrote afterwards; "he had the last word to his jury."

Sir Henry was silenced, but Solicitor Finch was seen to whisper to the foreman of the jury just before they retired. Weary, hungry, and docile, they took only half an hour to decide that Sir Henry Vane had been guilty of high treason not only in the charges of the indictment, but also in a long series of treasons from the very beginning of the reign of Charles II—January 30, 1649.

For ten racking hours Sir Henry had stood at the bar without intermission, denied all rest or respite, even food and drink. Nor in his pride did he ask consideration of his person, but only of his cause. Nevertheless, after hearing the verdict, he left the court in triumphant and almost jovial good spirits, in a kind of exultation that he had that day proved himself "worthy to suffer for the name of Christ," and had stood uncompromising and uncompromised as a witness to the cause. His trial, he felt, had been a success against great odds: "Neither flatteries before, nor threatening now could prevail upon me," he told a friend, "and I bless God that enabled me to make a stand for his cause; for I saw the Court resolved to run it down, and (through the assistance of God) I resolved they should run over my life and blood first."

The five days' respite before sentence was to be imposed he put to good use. On Wednesday, June 11, he returned to court prepared to put on record every bias, injustice, slight, or insult that the cause had received in his person, and to speak out again for laws consonant with both fact and truth. He would make the courtroom his platform. For like Charles I, he never accepted the jurisdiction or procedure of the court that tried him; "he never owned it for a legal trial to his last breath." And this time he would not be silenced: if the court would not hear him, the public could read him, for everything he had to say was in writing, ready for the printing press. Though he had been assured that at the proper time the court would hear whatever he had to say to justify an arrest of judgment, he had little faith that he would be allowed to speak freely. And his suspicions were verified. The court interrupted his arguments, snubbed his appeals, and negated his motions with neither patience nor courtesy, and the law duly proceeded amid much noise and confusion.

When after the opening formalities Sir Henry stood at the bar, the clerk asked him "what he had to say, why sentence of death should not be passed upon him." He first complained that he had not heard the indictment read in Latin, and after some squabbling the king's counsel with a shrug desired "that the prisoner might be satisfied in that point." Then Sir Henry asked again for legal counsel, but he was over-ruled by the court. He in turn shrugged, and "desisted from any further urging it." He also relinquished any further attempt to reargue the old legal questions. Instead, he submitted to the judges a long Bill of Exceptions and asked the judges to sign and seal it, in accordance with a statute of Edward I which provided that any man aggrieved by proceedings against him should write his exceptions and "desire the Justices to set their seal on it." Its purpose, as Justice Coke had explained, was to provide a record on which a defendant could appeal to a higher court on a plea of mistrial. By sealing the document, the judges would not approve the exceptions, but only verify that these were in fact the objections the accused had submitted. "And if the judge (or judges) deny to seal the exception, the party wronged may in the Writ of Error take issue thereupon, if he can prove by witnesses the judge or judges denied to seal it." Serjeant Keeling, who frequently "showed a very snappish property" towards the prisoner, tried to wrest the law book from Sir Henry's hands, whereat Sir Henry remarked that if their conditions were reversed he would not only allow Serjeant Keeling books, but would even find them for him. Sir Henry was so insistent upon his right to the Bill of Exceptions that after much dispute the judges consented that the statute on which he based his plea might be read aloud in open court. And though the statute seemed to favor the prisoner's petition, the judges nevertheless over-ruled it, deciding that the statute "was not allowable in criminal cases for life," for if it were, "every felon in Newgate might plead the same, and so there would be no gaol delivery."

His was no felon's case, Sir Henry responded indignantly, for felons were not confined for years without being charged or heard, as he had been. Besides, the king had already granted him his life if he were condemned; why then this haste in a matter of death, which is irrevocable, when civil questions of mere property were often indefinitely protracted? He was after all making this plea not only for his own sake, "but for theirs, and for posterity, that they might on a more leisurely and unprejudiced hearing of what may be said on all hands, prevent the bringing of innocent blood upon themselves and the land." Again the court over-ruled him. Would they then at least "give it as their common judgment . . . that what he desired was not his due by the law?" Thus pushed into a corner, each judge individually asserted that it was legal and right that Vane should "be denied the benefit of that act," mainly on the grounds that the act had not been called into practice for a hundred years.

So much for the Bill of Exceptions in which Sir Henry had itemized all his wrongs and all the legal errors and biases he had observed. Much of it was repetition: he had been illegally held prisoner; the jury was packed; the indictment was inadequate, the charges being uncertain and vaguely phrased, involving multitudes of unknown persons, and no sufficient overt act being alleged, since mere assembly without hostility does not constitute levying war; and so forth. He added that no allegation was directly proved by two witnesses, and he lined up a series of grievances that tended to show that there had been a conspiracy for his legal murder among his tenants, his enemies, and Royalists eager for his estates. But this long and trenchant attack on the whole judicial process under which he had suffered would be known only to his friends and posterity, who could do nothing about it.

Now Sir Henry had recourse to his last outpost of defense, the Petition of Both Houses. What it said was that since His Majesty was pleased to proceed only against the immediate murderers of his father, and since they had not found Vane or Lambert one of these, both Lords and Commons were "humble suitors to your Majesty that if they shall be attainted, that execution, as to their lives, may be remitted." And the Lord Chancellor had reported back that "his Majesty grants the desires in the said petition." Its purport could hardly be clearer, but after long disputation the court decided that since it was not a formal act of Parliament, they were "not bound to take notice" of it. Vane argued cogently that it was part of the bill it was appended to, which received His Majesty's royal assent, and was a matter of public record. To pacify him, the court "condescended to read it, and that was all."

In everything he had tried, Sir Henry had been rebuffed. Not that there is reason to question the integrity of his judges, who were no more arrogant, hostile, and contentious than judges in most trials for treason. They were subtle legalists, and they had answered Sir Henry's questions to their own satisfaction with arguments based on statute and precedent. But they had brushed aside all the broad and humane questions of the spirit of justice that the prisoner had raised. Yet once again Sir Henry tried to explain to his judges why his conscience demanded that he stand his ground, for his case was the cause of the whole people of England who, in the condemnation about to be passed on his person, would "be rendered to posterity murderers and rebels, and that upon record in a Court of Justice." And he begged once more that the unprecedented legal questions opened by the civil war be explored and settled in the light of full and disinterested debate. But his insistence was clearly exasperating his judges, and having exhausted his arguments, he resorted to eloquence. All the declarations and actions on both sides, he said, were openly

> contended for in the high places of the field, and written even with characters of blood. And out of the bowels of these public differences and disputes doth my particular case arise, for which I am called into question. But admitting it come to my lot to stand single, in the witness I am to give to this Glorious Cause, and to be left alone (as in sort I am) yet being upheld with the authority before asserted, and keeping myself in union and conjunction therewith, I am not afraid to bear my witness to it in this great presence, nor to seal it with my blood, if called thereunto.

The judges being as impervious to eloquence as to appeals to God's natural law, Sir Henry made one more desperate attempt to assert the authority of Parliament while the king was out of possession, but the judges stopped him in mid-sentence, refusing to admit that the king was ever out of possession. But, cried Sir Henry, the very words of the indictment ran thus, "*that he endeavored to keep out his Majesty;* and how could he keep him out of the realm if he were not out?"

But it was futile, Vane saw; "bent upon his condemnation," the judges would over-rule whatever he proposed. Resignedly he folded up his papers and put them away, appealing now only to the "righteous judgment of God who . . . must judge them as well as him" and reiterating his satisfaction to die upon this testimony, to which Serjeant Keeling insultingly answered, "So you may, Sir, in good time, by the grace of God." Vane did not reply, but stood patiently while the Chief Justice lectured him that "had not the prisoner's high crimes been heightened by his very ill deportment, he might have had some hopes of mercy." Then he intoned the grim formula itemizing the ferocious process of hanging, drawing, and quartering at Tyburn, the "ordinary place of execution for the meanest thieves and robbers."

Not for many days would he have to endure the anticipation of that agony: Saturday, June 14, would be his last.

23

Martyr and Witness (1662)

Sir Henry Vane and John Lambert, both exempted from amnesty, were arraigned on the same day, but unlike Vane, Lambert did not trouble the court with "seditious queries"; rather, he repented and recanted, extenuated his offenses, and so generally abased himself that he found high favor with his judges and his king. After he had been tried and convicted of treason, the Lord Chief Justice announced that the king had been pleased to remit the death penalty, and Lambert was returned to the Isle of Guernsey, where he was granted wide indulgence, with freedom to range the island so far as was consistent with security.

But when King Charles heard of Vane's conduct at both arraignment and trial, he was perturbed and indignant. On Saturday afternoon he wrote to Lord Chancellor Clarendon: Sir Henry, he said, was

> if I am rightly informed, so insolent as to justify all he had done, acknowledging no supreme power in England but a parliament, and many things to that purpose. . . . and if he has given new occasion to be hanged, certainly he is too dangerous a man to let live if we can honestly put him out of the way.

And when Vane's judges had reported at Hampton Court that morning, they had already shown the king an honest way to by-pass his promise and Parliament's petition. God himself, Justice Forster had said, "though full of mercy, yet intended his mercy only to the penitent." It could not be said that Vane was penitent, and the king was under no obligation to be more merciful than the Almighty himself.

But Charles must not have been altogether easy in his mind, for he was persuaded by some of Vane's family (probably his brother, Sir Walter) to remit the hanging, drawing, and quartering, and allow him to die like a gentleman by beheading on Tower Hill, the very scene of a well-remembered show of courage when the Earl of Strafford bowed his head to the axe. Many men recalled that Vane had been the "prime instrument" of his death, and believed that Vane now suffered principally for his sake; revenge has a long memory and it seemed fitting that he should die under the shadow of his guilt. Nor was the day set for his death without remembered significance, for it was the anniversary of the Battle of Naseby, to celebrate which Sir Harry himself had proposed a day of general thanksgiving seventeen years ago. As Vane pondered what he would say and how he would act on the scaffold, many such memories must have crowded in upon him.

Did he remember poor old Laud, his cause defeated and his powers withered, languishing for years in the Tower before he was tried and haled out to a harassed, unceremonious death? He must surely have remembered the brave words of Harrison and even the cracked Venner, as they defended the cause with their last breaths. Did his mind turn back to his royal adversary Charles, whose death he had partly caused, though he had neither intended nor condoned it? As Vane protested the unjust treatment he had endured, did he remember what Charles, long imprisoned without charges, had written in isolation at Carisbrooke Castle?

> Felons obtain more privilege than I,
> They are allow'd to answer ere they die.

Or how Charles, too, had proclaimed that it was not his life alone, but the freedom of the English people that was at stake in his trial, warning that all private liberty is threatened when law is abrogated by force. Did he recall how Charles, making his death a public sacrifice, suggested step by step his Master's progress to Calvary, as Vane was doing? Did he realize that Charles with his episcopal forms and rituals, like Vane with his inner light, cleared for himself a haven of rest and refuge from the brutality and turmoil of the world, while he awaited his simulacrum of a trial and his martyrdom for his kingdom and God's church? On that Thursday, as Vane composed in solitude the speech he hoped to be allowed to deliver on the scaffold, many names and moments from the past must have ironically echoed in his mind, as the whirligig of time had brought in its revenges.

He carefully wrote down his lines for the last scene in this *Theatrum Mundi*, knowing that with all his inner composure, he might still be an imperfect actor, for he was getting old and tired and under stress his memory sometimes hesitated: at his trial, his enemies had made note of his long pauses when interruptions had thrown him off the track. To make sure that his message would be heard, he gave a copy to a friend for safe-keeping, suspecting that even in those last moments when a man should hold center stage in peace and dignity, his utterance might somehow be prevented— King Charles, he would recall, had been so thickly hedged with soldiers that his voice could not reach and stir any spectators beyond them. On Tower Hill, Sir Henry would face a multitude—a good house, he might well have said, for he knew that a public execution is rightly a theatrical performance. On a platform raised high before a large crowd, he would enact his own acceptance and control of his death. "We do not know what to say to him," Justice Forster had growled at his arraignment, "but we know what to do to him." Well, Vane knew what would be done to him, but what he would say about it was in his own choice.

After all, everyone knew the old analogy—"all the world's a stage"—and knew that for centuries a gallows had been called a stage and a stage a scaffold; Shakespeare had apologized for the constriction of his "unworthy scaffold" that could not contain the vasty fields of France. And many must have realized that to make an execution a public theatrical ritual in which for a time the victim plays the leading role in his own way, *in coram populo*, is not only to dignify a squalid business but also to assuage the pain of it, for how many victims playing a role of courage to the death have in truth found that courage, and by moving their audiences have achieved a victory not only over themselves but over those who had doomed them? Charles and Strafford and Laud had managed to do it, and so had Harrison and the other brave regicides, to the embarrassment of the government. Well, Vane would do that, too: it would be seen, he said, that he did not shrink from death, but made death shrink from him. And when he did play the martyr on the scaffold, he had rehearsed the part well, for he knew precisely what he was doing. Up to the last, he would be acting his own composition. In his cell, he said as much to his friends. God had already brought him upon three stages before the court, he said, "and now was leading him to the fourth (his execution place) which was far easier and pleasanter to him than any of the other three." The destructive uncertainty was over, and he was ready to make his entrance and play the scene right up to the shattering stroke of release.

On Friday the thirteenth, when his friends and disciples were permitted to visit him to give him comfort, he received them "with very great cheerfulness, and with a composed frame of spirit," but it was he who proved to be the comforter. "I have not the least reluctancy or struggling in my spirit against death," he told them. "I desire not to live; but my will is resigned to God in all. Why are you troubled? I am not." And he tried to convey to his grieving children the peace that comes in the valley of Jehoshaphat when all striving is given over: "God now seems to take all into his own hands," he told them. "You will be deprived of my bodily presence, but Abraham's blessing shall come upon you." Furthermore, he told them, they should not grieve for him, for since his imprisonment he had experienced "ravishments of joy," and had found an inward peace, "a joy unspeakable and glorious."

A few of his friends, still unresigned, urged him to offer some submission to the king in order to save his life. They little understood either Vane's thirst for martyrdom or his pride of spirit: he would not deny his integrity or beg for his life. If the king was not more concerned for his own honor and his word than Vane was for his life, "he was very willing they should take it. Nay I declare (said he) that I value my life less in a good cause, than the king can do his promise." Some were so tactless as to offer a thousand pounds to ransom his life; but "if a thousand farthings would gain it, he would not give it. . . . for," he said, "I think the King himself is so sufficiently obliged to spare my life that it is fitter for him to do it, than my self to seek it." So much for the honor of the Stuarts: like father, like son. Though Strafford was shielded by Charles' promise, yet his head rolled, and what else could Vane expect?

In these last hours, Vane's mind ran much upon the glories of that blessedness towards which he was to depart with joy, returning home as the Lamb's wife after long separation. And he thought much of that day, not too long in the future, when Christ would return in glory to the earth to deliver the saints of Sion from their foes. Although he would not live to see it, the Lord would soon come bringing His vengeance—"vengeance upon the outward man of his saints, and vengeance upon the inward man of his and their enemies," sending a fire that would burn in the conscience of his enemies. "Men they may fight against; but this they cannot fight against." But even the fury of that day of wrath seems dimmed in his words; now all the burning is in the conscience. But the Lord will take care of all that; Sir Henry need not concern himself about it anymore.

But even departing to the embrace of Christ, Vane found it easier to talk about severing the ties of love than to do it. He bade his family farewell at last. He knew that he could see past them to Mount Sion, but he lingeringly kissed his children and spoke the words of severance with subdued resignation. "The Lord bless you," he said; "he will be a better Father to you: I must now forget that ever I knew you. . . . Be not you troubled, for I am going home to my Father."

Gossip had it that his farewell to Frances was a final, fleshly, conjugal embrace, and that with typical consideration for the good name of his wife and the child who might be born thereafter, he informed his jailer of what he had done. No one knows whether or not the tale is true. It is certain that no child was conceived that night, though years later his sons faced amiable but crude jests about it. To his enemies, the story evidenced hypocrisy and crassness; to his friends, his total unconcern about the death awaiting him. But one likes to think that if Sir Henry did make love to Lady Frances under that shadow, it meant that his vision of the spirit had not perverted him into contempt for the love and comfort to be found in this world; that he fully appreciated what he was to give up, and even in resigning it cherished it.

At midnight, the sheriff's chaplain brought him "the fatal message of death," the Order of Execution. Now he knew for sure that he would be spared the torment of slow butchery and would die the quick, clean death. He then fell asleep quietly, and after four hours awoke blithe and refreshed, his mind on eternity. "The Lord made it sufficient for me," he said, "and now I am going to sleep my last, after which I shall need sleep no more." And his mind worked happily in its old ways of allegorizing and drawing analogies: God had commanded Moses to go to the top of Mt. Pisgah and die, he told a friend, so now he bade Sir Henry go to the top of Tower Hill and die. And he gathered together his wife, his children, and his friends to share with him his prayer. As Puritan prayers go, it was not unduly long. He knew what he must say and do this morning, he said, for "it is my happiness that Death must not surprise me," but he prayed earnestly that God would give him strength to speak and act steadfastly.

> Most holy and gracious Father . . . shew thyself in a poor weak worm, by enabling him to stand against all the power of thy enemies. . . . We know not what interruptions may attend thy servant, but Lord, let thy power carry him in a holy triumph over all difficulties. . . . Good Lord, put words into his mouth that may daunt his enemies. . . . strengthen the faith and heart of thy poor servant, to undergo this day's work with joy and gladness. . . .

And after praying that the remnant of those faithful to the cause might be gathered together, and the poor handful of them lying in prison relieved, he called down blessings upon those near at hand:

> Let my poor family that is left desolate, let my dear wife and children be taken into thy care; be thou a husband, father, and master to them. Let the spirits of those that love me be drawn towards them.

Soon a sheriff's deputy came to tell Sir Henry that he would walk to the place of execution as gentle and noble prisoners customarily did. But then the sheriff himself came with a message that he was embarrassed to deliver—Charles had commanded that on the scaffold Sir Henry must not speak anything against His Majesty or the government. Vane's reply was not reassuring: he would make his speech as little offensive as possible "saving my faithfulness to the trust reposed in me, which I must discharge with a good conscience unto death, for I ever valued a man according to his faithfulness to the trust reposed in him, even on his Majesty's behalf." The government had been warned.

Having received the sheriff's promise that his servants would be allowed to attend him on the platform and be civilly treated, Vane announced that he was ready to set out, but the sheriff was not ready yet. Then occurred the first of many petty indignities and insults apparently calculated to unsettle Vane's composure and check his impulses to sedition: a messenger brought word that he was not to walk after all, but be dragged upon a sled at a horse's tail, the rough and humiliating conveyance of common felons. Sir Henry calmly replied, "Any way, how they please, for I long to be at home." And he walked cheerfully down the stone stairs to the courtyard and seated himself on the rude wooden hurdle. Sir Henry composed himself for his jolting ride as if he were commencing a royal progress, and at the touch of the lash the horse lurched forward. Prisoners peering out the windows of their cells called out to bless him, and as he was dragged up the Tower Hill road, crowds waved to him from the housetops and the windows, blessing him and crying out, "The Lord go with you!" And as well as he was able in these circumstances, bumping and rumbling over the cobblestones, he acknowledged their respect, "putting off his hat and bowing to them." Only one dissident voice is recorded: "Many suffered for a better cause," grumbled a tall dark man, to which Sir Henry pleasantly replied, "And many may suffer for a worse!" As he neared the scaffold, an exultant voice cried out, "You never sat in so glorious a seat!" and he answered, "It is so indeed," and rejoiced exceedingly.

As he mounted the steps to the scaffold, he heard a commotion behind him and, turning, saw that his servants were being held back and beaten to keep them from following him. "What?" he cried, "have I never a servant here?" Unattended, he stepped onto the scaffold, only to find himself pushed and jostled by a crowd, as old Laud had been when he protested, "I did think that I might have had room to die." He thrust his way among them, but found no open space for a "well-graced actor" to play his part; the spectators standing in the square could not distinguish him from the supernumeraries and friends standing near him. Voices were heard crying, "Which is the man to suffer? Which is Sir Henry Vane?" Sir Henry turned to the sheriff and said he hoped that they "would let him die like a gentleman and a Christian, and not crowded and pressed as he was."

The sheriff parted the crowd and pressed them back, leaving room for Sir Henry to step to the front of the scaffold and show himself to the people. He opened his cloak to expose his brilliant scarlet silk waistcoat, the color of victory and martyrdom flashing in the midst of the black of his suit and cloak; and as if he were going to speak a prologue (Anthony Wood said), he took off his hat and saluted the spectators on each side of the stage. Then he rested his hands on the railing, and took a "very serious, composed, and majestic view of the great multitude about him," for the square was crowded with viewers, many of them his friends and well-wishers. The sheriff called for silence and the roar subsided to a murmur; the audience was his to sway. Raising his hands, he fixed his auditors with his gaze and addressed them.

"Gentlemen, fellow-countrymen, and Christians!" he began. "The work which I am at this time called unto in this place (as upon a public theater) is to die, and receive a discharge, once and for all, out of prison." After he had recounted the sheriff's injunction to speak nothing against the government and his assurance that he would say only what became a Christian and a gentleman—that is, the truth—he supposed (quite rightly) that they would be surprised to hear him say that he was not "brought hither according to any known law of the land." He had been, he said, "run upon and destroyed contrary to right and the liberties of Magna Charta, under the form only of justice." And though he prayed that God would forgive all who had a hand in his death, it was nonetheless true that he had been denied his rights, and that the judges had refused to seal his Bill of Exceptions—

But here Sir John Robinson, Governor of the Tower (a talking, bragging bufflehead, Pepys thought him) interposed furiously, "Sir, you must not go on thus: you are railing against the judges, and it is a lie, and I am here to testify that it is false!" Sir Henry was not to be discomposed. "God will judge between you and me in this matter," he said quietly. "I speak but matter of fact, and cannot you bear that? 'Tis evident, the judges have refused to sign my Bill of—"

But a sudden deafening roll of drums and blare of trumpets drowned him out, not a fanfare, but a raucous, contemptuous squawking and blatting. Sir John had seen to it that whatever Sir Henry might speak against the government would not be heard. This was a new, barbarous, and "very indecent" practice, and was a

fair measure of the irrational fear of "fanatics." Vane had nothing to
say that he had not said without avail many times before, and
whatever influence he had once had was dispersed. As one
remembers Charles' evading his promise of amnesty, one is struck
not so much by his perfidy as by his belief that Vane's very
existence endangered him. No matter, his government had discovered a new way of highlighting a martyrdom, a new kind of affront
for Vane to transcend. Spared the agonizing, tearing desecration of
his flesh, which a timorous man might dread uncontrollably, Vane
was heaped with mean-minded indignities, which he could cope
with.

When the trumpeters stopped for breath, Vane laid his hand
upon his breast and mildly expostulated. "What mean you,
gentlemen? Is this your usage of me? Did you use all the rest so?"

> I had even done (as to that) could you have been patient, but
> seeing you cannot bear it, I shall only say this, that whereas the
> judges have refused to seal that with their hands that they have
> done, I am come to seal that with my blood that I have done.
> Therefore leaving this matter, which I perceive will not be borne,
> I judge it meet to give you some account of my life.

Briefly and simply he told of his careless youth, the wonderful
revelation of God's grace, which altered his very life, his emigration
to escape compulsion of his conscience, his induction into the Long
Parliament, and his efforts to conduct himself rightly amid change
and confusion. More searchingly than ever before, he laid bare his
fallibility and error.

> I shall not altogether excuse myself. I know that by many
> weaknesses and failures I have given occasion enough of the ill
> usage I have met with from men, though, in the main, the Lord
> knows the sincerity and integrity of my heart. . . . I know also
> that God is just in bringing this sentence and condemnation upon
> me for my sins; there is a body of sin and death in me deserves
> this sentence; and there is a similitude and likeness also that, as a
> Christian, God thinks me worthy to bear with my Lord in being
> . . . made a public sacrifice.

And then his audience knew that they were seeing a passion play.

Vane asserted too confidently perhaps that no man could rightly accuse him, in all his public actions, of defiling his hands with any man's blood or estate, or working his own interests. Then he began to vindicate the cause, to speak of the Solemn League and Covenant, which he fully assented to, though never approving the rigid way of prosecuting it with oppressive uniformity—

Again the trumpets blatted and blared. The sheriff tried to snatch the papers from which Vane was speaking, and Sir John Robinson, observing that some of the auditors were writing down Vane's words, stormed to the edge of the scaffold and furiously demanded that all writers surrender their notebooks, for "he treats of rebellion, and you write it!" Then the ritual broke down into riotous confusion. It was hard, Vane patiently said, that "he might not be suffered to speak—" and the trumpeters, now thrusting the bells of their trumpets in his face, blared him into silence. He was trying to read from his notes; Robinson and others were trying to snatch them from him, and whenever he got out a sentence or two, the trumpets screeched him down. At last, as Robinson made another attempt on his papers, Vane gave up the fight. Quickly he tore his notes into pieces and handed them surreptitiously to a friend, but the sheriff was too quick for him: he seized the fragments and then he and Robinson thrust their hands into Vane's pockets in an ignominious search for concealed papers. The spectators, it was said, were distressed to see "a prisoner so strangely handled in his dying words," but Vane knew what to do: he stood patient and composed, remembering the serene silence of his Lord when he was mocked and jeered and buffeted.

When the tumult stilled, he was allowed to pray in peace. He prayed at length, as enthusiasts of his persuasion were wont to do, informing the Lord of a great many things that He presumably already knew, but it was an honest prayer and humble, even a generous one. He knew now whence much human evil came. "Deliver us, O Lord, from the Evil One, deliver us from ourselves; take us out of our own dispose, our own liberty and power . . . and bring us into . . . the most holy immutable and righteous state of the sons of God, a freedom to good only, and not at all to evil." He prayed that the faithful might be delivered from bondage, and for himself he prayed that he might stand fast.

Thou knowest, O Lord, that in the faith of Jesus, and for the truth that is in Jesus, thy servant desires to die . . . in that way which men call heresy. . . . Now set thy seal to it, and remove the reproaches and calumnies with which thy servant is reproached, for thou knowest his innocency. Dear Father, thou sentest us into this world, but this world is not our home, we are strangers and pilgrims in it, as all our fathers were. We have no abode here.

He must speak, too, on behalf of the great nation wherein he has lived: "Lord, did we not exceed other nations in our day? Great things have been done by thee in the midst of us." And he prays that the sins of the whole nation may be forgiven, that it may endure what must be endured for its cleansing.

We are assured thou knowest our suffering case and condition, how it is with us. We desire to give no just occasion of offense, nor to provoke any, but in meekness to forgive our enemies. Thy servant that is now falling asleep doth heartily desire of thee that thou would forgive them, and not lay this to their charge.

Samuel Pepys heard a voice from the crowd ask why he did not pray for the king. "Nay," he answered, "you shall see I can pray for the King. I pray God bless him." And then, unhurried and with steady hands, he removed his cloak and his coat, and opened his shirt to bare his neck to the axe. And with that strange preoccupation with inconsequential things men exhibit in crises of great consequence, he recalled wryly that he had a "blister or issue" on his neck; be careful not to hurt it, he warned the headsman. Even as he fitted his head and neck to the receiving indentations of the block, he continued to pray: "Father, glorify thy servant in the sight of man, that he may glorify thee in the discharge of his duty to thee and to his country."

He spread his arms in the understood signal; the axe flashed overhead in the morning light, and then descended in a firm, efficient stroke that severed his head clean from his body. He had been altogether ready—even the unintelligent flesh accepted the blow and did not rebel. His body slumped still, and his head fell without so much as a tic or quiver of a muscle. Sir Henry had already gone into the world of light.

Epilogue

For days the patience and unshakable courage of Sir Henry Vane at his death was "talked on everywhere" as a miracle, and the populace that had hated him so bitterly now made a pious hero of him. Many agreed that the king had lost more by his death than he would "get again in a good while." And the "fanatics"—a term which in these days of enforced episcopal uniformity was blanketing all shades of dissenters—felt assured that "he had died as much a martyr as ever man did." Never in his life had he been so generally esteemed, and even the rather skeptical Pepys said that after his death it was believed that the bishops would "never be able to carry it as high as they do."

His Majesty had graciously consigned the sundered body to Vane's family, who laid it to rest in the vaults of Shipborne Church in Kent. With what improvised prayers his disciples commended his body to the earth and his soul to its Maker we do not know, but we may be sure that they would not have consoled his now aged mother, enduring his death in sorrow as she had once endured the pain of his birth in joy. She would once again have taken comfort in the familiar, consecrated words of the Prayer Book, knowing that her son would understand: he had never thought that forms of worship mattered enough that they should loosen the bonds of love. Besides, she knew that these ritual phrases said nothing that he would exclude from his own prayers. "O God," she read,

> whose mercies cannot be numbered; accept our prayers on behalf of the soul of thy servant departed, and grant him an entrance into the land of light and joy in the fellowship of thy saints; through Jesus Christ our Lord.

The king had refused to honor his promise of mercy, and now the stubborn Sir Harry was in his grave, and he slept well. John Lambert was just beginning to enjoy the royal clemency on the Isle of Guernsey, where he would rot in neglect and desuetude for nearly a third of a century; only after thirty years would death release him, his memory decayed and his troubled mind slipped from its moorings. The courses of rigor and mercy are no less strange and devious than the twistings of fate.

After his death, Vane's spirit was for a time still abroad in the land. His friends and disciples published the available accounts of his trial, including his own speeches that he was partly prevented from delivering; George Sikes wrote a life of Vane, more hagiological than biographical, much of which was devoted to expounding Sir Henry's religious teachings, so inspiring to the Fifth Monarchists and so comforting to the persecuted dissenters. Soon government agents were interrogating anyone who might lead them to "certain bookbinders and printers connected with the circulation of . . . Vane's trial and life," his *Retired Man's Meditations*, and other subversive books. The Fifth Monarchists and the Quakers and other sects continued to meet surreptitiously, as they had to, and wherever the fanatics were gathered together the government smelled sedition: rumors of planned uprisings proliferated, uprisings inspired by the martyred Vane and to be led by the fugitive Ludlow. Lady Vane herself was under suspicion, not only as a leader of the Seekers, but as one in conspiratorial correspondence with the wives of Wariston and Ludlow, and hence likely to know where these proscribed men might be found. Her letters were intercepted and read; even Vane's daughter, Albinia, wrote to her friend Anne Hutchinson in Scotland in cypher, for she knew that her letters were being scrutinized. Raby Castle was suspect as a center of infection, and Lady Vane's agent there, John Cock, was for several years under investigation as a very dangerous man. It was he, one agent learned, who had composed the eulogy on Vane and his sufferings which was printed as a kind of benediction at the end of the accounts of his trial. It began,

> Great Soul, ne'er understood
> Until deciphered by thy blood. . . .
> Dying, that liberty might live,
> The English Cause he doth retrieve;
> Stating it in no formal dress,
> But in the spirit of righteousness.
> Which he from th' earth perceiving fled
> Died, to return with it from the Dead.

But though Vane's death inspired his followers, it could not resurrect the cause. Begun with high and unselfish hopes, fought for with the fervor of a crusade for liberty, perverted into a self-righteous tyranny, it had finally soured and fallen apart; after Cromwell's death the center no longer held and the cause collapsed into chaos as its heroes were dispersed, in flight or struck down. Nor did that promised glorious Fifth Monarchy come to pass. Vane would never know that 1666 would come and go, marked by fire and plague and defeat, another "wonderful year," but with never a glimmer of a Messiah descending from the eastern heavens. Nor could he even have dreamed that the cause of government representative of the people and protecting their rights with a constitution would succeed—after a fashion—in the land that had hounded Anne Hutchinson into the wilderness. Or that with the slow shiftings of time, the idea that church and magistracy should be held apart would become almost too obvious to argue about; or that full religious toleration would finally be enjoyed when men would cease to consider theological differences important enough to fight over. Or that he would one day be revered in that new world not as a saint, but as the father of constitutional government and a champion of freedom.

Nor could he have guessed that in his own land, after a bloodless revolution, Parliament would one day again grasp its fundamental power, leaving to kings only their glory. Vane's good old cause was not dead; it only slept.

Nor was Vane himself dead; the courage and dignity of his death entitled him to speak to that future whose lineaments he had so confidently discerned and proclaimed. He had died knowing that when time had sickened—when the people were heartsick with violence and disillusioned with the utopia which presumably justified that violence—he, alone, friendless and stubborn, had still tried to force the nation along the visionary ways of the good old cause until he had seemed less a prophetic revolutionary than a deluded reactionary.

He died knowing, too, that in those confused times when England was tearing itself apart, under the pressures of daily actions and decisions, he had sometimes misread the rights and wrongs and had not always distinguished between the voice of the divine imperative and the voice of self-interest.

And yet he had been right all along in one supremely significant thing. The voice that spoke to him all his life, that antinomian voice from deeper levels of the mind than most men ever know, was right when it told him that the time had come at last for the fragile individual conscience to be shielded from the massive power of the state, that the integrity and freedom of man's inner life was the supreme value and worth the terrible price he and his age had paid for it. More than any other man of the Puritan revolution he had known that, fought for that, died for that. He had built only one monument, but it was higher than a pyramid, stronger than brass:

> to know
> Both spiritual power and civil, what each means,
> What severs each, thou hast learnt, which few have done.
> The bounds of either sword to thee we owe.
> Therefore on thy firm hand religion leans
> In peace and reckons thee her eldest son.

Bibliography

WORKS BY SIR HENRY VANE, JR.

Printed Speeches

1. *Sir Henry Vane His Speech in the House of Commons, at a Committee for the Bill Against Episcopal Government* (London, June 11, 1641). Reprinted in *Old Parliamentary History*, IX, 342.

2. *Three Speeches Spoken in Guildhall, Concerning His Majesty's Refusal of a Treaty of Peace.* . . . (November, 1642). Reprinted in *Old Parliamentary History*, XII, 17.

3. *Two Speeches Spoken at Common Hall, October 27, 1643, wherein is showed the readiness of the Scots to assist the Kingdom of England to the utmost of their power* (London, 1643).

4. *A Cunning Plot to Divide and Destroy the Parliament and the City of London, spoken at Common Hall* (London, January, 1644).

5. *Three Speeches Delivered in Guildhall, London on Tuesday, March 4 . . . Concerning the Treaty at Uxbridge* (London, 1645).

6. "Exhortation to His Children." Appended to *Pilgrimage into the Land of Promise* (London, 1664).

7. *The Speech Intended to Have been Spoken on the Scaffold.* Printed in *The Trial of Sir Henry Vane* (London, 1662).

Note: A speech attributed to young Vane in support of the Self-Denying Ordinance is reprinted by Clarendon in *History of the Rebellion.* Because it appears in no other source and because there are some internal problems, Samuel Rawson Gardiner pronounced it spurious.

The Speech against Richard Cromwell attributed to Vane in Oldmixon's *History of England under the House of Stuart* is generally agreed to be the work of some later writer.

Printed Books and Tracts

1. *A Brief Answer to a Certain Declaration*, 1637. Reprinted in *Hutchinson Papers* (see below, under *Primary Sources*).

2. *The Retired Man's Meditations* (London, 1655).

3. *A Healing Question Propounded* (London, 1656).

4. *Of Love of God and Union with God* (1657?). This work, attributed to Vane by Anthony Wood, is also listed by Sir Charles Firth among Vane's writings, but no other biographer gives evidence of familiarity with it. The British Museum does not have it, and our search in other major libraries has failed to turn it up.

5. *The Proceeds of the Protector . . . Against Sir Henry Vane, Knight* (London, 1658).

6. "A Needful Corrective or Balance in Popular Government." Letter to James Harrington (1659?).

7. *Two Treatises: Epistle General to the Mystical Body of Christ* and *The Face of the Times* (London, 1662).

8. *The Cause of the People of England Stated* (London, 1689). This work was apparently written between 1660 and 1662. A printer's note at the end of this treatise says that "Cause" should read "Case." While other scholars have followed the printer, it seems more reasonable to us that the title was intended as we have written it.

9. *A Pilgrimage into the Land of Promise* (London, 1664).

10. *The Trial of Sir Henry Vane, Knight*, with other occasional speeches, his prayers on the scaffold, etc. (London, 1662).
Note: A work called *Light Shining out of Darkness*, sometimes attributed to Vane, is clearly not his.

Letters

1. Vane's letters to his father from Vienna are found in the Public Record Office, reference SP 80–8.

2. A letter to his wife, written from the Scilly Isles, is appended to *Two Treatises* (see above, under *Printed Books and Tracts*).

3. Other letters are found in the *Calendar of State Papers*, the *Nickolls Papers*, the collected correspondence of Cromwell, and other scattered sources.

BIOGRAPHIES OF VANE
(listed according to date of publication)

Calendar of State Papers, Domestic Series. The reign of Charles I, 1662. *The Life and Death of Sir Henry Vane*. George Sikes (London).

1835. *The Life of Sir Henry Vane*. C. W. Upham (Boston).

1838. *Sir Henry Vane*. John Forster. In *Lives of Eminent British Statesmen*. Lardner's Encyclopedia, vol. 4 (London, 1831 et seq.).

1888. *The Life of Young Sir Henry Vane*. James K. Hosmer (Boston).

1905. *The Life of Sir Henry Vane*. W. W. Ireland (London).

1909. *Sir Henry Vane, Jr.* Melville King (Providence, R. I.).

1910. *The Life of Sir Henry Vane the Younger, Puritan Idealist.* F. J. C. Hearnshaw (London). Congregational Worthies Series, no. 2.

1913. *The Life of Sir Henry Vane the Younger.* John Willcock (London).

1970. *Sir Henry Vane the Younger.* Violet Rowe (London).

Note: Sir Charles Firth wrote the account of Vane in *DNB*. Also, J. H. Hexter's unpublished thesis, *The Rise of the Independent Party* in the Widener Archives, Harvard University, contains much valuable information about young Vane in Parliament.

PRIMARY SOURCES

Abbott, W. C. *The Writings and Speeches of Oliver Cromwell* (Harvard, 1937 et seq.).

Adams, Charles Francis, ed. *Antinomianism in the Colony of Massachusetts Bay* (Prince Society, 1894).

Alsted, John Henry. *The Beloved City.* Translated by Wm. Burton (London, 1643).

Anon. *A True Relation of the Late Battle Fought in New England* (London, 1637).

Aubrey, John. *Brief Lives.* Edited by O. L. Dick (Ann Arbor, 1957).

Baillie, Robert. *The Letters and Journals of.* Edited by David Laing. 3 vols. (Edinburgh, 1841–1842).

Baxter, Richard. *Reliquiae Baxterianae.* Edited by M. Sylvester (London, 1696).

Berkeley, Sir John. *Memoirs of.* In *A Narrative by John Ashburnham* (London, 1830).

Bradford, William. *Of Plymouth Plantation.* Edited by S. E. Morison (New York, 1963).

Bulstrode, Sir Richard. *Memoirs and Reflections upon the Reign and Government of King Charles I, and King Charles II* (London, 1721).

Burnet, Gilbert. *History of my Own Time.* Edited by O. Airy. 2 vols. (Oxford, 1897).

Calendar of State Papers, Domestic Series. The reign of Charles I, 1625–1649. 22 vols., 1858–1893. Addenda, 1 vol., 1629–1649 (London, 1897).

Calendar of State Papers, Domestic Series. Commonwealth and Protectorate, 1649–1660. 13 vols., 1875–1876.

Calendar of State Papers, Domestic Series. Reign of Charles II, 1660–1681. 22 vols., 1860–1921.

Calendar of State Papers, Venetian. Edited by H. F. Brown and A. B. Hind. Vols. 25–32 (London, 1900–1925).

Calendar of the Proceedings of the Committee for Compounding (1643–1660). Edited by M. A. E. Green. 5 vols. (London, 1889–1892).

Carte, Thomas. *A Collection of Original Papers and Letters, 1641–1648* (London, 1739).

Cary, H., ed. *Memorials of the Great Civil War, 1646–1652.* 2 vols. (London, 1842).

Clarendon, Edward Earl of. *The History of the Rebellion and the Civil Wars in England.* Edited by W. D. Macray. 6 vols. (Oxford, 1888).

Clarendon State Papers. Edited by R. Scope and T. Monkhouse. 3 vols. (Oxford, 1767–1786).

Commons, Journals of the House of. Vols. 2–8.

Cotton, John. *God's Promise to His Plantations* (London, 1634); *The Way of the Churches of Christ in New England* (London, 1645); *The Way of the Congregational Churches Cleared* (London, 1648).

Dalton, Charles. *History of the Wrays of Glentworth.* 2 vols. (London, 1880–1881).

Evelyn, John. *The Diary of.* Edited by E. S. DeBeer. 6 vols. (London, 1648).

Fairfax, Lord Thomas. *Short Memorials of* (London, 1699). Reprinted in Maseres, *Select Tracts.*

Ferdinand II, Emperor. *The Particular State of the Government.* Translated by R. W. (London, 1637). This work has a detailed description of Vienna as Vane would have seen it.

Firth, C. H., and Rait, C. S., eds. *Acts and Ordinances of the Interregnum, 1642–1660* (Oxford, 1906).

Firth, C. H., ed. *Selections from the Papers of William Clarke.* Camden Society, 4 vols. (London, 1891–1901).

Gardiner, S. R., ed. *The Constitutional Documents of the Puritan Revolution 1625–1660* (Oxford, 1899).

Gataker, Thomas. *Antinomianism Discovered and Confuted* (London, 1652).

Hall, J. D. *The Antinomian Controversy* [a collection of the documents] (Middleton, Conn., 1968).

Haller, William, and Davies, Godfrey. *The Leveller Tracts* (Gloucester, Mass., 1964).

Herbert, Sir Thomas. *Memoirs of the Two Last Years of the Reign of King Charles I.* Edited by G. N. (London, 1839).

Heylyn, Peter. *A Brief Relation of the Death and Suffering of the Most Reverend and Renowned Prelate, the Lord Archbishop of Canterbury* (Oxford, 1644).

Hobbes, Thomas. *Behemoth, History of the Causes of the Civil War in England.* Reprinted in Maseres, *Select Tracts.*

Holles, Denzil Lord. *Memoirs of.* Reprinted in Maseres, *Select Tracts.*

Howell, James. *Epistolae Ho-Elianae.* Edited by Joseph Jacobs (London, 1890).

Howell, T. B. *State Trials.* 21 vols. (1816).

Hutchinson, Lucy, *Memoirs of the Life of Colonel Hutchinson*. Edited by Julius Hutchinson. Revised and additional notes by C. H. Firth (London, 1906).

Hutchinson Papers. Edited by W. H. Whitmore and W. S. Appleton. 2 vols. (Prince Society, 1864).

Johnston, Sir Archibald of Wariston. *Diary of*. Edited by G. M. Paul et al. 3 vols. (Edinburgh, 1911 et seq.).

Laud, William. *History of the Troubles and Trials of the Most Reverend Father in God and Blessed Martyr*. Edited by Henry Wharton (London, 1694).

Leighton, Alexander. *Sion's Plea Against Prelacy* (London, 1628).

Lilburne, John. *London's Liberty in Chains Discovered* (London, 1646); *Jonah's Cry out of the Whale's Belly* (London, 1647); *An Impeachment of High Treason*. . . . (London, 1649); *The Legal, Fundamental Liberties of the People of England Revived* (1649).

Lilly, William. *Several Observations upon the Life and Death of King Charles* (London, 1651). Reprinted in Maseres, *Select Tracts*.

Lords, Journals of the House of.

Ludlow, Edmund. *Memoirs of* (London, 1751).

Maseres, Francis, ed. *Select Tracts Relating to the Civil War in England*. (London, 1815).

Mason, John. *A Brief History of the Pequot Wars*. . . . (Boston, 1736).

Massachusetts, The Founding of. A Selection from the Sources of the History and Settlement, 1628–1631 (Boston, 1930).

May, Thomas. *Breviary History of the Parliament of England* (London, 1655). Reprinted in Maseres, *Select Tracts*.

Mede, Joseph. *The Key of the Revelation*. Translated by Richard More (London, 1643).

Milton, John. *Complete Works*, Columbia edition. Edited by F. A. Patterson et. al. (New York, 1931–1938).

Montague, Richard. *A Gag for a New Gospel? No, a New Gag for an Old Goose* (London, 1624); *Apello Caesarem* (London, 1625).

Montereuil, Jean de, and the brothers de Bellièvre. *The Diplomatic Correspondence of*. Edited by J. G. Fotheringham. 2 vols. (Edinburgh, 1898–1899).

Nalson, John. *An Impartial Collection* (London, 1682).

Nicholas, Sir Edward. *Correspondence of*. Edited by Sir. G. F. Warner. Camden Society, 4 vols. (London, 1886, 1920).

Nickolls, J. *Original Letters and Papers of State* (London, 1743).

Oxinden Letters. Edited by Dorothy Gardiner (London, 1933).

Parliamentary or Constitutional History of England, by several hands (London, 1751). Generally referred to as *The Old Parliamentary History*.

Pepys, Samuel. *The Diary of*. Edited by H. B. Wheatley. 2 vols. (New York, 1946).

Prynne, William. *Histriomastix: The Player's Scourges* (London, 1633); *News from Ipswich* (Edinburgh, 1636?); *A Brief Justification of the Eleven Accused Members* (1647); *The Works of* (London, 1655).

Records of the Governor and Company of the Massachusetts Bay. Edited by N. B. Shurtleff (Boston, 1853).

Rushworth, John. *Historical Collections.* 7 vols. (London, 1659–1701).

Sanderson, William. *A Complete History of the Life and Reign of King Charles* (London, 1658).

Sanford, John Langton. *Studies and Illustrations of the Great Rebellion* (London, 1858).

Slingsby, Bethel. *A True and Impartial Narrative* (London, 1659).

Somers Tracts. Edited by Sir W. Scott. 13 vols. (London, 1809–1815).

Sprigge, Joshua. *Anglia Rediviva* (London, 1647).

Stubbe, Henry. *Malice Rebuked: A Vindication of Sir Henry Vane* (London, 1659).

Sydney Papers: A Journal of the Earl of Leicester and Original Letters of Algernon Sydney. Edited by R. W. Blencowe (London, 1825).

Thomason Tracts. This notable collection in the British Museum contains the news sheets of the time and the principal contemporary tracts.

Thurloe, John. *A Collection of State Papers.* Edited by Thomas Birch. 7 vols. (London, 1742).

Verney Family. *Memoirs of the.* Edited by Francis P. Verney. 2 vols. (London, 1894).

Walker, Clement. *The Complete History of Independency* (London, 1661).

Wallington, Nehemiah. *Historical Notices of the Reign of Charles I.* Edited by R. Webb. 2 vols. (London, 1869).

Walwyn, William. *The Bloody Project* (London, 1648).

Warwick, Sir Philip. *Memoirs of the Reign of King Charles I* (London, 1702).

Weld, Thomas. *Antinomians and Familists Condemned by the Synod of Elders in New England* (London, 1644).

Whitelocke, Bulstrode. *Memorials of English Affairs.* 4 vols. (Oxford, 1853).

Lovelace, Richard. *Poems of.* Edited by C. H. Wilkinson (Oxford, 1930). *The Bloody Tenent yet more Bloody* (London, 1652).

Willis-Bund, John W., ed. *A Selection of Cases from the State Trials.* 2 vols. (Cambridge, England, 1882).

Winthrop, John. *The History of New England, 1630–1649.* Edited by James Savage. 2 vols. (Boston, 1853).

Winthrop Papers. Vols. 2–4, 1623–1644 (Massachusetts Historical Society, 1929 et seq.).

Woodhouse, A. S. P. *Puritanism and Liberty,* 2d ed. (University of Chicago, 1950). A compilation of the army debates.

PARLIAMENTARY DIARIES

Manuscripts

D'Ewes, Sir Symonds. *A Journal of the Parliament.*

Whittaker, Lawrence. *Diary of Proceedings in the House of Commons.*

Yonge, Walter. *Journal of Proceedings in the House of Commons.*

Printed

Burton, Thomas. *Diary of.* Edited by J. T. Rutt. 4 vols. (London, 1828).

D'Ewes, Sir Simonds. *Journal.* Edited by W. Notestein (New Haven, 1923); *Journal.* Edited by W. H. Coates (New Haven, 1942).

Northcote, Sir John. *Notebook.* Edited by A. H. A. Hamilton (London, 1877).

Verney, Sir Ralph. *Notes of Proceedings in the Long Parliament.* Edited by J. Bruce. Camden Society (London, 1845).

POETRY ABOUT THE CIVIL WAR

Ault, Norman. *Seventeenth Century Lyrics* (New York, 1928).

Butler, Samuel. *Hudibras.* Edited by T. R. Nash. (New York, 1901).

Carew, Thomas. *The Poems of.* Edited by Rhodes Dunlap (Oxford, 1949).

Cartwright, William. *Plays and Poems.* Edited by G. Blakemore Evans (University of Wisconsin Press, 1951).

Cleveland, John. *The Poems of.* Edited by Brian Morris and Eleanor Withington (Oxford, 1967).

Fiske, John. *The Beginnings of New England and the Puritan Theocracy.* . . . (Boston, 1896).

printed, New York, 1967).

Denham, Sir John. *Poetical Works of.* Edited by Theodore H. Banks, Jr. (New Haven, 1928).

Habington, William. *The Poems of.* Edited by Kenneth Allott (London, 1948).

Herrick, Robert. *Complete Poems of.* Edited by J. Max Patrick (New York, 1963).

Lovelace, Richard. *Poems of.* Edited by C. H. Wilkinson (Oxford, 1930).

Milton, John (see above, under *Primary Sources*).

Randolph, Thomas. *Poetical and Dramatic Works of.* Edited by W. Carew Hazlitt (London, 1875).

Rumpe, The, or an exact collection of the choicest poems and songs relating to the late times (London, 1874).

Saintsbury, George. *Minor Poets of the Caroline Period* (Oxford, 1905).

Shirley, James. *Dramatic Works and Poems*. Edited by William Gifford (London, 1833).

Stanley, Thomas. *Poems and Translations*. Edited by G. M. Crump (Oxford, 1962).

Suckling, Sir John. *Poems and Letters*. Edited by Herbert Berry (Ontario, 1960).

Waller, Edmund. *Poems of*. Edited by G. T. Drury (London, 1893).

SECONDARY SOURCES

Adams, Charles Francis. *Three Episodes of Massachusetts History* (Boston, 1892).

Bosher, Robert S. *The Making of the Restoration Settlement* (New York, 1951).

Bourne, E. C. E. *The Anglicanism of William Laud* (London, 1947).

Brailsford, H. N. *The Levellers and the English Revolution* (Stanford University Press, 1961).

Burne, Alfred H., and Young, Peter. *The Great Civil War* (London, 1959).

Davies, Godfrey. *The Restoration of Charles II* (California, 1955).

Dow, George Francis. *Every Day Life in the Massachusetts Bay Colony* (Boston, 1935).

Ellis, George E. *Life of John Mason* in Library of American Biography. Vol. 13 (1848).

Firth, Sir Charles H. *Cromwell's Army*. New ed. with Introduction by P. H. Hardacre (London, 1961); *Oliver Cromwell* (London, 1953); *The Last Years of the Protectorate*, 1656–1658. 2 vols. (New York, 1964).

Fiske, John. *The Beginnings of New England and the Puritan Theocracy. . . .* (Boston, 1896).

Forshall, T. H. *Westminster School: Past and Present* (London, 1884).

Frank, Joseph. *The Beginnings of English Newspapers*, 1620–1660 (Harvard, 1961).

Gardiner, Samuel Rawson. *The Thirty Years War* (New York, 1891); *History of England from the Accession of James I to the Outbreak of the Civil War*. 10 vols. (London, 1883–1884); *History of the Great Civil War*, 1642–1649. 4 vols. (London, 1893); *History of the Commonwealth and Protectorate* 1649–1656. New ed., 4 vols. (London, 1903).

Glass, H. A. *The Barebone Parliament* (London, 1899).

Hallam, Henry. *The Constitutional History of England* (London, 1854).

Hexter, J. H. *The Reign of King Pym* (Cambridge, Mass., 1941).

Hill, Christopher. *Society and Puritanism in Pre-Revolutionary England* (New York, 1964); *Puritanism and Revolution* (London, 1965).

Hutchinson, Thomas. *The History of Massachusetts Bay* (Boston, 1795).

Judson, Margaret A. *The Political Thought of Sir Henry Vane the Younger* (Philadelphia, 1969).

Masson, David. *The Life of John Milton* (London, 1877 et seq.).

Morgan, Edmund S. *Roger Williams: The Church and the State* (New York, 1967).

Morrah, Patrick. *1660: The Year of Restoration* (London, 1960).

Northend, William D. *The Bay Colony* (Boston, 1896).

Ogg, David. *England in the Reign of Charles II.* 2 vols. (Oxford, 1955).

Oppenheim, M. A. *A History of the Administration of the Royal Navy 1509–1660* (London, 1896).

Powell, J. R. *The Navy in the English Civil War* (London, 1962).

Redlich, Josef. *The Procedure of the House of Commons* (London, 1908).

Roberts, Michael. *Gustavus Adolphus* (London, 1958).

Rogers, P. G. *The Fifth Monarchy Men* (London, 1966).

Rugg, Winifred K. *Unafraid: A Life of Anne Hutchinson* (Boston, 1930).

Rutman, Darret B. *Winthrop's Boston: Portrait of a Puritan Town, 1630–1649* (Chapel Hill, N.C., 1965).

Sargeant, John. *Annals of Westminster School* (London, 1898).

Shaw, William A. *A History of the English Church During the Civil Wars and under the Commonwealth* (London, 1900).

Skinner, Thomas. *The Life of General Monk* (London, 1723).

Trevor-Roper, H. R. *Archbishop Laud* (London, 1963); *The Crisis of the Seventeenth Century* (New York, 1968).

Vaughan, Allen T. *New England Frontier, Puritans and Indians, 1620–75* (Boston, 1965).

Walzer, Michael. *The Revolution of the Saints* (Harvard University Press, 1965).

Wedgwood, C. V. *A Coffin for King Charles* (New York, 1964); *The King's Peace* (New York, 1956); *The King's War, 1641–47* (New York, 1959); *Thomas Wentworth* (London, 1961).

Whitehill, Walter Muir. *Boston: A Topographical History* (Cambridge, Mass., 1968).

Wormald, B. H. G. *Clarendon* (Cambridge University Press, 1964).

Woolrych, Austin. *Battles of the English Civil War* (New York, 1961).

Index